JACOB RIIS
REVISITED

Francesco Cordasco received his B.A. (Sociology) from Columbia College, Columbia University; his M.A. and Doctorate from New York University; and a Diploma (Sociology) from the University of London where he studied at the Institute of Education, and at the London School of Economics. Presently, he is Professor of Education at Montclair State College, and has taught at New York University, the City University of New York, London University and the University of Puerto Rico. He is serving as educational consultant, Migration Division, Commonwealth of Puerto Rico, and has served as a consultant to the U. S. Office of Education; and to federal, state, and community antipoverty programs funded under the Economic Opportunity Act (1964).

Professor Cordasco has published numerous articles and reviews in professional journals, and is the author of books on ethnicity and social class stratification in American education; on educational sociology; and on urban education and the immigrant child.

A Fellow of the American Sociological Association, and a Fellow of the British Sociological Association, Professor Cordasco is a native of New York City.

JACOB RIIS REVISITED

Poverty and the Slum
in Another Era

EDITED
WITH AN INTRODUCTION BY
FRANCESCO CORDASCO

Anchor Books

DOUBLEDAY & COMPANY, INC.
GARDEN CITY, NEW YORK
1968

HOW THE OTHER HALF LIVES: *STUDIES AMONG THE TENEMENTS OF NEW YORK* was originally published in 1890 by Charles Scribner's Sons, New York; chapters 5, 6, 7, 9, 10, 11, 12, 14, 15, 18, 19, 23, and 24 have been omitted from the Anchor Books edition. THE CHILDREN OF THE POOR was originally published in 1892 by Charles Scribner's Sons, New York; chapters 3, 5, 9, 10, and 13 have been omitted from the Anchor Books edition. A TEN YEARS' WAR: *AN ACCOUNT OF THE BATTLE WITH THE SLUM IN NEW YORK* was originally published in 1900 by Houghton Mifflin Company, Boston and New York; chapters 5 and 6 have been omitted from the Anchor Books edition.

The Anchor Books edition is the first publication of
JACOB RIIS REVISITED.

Anchor Books edition: 1968

PREFACE

For some time I have been convinced that a set of readings which reflected American society's continuing concern with poverty and the poor would be of value: instructive not only in the historical perspective that such readings would afford, but more so in affirming the commitment of a free society to a constant dialogue on the dynamics of opportunity or its absence in the achievement of our social ideals. From a host of writers, I selected Jacob A. Riis whose books have a haunting relevance to many of our contemporary concerns with the "simple annals of the poor." This collection brings together selections from *How the Other Half Lives: Studies Among the Tenements of New York* (1890); *The Children of the Poor* (1892); and *A Ten Years' War: An Account of the Battle with the Slum in New York* (1900).

If the idea for this reader was born in my work in the urban ghettoes of American cities, it was refined and disciplined by Loretta Barrett of the Doubleday staff; and if the book has value, much of the credit must go to her. Grateful acknowledgment is made to Charles Scribner's Sons; and to Houghton Mifflin

Company for permission to republish the writings of
Jacob Riis. The photographs have come from the fol-
lowing archives: The Jacob A. Riis Collection, Mu-
seum of the City of New York; The Community
Service Society, New York; The George Eastman
House; The Bettmann Archive; Culver Pictures, Inc.;
The Byron Collection, Museum of the City of New
York; The Library of Congress.

F.C.

CONTENTS

I
HOW THE OTHER HALF LIVES
*Studies Among the Tenements
of New York*

II
THE CHILDREN OF THE POOR

III
A TEN YEARS' WAR
*An Account of the Battle
with the Slum in New York*

LIST OF PLATES

———

INTRODUCTION

Since the enactment of the Economic Opportunity Act of 1964, America has been preoccupied with poverty.[1] The creation of the Office of Economic Opportunity in 1964 was, in itself, a declaration of war on poverty; and out of the cornucopia of federal legislation (and the largess of the Congress) came a

[1] The best incisive commentary on the concern with poverty in the America of the 1960s is that of Thomas Gladwin, *Poverty, U.S.A.* (Boston: Little, Brown, 1967). A staggering bibliography reflects the extent of the engagement against poverty in theoretical, practical, and philosophical terms. The U. S. Office of Education has prepared a *Catalog of Selected Documents on the Disadvantaged: A Number and Author Index* (OE 37001) and a *Subject Index* (OE 37002) which is ". . . a collection of 1740 documents on the special education needs of the disadvantaged in support of the Elementary and Secondary Education Act of 1965." Since "disadvantaged" is one of the euphemisms coined by our age for "poor," the collection is a multifaceted portraiture of poverty in our time, and its impingement on the social institution which is the school. See also, Michael Harrington, *The Other America: Poverty in the United States* (New York: Macmillan, 1962); Robert E. Will and Harold G. Vatter, eds., *Poverty in Affluence* (New York: Harcourt, 1965); Louis A. Ferman, *et al.*, eds., *Poverty in America* (Ann Arbor; University of Michigan Press, 1966).

varied set of legal strategies to combat deprivation and to work toward what President Lyndon B. Johnson called "The Great Unfinished Work of Our Society."[2]

In the general affluence of the United States in the 1960s, Americans were starkly reminded of the plight of the negro, and the War on Poverty has been related to the Civil Rights struggle, and to concerns articulated within the matrix of revolutionary social interventions; in a sense, the struggle over civil rights may well have been the catalyst which brought about social awareness in its wake, and a paradoxically ambivalent commitment to social reformation which (in our time) saw poverty as a negro problem. Yet, in truth, poverty as a social reality has a very broad dimension both in contemporary America and in our nation's history,[3] and the Civil Rights movement has contributed a new sense of urgency to the continuing confrontation of poverty. Each age defines its own rationale and relates it to a social setting. Franklin Roosevelt's New Deal, in a world very different from ours, coined its own terminology, fashioned its own multiplicity of agencies and laws, and mapped broad lines of strategy to combat the social and psychological debilitation of the 1930s.

Serious public concern with the problem of poverty in America is not a new phenomenon. The nature of poverty, its structure, the very attitudes toward the poor, have varied from period to period, but serious concern has never been lacking. Central to any concern with the plight of the poor was the attitude toward poverty and the poor themselves. It might be argued that the shift of emphasis in attitude toward the poor, which saw them as *victims* and not as *causal*

---

[2] From *Message on Poverty*, March 16, 1964, in which President Johnson called for a national war on poverty.

[3] See, in this connection, Thomas Gladwin, "War Is an Extension of Politics," *op. cit.*, pp. 37–47.

agents of poverty, is the main dynamic of social reform
which undergirds contemporary effort, no less than it
did the policies of the New Deal and the tortuous
decades of social agitation and reform which lay behind
it in the historical mist of the progressive movement.
In this sense, a whole host of forgotten social reformers
takes on a new significance and their writings represent not an *ur*-period in the annals of poverty but
rather the very genesis of a philanthropic compassion
out of which new attitudes were born and new social
responsibilities were defined. It is in the cities of America in the late nineteenth century that the seeds of
our contemporary concern with impoverishment and
social injustice are correctly to be sought: in the Hull
House of Jane Addams; in the acidulous observations
of Lincoln Steffens; in the new sociology of the new
University of Chicago; in the abrasive literary vignettes
of Stephen Crane and Theodore Dreiser; and in the
chronicles and portraits of slum life given to us by
Jacob Riis.[4]

Jacob August Riis (1849–1914) was an unlikely candidate for the lifework he was to find in the slums of
New York City. A Danish immigrant, he arrived in
New York City penniless in 1870, lived in semipoverty
for some seven years, and drifted almost haphazardly
into newspaper work.[5] By 1886, he was a seasoned
reporter and he had learned his craft out of police

[4] See Robert H. Bremner, *From the Depths: The Discovery
of Poverty in the United States* (New York: New York Uni-
versity Press, 1956); Henry Steele Commager, "Introduction,"
Jane Addams, *Twenty Years at Hull House* (New York: New
American Library, 1960); and Richard Hofstadter, ed., *The
Progressive Movement, 1900–1915* (Englewood Cliffs, N.J.;
Prentice-Hall, 1963).

[5] The best biographical source is Riis's autobiography, *The
Making of an American* (New York: Macmillan, 1901). See
also, J. H. Holmes, "Jacob A. Riis," *Dictionary of American
Biography;* and the only full-length biographical study, Louise
Ware, *Jacob A. Riis* (New York: D. Appleton-Century, 1939).

precincts for the *New York Tribune,* eking out of the crimes and accidents he reported a mosaic of human degradation, misfortune, and misery. In the ghettoes of New York City's Lower East Side he recorded in hundreds of short, vivid pictures physical wretchedness, moral and spiritual degradation, and all the dynamics of the slum of his era: poignantly, sensationally, and in the crude journalistic idiom of his day. That he translated what he saw into a lifelong battle against the slum of the tenement districts and wrote a half dozen books calling for social and economic reform is explained not only by an age imbued with humanitarian motive, but equally by his simple refusal to accept the horrors of a social pathology which he recorded in microscopic detail, and from which he recoiled.

The growth of industrialism in the United States after the Civil War, the growth of the cities with overcrowding in their slums, and the increasing European immigration, brought in their wake terrible problems. By the late 1880s many American cities were haunted by the specter of a permanent pauper class. It was not crime or juvenile delinquency in the city slum, alone, which aroused serious concern. The wretchedness of life in the city tenements, the calloused indifference of employers in their exploitation of the child and adult poor, the corruption of city officials, all help explain the ferment of social reform: the plans for economic reform, ranging from Henry George's single tax to the Socialist plea for public ownership; utopian fiction, of which Edward Bellamy's *Looking Backward* (1888) is representative; the founding of the American Federation of Labor (1886), and the dynamic stirrings of trade unionism; the settlement-house movement, and a myriad of social-work programs. The engagement with poverty was very real. By the end of the nineteenth century, America was on all fronts, philosophic, economic, and social, struggling with the dynamics of urban poverty, with urban blight, and with what a later age was euphemistically to call "the culturally deprived."[6]

Jacob Riis was, then, part of a great movement for social reform. He was directly related to a number of organizations in New York City which were in the forefront of social welfare and reform, particularly with the work of the Charity Organization Society and that of the Children's Aid Society. The first of these had been organized in 1882 by Josephine Shaw Lowell and was active in housing and legislative reform. The Children's Aid Society, founded as early as 1853, conducted a continuing battle against the slum and its deleterious effect on children, moving many children out of the city for short periods of time.[7] It was out of these associations that Jacob Riis largely drew not the theoretic constructs of social reform but rather the idea of a concerted assault on the slum in the idiom and language of a journalistic reformer, and in this context that he published his first book, *How the Other Half Lives: Studies Among the Tenements of New York* (1890).

[6] Good accounts of the historical and social background are in A. M. Schlesinger, *The Rise of the City* (New York: Harper, 1933); H. U. Faulker, *The Quest for Social Justice* (New York: Knopf, 1931). See also Robert Ernst, *Immigrant Life in New York City, 1825–1863* (New York: Columbia University Press, 1949); Maldwyn Allen Jones, *American Immigration* (Chicago: Chicago University Press, 1960); Robert A. Woods, et al., *The Poor in Great Cities* (New York: Charles Scribner's Sons, 1895); Moses Rischin, *The Promised City* (Cambridge: Harvard University Press, 1962); Roy Lubove, *The Progressives and the Slums: Tenement House Reform in New York City, 1890–1917* (Ithaca: Cornell University Press, 1962).

[7] For examples of summer programs for the children of the poor, see F. Cordasco, "Summer Camp Education for Underprivileged Children," *School and Society*, vol. 93 (Summer 1965), pp. 299–300. See also Morris I. Berger, *The Settlement, the Immigrant and the Public School* (unpublished Ph.D. thesis, Columbia University, 1956); and Richard Hofstadter, *The Age of Reform* (New York: Knopf, 1955).

The ugly pictures which Riis sketched in his vignettes of the slum and the tenement poor were not new;[8] they had been done before, but what was new was the book's raucous cry for reform, the vividness of its description and its prescription for change. Riis described the "genesis of the tenements," and drew as a line of demarcation for his "The Other Half" the 37,316 tenement houses which harbored the poor. The quality of his writing sought a sharp delineation of the pauperism and the crime, the degradation and the vice, and all was pointed up in the sharp staccato of a reporter's penchant for statistics:

. . . The commonest keeper soon learns to pick out almost at sight the "cases" that will leave the penitentiary, the workhouse, the almshouse, only to return again and again, each time more hopeless, to spend their wasted lives in the bondage of the island.

The alcoholic cells in Bellevue Hospital are a way station for a goodly share of them on their journeys back and forth across the East River. Last year they held altogether 3694 prisoners, considerably more than one-fourth of the whole number of 13,813 patients that went in through the hospital gates. The average daily census of all the prisons, hospitals, workhouses, and asylums in the charge of the Department of Charities and Correction last year was about 14,000 and about one employee was required for every ten of this army to keep its machinery running smoothly. The total number admitted in

[8] Charles Loring Brace, *The Dangerous Classes of New York and Twenty Years' Work Among Them* (New York: Wynkoop and Hallenbeck, 1880). For an early picture of the English poor, see Henry Meyhew, *London Labour and the London Poor: The Condition and Earnings of Those That Will Work, Cannot Work, and Will Not Work* (London: Charles Griffin, 1851).

1889 to all the jails and institutions in the city and on the islands was 138,332. To the almshouse alone 38,600 were admitted, 9765 were there to start the new year with, and 553 were born with the dark shadow of the poorhouse overhanging their lives, making a total of 48,918. . . . The first cost of maintaining our standing army of paupers, criminals, and sick poor by direct taxation was last year $7,156,112.94. (*How the Other Half Lives,* 1890 edition, pp. 261–63).

How the Other Half Lives described the horrible conditions which Riis found in the tenements, and drew particular attention to the plight of neglected and abandoned children (he called vagabond children "street arabs"); it applauded the efforts of those agencies (*e.g.,* The Society for the Prevention of Cruelty to Children) which were engaged in confronting the stark terror of a city in which nearly a half million people (in a population of a million and a half) were begging for food and in which one person of every ten who died was buried a pauper in Potter's Field.[9]

For Riis the *bête noire* of this social pathology was the tenement against which he offered no sophisticated theories for social reform. The only effective remedies were to be provided by law, by the remodeling of old houses, and by model housing built on new plans.[10] The graphic quality of *How the Other Half*

[9] The book was illustrated with many photographs most of which Riis took himself. For an interesting description of his techniques see his *The Making of an American* (New York: Macmillan, 1901), pp. 264–74.

[10] The intricacies of tenement house reform in New York City are best described in James Ford, *Slums and Housing with Special Reference to New York City* (Cambridge: Harvard University Press, 1936). Ford notes, "During this period (1890s) Jacob A. Riis probably had greater influence than any other publicist in calling attention in a graphic manner to the evils of slum dwelling and in developing the public opinion which

Lives; its muscular Christianity, cast in the mold of the nineteenth century evangelism and individualism of Charles Kingsley; and the simplicity of its patterns of reform made the book an immediate success.[11] In essence, it became the prototype of all of the books which Riis was to write against the tenement.[12] The basic ingredients were always the same, and in holding up a mirror to his age, he awakened conscience and became a significant part of that age's reform. By 1900 (when Riis reviewed the history of the struggle in *The Ten Years' War*), significant gains had been achieved. The work of the Gilder Commission of 1894 outlawed the old rear tenements in the Tenement House Law of 1895.[13] The notorious Mulberry Bend was demolished and replaced with Mulberry Bend Park.[14] In 1900 the New York State Tenement Commis-

---

was necessary to bring about the drastic changes in tenement house legislation that occurred in 1901" (p. 197). For a contemporary account of proposed reforms, see "Tenement House Ordinances: Proposed by the Tenement House Ordinances Committee of the Charity Organization Society," *Charities,* vol. III (July 1, 1899), pp. 2–6.

[11] *The Christian Union* spoke of *How the Other Half Lives* as ". . . these companion pictures, dark and ominous in line and color, ought to stir in the prosperous, the happy, and the indolent a sense of misery of a large part of their fellow beings, and stimulate them to practical action." "In Darkest New York," *The Christian Union,* vol. 42 (November 27, 1890), p. 703. See also *The Nation,* vol. 52 (February 5, 1891); *The Independent* (January 1, 1891), p. 19; *The Dial* (April 1891), p. 364; *The Critic* (December 27, 1890), p. 332.

[12] *The Children of the Poor* (1892); *Out of Mulberry Bend* (1898); *A Ten Years' War* (1900); *The Battle with the Slum* (1902); *Children of the Tenements* (1903).

[13] See Joseph Lee, "Preventive Work: American Philanthropy of the 19th Century," *The Charities Review,* vol. 10 (December 1900), p. 481. See also Chapter 497, Laws (New York) of 1894.

[14] For the opening of the Park, see the New York *Times,* June 16, 1897, p. 7.

sion presented its report to the Legislature, and the Tenement House Law of 1901 was enacted, representing in its provisions the first major advance in the fight against the tenement slum. According to this law all tenements built after 1901 had to provide for light and ventilation in all rooms as well as in public halls. Only seventy per cent of the lot could be occupied by the building which was also limited in height to one half times the width of the street. No room of less than seventy square feet was to be permitted. Large courts, twelve feet wide, were provided in place of the small air shafts, and a twenty-four-foot-wide court was to be in the center of the building. Non-fireproof buildings were limited to six stories, and fire escapes were forbidden in air shafts. Stairs and hallways were to be completely fireproof in buildings of five stories or more.[15] In large measure, the Law of 1901 was due to the efforts of Jacob Riis. In the New York City of today thousands of old-law tenements (built before the Law of 1901, and outside the purview of the law) still stand as grim evidence of the horrors against which Jacob Riis fought and won.

How instructive is Jacob Riis to our age, to its "Great Society," and to the contemporary patterns of social reform? Alongside much of the effort of our age his reforms may appear relatively small; the crusade he waged against the tenement could be regarded as but a miniscule part of what the Demonstration Cities and Metropolitan Development Act (1966) set out to provide in our cities in our time; and it might be cogently argued that Riis suffered all of the prejudices of his day and that in his books the immigrant tenement poor are at best crude caricatures, and that his concept of "Americanization" and his call for restrictive immi-

[15] Robert W. DeForest, "Recent Progress in Tenement House Reform," *The Annals of the American Academy of Political and Social Science,* vol. 23 (January–June 1904), pp. 109 ff. See also James Ford, *op. cit.*

gration were the harbingers of the isolationism and
quotas of subsequent decades. Yet all of these misgivings would miss the point and deny us the full measure
of the man. Jacob Riis was part of a reform age. With
this age, he shared what we call "commitment": the
restiveness of an age which saw trade unionism, humanitarian reformers, the churches, its creative literature, even the schools, jointly engaged in a massive
assault against social ills, and with a buoyant optimism
which prophesied inevitable change and melioration,
the last phases of what the historian James Bury called
the "idea of progress."

There may be many answers, but none is more appropriate than the eulogy written a long time ago by
the charismatic Theodore Roosevelt who was a witness to the modest endeavors of Jacob Riis:

> Jacob Riis was one of those men who by his writings
> contributed most to raising the standard of unself-
> ishness, of disinterestedness, of sane and kindly
> good citizenship, in this country. But in addition to
> this he was one of the few great writers for clean
> and decent living and for upright conduct who was
> also a great doer. He never wrote sentences which
> he did not in good faith try to act whenever he
> could find the opportunity for action.[16]

[16] "Jacob Riis," *The Outlook*, vol. 57 (June 6, 1914), p.
284.

I

HOW THE OTHER HALF LIVES
Studies Among the Tenements
of New York

INTRODUCTION

————

Long ago it was said that "one half of the world does not know how the other half lives." That was true then. It did not know because it did not care. The half that was on top cared little for the struggles, and less for the fate of those who were underneath, so long as it was able to hold them there and keep its own seat. There came a time when the discomfort and crowding below were so great, and the consequent upheavals so violent, that it was no longer an easy thing to do, and then the upper half fell to inquiring what was the matter. Information on the subject has been accumulating rapidly since, and the whole world has had its hands full answering for its old ignorance.

In New York, the youngest of the world's great cities, that time came later than elsewhere, because the crowding had not been so great. There were those who believed that it would never come; but their hopes were vain. Greed and reckless selfishness wrought like results here as in the cities of older lands. "When the great riot occurred in 1863," so reads the testimony of the Secretary of the Prison Association of New York before a legislative committee appointed to investigate causes of the increase of crime in the State twenty-five years ago, "every hiding place and nursery of crime discovered itself by immediate and active participation in the operations of the mob. Those very places and domiciles, and all that are like them, are today nurseries of crime, and of the vices and disorderly courses which lead to crime. By far the largest part

—eighty per cent at least—of crimes against property and against the person are perpetrated by individuals who have either lost connection with home life, or never had any, or whose *homes had ceased to be sufficiently separate, decent, and desirable to afford what are regarded as ordinary wholesome influences of home and family.* . . . The younger criminals seem to come almost exclusively from the worst tenement house districts, that is, when traced back to the very places where they had their homes in the city here." Of one thing New York made sure at that early stage of the inquiry: the boundary line of the Other Half lies through the tenements.

It is ten years and over, now, since that line divided New York's population evenly. Today three-fourths of its people live in the tenements, and the nineteenth century drift of the population to the cities is sending ever-increasing multitudes to crowd them. The fifteen thousand tenant houses that were the despair of the sanitarian in the past generation have swelled into thirty-seven thousand, and more than twelve hundred thousand persons call them home. The one way out he saw—rapid transit to the suburbs—has brought no relief. We know now that there is no way out; that the "system" that was the evil offspring of public neglect and private greed has come to stay, a storm center forever of our civilization. Nothing is left but to make the best of a bad bargain.

What the tenements are and how they grew to what they are, we shall see hereafter. The story is dark enough, drawn from the plain public records, to send a chill to any heart. If it shall appear that the sufferings and the sins of the "other half," and the evil they breed, are but as a just punishment upon the community that gave it no other choice, it will be because that is the truth. The boundary line lies there because, while the forces for good on one side vastly outweigh the bad—it were not well otherwise—in the tenements all the influences make for evil; because they are the hotbeds of the epidemics that carry death to rich and poor alike; the nurseries of pauperism and crime that fill our jails and police courts; that throw off a scum of forty thousand human wrecks to the island asylums and workhouses year by year; that turned out in the last eight years a round half million beggars to prey upon our charities; that maintain a standing army of ten thousand tramps with all that that implies; because, above all, they touch the family life with deadly moral contagion. This is their worst crime, inseparable from the system. That we have to own it the child of our own wrong does not excuse it, even though it gives it claim upon our utmost patience and tenderest charity.

What are you going to do about it is the question of today. It was asked once of our city in taunting defiance by a band of political cutthroats, the legitimate outgrowth of life on the tenement-house level.* Law and order found the answer then and prevailed. With our enormously swelling population held in this galling bondage, will that answer always be given? It will depend on how fully the situation that prompted the challenge is grasped. Forty per cent of the distress among the poor, said a recent official report, is due to drunkenness. But the first legislative committee ever appointed to probe this sore went deeper down and uncovered its roots. The "conclusion forced itself upon it that certain conditions and associations of human life and habitation are the prolific parents of corresponding habits and morals," and it recommended "the prevention of drunkenness by providing for every man a clean and comfortable home." Years after, a sanitary inquiry brought to light the fact that "more than one-half of the tenements with two-thirds of their population were held by owners who made the keeping of them a business, *generally a speculation.* The owner was seeking a certain percentage on his outlay, and that percentage very rarely fell below

* The Tweed band of municipal robbers.

fifteen per cent, and frequently exceeded thirty.* . . .
The complaint was universal among the tenants
that they were entirely uncared for, and that the only
answer to their requests to have the place put in order
by repairs and necessary improvements was that they
must pay their rent or leave. The agent's instructions
were simple but emphatic: 'Collect the rent in advance,
or, failing, eject the occupants.'" Upon such a stock
grew this upas tree. Small wonder the fruit is bitter.
The remedy that shall be an effective answer to the
coming appeal for justice must proceed from the public conscience. Neither legislation nor charity can
cover the ground. The greed of capital that wrought
the evil must itself undo it, as far as it can now be
undone. Homes must be built for the working masses
by those who employ their labor; but tenements
must cease to be "good property" in the old, heartless sense. "Philanthropy and five per cent" is the
penance exacted.

If this is true from a purely economic point of view,
what then of the outlook from the Christian standpoint? Not long ago a great meeting was held in this
city, of all denominations of religious faith, to discuss
the question how to lay hold of these teeming masses
in the tenements with Christian influences, to which
they are now too often strangers. Might not the con-
ference have found in the warning of one Brooklyn
builder, who has invested his capital on this plan and
made it pay more than a money interest, a hint worth
heeding: "How shall the love of God be understood
by those who have been nurtured in sight only of the
greed of man?"

* Forty per cent was declared by witnesses before a Senate
Committee to be a fair average interest on tenement property.
Instances were given of its being one hundred per cent and
over.

GENESIS OF
THE TENEMENT

The first tenement New York knew bore the mark of Cain from its birth, though a generation passed before the writing was deciphered. It was the "rear house," infamous ever after in our city's history. There had been tenant houses before, but they were not built for the purpose. Nothing would probably have shocked their original owners more than the idea of their harboring a promiscuous crowd; for they were the decorous homes of the old Knickerbockers, the proud aristocracy of Manhattan in the early days.

It was the stir and bustle of trade, together with the tremendous immigration that followed upon the war of 1812 that dislodged them. In thirty-five years the city of less than a hundred thousand came to harbor half a million souls, for whom homes had to be found. Within the memory of men not yet in their prime, Washington had moved from his house on Cherry Hill as too far out of town to be easily reached. Now the old residents followed his example; but they moved in a different direction and for a different reason. Their comfortable dwellings in the once fashionable streets along the East River front fell into the hands of real estate agents and boardinghouse keepers; and here, says the report to the Legislature of 1857, when the evils engendered had excited just alarm, "in its beginning, the tenant house became a real blessing to that class of industrious poor whose small earnings limited their expenses, and whose employment in workshops, stores, or about the warehouses and thoroughfares, render a near residence of much importance." Not for long, however. As business increased, and the city grew with rapid strides, the necessities of the poor became the opportunity of their wealthier neighbors, and the stamp was set upon the old houses, suddenly become valuable, which the best thought and effort of a later age have vainly struggled to efface. Their "*large rooms were partitioned into several smaller ones*, without regard to light or ventilation, the rate of rent being lower in proportion to space or height from the street; and they soon became filled from cellar to garret with a class of tenantry living from hand to mouth, loose in morals, improvident in habits, degraded, and squalid as beggary itself." It was thus the dark bedroom, prolific of untold depravities, came into the world. It was destined to survive the old houses. In their new role, says the old report, eloquent in its indignant denunciation of "evils more destructive than wars," "they were not intended to last. Rents were fixed high enough to cover damage and abuse from this class, from whom nothing was expected, and the most was made of them while they lasted. Neatness, order, cleanliness, were never dreamed of in connection with the tenant-house system, as it spread its localities from year to year; while reckless slovenliness, discontent, privation, and ignorance were left to work out their invariable results, until the entire premises reached the level of tenant-house dilapidation, containing, but sheltering not, the miserable hordes that crowded beneath moldering, water-rotted roofs or burrowed among the rats of clammy cellars." Yet so illogical is human greed that, at a later day, when called to account, "the proprietors frequently urged the filthy habits of the tenants as an excuse for the condition of their property, utterly losing sight of the fact that it was the tolerance of those habits which was the real evil, and that for this they themselves were alone responsible."

Still the pressure of the crowds did not abate, and

in the old garden where the stolid Dutch burgher grew his tulips or early cabbages a rear house was built, generally of wood, two stories high at first. Presently it was carried up another story, and another. Where two families had lived ten moved in. The front house followed suit, if the brick walls were strong enough. The question was not always asked, judging from complaints made by a contemporary witness, that the old buildings were "often carried up to a great height without regard to the strength of the foundation walls." It was rent the owner was after; nothing was said in the contract about either the safety or the comfort of the tenants. The garden gate no longer swung on its rusty hinges. The shell-paved walk had become an alley; what the rear house had left of the garden, a "court." Plenty such are yet to be found in the Fourth Ward, with here and there one of the original rear tenements.

Worse was to follow. It was "soon perceived by estate owners and agents of property that a greater percentage of profits could be realized by the conversion of houses and blocks into barracks, and dividing their space into smaller proportions capable of containing human life within four walls. . . . Blocks were rented of real estate owners, or 'purchased on time,' or taken in charge at a percentage, and held for underletting." With the appearance of the middleman, wholly irresponsible, and utterly reckless and unrestrained, began the era of tenement building which turned out such blocks as Gotham Court, where, in one cholera epidemic that scarcely touched the clean wards, the tenants died at the rate of one hundred and ninety-five to the thousand of population; which forced the general mortality of the city up from 1 in 41.83 in 1815, to 1 in 27.33 in 1855, a year of unusual freedom from epidemic disease, and which wrung from the early organizers of the Health Department this wail: "There are numerous examples of tenement houses in which are lodged several hundred people that have a *pro rata* allotment of ground area scarcely equal to two square yards upon the city lot, courtyards and all included." The tenement-house population had swelled to half a million souls by that time, and on the East Side, in what is still the most densely populated district in all the world, China not excluded, it was packed at the rate of 290,000 to the square mile, a state of affairs wholly unexampled. The utmost cupidity of other lands and other days had never contrived to herd much more than half that number within the same space. The greatest crowding of Old London was at the rate of 175,816. Swine roamed the streets and gutters as their principal scavengers.* The death of a child in a tenement was registered at the Bureau of Vital Statistics as "plainly due to suffocation in the foul air of an unventilated apartment," and the Senators, who had come down from Albany to find out what was the matter with New York, reported that "there are annually cut off from the population by disease and death enough human beings to people a city, and enough human labor to sustain it." And yet experts had testified that, as compared with uptown, rents were from twenty-five to thirty per cent higher in the worst slums of the lower wards, with such accommodations as were enjoyed, for instance, by a "family with boarders" in Cedar Street, who fed hogs in the cellar that contained eight or ten loads of manure; or "one room 12 × 12 with five families living in it, comprising twenty persons of both sexes and all ages, with only two beds, without partition, screen, chair, or table." The rate of rent has been successfully maintained to the present day, though the hog at least has been eliminated.

Lest anybody flatter himself with the notion that these were evils of a day that is happily past and may safely be forgotten, let me mention here three

---

* It was not until the winter of 1867 that owners of swine were prohibited by ordinance from letting them run at large in the built-up portions of the city.

very recent instances of tenement-house life that came under my notice. One was the burning of a rear house in Mott Street, from appearances one of the original tenant houses that made their owners rich. The fire made homeless ten families, who had paid an average of $5 a month for their mean little cubbyholes. The owner himself told me that it was *fully* insured for $800, though it brought him in $600 a year rent. He evidently considered himself especially entitled to be pitied for losing such valuable property. Another was the case of a hard-working family of man and wife, young people from the old country, who took poison together in a Crosby Street tenement because they were "tired." There was no other explanation, and none was needed when I stood in the room in which they had lived. It was in the attic with sloping ceiling and a single window so far out on the roof that it seemed not to belong to the place at all. With scarcely room enough to turn around in they had been compelled to pay five dollars and a half a month in advance. There were four such rooms in that attic, and together they brought in as much as many a handsome little cottage in a pleasant part of Brooklyn. The third instance was that of a colored family of husband, wife, and baby in a wretched rear rookery in West Third Street. Their rent was eight dollars and a half for a single room on the top story, so small that I was unable to get a photograph of it even by placing the camera outside the open door. Three short steps across either way would have measured its full extent.

There was just one excuse for the early tenement-house builders, and their successors may plead it with nearly as good right for what it is worth. "Such," says an official report, "is the lack of house room in the city that any kind of tenement can be immediately crowded with lodgers, if there is space offered." Thousands were living in cellars. There were three hundred underground lodginghouses in the city when the Health Department was organized. Some fifteen years before that the old Baptist Church in Mulberry Street, just off Chatham Street, had been sold, and the rear half of the frame structure had been converted into tenements that with their swarming population became the scandal even of that reckless age. The wretched pile harbored no less than forty families, and the annual rate of deaths to the population was officially stated to be 75 in 1000. These tenements were an extreme type of very many, for the big barracks had by this time spread east and west and far up the island into the sparsely settled wards. Whether or not the title was clear to the land upon which they were built was of less account than that the rents were collected. If there were damages to pay, the tenant had to foot them. Cases were "very frequent when property was in litigation, and two or three different parties were collecting rents." Of course under such circumstances "no repairs were ever made."

The climax had been reached. The situation was summed up by the Society for the Improvement of the Condition of the Poor in these words: "Crazy old buildings, crowded rear tenements in filthy yards, dark, damp basements, leaking garrets, shops, out-houses, and stables* converted into dwellings, though scarcely fit to shelter brutes, are habitations of thousands of our fellow beings in this wealthy, Christian city." "The city," says its historian, Mrs. Martha Lamb, commenting on the era of aqueduct building between 1835 and 1845, "was a general asylum for vagrants." Young vagabonds, the natural offspring of such "home" conditions, overran the streets. Juvenile crime increased fearfully year by year. The Children's Aid Society and kindred philanthropic organizations were yet unborn, but in the city directory was to be found the address of the "American Society for the Promotion of Education in Africa."

---

* "A lot 50 × 60, contained twenty stables, rented for dwellings at $15 a year each; cost of the whole $600."

THE AWAKENING

The dread of advancing cholera, with the guilty
knowledge of the harvest field that awaited the plague
in New York's slums, pricked the conscience of the
community into action soon after the close of the war.
A citizens' movement resulted in the organization of a
Board of Health and the adoption of the "Tenement-
House Act" of 1867, the first step toward remedial
legislation. A thorough canvass of the tenements had
been begun already in the previous year; but the
cholera first, and next a scourge of smallpox, delayed
the work, while emphasizing the need of it, so that
it was 1869 before it got fairly under way and began
to tell. The dark bedroom fell under the ban first.
In that year the Board ordered the cutting of more
than forty-six thousand windows in interior rooms,
chiefly for ventilation—for little or no light was to be
had from the dark hallways. Air shafts were unknown.
The saw had a job all that summer; by early fall nearly
all the orders had been carried out. Not without opposition; obstacles were thrown in the way of the officials on the one side by the owners of the tenements,
who saw in every order to repair or clean up only an
item of added expense to diminish their income from
the rent; on the other side by the tenants themselves,
who had sunk, after a generation of unavailing protest, to the level of their surroundings, and were at
last content to remain there.

The tenements had bred their Nemesis, a proletariat
ready and able to avenge the wrongs of their crowds.

Already it taxed the city heavily for the support of its jails and charities. The basis of opposition, curiously enough, was the same at both extremes; owner and tenant alike considered official interference an infringement of personal rights and a hardship. It took long years of weary labor to make good the claim of the sunlight to such corners of the dens as it could reach at all. Not until five years after did the department succeed at last in ousting the "cave dwellers" and closing some five hundred and fifty cellars south of Houston Street, many of them below tidewater, that had been used as living apartments. In many instances the police had to drag the tenants out by force.

The work went on; but the need of it only grew with the effort. The Sanitarians were following up an evil that grew faster than they went; like a fire, it could only be headed off, not chased, with success. Official reports, read in the churches in 1879, characterized the younger criminals as victims of low social conditions of life and unhealthy, overcrowded lodgings, brought up in "an atmosphere of actual darkness, moral and physical." This after the saw had been busy in the dark corners ten years! "If we could see the air breathed by these poor creatures in their tenements," said a well-known physician, "it would show itself to be fouler than the mud of the gutters." Little improvement was apparent despite all that had been done. "The new tenements that have been recently built have been usually as badly planned as the old, with dark and unhealthy rooms, often over wet cellars, where extreme overcrowding is permitted," was the verdict of one authority. These are the houses that today perpetuate the worst traditions of the past, and they are counted by thousands. The Five Points had been cleansed, as far as the immediate neighborhood was concerned, but the Mulberry Street Bend was fast outdoing it in foulness not a stone's throw away, and new centers of corruption were continually springing up and getting the upper hand whenever vigilance was relaxed for ever so short a time. It is one of the curses of the tenement-house system that the worst houses exercise a leveling influence upon all the rest, just as one bad boy in a schoolroom will spoil the whole class. It is one of the ways the evil that was "the result of forgetfulness of the poor," as the Council of Hygiene mildly put it, has of avenging itself.

The determined effort to head it off by laying a strong hand upon the tenement builders that has been the chief business of the Health Board of recent years dates from this period. The era of the air shaft has not solved the problem of housing the poor, but it has made good use of limited opportunities. Over the new houses, sanitary law exercises full control. But the old remain. They cannot be summarily torn down, though in extreme cases the authorities can order them cleared. The outrageous overcrowding, too, remains. It is characteristic of the tenements. Poverty, their badge and typical condition, invites—compels it. All efforts to abate it result only in temporary relief. As long as they exist, it will exist with them. And the tenements will exist in New York forever.

Today, what is a tenement? The law defines it as a house "occupied by three or more families, living independently and doing their cooking on the premises; or by more than two families on a floor, so living and cooking and having a common right in the halls, stairways, yards, etc." That is the legal meaning, and includes flats and apartment houses, with which we have nothing to do. In its narrower sense the typical tenement was thus described when last arraigned before the bar of public justice: "It is generally a brick building from four to six stories high on the street, frequently with a store on the first floor which, when used for the sale of liquor, has a side opening for the benefit of the inmates and to evade the Sunday law; four families occupy each floor, and a set of rooms consists of one or two dark closets, used as bedrooms, with a living

room twelve feet by ten. The staircase is too often
a dark well in the center of the house, and no direct
through ventilation is possible, each family being separated from the other by partitions. Frequently the
rear of the lot is occupied by another building of three
stories high with two families on a floor." The picture
is nearly as true today as ten years ago, and will be
for a long time to come. The dim light admitted by
the air shaft shines upon greater crowds than ever.
Tenements are still "good property," and the poverty
of the poor man his destruction. A barrack downtown
where he *has to live* because he is poor brings in a
third more rent than a decent flat house in Harlem.
The statement once made a sensation that between
seventy and eighty children had been found in one
tenement. It no longer excites even passing attention,
when the sanitary police report counting 101 adults
and 91 children in a Crosby Street house, one of twins,
built together. The children in the other, if I am not
mistaken, numbered 89, a total of 180 for two tenements! Or when a midnight inspection in Mulberry
Street unearths a hundred and fifty "lodgers" sleeping
on filthy floors in two buildings. In spite of brownstone
trimmings, plate-glass and mosaic vestibule floors, the
water does not rise in summer to the second story,
while the beer flows unchecked to the all-night pic-
nics on the roof. The saloon with the side door and the
landlord divide the prosperity of the place between
them, and the tenant, in sullen submission, foots the
bills.

Where are the tenements of today? Say rather: where
are they not? In fifty years they have crept up from
the Fourth Ward slums and the Five Points the whole
length of the island, and have polluted the Annexed
District to the Westchester line. Crowding all the
lower wards, wherever business leaves a foot of ground
unclaimed; strung along both rivers, like ball and chain
tied to the foot of every street, and filling up Harlem
with their restless, pent-up multitudes, they hold within

their clutch the wealth and business of New York, hold them at their mercy in the day of mob rule and wrath. The bulletproof shutters, the stacks of hand grenades, and the Gatling guns of the Subtreasury are tacit admissions of the fact and of the quality of the mercy expected. The tenements today are New York, harboring three-fourths of its population. When another generation shall have doubled the census of our city, and to that vast army of workers, held captive by poverty, the very name of home shall be as a bitter mockery, what will the harvest be?

THE MIXED CROWD

When once I asked the agent of a notorious Fourth Ward alley how many people might be living in it, I was told: One hundred and forty families, one hundred Irish, thirty-eight Italian, and two that spoke the German tongue. Barring the agent herself, there was not a native-born individual in the court. The answer was characteristic of the cosmopolitan character of lower New York, very nearly so of the whole of it, wherever it runs to alleys and courts. One may find for the asking an Italian, a German, a French, African, Spanish, Bohemian, Russian, Scandinavian, Jewish, and Chinese colony. Even the Arab, who peddles "holy earth" from the Battery as a direct importation from Jerusalem, has his exclusive preserves at the lower end of Washington Street. The one thing you shall vainly ask for in the chief city of America is a distinctively American community. There is none; certainly not among the tenements. Where have they gone to, the old inhabitants? I put the question to one who might fairly be presumed to be of the number, since I had found him sighing for the "good old days" when the legend "no Irish need apply" was familiar in the advertising columns of the newspapers. He looked at me with a puzzled air. "I don't know," he said. "I wish I did. Some went to California in '49, some to the war and never came back. The rest, I expect, have gone to heaven, or somewhere. I don't see them 'round here."

Whatever the merit of the good man's conjectures,

his eyes did not deceive him. They are not here. In their place has come this queer conglomerate mass of heterogeneous elements, ever striving and working like whisky and water in one glass, and with the like result: final union and a prevailing taint of whisky. The once unwelcome Irishman has been followed in his turn by the Italian, the Russian Jew, and the Chinaman, and has himself taken a hand at opposition, quite as bitter and quite as ineffectual, against these later hordes. Wherever these have gone, they have crowded him out, possessing the block, the street, the ward with their denser swarms. But the Irishman's revenge is complete. Victorious in defeat over his recent as over his more ancient foe, the one who opposed his coming no less than the one who drove him out, he dictates to both their politics, and, secure in possession of the offices, returns the native his greeting with interest, while collecting the rents of the Italian whose house he has bought with the profits of his saloon. As a landlord he is picturesquely autocratic. An amusing instance of his methods came under my notice while writing these lines. An inspector of the Health Department found an Italian family paying a man with a Celtic name twenty-five dollars a month for three small rooms in a ramshackle rear tenement—more than twice what they were worth—and expressed his astonishment to the tenant, an ignorant Sicilian laborer. He replied that he had once asked the landlord to reduce the rent, but he would not do it.

"Well! What did he say?" asked the inspector.

"'Damma, man!' he said; 'if you speaka thata way to me, I fira you and your things in the streeta.'" And the frightened Italian paid the rent.

In justice to the Irish landlord it must be said that like an apt pupil he was merely showing forth the result of the schooling he had received, re-enacting, in his own way, the scheme of the tenements. It is only his frankness that shocks. The Irishman does not naturally take kindly to tenement life, though with characteristic versatility he adapts himself to its conditions at once. It does violence, nevertheless, to the best that is in him, and for that very reason of all who come within its sphere soonest corrupts him. The result is a sediment, the product of more than a generation in the city's slums, that, as distinguished from the larger body of his class, justly ranks at the foot of tenement dwellers, the so-called "low Irish."

It is not to be assumed, of course, that the whole body of the population living in the tenements, of which New Yorkers are in the habit of speaking vaguely as "the poor," or even the larger part of it, is to be classed as vicious or as poor in the sense of verging on beggary.

New York's wage earners have no other place to live, more is the pity. They are truly poor for having no better homes; waxing poorer in purse as the exorbitant rents to which they are tied, as ever was serf to soil, keep rising. The wonder is that they are not all corrupted, and speedily, by their surroundings. If, on the contrary, there be a steady working up, if not out of the slough, the fact is a powerful argument for the optimist's belief that the world is, after all, growing better, not worse, and would go far toward disarming apprehension, were it not for the steadier growth of the sediment of the slums and its constant menace. Such an impulse toward better things there certainly is. The German ragpicker of thirty years ago, quite as low in the scale as his Italian successor, is the thrifty tradesman or prosperous farmer of today.*

The Italian scavenger of our time is fast graduating into exclusive control of the corner fruit stands, while

---

* The Sheriff Street Colony of ragpickers, long since gone, is an instance in point. The thrifty Germans saved up money during years of hard work in squalor and apparently wretched poverty to buy a township in a Western State, and the whole colony moved out there in a body. There need be no doubt about their thriving there.

his black-eyed boy monopolizes the bootblacking industry in which a few years ago he was an intruder. The Irish hod carrier in the second generation has become a bricklayer, if not the Alderman of his ward, while the Chinese coolie is in almost exclusive possession of the laundry business. The reason is obvious. The poorest immigrant comes here with the purpose and ambition to better himself and, given half a chance, might be reasonably expected to make the most of it. To the false plea that he prefers the squalid homes in which his kind are housed there could be no better answer. The truth is, his half chance has too long been wanting, and for the bad result he has been unjustly blamed.

As emigration from east to west follows the latitude, so does the foreign influx in New York distribute itself along certain well-defined lines that waver and break only under the stronger pressure of a more gregarious race or the encroachments of inexorable business. A feeling of dependence upon mutual effort, natural to strangers in a strange land, unacquainted with its language and customs, sufficiently accounts for this.

The Irishman is the true cosmopolitan immigrant. All-pervading, he shares his lodging with perfect impartiality with the Italian, the Greek, and the "Dutchman," yielding only to sheer force of numbers, and objects equally to them all. A map of the city, colored to designate nationalities, would show more stripes than on the skin of a zebra, and more colors than any rainbow. The city on such a map would fall into two great halves, green for the Irish prevailing in the West Side tenement districts, and blue for the Germans on the East Side. But intermingled with these ground colors would be an odd variety of tints that would give the whole the appearance of an extraordinary crazy quilt. From down in the Sixth Ward, upon the site of the old Collect Pond that in the days of the fathers drained the hills which are no more, the red of the Italian would be seen forcing its way northward along the line of Mulberry Street to the quarter of the French purple on Bleecker Street and South Fifth Avenue, to lose itself and reappear, after a lapse of miles, in the "Little Italy" of Harlem, east of Second Avenue. Dashes of red, sharply defined, would be seen strung through the Annexed District, northward to the city line. On the West Side the red would be seen overrunning the old Africa of Thompson Street, pushing the black of the negro* rapidly uptown, against querulous but unavailing protests, occupying his home, his church, his trade and all, with merciless impartiality. There is a church in Mulberry Street that has stood for two generations as a sort of milestone of these migrations. Built originally for the worship of staid New Yorkers of the "old stock," it was engulfed by the colored tide, when the draft riots drove the negroes out of reach of Cherry Street and the Five Points. Within the past decade the advance wave of the Italian onset reached it, and today the arms of United Italy adorn its front. The negroes have made a stand at several points along Seventh and Eighth Avenues; but their main body, still pursued by the Italian foe, is on the march yet, and the black mark will be found overshadowing today many blocks on the East Side, with One Hundredth Street as the center, where colonies of them have settled recently.

Hardly less aggressive than the Italian, the Russian and Polish Jew, having overrun the district between Rivington and Division Streets, east of the Bowery, to the point of suffocation, is filling the tenements of the old Seventh Ward to the river front, and disputing with the Italian every foot of available space in the back alleys of Mulberry Street. The two races, differing

---

* "Negro" was not officially capitalized until the New York *Times* announced in an editorial that it would add "Negro" to its list of words to be capitalized. ("Negro with a Capital 'N,' " New York *Times*, March 7, 1930.)

hopelessly in much, have this in common: they carry their slums with them wherever they go, if allowed to do it. Little Italy already rivals its parent, the "Bend," in foulness. Other nationalities that begin at the bottom make a fresh start when crowded up the ladder. Happily both are manageable, the one by rabbinical, the other by the civil law. Between the dull gray of the Jew, his favorite color, and the Italian red, would be seen squeezed in on the map a sharp streak of yellow, marking the narrow boundaries of Chinatown. Dovetailed in with the German population, the poor but thrifty Bohemian might be picked out by the somber hue of his life as of his philosophy, struggling against heavy odds in the big human beehives of the East Side. Colonies of his people extend northward, with long lapses of space, from below the Cooper Institute more than three miles. The Bohemian is the only foreigner with any considerable representation in the city who counts no wealthy man of his race, none who has not to work hard for a living, or has got beyond the reach of the tenement.

Down near the Battery the West Side emerald would be soiled by a dirty stain, spreading rapidly like a splash of ink on a sheet of blotting paper, headquarters of the Arab tribe, that in a single year has swelled from the original dozen to twelve hundred, intent, every mother's son, on trade and barter. Dots and dashes of color here and there would show where the Finnish sailors worship their djumala (God), the Greek peddlers the ancient name of their race, and the Swiss the goddess of thrift. And so on to the end of the long register, all toiling together in the galling fetters of the tenement. Were the question raised Who makes the most of life thus mortgaged, who resists most stubbornly its leveling tendency—knows how to drag even the barracks upward a part of the way at least toward the ideal plane of the home—the palm must be unhesitatingly awarded the Teuton. The Italian and the poor Jew rise only by compulsion. The

Chinaman does not rise at all; here, as at home, he simply remains stationary. The Irishman's genius runs to public affairs rather than domestic life; wherever he is mustered in force, the saloon is the gorgeous center of political activity. The German struggles vainly to learn his trick; his Teutonic wit is too heavy, and the political ladder he raises from his saloon usually too short or too clumsy to reach the desired goal. The best part of his life is lived at home, and he makes himself a home independent of the surroundings, giving the lie to the saying, unhappily become a maxim of social truth, that pauperism and drunkenness naturally grow in the tenements. He makes the most of his tenement, and it should be added that whenever and as soon as he can save up money enough, he gets out and never crosses the threshold of one again.

THE DOWNTOWN
BACK ALLEYS

Down below Chatham Square, in the old Fourth
Ward, where the cradle of the tenement stood, we
shall find New York's Other Half at home, receiving
such as care to call and are not afraid. Not all of it, to
be sure, there is not room for that; but a fairly representative gathering, representative of its earliest and
worst traditions. There is nothing to be afraid of. In
this metropolis, let it be understood, there is no public
street where the stranger may not go safely by day
and by night, provided he knows how to mind his own
business and is sober. His coming and going will excite
little interest, unless he is suspected of being a truant
officer, in which case he will be impressed with the
truth of the observation that the American stock is
dying out for want of children. If he escapes this
suspicion and the risk of trampling upon, or being
himself run down by the bewildering swarms of
youngsters that are everywhere or nowhere as the
exigency and their quick scent of danger direct, he
will see no reason for dissenting from that observation.
Glimpses caught of the parents watching the youngsters play from windows or open doorways will soon
convince him that the native stock is in no way involved.

Leaving the Elevated Railroad where it dives under
the Brooklyn Bridge at Franklin Square, scarce a dozen
steps will take us where we wish to go. With its rush
and roar echoing yet in our ears, we have turned the
corner from prosperity to poverty. We stand upon the

domain of the tenement. In the shadow of the great
stone abutments the old Knickerbocker houses linger
like ghosts of a departed day. Down the winding slope
of Cherry Street—proud and fashionable Cherry Hill
that was—their broad steps, sloping roofs, and dormer
windows are easily made out; all the more easily for
the contrast with the ugly barracks that elbow them
right and left. These never had other design than to
shelter, at as little outlay as possible, the greatest
crowds out of which rent could be wrung. They were
the bad afterthought of a heedless day. The years have
brought to the old houses unhonored age, a querulous
second childhood that is out of tune with the time,
their tenants, the neighbors, and cries out against them
and against you in fretful protest in every step on their
rotten floors or squeaky stairs. Good cause have they
for their fretting. This one, with its shabby front and
poorly patched roof, what glowing firesides, what
happy children may it once have owned? Heavy feet,
too often with unsteady step, for the pothouse is next
door—where is it not next door in these slums?—have
worn away the brownstone steps since; the broken
columns at the door have rotted away at the base. Of
the handsome cornice barely a trace is left. Dirt and
desolation reign in the wide hallway, and danger lurks
on the stairs. Rough pine boards fence off the roomy
fireplaces—where coal is bought by the pail at the
rate of twelve dollars a ton, these have no place. The
arched gateway leads no longer to a shady bower on
the banks of the rushing stream, inviting to daydreams
with its gentle repose, but to a dark and nameless
alley, shut in by high brick walls, cheerless as the lives
of those they shelter. The wolf knocks loudly at the
gate in the troubled dreams that come to this alley,
echoes of the day's cares. A horde of dirty children
play about the dripping hydrant, the only thing in the
alley that thinks enough of its chance to make the
most of it: it is the best it can do. These are the children of the tenements, the growing generation of the

slums; this their home. From the great highway overhead, along which throbs the life-tide of two great
cities, one might drop a pebble into half a dozen such
alleys.

One yawns just across the street; not very broadly,
but it is not to blame. The builder of the old gateway
had no thought of its ever becoming a public thoroughfare. Once inside it widens, but only to make room for
a big boxlike building with the worn and greasy look
of the slum tenement that is stamped alike on the
houses and their tenants down here, even on the homeless cur that romps with the children in yonder building lot, with an air of expectant interest plainly betraying the forlorn hope that at some stage of the game a
meat bone may show up in the role of "It." Vain hope,
truly! Nothing more appetizing than a bare-legged
ragamuffin appears. Meat bones, not long since picked
clean, are as scarce in Blind Man's Alley as elbowroom
in any Fourth Ward backyard. The shouts of the children come hushed over the housetops, as if apologizing
for the intrusion. Few glad noises make this old alley
ring. Morning and evening it echoes with the gentle,
groping tap of the blind man's staff as he feels his way
to the street. Blind Man's Alley bears its name for a
reason. Until little more than a year ago its dark burrows harbored a colony of blind beggars, tenants of a
blind landlord, old Daniel Murphy, whom every child
in the ward knows, if he never heard of the President
of the United States. "Old Dan" made a big fortune—
he told me once four hundred thousand dollars—out of
his alley and the surrounding tenements, only to grow
blind himself in extreme old age, sharing in the end the
chief hardship of the wretched beings whose lot he had
stubbornly refused to better that he might increase
his wealth. Even when the Board of Health at last
compelled him to repair and clean up the worst of the
old buildings, under threat of driving out the tenants
and locking the doors behind them, the work was
accomplished against the old man's angry protests. He

appeared in person before the Board to argue his case, and his argument was characteristic.

"I have made my will," he said. "My monument stands waiting for me in Calvary. I stand on the very brink of the grave, blind and helpless, and now (here the pathos of the appeal was swept under in a burst of angry indignation) do you want me to build and get skinned, skinned? These people are not fit to live in a nice house. Let them go where they can, and let my house stand."

In spite of the genuine anguish of the appeal, it was downright amusing to find that his anger was provoked less by the anticipated waste of luxury on his tenants than by distrust of his own kind, the builder. He knew intuitively what to expect. The result showed that Mr. Murphy had gauged his tenants correctly. The cleaning up process apparently destroyed the home feeling of the alley; many of the blind people moved away and did not return. Some remained, however, and the name has clung to the place.

Some idea of what is meant by a sanitary "cleaning up" in these slums may be gained from the account of a mishap I met with once, in taking a flashlight picture of a group of blind beggars in one of the tenements down here. With unpracticed hands I managed to set fire to the house. When the blinding effect of the flash had passed away and I could see once more, I discovered that a lot of paper and rags that hung on the wall were ablaze. There were six of us, five blind men and women who knew nothing of their danger, and myself, in an attic room with a dozen crooked, rickety stairs between us and the street, and as many households as helpless as the one whose guest I was all about us. The thought How were they ever to be got out? made my blood run cold as I saw the flames creeping up the wall, and my first impulse was to bolt for the street and shout for help. The next was to smother the fire myself, and I did, with a vast deal of trouble. Afterward, when I came down to the street

I told a friendly policeman of my trouble. For some reason he thought it rather a good joke, and laughed immoderately at my concern lest even then sparks should be burrowing in the rotten wall that might yet break out in flame and destroy the house with all that were in it. He told me why, when he found time to draw breath. "Why, don't you know," he said, "that house is the Dirty Spoon? It caught fire six times last winter, but it wouldn't burn. The dirt was so thick on the walls, it smothered the fire!" Which, if true, shows that water and dirt, not usually held to be harmonious elements, work together for the good of those who insure houses.

Sunless and joyless though it be, Blind Man's Alley has that which its compeers of the slums vainly yearn for. It has a payday. Once a year sunlight shines into the lives of its forlorn crew, past and present. In June, when the Superintendent of Out-door Poor distributes the twenty thousand dollars annually allowed the poor blind by the city, in halfhearted recognition of its failure to otherwise provide for them, Blind Man's Alley takes a day off and goes to "see" Mr. Blake. That night it is noisy with unwonted merriment. There is scraping of squeaky fiddles in the dark rooms, and cracked old voices sing long-forgotten songs. Even the blind landlord rejoices, for much of the money goes into his coffers.

From their perch up among the rafters Mrs. Gallagher's blind boarders might hear, did they listen, the tramp of the policeman always on duty in Gotham Court, half a stone's throw away. His beat, though it takes in but a small portion of a single block, is quite as lively as most larger patrol rounds. A double row of five-story tenements, back to back under a common roof, extending back from the street two hundred and thirty-four feet, with barred openings in the dividing wall, so that the tenants may see but cannot get at each other from the stairs, makes the "court." Alleys—one wider by a couple of feet than the other, whence

the distinction Single and Double Alley—skirt the barracks on either side. Such, briefly, is the tenement that
has challenged public attention more than any other
in the whole city and tested the power of sanitary law
and rule for forty years. The name of the pile is not
down in the City Directory, but in the public records
it holds an unenviable place. It was here the mortality
rose during the last great cholera epidemic to the unprecedented rate of 195 in 1000 inhabitants. In its
worst days a full thousand could not be packed into
the court, though the number did probably not fall far
short of it. Even now, under the management of men
of conscience, and an agent, a King's Daughter, whose
practical energy, kindliness and good sense have done
much to redeem its foul reputation, the swarms it
shelters would make more than one fair-sized country
village. The mixed character of the population, by this
time about equally divided between the Celtic and
the Italian stock, accounts for the iron bars and the
policeman. It was an eminently Irish suggestion that
the latter was to be credited to the presence of two
German families in the court, who "made trouble all
the time." A Chinaman whom I questioned as he hurried past the iron gate of the alley put the matter in a
different light. "Lem Ilish velly bad," he said. Gotham
Court has been the entering wedge for the Italian
hordes, which until recently had not attained a foot-
hold in the Fourth Ward, but are now trailing across
Chatham Street from their stronghold in "the Bend"
in ever-increasing numbers, seeking, according to their
wont, the lowest level.

It is curious to find that this notorious block, whose
name was so long synonymous with all that was desperately bad, was originally built (in 1851) by a benevolent Quaker for the express purpose of rescuing the
poor people from the dreadful rookeries they were then
living in. How long it continued a model tenement is
not on record. It could not have been very long, for
already in 1862, ten years after it was finished, a sani-

tary official counted 146 cases of sickness in the court, including "all kinds of infectious disease," from small-pox down, and reported that of 138 children born in it in less than three years 61 had died, mostly before they were one year old. Seven years later the inspector of the district reported to the Board of Health that "nearly ten per cent of the population is sent to the public hospitals each year." When the alley was finally taken in hand by the authorities, and, as a first step toward its reclamation, the entire population was driven out by the police, experience dictated, as one of the first improvements to be made, the putting in of a kind of sewer grating, so constructed, as the official report patiently puts it, "as to prevent the ingress of persons disposed to make a hiding place" of the sewer and the cellars into which they opened. The fact was that the big vaulted sewers had long been a runway for thieves —the Swamp Angels—who through them easily escaped when chased by the police, as well as a storehouse for their plunder. The sewers are there today; in fact the two alleys are nothing but the roofs of these enor-mous tunnels in which a man may walk upright the full distance of the block and into the Cherry Street sewer —if he likes the fun and is not afraid of rats. Could their grimy walls speak, the big canals might tell many a startling tale. But they are silent enough, and so are most of those whose secrets they might betray. The floodgates connecting with the Cherry Street main are closed now, except when the water is drained off. Then there were no gates, and it is on record that the sewers were chosen as a shortcut habitually by residents of the court whose business lay on the line of them, near a manhole, perhaps, in Cherry Street, or at the river mouth of the big pipe when it was clear at low tide. "Me Jimmy," said one wrinkled old dame, who looked in while we were nosing about under Double Alley, "he used to go to his work along down Cherry Street that way every morning and come back at night." The associations must have been congenial. Probably "Jimmy" himself fitted into the landscape.

Halfway back from the street in this latter alley is a tenement, facing the main building, on the west side of the way, that was not originally part of the court proper. It stands there a curious monument to a Quaker's revenge, a living illustration of the power of hate to perpetuate its bitter fruit beyond the grave. The lot upon which it is built was the property of John Wood, brother of Silas, the builder of Gotham Court. He sold the Cherry Street front to a man who built upon it a tenement with entrance only from the street. Mr. Wood afterward quarreled about the partition line with his neighbor, Alderman Mullins, who had put up a long tenement barrack on his lot after the style of the Court, and the Alderman knocked him down. Tradition records that the Quaker picked himself up with the quiet remark, "I will pay thee for that, friend Alderman," and went his way. His manner of paying was to put up the big building in the rear of 34 Cherry Street with an immense blank wall right in front of the windows of Alderman Mullins's tenements, shutting out effectually light and air from them. But as he had no access to the street from his building for many years, it could not be let or used for anything, and remained vacant until it passed under the management of the Gotham Court property. Mullins's Court is there yet, and so is the Quaker's vengeful wall that has cursed the lives of thousands of innocent people since. At its farther end, the alley between the two that begins inside the Cherry Street tenement, six or seven feet wide, narrows down to less than two feet. It is barely possible to squeeze through; but few care to do it, for the rift leads to the jail of the Oak Street police station, and therefore is not popular with the growing youth of the district.

There is crape on the door of the Alderman's court as we pass out, and upstairs in one of the tenements preparations are making for a wake. A man lies dead in the hospital who was cut to pieces in a "can racket" in the alley on Sunday. The sway of the excise law is not extended to these back alleys. It would matter little if it were. There are secret byways, and some it is not held worthwhile to keep secret, along which the "growler" wanders at all hours and all seasons unmolested. It climbed the stairs so long and so often that day that murder resulted. It is nothing unusual on Cherry Street, nothing to "make a fuss" about. Not a week before, two or three blocks up the street, the police felt called upon to interfere in one of these can rackets at two o'clock in the morning, to secure peace for the neighborhood. The interference took the form of a general fusillade, during which one of the disturbers fell off the roof and was killed. There was the usual wake and nothing more was heard of it. What, indeed, was there to say?

The "Rock of Ages" is the name over the door of a low saloon that blocks the entrance to another alley, if possible more forlorn and dreary than the rest, as we pass out of the Alderman's court. It sounds like a jeer from the days, happily past, when the "wickedest man in New York" lived around the corner a little way and boasted of his title. One cannot take many steps in Cherry Street without encountering some relic of past or present prominence in the ways of crime, scarce one that does not turn up specimen bricks of the coming thief. The Cherry Street tough is all-pervading. Ask Superintendent Murray, who, as captain of the Oak Street squad, in seven months secured convictions for theft, robbery, and murder aggregating no less than five hundred and thirty years of penal servitude, and he will tell you his opinion that the Fourth Ward, even in the last twenty years, has turned out more criminals than all the rest of the city together.

But though the "Swamp Angels" have gone to their reward, their successors carry on business at the old stand as successfully, if not as boldly. There goes one who was once a shining light in thiefdom. He has reformed since, they say. The policeman on the corner, who is addicted to a professional unbelief in reform of any kind, will tell you that while on the Island once he sailed away on a shutter, paddling along until he was picked up in Hell Gate by a schooner's crew, whom he persuaded that he was a fanatic performing some sort of religious penance by his singular expedition. Over yonder, Tweed, the archthief, worked in a brush shop and earned an honest living before he took to politics. As we stroll from one narrow street to another, the odd contrast between the low, old-looking houses in front and the towering tenements in the backyards grows even more striking, perhaps because we expect and are looking for it. Nobody who was not would suspect the presence of the rear houses, though they have been there long enough. Here is one seven stories high behind one with only three floors. Take a look into this Roosevelt Street alley; just about one step wide, with a five-story house on one side that gets its light and air—God help us for pitiful mockery!—from this slit between brick walls. There are no windows in the wall on the other side; it is perfectly blank. The fire escapes of the long tenement fairly touch it; but the rays of the sun, rising, setting, or at high noon, never do. It never shone into the alley from the day the devil planned and man built it. There was once an English doctor who experimented with the sunlight in the soldiers' barracks, and found that on the side that was shut off altogether from the sun the mortality was one hundred per cent greater than on the light side, where its rays had free access. But then soldiers are of some account, have a fixed value, if not a very high one. The people who live here have not. The horse that pulls the dirt cart one of these laborers loads and unloads is of ever so much more account to the employer of his labor than he and all that belongs to him. Ask the owner; he will not attempt to deny it, if the horse is worth anything.

The man, too, knows it. It is the one thought that occasionally troubles the owner of the horse in the enjoyment of his prosperity, built of and upon the successful assertion of the truth that all men are created equal.

With what a shock did the story of yonder Madison Street alley come home to New Yorkers one morning, eight or ten years ago, when a fire that broke out after the men had gone to their work swept up those narrow stairs and burned up women and children to the number of a full half score. There were fire escapes, yes! but so placed that they could not be reached. The firemen had to look twice before they could find the opening that passes for a thoroughfare; a stout man would never venture in. Some wonderfully heroic rescues were made at that fire by people living in the adjoining tenements. Danger and trouble—of the imminent kind, not the everyday sort that excites neither interest nor commiseration—run even this common clay into heroic molds on occasion; occasions that help us to remember that the gap that separates the man with the patched coat from his wealthy neighbor is, after all, perhaps but a tenement. Yet, what a gap! And of whose making? Here, as we stroll along Madison Street, workmen are busy putting the finishing touches to the brownstone front of a tall new tenement. This one will probably be called an apartment house. They are carving satyrs' heads in the stone, with a crowd of gaping youngsters looking on in admiring wonder. Next door are two other tenements, likewise with brownstone fronts, fair to look at. The youngest of the children in the group is not too young to remember how their army of tenants was turned out by the health officers because the houses had been condemned as unfit for human beings to live in. The owner was a wealthy builder who "stood high in the community." Is it only in our fancy that the sardonic leer on the stone faces seems to list that way? Or is it an introspective grin? We will not ask if the new house belongs to the same builder. He, too, may have reformed.

We have crossed the boundary of the Seventh Ward. Penitentiary Row, suggestive name for a block of Cherry Street tenements, is behind us. Within recent days it has become peopled wholly with Hebrews, the overflow from Jewtown adjoining, peddlers and tailors, all of them. It is odd to read this legend from other days over the door: "No peddlers allowed in this house." These thrifty people are not only crowding into the tenements of this once exclusive district—they are buying them. The Jew runs to real estate as soon as he can save up enough for a deposit to clinch the bargain. As fast as the old houses are torn down, towering structures go up in their place, and Hebrews are found to be the builders. Here is a whole alley nicknamed after the intruder, Jews' Alley. But abuse and ridicule are not weapons to fight the Israelite with. He pockets them quietly with the rent and bides his time. He knows from experience, both sweet and bitter, that all things come to those who wait, including the houses and lands of their persecutors.

Here comes a pleasure party, as gay as any on the avenue, though the carryall is an ash cart. The father is the driver and he has taken his brown-legged boy for a ride. How proud and happy they both look up there on their perch! The queer old building they have halted in front of is "The Ship," famous for fifty years as a ramshackle tenement filled with the oddest crowd. No one knows why it is called "The Ship," though there is a tradition that once the river came clear up here to Hamilton Street, and boats were moored alongside it. More likely it is because it is as bewildering inside as a crazy old ship, with its ups and downs of ladders parading as stairs, and its unexpected pitfalls. But Hamilton Street, like Water Street, is not what it was. The missions drove from the latter the worst of its dives. A sailors' mission has lately made its appearance in Hamilton Street, but there are no dives there, nothing worse than the ubiquitous saloon and tough tenements.

Enough of them everywhere. Suppose we look into one? No—Cherry Street. Be a little careful, please! The hall is dark and you might stumble over the children pitching pennies back there. Not that it would hurt them; kicks and cuffs are their daily diet. They have little else. Here where the hall turns and dives into utter darkness is a step, and another, another. A flight of stairs. You can feel your way, if you cannot see it. Close? Yes! What would you have? All the fresh air that ever enters these stairs comes from the hall door that is forever slamming, and from the windows of dark bedrooms that in turn receive from the stairs their sole supply of the elements God meant to be free, but man deals out with such niggardly hand. That was a woman filling her pail by the hydrant you just bumped against. The sinks are in the hallway, that all the tenants may have access—and all be poisoned alike by their summer stenches. Hear the pump squeak! It is the lullaby of tenement-house babes. In summer, when a thousand thirsty throats pant for a cooling drink in this block, it is worked in vain. But the saloon, whose open door you passed in the hall, is always there. The smell of it has followed you up. Here is a door. Listen! That short hacking cough, that tiny, helpless wail—what do they mean? They mean that the soiled bow of white you saw on the door downstairs will have another story to tell—Oh! a sadly familiar story—before the day is at an end. The child is dying with measles. With half a chance it might have lived; but it had none. That dark bedroom killed it.

"It was took all of a suddint," says the mother, smoothing the throbbing little body with trembling hands. There is no unkindness in the rough voice of the man in the jumper, who sits by the window grimly smoking a clay pipe, with the little life ebbing out in his sight, bitter as his words sound: "Hush, Mary! If we cannot keep the baby, need we complain—such as we?"

Such as we! What if the words ring in your ears as we grope our way up the stairs and down from floor to floor, listening to the sounds behind the closed doors—some of quarreling, some of coarse songs, more of profanity. They are true. When the summer heats come with their suffering, they have meaning more terrible than words can tell. Come over here. Step carefully over this baby—it is a baby, in spite of its rags and dirt—under these iron bridges called fire escapes, but loaded down, despite the incessant watchfulness of the firemen, with broken household goods, with wash tubs and barrels, over which no man could climb from a fire. This gap between dingy brick walls is the yard. That strip of smoke-colored sky up there is the heaven of these people. Do you wonder the name does not attract them to the churches? That baby's parents live in the rear tenement here. She is at least as clean as the steps we are now climbing. There are plenty of houses with half a hundred such in. The tenement is much like the one in front we just left, only fouler, closer, darker—we will not say more cheerless. The word is a mockery. A hundred thousand people lived in rear tenements in New York last year. Here is a room neater than the rest. The woman, a stout matron with hard lines of care in her face, is at the wash tub. "I try to keep the childer clean," she says, apologetically, but with a hopeless glance around. The spice of hot soapsuds is added to the air already tainted with the smell of boiling cabbage, of rags and uncleanliness all about. It makes an overpowering compound. It is Thursday, but patched linen is hung upon the pulley line from the window. There is no Monday cleaning in the tenements. It is wash day all the week round, for a change of clothing is scarce among the poor. They are poverty's honest badge, these perennial lines of rags hung out to dry, those that are not the washerwoman's professional shingle. The true line to be drawn between pauperism and honest poverty is the clothesline. With it begins the effort to be clean that is the first and the best evidence of a desire to be honest.

What sort of an answer, think you, would come from these tenements to the question "Is life worth living?" were they heard at all in the discussion? It may be that this, cut from the last report but one of the Association for the Improvement of the Condition of the Poor, a long name for a weary task, has a suggestion of it: "In the depth of winter the attention of the Association was called to a Protestant family living in a garret in a miserable tenement in Cherry Street. The family's condition was most deplorable. The man, his wife, and three small children shivering in one room through the roof of which the pitiless winds of winter whistled. The room was almost barren of furniture; the parents slept on the floor, the elder children in boxes, and the baby was swung in an old shawl attached to the rafters by cords by way of a hammock. The father, a seaman, had been obliged to give up that calling because he was in consumption, and was unable to provide either bread or fire for his little ones."

Perhaps this may be put down as an exceptional case, but one that came to my notice some months ago in a Seventh Ward tenement was typical enough to escape that reproach. There were nine in the family: husband, wife, an aged grandmother, and six children; honest, hard-working Germans, scrupulously neat, but poor. All nine lived in two rooms, one about ten feet square that served as parlor, bedroom, and eating room, the other a small hall room made into a kitchen. The rent was seven dollars and a half a month, more than a week's wages for the husband and father, who was the only breadwinner in the family. That day the mother had thrown herself out of the window, and was carried up from the street dead. She was "discour-

aged," said some of the other women from the tenement, who had come in to look after the children
while a messenger carried the news to the father at
the shop. They went stolidly about their task, although
they were evidently not without feeling for the dead
woman. No doubt she was wrong in not taking life
philosophically, as did the four families a city missionary found housekeeping in the four corners of one
room. They got along well enough together until one
of the families took a boarder and made trouble.
Philosophy, according to my optimistic friend, naturally inhabits the tenements. The people who live
there come to look upon death in a different way from
the rest of us—do not take it as hard. He has never
found time to explain how the fact fits into his general
theory that life is not unbearable in the tenements.
Unhappily for the philosophy of the slums, it is too
apt to be of the kind that readily recognizes the saloon, always handy, as the refuge from every trouble,
and shapes its practice according to the discovery.

THE CHEAP
LODGINGHOUSES

When it comes to the question of numbers with this
tramps' army, another factor of serious portent has to
be taken into account: the cheap lodginghouses. In
the caravanseries that line Chatham Street and the
Bowery, harboring nightly a population as large as
that of many a thriving town, a homemade article of
tramp and thief is turned out that is attracting the
increasing attention of the police, and offers a field for
the missionary's labors beside which most others seem
of slight account. Within a year they have been
stamped as nurseries of crime by the chief of the Secret Police,* the sort of crime that feeds especially
on idleness and lies ready to the hand of fatal opportunity. In the same strain one of the justices on the
police-court bench sums up his long experience as a
committing magistrate: "The ten-cent lodginghouses
more than counterbalance the good done by the free
reading room, lectures, and all other agencies of reform. Such lodginghouses have caused more destitution, more beggary and crime than any other agency
I know of." A very slight acquaintance with the subject is sufficient to convince the observer that neither
authority overstates the fact. The two officials had
reference, however, to two different grades of lodginghouses. The cost of a night's lodging makes the difference. There is a wider gap between the "hotel"—they

* Inspector Byrnes on Lodginghouses, in the North American
Review, September 1889.

are all hotels—that charges a quarter and the one that furnishes a bed for a dime than between the bridal suite and the everyday hall bedroom of the ordinary hostelry.

The metropolis is to lots of people like a lighted candle to the moth. It attracts them in swarms that come year after year with the vague idea that they can get along here if anywhere; that something is bound to turn up among so many. Nearly all are young men, unsettled in life, many—most of them, perhaps —fresh from good homes, beyond a doubt with honest hopes of getting a start in the city and making a way for themselves. Few of them have much money to waste while looking around, and the cheapness of the lodging offered is an object. Fewer still know anything about the city and its pitfalls. They have come in search of crowds, of "life," and they gravitate naturally to the Bowery, the great democratic highway of the city, where the twenty-five-cent lodginghouses take them in. In the alleged reading rooms of these great barracks, that often have accommodations, such as they are, for two, three, and even four hundred guests, they encounter three distinct classes of associates: the great mass adventurers like themselves, waiting there for something to turn up; a much smaller class of respectable clerks or mechanics, who, too poor or too lonely to have a home of their own, live this way from year to year; and lastly the thief in search of recruits for his trade. The sights the young stranger sees and the company he keeps in the Bowery are not of a kind to strengthen any moral principle he may have brought away from home, and by the time his money is gone, with no work yet in sight, and he goes down a step, a long step, to the fifteen-cent lodging-house, he is ready for the tempter whom he finds waiting for him there, reinforced by the contingent of ex-convicts returning from the prisons after having served out their sentences for robbery or theft. Then it is that the something he has been waiting for turns up. The police returns have the record of it. "In nine cases out of ten," says Inspector Byrnes, "he turns out a thief, or a burglar, if, indeed, he does not sooner or later become a murderer." As a matter of fact, some of the most atrocious of recent murders have been the result of schemes of robbery hatched in these houses, and so frequent and bold have become the depredations of the lodginghouse thieves, that the authorities have been compelled to make a public demand for more effective laws that shall make them subject at all times to police regulation.

Inspector Byrnes observes that in the last two or three years at least four hundred young men have been arrested for petty crimes that originated in the lodginghouses, and that in many cases it was their first step in crime. He adds his testimony to the notorious fact that three-fourths of the young men called on to plead to generally petty offenses in the courts are under twenty years of age, poorly clad, and without means. The bearing of the remark is obvious. One of the, to the police, well-known thieves who lived, when out of jail, at the Windsor, a well-known lodginghouse in the Bowery, went to Johnstown after the flood and was shot and killed there while robbing the dead.

An idea of just how this particular scheme of corruption works, with an extra touch of infamy thrown in, may be gathered from the story of David Smith, the "New York Fagin," who was convicted and sent to prison last year through the instrumentality of the Society for the Prevention of Cruelty to Children. Here is the account from the Society's last report:

"The boy, Edward Mulhearn, fourteen years old, had run away from his home in Jersey City, thinking he might find work and friends in New York. He may have been a trifle wild. He met Smith on the Bowery and recognized him as an acquaintance. When Smith offered him a supper and bed he was only too glad to accept. Smith led the boy to a vile lodginghouse on the

Bowery, where he introduced him to his 'pals' and
swore he would make a man of him before he was a
week older. Next day he took the unsuspecting Edward all over the Bowery and Grand Street, showed
him the sights and drew his attention to the careless
way the ladies carried their bags and purses and the
easy thing it was to get them. He induced Edward
to try his hand. Edward tried and won. He was richer
by three dollars! It did seem easy. 'Of course it is,'
said his companion. From that time Smith took the
boy on a number of thieving raids, but he never
seemed to become adept enough to be trusted out of
range of the 'Fagin's' watchful eye. When he went out
alone he generally returned empty-handed. This did
not suit Smith. It was then he conceived the idea of
turning this little inferior thief into a superior beggar.
He took the boy into his room and burned his arms
with a hot iron. The boy screamed and entreated in
vain. The merciless wretch pressed the iron deep into
the tender flesh, and afterward applied acid to the
raw wound.

"Thus prepared, with his arm inflamed, swollen,
and painful, Edward was sent out every day by this
fiend, who never let him out of his sight, and threatened to burn his arm off if he did not beg money
enough. He was instructed to tell people the wound
had been caused by acid falling upon his arm at the
works. Edward was now too much under the man's
influence to resist or disobey him. He begged hard
and handed Smith the pennies faithfully. He received
in return bad food and worse treatment."

The reckoning came when the wretch encountered
the boy's father, in search of his child, in the Bowery,
and fell under suspicion of knowing more than he
pretended of the lad's whereabouts. He was found in
his den with a half dozen of his chums reveling on the
proceeds of the boy's begging for the day.

The twenty-five-cent lodginghouse keeps up the
pretense of a bedroom, though the head-high parti-

tion enclosing a space just large enough to hold a cot and a chair and allow the man room to pull off his clothes is the shallowest of all pretenses. The fifteen-cent bed stands boldly forth without screen in a room full of bunks with sheets as yellow and blankets as foul. At the ten-cent level the locker for the sleeper's clothes disappears. There is no longer need of it. The tramp limit is reached, and there is nothing to lock up save, on general principles, the lodger. Usually the ten- and seven-cent lodgings are different grades of the same abomination. Some sort of an apology for a bed, with mattress and blanket, represents the aristo-cratic purchase of the tramp who, by a lucky stroke of beggary, has exchanged the chance of an empty box or ash-barrel for shelter on the quality floor of one of these "hotels." A strip of canvas, strung between rough timbers, without covering of any kind, does for the couch of the seven-cent lodger who prefers the questionable comfort of a red-hot stove close to his elbow to the revelry of the stale-beer dive. It is not the most secure perch in the world. Uneasy sleepers roll off at intervals, but they have not far to fall to the next tier of bunks, and the commotion that ensues is speedily quieted by the boss and his club. On cold winter nights, when every bunk had its tenant, I have stood in such a lodging room more than once, and listening to the snoring of the sleepers like the regular strokes of an engine, and the slow creaking of the beams under their restless weight, imagined myself on shipboard and experienced the very real nausea of seasickness. The one thing that did not favor the de-ception was the air; its character could not be mis-taken.

The proprietor of one of these seven-cent houses was known to me as a man of reputed wealth and respectability. He "ran" three such establishments and made, it was said, $8000 a year clear profit on his in-vestment. He lived in a handsome house quite near to the stylish precincts of Murray Hill, where the nature of his occupation was not suspected. A notice that was posted on the wall of the lodgers' room suggested at least an effort to maintain his uptown standing in the slums. It read: "No swearing or loud talking after nine o'clock." Before nine no exceptions were taken to the natural vulgarity of the place; but that was the limit.

There are no licensed lodginghouses known to me which charge less than seven cents for even such a bed as this canvas strip, though there are unlicensed ones enough where one may sleep on the floor for five cents a spot, or squat in a sheltered hallway for three. The police station lodginghouse, where the soft side of a plank is the regulation couch, is next in order. The manner in which this police bed is "made up" is interesting in its simplicity. The loose planks that make the platform are simply turned over, and the job is done, with an occasional coat of whitewash thrown in to sweeten things. I know of only one easier way, but, so far as I am informed, it has never been introduced in this country. It used to be practiced, if report spoke truly, in certain old-country towns. The "bed" was represented by clotheslines stretched across the room upon which the sleepers hung by the armpits for a penny a night. In the morning the boss woke them up by simply untying the line at one end and letting it go with its load; a labor-saving device certainly, and highly successful in attaining the desired end.

According to the police figures, 4,974,025 separate lodgings were furnished last year by these dormitories, between two and three hundred in number, and, adding the 147,634 lodgings furnished by the station houses, the total of the homeless army was 5,121,659, an average of over fourteen thousand homeless men* for every night in the year! The health officers, professional optimists always in matters that trench upon

* Deduct 69,111 women lodgers in the police stations.

their official jurisdiction, insist that the number is not quite so large as here given. But, apart from any slight discrepancy in the figures, the more important fact remains that last year's record of lodgers is an all-round increase over the previous year's of over three hundred thousand, and that this has been the ratio of growth of the business during the last three years, the period of which Inspector Byrnes complains as turning out so many young criminals with the lodginghouse stamp upon them. More than half of the lodginghouses are in the Bowery district, that is to say, the Fourth, Sixth, and Tenth Wards, and they harbor nearly three-fourths of their crowds. The calculation that more than nine thousand homeless young men lodge nightly along Chatham Street and the Bowery, between the City Hall and the Cooper Union, is probably not far out of the way. The City Missionary finds them there far less frequently than the thief in need of helpers. Appropriately enough, nearly one-fifth of all the pawnshops in the city and one-sixth of all the saloons are located here, while twenty-seven per cent of all the arrests on the police books have been credited to the district for the last two years.

About election time, especially in presidential elections, the lodginghouses come out strong on the side of the political boss who has the biggest "barrel." The victory in political contests, in the three wards I have mentioned of all others, is distinctly to the general with the strongest battalions, and the lodginghouses are his favorite recruiting ground. The colonization of voters is an evil of the first magnitude, none the less because both parties smirch their hands with it, and for that reason next to hopeless. Honors are easy, where the two "machines," intrenched in their strongholds, outbid each other across the Bowery in open rivalry as to who shall commit the most flagrant frauds at the polls. Semioccasionally a champion offender is caught and punished, as was, not long ago, the proprietor of one of the biggest Bowery lodginghouses.

But such scenes are largely spectacular, if not
prompted by some hidden motive of revenge that survives from the contest. Beyond a doubt Inspector
Byrnes speaks by the card when he observes that
"usually this work is done in the interest of some local
political boss, who stands by the owner of the house,
in case the latter gets into trouble." For standing by,
read twisting the machinery of outraged justice so that
its hand shall fall not too heavily upon the culprit, or
miss him altogether. One of the houses that achieved
profitable notoriety in this way in many successive
elections, a notorious tramps' resort in Houston Street,
was lately given up, and has most appropriately been
turned into a bar-factory, thus still contributing,
though in a changed form, to the success of "the
cause." It must be admitted that the black tramp who
herds in the West Side "hotels" is more discriminating
in this matter of electioneering than his white brother.
He at least exhibits some real loyalty in invariably
selling his vote to the Republican bidder for a dollar,
while he charges the Democratic boss a dollar and a
half. In view of the well-known facts, there is a good
deal of force in the remark made by a friend of ballot
reform during the recent struggle over that hotly con-
tested issue, that real ballot reform will do more to
knock out cheap lodginghouses than all the regulations
of police and health officers together.

The experiment made by a well-known stove manufacturer a winter or two ago in the way of charity
might have thrown much desired light on the question
of the number of tramps in the city, could it have
been carried to a successful end. He opened a sort of
breakfast shop for the idle and unemployed in the
region of Washington Square, offering to all who had
no money a cup of coffee and a roll for nothing. The
first morning he had a dozen customers, the next about
two hundred. The number kept growing until one
morning, at the end of two weeks, found by actual
count 2014 shivering creatures in line waiting their

turn for a seat at his tables. The shop was closed that day. It was one of the rare instances of too great a rush of custom wrecking a promising business, and the great problem remained unsolved.

THE COLOR LINE
IN NEW YORK

The color line must be drawn through the tenements to give the picture its proper shading. The landlord does the drawing, does it with an absence of pretense, a frankness of despotism, that is nothing if not brutal. The Czar of all the Russias is not more absolute upon his own soil than the New York landlord in his dealings with colored tenants. Where he permits them to live, they go; where he shuts the door, stay out. By his grace they exist at all in certain localities; his ukase banishes them from others. He accepts the responsibility, when laid at his door, with unruffled complacency. It is business, he will tell you. And it is. He makes the prejudice in which he traffics pay him well, and that, as he thinks it quite superfluous to tell you, is what he is there for.

That his pencil does not make quite as black a mark as it did, that the hand that wields it does not bear down as hard as only a short half dozen years ago, is the hopeful sign of an awakening public conscience under the stress of which the line shows signs of wavering. But for this the landlord deserves no credit. It has come, is coming about despite him. The line may not be wholly effaced while the name of the negro, alone among the world's races, is spelled with a small n. Natural selection will have more or less to do beyond a doubt in every age with dividing the races; only so, it may be, can they work out together their highest destiny. But with the despotism that deliberately assigns to the defenseless black the lowest level for the purpose of robbing him there that has nothing to do. Of such slavery, different only in degree from the other kind that held him as a chattel, to be sold or bartered at the will of his master, this century, if signs fail not, will see the end in New York.

Ever since the war New York has been receiving the overflow of colored population from the southern cities. In the last decade this migration has grown to such proportions that it is estimated that our blacks have quite doubled in number since the Tenth Census. Whether the exchange has been of advantage to the negro may well be questioned. Trades of which he had practical control in his southern home are not open to him here. I know that it may be answered that there is no industrial proscription of color; that it is a matter of choice. Perhaps so. At all events he does not choose then. How many colored carpenters or masons has anyone seen at work in New York? In the South there are enough of them and, if the testimony of the most intelligent of their people is worth anything, plenty of them have come here. As a matter of fact the colored man takes in New York, without a struggle, the lower level of menial service for which his past traditions and natural love of ease perhaps as yet fit him best. Even the colored barber is rapidly getting to be a thing of the past. Along shore, at any unskilled labor, he works unmolested; but he does not appear to prefer the job. His sphere thus defined, he naturally takes his stand among the poor, and in the homes of the poor. Until very recent times—the years since a change was wrought can be counted on the fingers of one hand—he was practically restricted in the choice of a home to a narrow section on the West Side, that nevertheless had a social top and bottom to it—the top in the tenements on the line of Seventh Avenue as far north as Thirty-second Street, where he was allowed to occupy the houses of unsavory reputation which the police had cleared and for which decent white tenants could not be found; the bottom in the vile rookeries of Thompson Street and South Fifth Avenue, the old "Africa" that is now fast becoming a modern Italy. Today there are black colonies in Yorkville and Morrisania. The encroachment of business and the Italian below, and the swelling of the population above, have been the chief agents in working out his second emancipation, a very real one, for with his cutting loose from the old tenements there has come a distinct and gratifying improvement in the tenant, that argues louder than theories or speeches the influence of vile surroundings in debasing the man. The colored citizen whom this year's census man found in his Ninety-ninth Street "flat" is a very different individual from the "nigger" his predecessor counted in the black-and-tan slums of Thompson and Sullivan Streets. There is no more clean and orderly community in New York than the new settlement of colored people that is growing up on the East Side from Yorkville to Harlem.

Cleanliness is the characteristic of the negro in his new surroundings, as it was his virtue in the old. In this respect he is immensely the superior of the lowest of the whites, the Italians and the Polish Jews, below whom he has been classed in the past in the tenant scale. Nevertheless, he has always had to pay higher rents than even these for the poorest and most stinted rooms. The exceptions I have come across, in which the rents, though high, have seemed more nearly on a level with what was asked for the same number and size of rooms in the average tenement, were in the case of tumble-down rookeries in which no one else would live, and were always coupled with the condition that the landlord should "make no repairs." It can readily be seen that his profits were scarcely curtailed by his "humanity." The reason advanced for this systematic robbery is that white people will not live in the same house with colored tenants, or even in a house recently occupied by negroes, and that consequently its selling value is injured. The prejudice undoubtedly exists, but it is not lessened by the house agents, who have set up the maxim "once a colored house, always a colored house."

There is method in the maxim, as shown by an inquiry made last year by the *Real Estate Record*. It proved agents to be practically unanimous in the endorsement of the negro as a clean, orderly, and "profitable" tenant. Here is the testimony of one of the largest real estate firms in the city: "We would rather have negro tenants in our poorest class of tenements than the lower grades of foreign white people. We find the former cleaner than the latter, and they do not destroy the property so much. We also get higher prices. We have a tenement on Nineteenth Street, where we get $10 for two rooms which we could not get more than $7.50 for from white tenants previously. We have a four-story tenement on our books on Thirty-third Street, between Sixth and Seventh Avenues, with four rooms per floor—a parlor, two bedrooms, and a kitchen. We get $20 for the first floor, $24 for the second, $23 for the third and $20 for the fourth, in all $87 or $1044 per annum. The size of the building is only 21 × 55." Another firm declared that in a specified instance they had saved fifteen to twenty per cent on the gross rentals since they changed from white to colored tenants. Still another gave the following case of a front and rear tenement that had formerly been occupied by tenants of a "low European type," who had been turned out on account of filthy habits and poor pay. The negroes proved cleaner, better, and steadier tenants. Instead, however, of having their rents reduced in consequence, the comparison stood as follows:

Rents under White Tenants

				Per month
Front—	1st floor	(store, etc.)		$21
	2d "			13
	3d "			13
	4th "	(and rear)		21
Rear—	2d "			12
	3d "			12
	4th "	(see front)		—
Rear house—1st "				8
	2d "			10
	3d "			9
	4th "			8
Total				$127

Rents under Colored Tenants

			Per month
Front—	1st floor	(store, etc.)	$21
	2d "		14
	3d "		14
	4th "		14
Rear—	2d "		12
	3d "		13
	4th "		13
Rear house—1st "			10
	2d "		12
	3d "		11
	4th "		10
Total			$144

An increased rental of $17 per month, or $204 a year, and an advance of nearly thirteen and one-half per cent on the gross rental "in favor" of the colored tenant. Profitable, surely!

I have quoted these cases at length in order to let in light on the quality of this landlord despotism that has purposely confused the public mind, and for its own selfish ends is propping up a waning prejudice. It will be cause for congratulation if indeed its time has come at last. Within a year, I am told by one of the most intelligent and best informed of our colored citizens, there has been evidence, simultaneous with the colored hegira from the low downtown tenements, of a movement toward less exorbitant rents. I cannot pass from this subject without adding a leaf from my own experience that deserves a place in this record, though, for the credit of humanity, I hope as an extreme case. It was last Christmas that I had occasion to visit the home of an old colored woman in Sixteenth Street, as the almoner of generous friends out of town who wished me to buy her a Christmas dinner. The old woman lived in a wretched shanty, occupying two mean, dilapidated rooms at the top of a sort of hen ladder that went by the name of stairs. For these she paid ten dollars a month out of her hard-earned wages as a scrubwoman. I did not find her in and, being informed that she was "at the agent's," went around to hunt her up. The agent's wife appeared, to report that Ann was out. Being in a hurry it occurred to me that I might save time by making her employer the purveyor of my friend's bounty, and proposed to entrust the money, two dollars, to her to be expended for Old Ann's benefit. She fell in with the suggestion at once, and confided to me in the fullness of her heart that she liked the plan, inasmuch as "I generally find her a Christmas dinner myself, and this money—she owes Mr. —— (her husband, the agent) a lot of rent." Needless to state that there was a change of program then and there, and that Ann was saved from the sort of Christmas cheer that woman's charity would have spread before her. When I had the old soul comfortably installed in her own den, with a chicken and "fixin's" and a bright fire in her stove, I asked her how much she owed of her rent. Her answer was that she did not really owe anything, her month not being quite up, but that the amount yet unpaid was—two dollars!

Poverty, abuse, and injustice alike the negro accepts with imperturbable cheerfulness. His philosophy is of the kind that has no room for repining. Whether he lives in an Eighth Ward barrack or in a tenement with a brownstone front and pretensions to the title of "flat," he looks at the sunny side of life and enjoys it. He loves fine clothes and good living a good deal more than he does a bank account. The proverbial rainy day it would be rank ingratitude, from his point of view, to look for when the sun shines unclouded in a clear sky. His home surroundings, except when he is utterly depraved, reflect his blithesome temper. The poorest negro housekeeper's room in New York is bright with gaily colored prints of his beloved "Abe Linkum," General Grant, President Garfield, Mrs. Cleveland, and other national celebrities, and cheery with flowers and singing birds. In the art of putting the best foot foremost, of disguising his poverty by making a little go a long way, our negro has no equal. When a fair share of prosperity is his, he knows how to make life and home very pleasant to those about him. Pianos and parlor furniture abound in the up-town homes of colored tenants and give them a very prosperous air. But even where the wolf howls at the door, he makes a bold and gorgeous front. The amount of "style" displayed on fine Sundays on Sixth and Seventh Avenues by colored holiday makers would turn a pessimist black with wrath. The negro's great ambition is to rise in the social scale to which his color has made him a stranger and an outsider, and he is quite willing to accept the shadow for the substance where that is the best he can get. The claw-hammer coat and white tie of a waiter in a first-class summer hotel, with the chance of taking his ease in six months of winter, are to him the next best thing to mingling with the white quality he serves, on equal terms. His festive gatherings, pre-eminently his cakewalks, at

which a sugared and frosted cake is the proud prize
of the couple with the most aristocratic step and carriage, are comic mixtures of elaborate ceremonial and
the joyous abandon of the natural man. With all his
ludicrous incongruities, his sensuality and his lack of
moral accountability, his superstition and other faults
that are the effect of temperament and of centuries of
slavery, he has his eminently good points. He is loyal
to the backbone, proud of being an American and of
his new-found citizenship. He is at least as easily
molded for good as for evil. His churches are crowded
to the doors on Sunday nights when the colored colony
turns out to worship. His people own church property
in this city upon which they have paid half a million
dollars out of the depth of their poverty, with comparatively little assistance from their white brethren.
He is both willing and anxious to learn, and his intel-
lectual status is distinctly improving. If his emotions
are not very deeply rooted, they are at least sincere
while they last, and until the tempter gets the upper
hand again.

Of all the temptations that beset him, the one that
troubles him and the police most is his passion for
gambling. The game of policy is a kind of unlawful
penny lottery specially adapted to his means, but
patronized extensively by poor white players as well.
It is the meanest of swindles, but reaps for its backers
rich fortunes wherever colored people congregate. Between the fortuneteller and the policy shop, closely
allied frauds always, the wages of many a hard day's
work are wasted by the negro; but the loss causes him
few regrets. Penniless, but with undaunted faith in his
ultimate "luck," he looks forward to the time when he
shall once more be able to take a hand at "beating
policy." When periodically the negro's lucky numbers,
4-11-44, come out on the slips of the alleged daily
drawings that are supposed to be held in some far-off
Western town, intense excitement reigns in Thompson
Street and along the Avenue, where someone is al-

ways the winner. An immense impetus is given then to the bogus business that has no existence outside of the cigar stores and candy shops where it hides from the law, save in some cunning Bowery "broker's" back office, where the slips are printed and the "winnings" apportioned daily with due regard to the backer's interests.

It is a question whether "Africa" has been improved by the advent of the Italian, with the tramp from the Mulberry Street Bend in his train. The moral turpitude of Thompson Street has been notorious for years, and the mingling of the three elements does not seem to have wrought any change for the better. The borderland where the white and black races meet in common debauch, the aptly named black-and-tan saloon, has never been debatable ground from a moral standpoint. It has always been the worst of the desperately bad. Than this commingling of the utterly depraved of both sexes, white and black, on such ground, there can be no greater abomination. Usually it is some foul cellar dive, perhaps run by the political "leader" of the district, who is "in with" the police. In any event it gathers to itself all the lawbreakers and all the human wrecks within reach. When a fight breaks out during the dance a dozen razors are handy in as many bootlegs, and there is always a job for the surgeon and the ambulance. The black "tough" is as handy with the razor in a fight as his peaceably inclined brother is with it in pursuit of his honest trade. As the Chinaman hides his knife in his sleeve and the Italian his stiletto in the bosom, so the negro goes to the ball with a razor in his bootleg, and on occasion does as much execution with it as both of the others together. More than three-fourths of the business the police have with the colored people in New York arises in the black-and-tan district, now no longer fairly representative of their color.

I have touched briefly upon such facts in the negro's life as may serve to throw light on the social condition

of his people in New York. If, when the account is
made up between the races, it shall be claimed that
he falls short of the result to be expected from
twenty-five years of freedom, it may be well to turn to
the other side of the ledger and see how much of the
blame is borne by the prejudice and greed that have
kept him from rising under a burden of responsibility
to which he could hardly be equal. And in this view
he may be seen to have advanced much farther and
faster than before suspected, and to promise, after all,
with fair treatment, quite as well as the rest of us, his
white-skinned fellow citizens, had any right to expect.

WAIFS OF THE
CITY'S SLUMS

First among these barriers is the Foundling Asylum. It stands at the very outset of the waste of life that goes on in a population of nearly two millions of people; powerless to prevent it, though it gather in the outcasts by night and by day. In a score of years an army of twenty-five thousand of these forlorn little waifs have cried out from the streets of New York in arraignment of a Christian civilization under the blessings of which the instinct of motherhood even was smothered by poverty and want. Only the poor abandon their children. The stories of richly dressed foundlings that are dished up in the newspapers at intervals are pure fiction. Not one instance of even a well-dressed infant having been picked up in the streets is on record. They come in rags, a newspaper often the only wrap, semioccasionally one in a clean slip with some evidence of loving care; a little slip of paper pinned on, perhaps, with some such message as this I once read, in a woman's trembling hand: "Take care of Johnny, for God's sake. I cannot." But even that is the rarest of all happenings.

The city divides with the Sisters of Charity the task of gathering them in. The real foundlings, the children of the gutter that are picked up by the police, are the city's wards. In midwinter, when the poor shiver in their homes, and in the dog days when the fierce heat and foul air of the tenements smother their babies by thousands they are found, sometimes three and four in a night, in hallways, in areas and on the doorsteps of the rich, with whose comfort in luxurious homes the wretched mother somehow connects her own misery. Perhaps, as the drowning man clutches at a straw, she hopes that these happier hearts may have love to spare even for her little one. In this she is mistaken. Unauthorized babies especially are not popular in the abodes of the wealthy. It never happens outside of the storybooks that a baby so deserted finds home and friends at once. Its career, though rather more official, is less romantic, and generally brief. After a night spent at Police Headquarters, it travels up to the Infants' Hospital on Randall's Island in the morning, fitted out with a number and a bottle that seldom see much wear before they are laid aside for a fresh recruit. Few outcast babies survive their desertion long. Murder is the true name of the mother's crime in eight cases out of ten. Of 508 babies received at the Randall's Island Hospital last year 333 died, 65.55 per cent. But of the 508 only 170 were picked up in the streets, and among these the mortality was much greater, probably nearer ninety per cent, if the truth were told. The rest were born in the hospitals. The high mortality among the foundlings is not to be marveled at. The wonder is, rather, that any survive. The stormier the night, the more certain is the police nursery to echo with the feeble cries of abandoned babes. Often they come half dead from exposure. One live baby came in a little pine coffin which a policeman found an inhuman wretch trying to bury in an uptown lot. But many do not live to be officially registered as a charge upon the county. Seventy-two dead babies were picked up in the streets last year. Some of them were doubtless put out by very poor parents to save funeral expenses. In hard times the number of dead and live foundlings always increases very noticeably. But whether traveling by way of the morgue or the Infants' Hospital, the little army of waifs meets, reunited soon, in the trench in the potter's field where, if no medical student is in need of a subject, they are laid in squads of a dozen.

Most of the foundlings come from the East Side, where they are left by young mothers without wedding ring or other name than their own to bestow upon the baby, returning from the island hospital to face an unpitying world with the evidence of their shame. Not infrequently they wear the bed-tick regimentals of the Public Charities, and thus their origin is easily enough traced. Oftener no ray of light penetrates the gloom, and no effort is made to probe the mystery of sin and sorrow. This also is the policy pursued in the great Foundling Asylum of the Sisters of Charity in Sixty-eighth Street, known all over the world as Sister Irene's Asylum. Years ago the crib that now stands just inside the street door, under the great main portal, was placed outside at night; but it filled up too rapidly. The babies took to coming in little squads instead of in single file, and in self-defense the sisters were forced to take the cradle in. Now the mother must bring her child inside and put it in the crib where she is seen by the sister on guard. No effort is made to question her, or discover the child's antecedents, but she is asked to stay and nurse her own and another baby. If she refuses, she is allowed to depart unhindered. If willing, she enters at once into the great family of the good Sister who in twenty-one years has gathered as many thousand homeless babies into her fold. One was brought in when I was last in the asylum, in the middle of July, that received in its crib the number 20715. The death rate is, of course, lowered a good deal where exposure of the child is prevented. Among the eleven hundred infants in the asylum, it was something over nineteen per cent last year; but among those actually received in the twelvemonth nearer twice that figure. Even the nineteen per cent, remarkably low for a Foundling Asylum, was equal to the startling death rate of Gotham Court in the cholera scourge.

Four hundred and sixty mothers, who could not or would not keep their own babies, did voluntary penance for their sin in the asylum last year by nursing a strange waif besides their own until both should be strong enough to take their chances in life's battle. An even larger number than the eleven hundred were "pay babies," put out to be nursed by "mothers" outside the asylum. The money thus earned pays the rent of hundreds of poor families. It is no trifle, quite half of the quarter of a million dollars contributed annually by the city for the support of the asylum. The procession of these nurse-mothers, when they come to the asylum on the first Wednesday of each month to receive their pay and have the babies inspected by the sisters, is one of the sights of the city. The nurses, who are under strict supervision, grow to love their little charges and part from them with tears when, at the age of four or five, they are sent to Western homes to be adopted. The sisters carefully encourage the home feeling in the child as their strongest ally in seeking its mental and moral elevation, and the toddlers depart happy to join their "papas and mammas" in the faraway, unknown home.

An infinitely more fiendish, if to surface appearances less deliberate, plan of child murder than desertion has flourished in New York for years under the title of baby farming. The name, put into plain English, means starving babies to death. The law has fought this most heinous of crimes by compelling the registry of all baby farms. As well might it require all persons intending murder to register their purpose with time and place of the deed under the penalty of exemplary fines. Murderers do not hang out a shingle. "Baby farms," said once Mr. Elbridge T. Gerry, the President of the Society charged with the execution of the law that was passed through his efforts, "are concerns by means of which persons, usually of disreputable character, eke out a living by taking two, or three, or four babies to board. They are the charges of outcasts, or illegitimate children. They feed them on sour milk, and give them paregoric to keep them quiet, until they die, when they get some young medical man without experience to sign a certificate to the Board of Health that the child died of inanition, and so the matter ends. The baby is dead, and there is no one to complain." A handful of baby farms have been registered and licensed by the Board of Health with the approval of the Society for the Prevention of Cruelty to Children in the last five years, but none of this kind. The devil keeps the only complete register to be found anywhere. Their trace is found oftenest by the coroner or the police; sometimes they may be discovered hiding in the advertising columns of certain newspapers, under the guise of the scarcely less heartless traffic in helpless children that is dignified with the pretense of adoption—for cash. An idea of how this scheme works was obtained through the disclosures in a celebrated divorce case, a year or two ago. The society has among its records a very recent case* of a baby a week old (Baby "Blue Eyes") that was offered for sale—adoption, the dealer called it—in a newspaper. The agent bought it after some haggling for a dollar, and arrested the woman slave trader; but the law was powerless to punish her for her crime. Twelve unfortunate women awaiting dishonored motherhood were found in her house.

One gets a glimpse of the frightful depths to which human nature, perverted by avarice bred of ignorance and rasping poverty, can descend, in the mere suggestion of systematic insurance *for profit* of children's lives. A woman was put on trial in this city last year for incredible cruelty in her treatment of a stepchild. The evidence aroused a strong suspicion that a pitifully small amount of insurance on the child's life was one of the motives for the woman's savagery. A little

* Society for the Prevention of Cruelty to Children, Case 42,028, May 16, 1889.

investigation brought out the fact that three companies that were in the business of insuring children's
lives, for sums varying from $17 up, had issued not
less than a million such policies! The premiums ranged
from five to twenty-five cents a week. What untold
horrors this business may conceal was suggested by a
formal agreement entered into by some of the companies, "for the purpose of preventing speculation in
the insurance of children's lives." By the terms of this
compact, "no higher premium than ten cents could be
accepted on children under six years old." Barbarism
forsooth! Did ever heathen cruelty invent a more
fiendish plot than the one written down between the
lines of this legal paper?

It is with a sense of glad relief that one turns from
this misery to the brighter page of the helping hands
stretched forth on every side to save the young and
the helpless. New York is, I firmly believe, the most
charitable city in the world. Nowhere is there so eager
a readiness to help, when it is known that help is
worthily wanted; nowhere are such armies of devoted
workers, nowhere such abundance of means ready to
the hand of those who know the need and how rightly
to supply it. Its poverty, its slums, and its suffering are
the result of unprecedented growth with the consequent disorder and crowding, and the common penalty of metropolitan greatness. If the structure shows
signs of being top-heavy, evidences are not wanting—
they are multiplying day by day—that patient toilers
are at work among the underpinnings. The day nurseries, the numberless kindergartens and charitable
schools in the poor quarters, the Fresh Air Funds, the
thousand and one charities that in one way or another
reach the homes and the lives of the poor with sweetening touch, are proof that if much is yet to be done, if
the need only grows with the effort, hearts and hands
will be found to do it in ever-increasing measure. Black
as the cloud is it has a silver lining, bright with prom-

ise. New York is today a hundredfold cleaner, better, purer, city than it was even ten years ago.

Two powerful agents that were among the pioneers in this work of moral and physical regeneration stand in Paradise Park today as milestones on the rocky, up-hill road. The handful of noble women, who braved the foul depravity of the Old Brewery to rescue its child victims, rolled away the first and heaviest boulder, which legislatures and city councils had tackled in vain. The Five Points Mission and the Five Points House of Industry have accomplished what no machinery of government availed to do. Sixty thousand children have been rescued by them from the streets and had their little feet set in the better way. Their work still goes on, increasing and gathering in the waifs, instructing and feeding them, and helping their parents with advice and more substantial aid. Their charity knows not creed or nationality. The House of Industry is an enormous nursery school with an average of more than four hundred day scholars and constant boarders—"outsiders" and "insiders." Its influence is felt for many blocks around in that crowded part of the city. It is one of the most touching sights in the world to see a score of babies, rescued from homes of brutality and desolation, where no other blessing than a drunken curse was ever heard, saying their prayers in the nursery at bedtime. Too often their white night-gowns hide tortured little bodies and limbs cruelly bruised by inhuman hands. In the shelter of this fold they are safe, and a happier little group one may seek long and far in vain.

THE STREET
ARAB

———

Not all the barriers erected by society against its nether life, not the labor of unnumbered societies for the rescue and relief of its outcast waifs, can dam the stream of homelessness that issues from a source where the very name of home is a mockery. The street Arab is as much of an institution in New York as Newspaper Row, to which he gravitates naturally, following his Bohemian instinct. Crowded out of the tenements to shift for himself, and quite ready to do it, he meets there the host of adventurous runaways from every State in the Union and from across the sea, whom New York attracts with a queer fascination, as it attracts the older emigrants from all parts of the world. A census of the population in the Newsboys' Lodginghouse on any night will show such an odd mixture of small humanity as could hardly be got together in any other spot. It is a mistake to think that they are helpless little creatures, to be pitied and cried over because they are alone in the world. The unmerciful "guying" the good man would receive, who went to them with such a program, would soon convince him that that sort of pity was wasted, and would very likely give him the idea that they were a set of hardened little scoundrels, quite beyond the reach of missionary effort.

But that would only be his second mistake. The street Arab has all the faults and all the virtues of the lawless life he leads. Vagabond that he is, acknowledging no authority and owing no allegiance to anybody or anything, with his grimy fist raised against society whenever it tries to coerce him, he is as bright and sharp as the weasel, which, among all the predatory beasts, he most resembles. His sturdy independence, love of freedom and absolute self-reliance, together with his rude sense of justice that enables him to govern his little community, not always in accordance with municipal law or city ordinances, but often a good deal closer to the saving line of "doing to others as one would be done by"—these are strong handles by which those who know how can catch the boy and make him useful. Successful bankers, clergymen, and lawyers all over the country, statesmen in some instances of national repute, bear evidence in their lives to the potency of such missionary efforts. There is scarcely a learned profession, or branch of honorable business, that has not in the last twenty years borrowed some of its brightest light from the poverty and gloom of New York's streets.

Anyone whom business or curiosity has taken through Park Row or across Printing House Square in the midnight hour, when the air is filled with the roar of great presses spinning with printers' ink on endless rolls of white paper the history of the world in the twenty-four hours that have just passed away, has seen little groups of these boys hanging about the newspaper offices; in winter, when snow is on the streets, fighting for warm spots around the grated vent holes that let out the heat and steam from the underground press rooms with their noise and clatter, and in summer playing craps and 7–11 on the curb for their hardearned pennies, with all the absorbing concern of hardened gamblers. This is their beat. Here the agent of the Society for the Prevention of Cruelty to Children finds those he thinks too young for "business," but does not always capture them. Like rabbits in their burrows, the little ragamuffins sleep with at least one eye open, and every sense alert to the approach of danger: of their enemy, the policeman, whose chief business in life is to move them on, and of the agent bent on robbing them of their cherished freedom. At the first warning shout they scatter and are off. To pursue them would be like chasing the fleet-footed mountain goat in his rocky fastnesses. There is not an open door, a hidden turn or runway which they do not know, with lots of secret passages and shortcuts no one else ever found. To steal a march on them is the only way. There is a coal chute from the sidewalk to the boiler room in the subcellar of the post office which the Society's officer found the boys had made into a sort of toboggan slide to a snug berth in wintry weather. They used to slyly raise the cover in the street, slide down in single file, and snuggle up to the warm boiler out of harm's way, as they thought. It proved a trap, however. The agent slid down himself one cold night—there was no other way of getting there—and landing right in the midst of the sleeping colony, had it at his mercy. After repeated raids upon their headquarters, the boys forsook it last summer, and were next found herding under the shore end of one of the East River banana docks, where they had fitted up a regular club-room that was shared by thirty or forty homeless boys and about a million rats.

Newspaper Row is merely their headquarters. They are to be found all over the city, these street Arabs, where the neighborhood offers a chance of picking up a living in the daytime and of "turning in" at night with a promise of security from surprise. In warm weather a truck in the street, a convenient outhouse, or a dugout in a hay barge at the wharf make good bunks. Two were found making their nest once in the end of a big iron pipe up by the Harlem Bridge, and an old boiler at the East River served as an elegant flat for another couple, who kept house there with a thief the police had long sought, little suspecting that he was hiding under their very noses for months together. When the Children's Aid Society first opened its lodginghouses, and with some difficulty persuaded the boys that their charity was no "pious dodge" to trap them into a treasonable "Sunday-school racket," its managers overheard a laughable discussion among the boys in their unwontedly comfortable beds—perhaps the first some of them had ever slept in—as to the relative merits of the different styles of their everyday berths. Preferences were divided between the steam grating and a sandbox; but the weight of the evidence was decided to be in favor of the sandbox, because, as its advocate put it, "you could curl all up in it." The new "find" was voted a good way ahead of any previous experience, however. "My eyes, ain't it nice!" said one of the lads, tucked in under his blanket up to the chin, and the roomful of boys echoed the sentiment. The compact silently made that night between the street Arabs and their hosts has never been broken. They have been fast friends ever since.

Whence this army of homeless boys is a question often asked. The answer is supplied by the procession of mothers that go out and in at police headquarters the year round, inquiring for missing boys, often not until they have been gone for weeks and months, and then sometimes rather as a matter of decent form than from any real interest in the lad's fate. The stereotyped promise of the clerks who fail to find his name on the books among the arrests, that he "will come back when he gets hungry," does not always come true. More likely he went away because he was hungry. Some are orphans, actually or in effect, thrown upon the world when their parents were "sent up" to the island or to Sing Sing, and somehow overlooked by the Society, which thenceforth became the enemy to be shunned until growth and dirt and the hardships of the street, that make old early, offer some hope of successfully floating the lie that they are "sixteen." A drunken father explains the matter in other cases, as in that of John and Willie, aged ten and eight, picked up by the police. They "didn't live nowhere," never went to school, could neither read nor write.

Their twelve-year-old sister kept house for the father, who turned the boys out to beg, or steal, or starve. Grinding poverty and hard work beyond the years of the lad; blows and curses for breakfast, dinner, and supper; all these are recruiting agents for the homeless army. Sickness in the house, too many mouths to feed:

"We wuz six," said an urchin of twelve or thirteen I came across in the Newsboys' Lodginghouse, "and we ain't got no father. Some on us had to go." And so he went, to make a living by blacking boots. The going is easy enough. There is very little to hold the boy who has never known anything but a home in a tenement. Very soon the wild life in the streets holds him fast, and thenceforward by his own effort there is no escape. Left alone to himself, he soon enough finds a place in the police books, and there would be no other answer to the second question, What becomes of the boy, than that given by the criminal courts every day in the week.

But he is not left alone. Society in our day has no such suicidal intention. Right here, at the parting of the ways, it has thrown up the strongest of all its defenses for itself and for the boy. What the Society for the Prevention of Cruelty to Children is to the baby waif, the Children's Aid Society is to the homeless boy at this real turning point in his career. The good it has done cannot easily be overestimated. Its lodging-houses, its schools, and its homes block every avenue of escape with their offer of shelter upon terms which the boy soon accepts as on the whole cheap and fair. In the great Duane Street lodginghouse for newsboys, they are succinctly stated in a "notice" over the door that reads thus: "Boys who swear and chew tobacco cannot sleep here." There is another unwritten condition, viz.: that the boy shall be really without a home; but upon this the managers wisely do not insist too obstinately, accepting without too close inquiry his account of himself where that seems advisable, well knowing that many a home that sends forth such lads far less deserves the name than the one they are able to give them.

With these simple preliminaries the outcast boy may enter. Rags do not count; to ignorance the door is only opened wider. Dirt does not survive long, once within the walls of the lodginghouse. It is the settled belief of the men who conduct them that soap and water are as powerful moral agents in their particular field as preaching, and they have experience to back them. The boy may come and go as he pleases, so long as he behaves himself. No restraint of any sort is put on his independence. He is as free as any other guest at a hotel, and, like him, he is expected to pay for what he gets. How wisely the men planned who laid the foundation of this great rescue work and yet carry it on is shown by no single feature of it better than by this. No pauper was ever bred within these houses. Nothing would have been easier with such material, or more fatal. But charity of the kind that pauperizes is furthest from their scheme. Self-help is its very keynote, and it strikes a response in the boy's sturdiest trait that raises him at once to a level with the effort made in his behalf. Recognized as an independent trader, capable of and bound to take care of himself, he is in a position to ask trust if trade has gone against him and he cannot pay cash for his "grub" and his bed, and to get it without question. He can even have the loan of the small capital required to start him in business with a bootblack's kit, or an armful of papers, if he is known or vouched for; but every cent is charged to him as carefully as though the transaction involved as many hundreds of dollars, and he is expected to pay back the money as soon as he has made enough to keep him going without it. He very rarely betrays the trust reposed in him. Quite on the contrary, around this sound core of self-help, thus encouraged, habits of thrift and ambitious industry are seen to grow up in a majority of instances. The boy is "growing" a character, and he goes out to the man's work in life with that which for him is better than if he had found a fortune.

Six cents for his bed, six for his breakfast of bread and coffee, and six for his supper of pork and beans, as much as he can eat, are the rates of the boys' "hotel" for those who bunk together in the great dormitories that sometimes hold more than a hundred berths, two tiers high, made of iron, clean and neat. For the "upper ten," the young financiers who early take the lead among their fellows, hire them to work for wages and add a share of their profits to their own, and for the lads who are learning a trade and getting paid by the week, there are ten-cent beds with a locker and with curtains hung about. Night schools and Sunday night meetings are held in the building and are always well attended, in winter especially, when the lodginghouses are crowded. In summer the tow-path and the country attract their share of the bigger boys. The "Sunday-school racket" has ceased to have terror for them. They follow the proceedings with the liveliest interest, quick to detect cant of any sort, should any stray in. No one has any just conception of what congregational singing is until he has witnessed a roomful of these boys roll up their sleeves and start in on "He is the lily of the valley." The swinging trapeze in the gymnasium on the top floor is scarcely more popular with the boys than this tremendously vocal worship. The street Arab puts his whole little soul into what interests him for the moment, whether it be pulverizing a rival who has done a mean trick to a smaller boy, or attending at the "gospel shop" on Sundays. This characteristic made necessary some extra supervision when recently the lads in the Duane Street Lodginghouse "chipped in" and bought a set of boxing gloves. The trapeze suffered a temporary eclipse until this new toy had been tested to the extent of several miniature black eyes upon which soap had no effect, and sundry little scores had been settled that evened things up, as it were, for a fresh start.

I tried one night, not with the best of success I confess, to photograph the boys in their washroom, while they were cleaning up for supper. They were quite turbulent, to the disgust of one of their number who assumed, unasked, the office of general manager of the show, and expressed his mortification to me in very polite language. "If they would only behave, sir!" he complained, "you could make a good picture."

"Yes," I said, "but it isn't in them, I suppose."

"No, b'gosh!" said he, lapsing suddenly from grace under the provocation, "them kids ain't got no sense, nohow!"

The Society maintains five of these boys' lodging-houses, and one for girls, in the city. The Duane Street Lodginghouse alone has sheltered since its foundation in 1855 nearly a quarter of a million different boys, at a total expense of a good deal less than half a million dollars. Of this amount, up to the beginning of the present year, the boys and the earnings of the house had contributed no less than $172,776.38. In all of the lodginghouses together, 12,153 boys and girls were sheltered and taught last year. The boys saved up no inconsiderable amount of money in the savings banks provided for them in the houses, a simple system of lockboxes that are emptied for their benefit once a month. Besides these, the Society has established and operates in the tenement districts twenty-one industrial schools, co-ordinate with the public schools in authority, for the children of the poor who cannot find room in the city's schoolhouses, or are too ragged to go there; two free reading rooms, a dressmaking and typewriting school, and a laundry for the instruction of girls; a sick-children's mission in the city and two on the seashore, where poor mothers may take their babies; a cottage by the sea for crippled girls, and a brush factory for crippled boys in Forty-fourth Street. The Italian school in Leonard Street alone had an average attendance of over six hundred pupils last year. The daily average attendance at all of them was 4105, while 11,331 children were registered and taught. When the fact that there were among these 1132 children of drunken parents and 416 that had been found begging in the street is contrasted with the showing of $1337.21 deposited in the school savings banks by 1745 pupils, something like an adequate idea is gained of the scope of the Society's work in the city.

A large share of it, in a sense the largest, certainly that productive of the happiest results, lies outside of the city, however. From the lodginghouses and the schools are drawn the battalions of young emigrants that go every year to homes in the Far West, to grow up self-supporting men and women safe from the temptations and the vice of the city. Their number runs far up in the thousands. The Society never loses sight of them. The records show that the great mass, with this start given them, become useful citizens, an honor to the communities in which their lot is cast. Not a few achieve place and prominence in their new surroundings. Rarely bad reports come of them. Occasionally one comes back, lured by homesickness even for the slums; but the briefest stay generally cures the disease for good. I helped once to see a party off for Michigan, the last sent out by that great friend of the homeless children, Mrs. Astor, before she died. In the party was a boy who had been an "Insider" at the Five Points House of Industry, and brought along as his only baggage a padlocked and iron-bound box that contained all his wealth, two little white mice of the friendliest disposition. They were going with him out to live on the fat of the land in the fertile West, where they would never be wanting for a crust. Alas! for the best-laid plans of mice and men. The Western diet did not agree with either. I saw their owner some months later in the old home at the Five Points. He had come back, walking part of the way, and was now pleading to be sent out once more. He had at last had enough of the city. His face fell when I asked him about the mice. It was a sad story, indeed. "They had so much corn to eat," he said, "and they couldn't stand it. They burned all up inside, and then they busted."

Mrs. Astor set an example during her noble and useful life in gathering every year a company of homeless boys from the streets and sending them to good homes, with decent clothes on their backs—she had sent out no less than thirteen hundred when she died, and left funds to carry on her work—that has been followed by many who, like her, had the means and the heart for such a labor of love. Most of the lodging-houses and school buildings of the society were built by some one rich man or woman who paid all the bills, and often objected to have even the name of the giver made known to the world. It is one of the pleasant experiences of life that give one hope and courage in the midst of all this misery to find names that stand to the unthinking mass only for money-getting and grasping associated with such unheralded benefactions that carry their blessings down to generations yet unborn. It is not so long since I found the carriage of a woman, whose name is synonymous with millions, standing in front of the boys' lodginghouse in Thirty-fifth Street. Its owner was at that moment busy with a surgeon making a census of the crippled lads in the brush shop, the most miserable of all the Society's charges, as a preliminary to fitting them out with artificial limbs.

Farther uptown than any reared by the Children's Aid Society, in Sixty-seventh Street, stands a lodging-house intended for boys of a somewhat larger growth than most of those whom the Society shelters. Unlike the others, too, it was built by the actual labor of the young men it was designed to benefit. In the day when more of the boys from our streets shall find their way to it and to the New York Trade Schools, of which it is a kind of home annex, we shall be in a fair way of solving in the most natural of all ways the question what to do with this boy, in spite of the ignorant opposition of the men whose tyrannical policy is now to blame for the showing that, out of twenty-three millions of dollars paid annually to mechanics in the building trades in this city, less than six millions go to the workman born in New York, while his boy roams the streets with every chance of growing up a vagabond and next to none of becoming an honest artisan. Colonel Auchmuty is a practical philanthropist to whom the growing youth of New York will one day owe a debt of gratitude not easily paid. The progress of the system of trade schools established by him, at which a young man may acquire the theory as well as the practice of a trade in a few months at a merely nominal outlay, has not been nearly as rapid as was to be desired, though the fact that other cities are copying the model, with their master mechanics as the prime movers in the enterprise, testifies to its excellence. But it has at last taken a real start, and with union men and even the officers of unions now sending their sons to the trade schools to be taught,* one may perhaps be permitted to hope that an era of better sense is dawning that shall witness a rescue work upon lines which, when the leaven has fairly had time to work, will put an end to the existence of the New York street Arab, of the native breed at least.

* Colonel Auchmuty's own statement.

THE WORKING GIRLS
OF NEW YORK

Of the harvest of tares, sown in iniquity and reaped in wrath, the police returns tell the story. The pen that wrote the "Song of the Shirt" is needed to tell of the sad and toil-worn lives of New York's working women. The cry echoes by night and by day through its tenements:

> Oh, God! that bread should be so dear,
> And flesh and blood so cheap!

Six months have not passed since at a great public meeting in this city, the Working Women's Society reported: "It is a known fact that men's wages cannot fall below a limit upon which they can exist, but woman's wages have no limit, since the paths of shame are always open to her. It is simply impossible for any woman to live without assistance on the low salary a saleswoman earns, without depriving herself of real necessities. . . . It is inevitable that they must in many instances resort to evil." It was only a few brief weeks before that verdict was uttered, that the community was shocked by the story of a gentle and refined woman who, left in direst poverty to earn her own living alone among strangers, threw herself from her attic window, preferring death to dishonor. "I would have done any honest work, even to scrubbing," she wrote, drenched and starving, after a vain search for work in a driving storm. She had tramped the streets for weeks on her weary errand, and the only living wages that were offered her were the wages of sin. The ink was not dry upon her letter before a woman in an East Side tenement wrote down her reason for self-murder: "Weakness, sleeplessness, and yet obliged to work. My strength fails me. Sing at my coffin: 'Where does the soul find a home and rest?'" Her story may be found as one of two typical "cases of despair" in one little church community, in the *City Mission Society's Monthly* for last February. It is a story that has many parallels in the experience of every missionary, every police reporter, and every family doctor whose practice is among the poor.

It is estimated that at least one hundred and fifty thousand women and girls earn their own living in New York; but there is reason to believe that this estimate falls far short of the truth when sufficient account is taken of the large number who are not wholly dependent upon their own labor, while contributing by it to the family's earnings. These alone constitute a large class of the women wage earners, and it is characteristic of the situation that the very fact that some need not starve on their wages condemns the rest to that fate. The pay they are willing to accept all have to take. What the "everlasting law of supply and demand," which serves as such a convenient gag for public indignation, has to do with it, one learns from observation all along the road of inquiry into these real woman's wrongs. To take the case of the saleswomen for illustration: The investigation of the Working Women's Society disclosed the fact that wages averaging from $2 to $4.50 a week were reduced by excessive fines, "the employers placing a value upon time lost that is not given to services rendered." A little girl, who received two dollars a week, made cash sales amounting to $167 in a single day, while the receipts of a fifteen-dollar male clerk in the same department footed up only $125; yet for some trivial mistake the girl was fined sixty cents out of her two dollars. The practice prevailed in some stores of dividing the fines between the superintendent and the timekeeper at the end of the year. In one instance they amounted to $3000, and "the superintendent was heard to charge the timekeeper with not being strict enough in his duties." One of the causes for fine in a certain large store was sitting down. The law requiring seats for saleswomen, generally ignored, was obeyed faithfully in this establishment. The seats were there, but the girls were fined when found using them.

Cash girls receiving $1.75 a week for work that at certain seasons lengthened their day to sixteen hours were sometimes required to pay for their aprons. A common cause for discharge from stores in which, on account of the oppressive heat and lack of ventilation, "girls fainted day after day and came out looking like corpses," was too long service. No other fault was found with the discharged saleswomen than that they had been long enough in the employ of the firm to justly expect an increase of salary. The reason was even given with brutal frankness, in some instances.

These facts give a slight idea of the hardships and the poor pay of a business that notoriously absorbs child labor. The girls are sent to the store before they have fairly entered their teens, because the money they can earn there is needed for the support of the family. If the boys will not work, if the street tempts them from home, among the girls at least there must be no drones. To keep their places they are told to lie about their age and to say that they are over fourteen. The precaution is usually superfluous. The Women's Investigating Committee found the majority of the children employed in the stores to be under age, but heard only in a single instance of the truant officers calling. In that case they came once a year and sent the youngest children home; but in a month's time they were all back in their places, and were not again disturbed. When it comes to the factories, where hard bodily labor is added to long hours, stifling rooms, and starvation wages, matters are even worse. The legislature has passed laws to prevent the employment of children, as it has forbidden saloonkeepers to sell them beer, and it has provided means of enforcing its mandate, so efficient, that the very number of factories in New York is *guessed* at as in the neighborhood of twelve thousand. Up till this summer, a single inspector was charged with the duty of keeping the run of them all, and of seeing to it that the law was respected by the owners.

Sixty cents is put as the average day's earnings of the 150,000, but into this computation enters the stylish "cashier's" two dollars a day, as well as the thirty cents of the poor little girl who pulls threads in an East Side factory, and, if anything, the average is probably too high. Such as it is, however, it represents board, rent, clothing, and "pleasure" to this army of workers. Here is the case of a woman employed in the manufacturing department of a Broadway house. It stands for a hundred like her own. She averages three dollars a week. Pays $1.50 for her room; for breakfast she has a cup of coffee; lunch she cannot afford. One meal a day is her allowance. This woman is young, she is pretty. She has "the world before her." Is it anything less than a miracle if she is guilty of nothing worse than the "early and improvident marriage," against which moralists exclaim as one of the prolific causes of the distress of the poor? Almost any door might seem to offer welcome escape from such slavery as this. "I feel so much healthier since I got three square meals a day," said a lodger in one of the Girls' Homes. Two young sewing girls came in seeking domestic service, so that they might get enough to eat. They had been only half fed for some time, and starvation had driven them to the one door at which the pride of the American-born girl will not permit her to knock, though poverty be the price of her independence.

The tenement and the competition of public institutions and farmers' wives and daughters, have done the tyrant shirt to death, but they have not bettered

the lot of the needle women. The sweater of the East
Side has appropriated the flannel shirt. He turns them
out today at forty-five cents a dozen, paying his Jewish
workers from twenty to thirty-five cents. One of these
testified before the State Board of Arbitration, during
the shirtmakers' strike, that she worked eleven hours
in the shop and four at home, and had never in the
best of times made over six dollars a week. Another
stated that she worked from 4 o'clock in the morning
to 11 at night. These girls had to find their own thread
and pay for their own machines out of their wages.
The white shirt has gone to the public and private institutions that shelter large numbers of young girls,
and to the country. There are not half as many shirtmakers in New York today as only a few years ago,
and some of the largest firms have closed their city
shops. The same is true of the manufacturers of under-
wear. One large Broadway firm has nearly all its work
done by farmers' girls in Maine, who think themselves
well off if they can earn two or three dollars a week to
pay for a Sunday silk, or the wedding outfit, little
dreaming of the part they are playing in starving their
city sisters. Literally, they sew "with double thread,
a shroud as well as a shirt." Their pin money sets the
rate of wages for thousands of poor sewing girls in
New York. The average earnings of the worker on un-
derwear today do not exceed the three dollars which
her competitor among the Eastern hills is willing to
accept as the price of her play. The shirtmaker's pay
is better only because the very finest custom work is
all there is left for her to do.

Calico wrappers at a dollar and a half a dozen—the
very expert sewers able to make from eight to ten,
the common run five or six—neckties at from 25 to 75
cents a dozen, with a dozen as a good day's work, are
specimens of women's wages. And yet people persist
in wondering at the poor quality of work done in the
tenements! Italian cheap labor has come of late also to
possess this poor field, with the sweater in its train.

There is scarce a branch of woman's work outside of
the home in which wages, long since at low-water
mark, have not fallen to the point of actual starvation.
A case was brought to my notice recently by a woman
doctor, whose heart as well as her lifework is with the
poor, of a widow with two little children she found at
work in an East Side attic, making paper bags. Her
father, she told the doctor, had made good wages at
it; but she received only five cents for six hundred of
the little three-cornered bags, and her fingers had to
be very swift and handle the paste brush very deftly
to bring her earnings up to twenty-five and thirty cents
a day. She paid four dollars a month for her room. The
rest went to buy food for herself and the children.
The physician's purse, rather than her skill, had heal-
ing for their complaint.

I have aimed to set down a few dry facts merely.
They carry their own comment. Back of the shop with
its weary, grinding toil—the home in the tenement, of
which it was said in a report of the State Labor Bureau: "Decency and womanly reserve cannot be maintained there—what wonder so many fall away from
virtue?" Of the outlook, what? Last Christmas Eve my
business took me to an obscure street among the West
Side tenements. An old woman had just fallen on the
doorstep, stricken with paralysis. The doctor said she
would never again move her right hand or foot. The
whole side was dead. By her bedside, in their cheerless
room, sat the patient's aged sister, a hopeless cripple,
in dumb despair. Forty years ago the sisters had come,
five in number then, with their mother, from the North
of Ireland to make their home and earn a living among
strangers. They were lace embroiderers and found
work easily at good wages. All the rest had died as the
years went by. The two remained and, firmly resolved
to lead an honest life, worked on though wages fell
and fell as age and toil stiffened their once nimble fingers and dimmed their sight. Then one of them
dropped out, her hands palsied and her courage gone.

Still the other toiled on, resting neither by night nor by day, that the sister might not want. Now that she too had been stricken, as she was going to the store for the work that was to keep them through the holidays, the battle was over at last. There was before them starvation, or the poorhouse. And the proud spirits of the sisters, helpless now, quailed at the outlook.

These were old, with life behind them. For them nothing was left but to sit in the shadow and wait. But of the thousands who are traveling the road they trod to the end, with the hot blood of youth in their veins, with the love of life and of the beautiful world to which not even sixty cents a day can shut their eyes— who is to blame if their feet find the paths of shame that are "always open to them?" The very paths that have effaced the saving "limit," and to which it is declared to be "inevitable that they must in many instances resort." Let the moralist answer. Let the wise economist apply his rule of supply and demand, and let the answer be heard in this city of a thousand charities where justice goes begging.

To the everlasting credit of New York's working girl let it be said that, rough though her road be, all but hopeless her battle with life, only in the rarest instances does she go astray. As a class she is brave, virtuous, and true. New York's army of profligate women is not, as in some foreign cities, recruited from her ranks. She is as plucky as she is proud. That "American girls never whimper" became a proverb long ago, and she accepts her lot uncomplainingly, doing the best she can and holding her cherished independence cheap at the cost of a meal, or of half her daily ration, if need be. The home in the tenement and the traditions of her childhood have neither trained her to luxury nor predisposed her in favor of domestic labor in preference to the shop. So, to the world she presents a cheerful, uncomplaining front that sometimes deceives it. Her courage will not be without its reward. Slowly, as the conviction is thrust upon society that woman's work must enter more and more into its planning, a better day is dawning. The organization of working girls' clubs, unions, and societies with a community of interests, despite the obstacles to such a movement, bears testimony to it, as to the devotion of the unselfish women who have made their poorer sister's cause their own, and will yet wring from an unfair world the justice too long denied her.

PAUPERISM
IN THE TENEMENTS

The reader who has followed with me the fate of the Other Half thus far, may not experience much of a shock at being told that in eight years 135,595 families in New York were registered as asking or receiving charity. Perhaps, however, the intelligence will rouse him that for five years past one person in every ten who died in this city was buried in the potter's field. These facts tell a terrible story. The first means that in a population of a million and a half, very nearly, if not quite, half a million persons were driven, or chose, to beg for food, or to accept it in charity at some period of the eight years, if not during the whole of it. There is no mistake about these figures. They are drawn from the records of the Charity Organization Society, and represent the time during which it has been in existence. It is not even pretended that the record is complete. To be well within the limits, the Society's statisticians allow only three and a half to the family, instead of the four and a half that are accepted as the standard of calculations which deal with New York's population as a whole. They estimate upon the basis of their everyday experience that, allowing for those who have died, moved away, or become for the time being at least self-supporting, eighty-five per cent of the registry are still within, or lingering upon, the borders of dependence. Precisely how the case stands with this great horde of the indigent is shown by a classification of 5169 cases that were investigated by the Society in one year. This was the way it turned out: 327 worthy of continuous relief, or 6.4 per cent; 1269 worthy of temporary relief, or 24.4 per cent; 2698 in need of work, rather than relief, or 52.2 per cent; 875 unworthy of relief, or 17 per cent.

That is, nearly six and a half per cent of all were utterly helpless—orphans, cripples, or the very aged; nearly one-fourth needed just a lift to start them on the road to independence, or to permanent pauperism, according to the wisdom with which the lever was applied. More than half were destitute because they had no work and were unable to find any, and one-sixth were frauds, professional beggars, training their children to follow in their footsteps—a veritable "tribe of Ishmael," tightening its grip on society as the years pass, until society shall summon up pluck to say with Paul, "if any man will not work neither shall he eat," and stick to it. It is worthy of note that almost precisely the same results followed a similar investigation in Boston. There were a few more helpless cases of the sort true charity accounts it a gain to care for, but the proportion of a given lot that was crippled for want of work, or unworthy, was exactly the same as in this city. The bankrupt in hope, in courage, in purse, and in purpose, are not peculiar to New York. They are found the world over, but we have our full share. If further proof were wanted, it is found in the prevalence of pauper burials. The potter's field stands ever for utter, hopeless surrender. The last the poor will let go, however miserable their lot in life, is the hope of a decent burial. But for the five years ending with 1888 the average of burials in the potter's field has been 10.03 per cent of all. In 1889 it was 9.64. In that year the proportion to the total mortality of those who died in hospitals, institutions, and in the almshouse was as 1 in 5.

The 135,595 families inhabited no fewer than 31,-000 different tenements. I say tenements advisedly, though the society calls them buildings, because at least ninety-nine per cent were found in the big barracks, the rest in shanties scattered here and there, and now and then a fraud or an exceptional case of distress in a dwelling house of better class. Here, undoubtedly, allowance must be made for the constant moving about of those who live on charity, which enables one active beggar to blacklist a dozen houses in the year. Still the great mass of the tenements are shown to be harboring alms seekers. They might almost as safely harbor the smallpox. That scourge is not more contagious than the alms seeker's complaint. There are houses that have been corrupted through and through by this pestilence, until their very atmosphere breathes beggary. More than a hundred and twenty pauper families have been reported from time to time as living in one such tenement.

The truth is that pauperism grows in the tenements as naturally as weeds in a garden lot. A moral distemper, like crime, it finds there its most fertile soil. All the surroundings of tenement-house life favor its growth, and where once it has taken root it is harder to dislodge than the most virulent of physical diseases. The thief is infinitely easier to deal with than the pauper, because the very fact of his being a thief presupposes some bottom to the man. Granted that it is bad, there is still something, a possible handle by which to catch him. To the pauper there is none. He is as hopeless as his own poverty. I speak of the *pauper*, not of the honestly poor. There is a sharp line between the two; but athwart it stands the tenement, all the time blurring and blotting it out. "It all comes down to character in the end," was the verdict of a philanthropist whose life has been spent wrestling with this weary problem. And so it comes down to the tenement, the destroyer of individuality and character everywhere. "In nine years," said a wise and charitable physician, sadly, to me, "I have known of but a single case of permanent improvement in a poor tenement family." I have known of some whose experience, extending over an even longer stretch, was little better.

The beggar follows the "tough's" rule of life that the world owes him a living, but his scheme of collecting it stops short of violence. He has not the pluck to rob even a drunken man. His highest flights take in at most an unguarded clothesline, or a little child sent to buy bread or beer with the pennies he clutches tightly as he skips along. Even then he prefers to attain his end by stratagem rather than by force, though occasionally, when the coast is clear, he rises to the height of the bully. The ways he finds of "collecting" under the cloak of undeserved poverty are numberless, and often reflect credit on the man's ingenuity, if not on the man himself. I remember the shock with which my first experience with his kind—her kind, rather, in this case: the beggar was a woman—came home to me. On my way to and from the office I had been giving charity regularly, as I fondly believed, to an old woman who sat in Chatham Square with a baby done up in a bundle of rags, moaning piteously in sunshine and rain, "Please, help the poor." It was the baby I pitied and thought I was doing my little to help, until one night I was just in time to rescue it from rolling out of her lap, and found the bundle I had been wasting my pennies upon just rags and nothing more, and the old hag dead drunk. Since then I have encountered bogus babies, borrowed babies, and drugged babies in the streets, and fought shy of them all. Most of them, I am glad to say, have been banished from the street since; but they are still occasionally to be found. It was only last winter that the officers of the Society for the Prevention of Cruelty to Children arrested an Italian woman who was begging along Madison Avenue with a poor little wreck of a girl, whose rags and pinched face were calculated to tug hard at the purse strings of a miser. Over five dollars in nickels and pennies were taken from the woman's pockets, and when her story of poverty and hunger was investigated at the family's home in a Baxter Street tenement, bankbooks turned up that showed the Masonis to be regular pauper capitalists, able to draw their check for three thousand dollars, had they been so disposed. The woman was fined $250, a worse punishment undoubtedly than to have sent her to prison for the rest of her natural life. Her class has, unhappily, representatives in New York that have not yet been brought to grief.

Nothing short of making street begging a crime has availed to clear our city of this pest to an appreciable extent. By how much of an effort this result has been accomplished may be gleaned from the fact that the Charity Organization Society alone, in five years, caused the taking up of 2594 street beggars, and the arrest and conviction of 1474 persistent offenders. Last year it dealt with 612 perambulating mendicants. The police report only 19 arrests for begging during the year 1889, but the real facts of the case are found under the heading "vagrancy." In all, 2633 persons were charged with this offense, 947 of them women. A goodly proportion of these latter came from the low groggeries of the Tenth Ward, where a peculiar variety of the female tramp-beggar is at home, the "scrub." The scrub is one degree perhaps above the average pauper in this, that she is willing to work at least one day in the week, generally the Jewish Sabbath. The orthodox Jew can do no work of any sort from Friday evening till sunset on Saturday, and this interim the scrub fills out in Ludlow Street. The pittance she receives for this vicarious sacrifice of herself upon the altar of the ancient faith buys her rum for at least two days of the week at one of the neighborhood "morgues." She lives through the other four by begging. There are distilleries in Jewtown, or just across its borders, that depend almost wholly on her custom. Recently, when one in Hester Street was raided because the neighbors had complained of the boisterous hilarity of the hags over their beer, thirty-two aged "scrubs" were marched off to the station house.

It is curious to find preconceived notions quite upset in a review of the nationalities that go to make up this squad of street beggars. The Irish head the list with fifteen per cent, and the native American is only a little way behind with twelve per cent, while the Italian, who in his own country turns beggary into a fine art, has less than two per cent. Eight per cent were Germans. The relative prevalence of the races in our population does not account for this showing. Various causes operate, no doubt, to produce it. Chief among them is, I think, the tenement itself. It has no power to corrupt the Italian, who comes here in almost every instance to work—no beggar would ever emigrate from anywhere unless forced to do so. He is distinctly on its lowest level from the start. With the Irishman the case is different. The tenement, especially its lowest type, appears to possess a peculiar affinity for the worse nature of the Celt, to whose best and strongest instincts it does violence, and soonest and most thoroughly corrupts him. The "native" twelve per cent represent the result of this process, the hereditary beggar of the second or third generation in the slums.

The blind beggar alone is winked at in New York's streets, because the authorities do not know what else to do with him. There is no provision for him anywhere after he is old enough to strike out for himself. The annual pittance of thirty or forty dollars which he receives from the city serves to keep his landlord in good humor; for the rest his misfortune and his thin disguise of selling pencils on the street corners must provide. Until the city affords him some systematic way of earning his living by work (as Philadelphia has done, for instance), to banish him from the street would be tantamount to sentencing him to death by starvation. So he possesses it in peace, that is, if he is blind in good earnest, and begs without "encumbrance." Professional mendicancy does not hesitate to make use of the greatest of human afflictions as a pretense for enlisting the sympathy upon which it thrives. Many New Yorkers will remember the French schoolmaster who was "blinded by a shell at the siege of Paris," but miraculously recovered his sight when arrested and deprived of his children by the officers of Mr. Gerry's society. When last heard of he kept a "museum" in Hartford, and acted the overseer with financial success. His sign with its pitiful tale, which was a familiar sight in our streets for years and earned for him the capital upon which he started his business, might have found a place among the curiosities exhibited there, had it not been kept in a different sort of museum here as a memento of his rascality. There was another of his tribe, a woman, who begged for years with a deformed child in her arms, which she was found to have hired at an almshouse in Genoa for fifteen francs a month. It was a good investment, for she proved to be possessed of a comfortable fortune. Some time before that, the Society for the Prevention of Cruelty to Children, which found her out, had broken up the dreadful padrone system, a real slave trade in Italian children, who were bought of poor parents across the sea and made to beg their way on foot through France to the port whence they were shipped to this city, to be beaten and starved here by their cruel masters and sent out to beg, often after merciless mutilation to make them "take" better with a pitying public.

But, after all, the tenement offers a better chance of fraud on impulsive but thoughtless charity than all the wretchedness of the street, and with fewer risks. To the tenderhearted and unwary it is, in itself, the strongest plea for help. When such a cry goes up as was heard recently from a Mott Street den, where the family of a "sick" husband, a despairing mother, and half a dozen children in rags and dirt were destitute of the "first necessities of life," it is not to be wondered at that a stream of gold comes pouring in to relieve. It happens too often, as in that case, that a little critical inquiry or reference to the "black list" of the Charity Organization Society, justly dreaded only by the frauds, discovers the "sickness" to stand for laziness, and the destitution to be the family's stock in trade; and the community receives a shock that for once is downright wholesome, if it imposes a check on an undiscriminating charity that is worse than none at all.

The case referred to furnished an apt illustration of how thoroughly corrupting pauperism is in such a setting. The tenement woke up early to the gold mine that was being worked under its roof, and before the day was three hours old the stream of callers who responded to the newspaper appeal found the alley blocked by a couple of "toughs," who exacted toll of a silver quarter from each tearful sympathizer with the misery in the attic.

A volume might be written about the tricks of the professional beggar, and the uses to which he turns the tenement in his trade. The Boston "widow" whose husband turned up alive and well after she had buried him seventeen times with tears and lamentation, and made the public pay for the weekly funerals, is not without representatives in New York. The "gentleman tramp" is a familiar type from our streets, and the "once respectable Methodist" who patronized all the revivals in town with his profitable story of repentance, only to fall from grace into the saloon door nearest the church after the service was over, merely transferred the scene of his operations from the tenement to the church as the proper setting for his specialty. There is enough of real suffering in the homes of the poor to make one wish that there were some effective way of enforcing Paul's plan of starving the drones into the paths of self-support: no work, nothing to eat.

The message came from one of the Health Department's summer doctors, last July, to The King's Daughters' Tenement-House Committee, that a family with a sick child was absolutely famishing in an uptown tenement. The address was not given. The doctor had forgotten to write it down, and before he could be found and a visitor sent to the house the baby was dead, and the mother had gone mad. The nurse found the father, who was an honest laborer long out of work, packing the little corpse in an orange-box partly filled with straw, that he might take it to the morgue for pauper burial. There was absolutely not a crust to eat in the house, and the other children were crying for food. The great immediate need in that case, as in more than half of all according to the record, was work and living wages. Alms do not meet the emergency at all. They frequently aggravate it, degrading and pauperizing where true help should aim at raising the sufferer to self-respect and self-dependence. The experience of the Charity Organization Society in raising, in eight years, 4500 families out of the rut of pauperism into proud, if modest, independence, without alms, but by a system of "friendly visitation," and the work of the Society for Improving the Condition of the Poor and kindred organizations along the same line, shows what can be done by well-directed effort. It is estimated that New York spends in public and private charity every year a round $8,000,000. A small part of this sum intelligently invested in a great labor bureau that would bring the seeker of work and the one with work to give together under auspices offering some degree of mutual security would certainly repay the amount of the investment in the saving of much capital now worse than wasted, and would be prolific of the best results. The ultimate and greatest need, however, the real remedy, is to remove the cause—the tenement that was built for "a class of whom nothing was expected," and which has come fully up to the expectation. Tenement-house reform holds the key to the problem of pauperism in the city. We can never get rid of either the tenement or the pauper. The two will always exist together in New York. But by reforming the one, we can do more toward exterminating the other than can be done by all other means together that have yet been invented, or ever will be.

THE WRECKS
AND THE WASTE

Pauperdom is to blame for the unjust yoking of poverty with punishment, "charities" with "correction," in our municipal ministering to the needs of the Nether Half. The shadow of the workhouse points like a scornful finger toward its neighbor, the almshouse, when the sun sets behind the teeming city across the East River, as if, could its stones speak, it would say before night drops its black curtain between them: "You and I are brothers. I am not more bankrupt in moral purpose than you. A common parent begat us. Twin breasts, the tenement and the saloon, nourished us. Vice and unthrift go hand in hand. Pauper, behold thy brother!" And the almshouse owns the bitter relationship in silence.

Over on the islands that lie strung along the river and far up the Sound the Nether Half hides its deformity, except on show days, when distinguished visitors have to be entertained and the sore is uncovered by the authorities with due municipal pride in the exhibit. I shall spare the reader the sight. The aim of these pages has been to lay bare its source. But a brief glance at our proscribed population is needed to give background and tone to the picture. The review begins with the Charity Hospital with its thousand helpless human wrecks; takes in the penitentiary, where the "tough" from Battle Row and Poverty Gap is made to earn behind stone walls the living the world owes him; a thoughtless, jolly convict band with opportunity at last "to think" behind the iron bars, but little desire to improve it; governed like unruly boys, which in fact most of them are. Three of them were taken from the dinner table while I was there one day, for sticking pins into each other, and were set with their faces to the wall in sight of six hundred of their comrades for punishment. Pleading incessantly for tobacco, when the keeper's back is turned, as the next best thing to the whisky they cannot get, though they can plainly make out the saloon-signs across the stream where they robbed or "slugged" their way to prison. Every once in a while the longing gets the best of some prisoner from the penitentiary or the workhouse, and he risks his life in the swift currents to reach the goal that tantalizes him with the promise of "just one more drunk." The chances are at least even of his being run down by some passing steamer and drowned, even if he is not overtaken by the armed guards who patrol the shore in boats, or his strength does not give out.

This workhouse comes next, with the broken-down hordes from the dives, the lodginghouses, and the tramps' nests, the "hellbox"* rather than the repair shop of the city. In 1889 the registry at the workhouse footed up 22,477, of whom some had been there as many as twenty times before. It is the popular summer resort of the slums, but business is brisk at this stand the year round. Not a few of its patrons drift back periodically without the formality of a commitment, to take their chances on the island when there is no escape from the alternative of work in the city. Work, but not too much work, is the motto of the establishment. The "workhouse step" is an institution that must be observed on the island, in order to draw any comparison between it and the snail's pace that shall do justice to the snail. Nature and man's art have made these islands beautiful; but weeds grow luxuriantly

* In printing-offices the broken, worn-out, and useless type is thrown into the "hellbox," to be recast at the foundry.

in their gardens, and spiders spin their cobwebs unmolested in the borders of sweet-smelling box. The
work which two score of hired men could do well is
too much for these thousands.

Rows of old women, some smoking stumpy, black
clay pipes, others knitting or idling, all grumbling, sit
or stand under the trees that hedge in the almshouse,
or limp about in the sunshine, leaning on crutches
or bean-pole staffs. They are a "growler-gang" of
another sort than may be seen in session on the rocks
of the opposite shore at that very moment. They
grumble and growl from sunrise to sunset, at the
weather, the breakfast, the dinner, the supper; at
pork and beans as at corned beef and cabbage; at
their Thanksgiving dinner as at the half rations of
the sick ward; at the past that had no joy, at the present whose comfort they deny, and at the future without promise. The crusty old men in the next building
are not a circumstance to them. The warden, who was
in charge of the almshouse for many years, had become so snappish and profane by constant association
with a thousand cross old women that I approached
him with some misgivings to request his permission to
"take" a group of a hundred or so who were within
shot of my camera. He misunderstood me.

"Take them?" he yelled. "Take the thousand of
them and be welcome. They will never be still, by ——,
till they are sent up on Hart's Island in a box, and I'll
be blamed if I don't think they will growl then at the
style of the funeral."

And he threw his arms around me in an outburst of
enthusiasm over the wondrous good luck that had sent
a friend indeed to his door. I felt it to be a painful
duty to undeceive him. When I told him that I simply
wanted the old women's picture, he turned away in
speechless disgust, and to his dying day, I have no
doubt, remembered my call as the day of the champion fool's visit to the island.

When it is known that many of these old people

have been sent to the almshouse to die by their heartless children, for whom they had worked faithfully as long as they were able, their growling and discontent is not hard to understand. Bitter poverty threw them all "on the county," often on the wrong county at that. Very many of them are old-country poor, sent, there is reason to believe, to America by the authorities to get rid of the obligation to support them. "The almshouse," wrote a good missionary, "affords a sad illustration of St. Paul's description of the 'last days.' The class from which comes our poorhouse population is to a large extent 'without natural affection.'" I was reminded by his words of what my friend, the doctor, had said to me a little while before: "Many a mother has told me at her child's deathbed, 'I cannot afford to lose it. It costs too much to bury it.' And when the little one did die there was no time for the mother's grief. The question crowded on at once, 'where shall the money come from?' Natural feelings and affections are smothered in the tenements." The doctor's experience furnished a sadly appropriate text for the priest's sermon.

Pitiful as these are, sights and sounds infinitely more saddening await us beyond the gate that shuts this world of woe off from one whence the light of hope and reason have gone out together. The shuffling of many feet on the macadamized roads heralds the approach of a host of women, hundreds upon hundreds—beyond the turn in the road they still keep coming, marching with the faltering step, the unseeing look and the incessant, senseless chatter that betrays the darkened mind. The lunatic women of the Blackwell's Island Asylum are taking their afternoon walk. Beyond, on the wide lawn, moves another still stranger procession, a file of women in the asylum dress of dull gray, hitched to a queer little wagon that, with its gaudy adornments, suggests a cross between a baby carriage and a circus chariot. One crazy woman is strapped in the seat; forty tug at the rope to which

they are securely bound. This is the "chain gang," so
called once in scoffing ignorance of the humane purpose the contrivance serves. These are the patients
afflicted with suicidal mania, who cannot be trusted at
large for a moment with the river in sight, yet must
have their daily walk as a necessary part of their
treatment. So this wagon was invented by a clever
doctor to afford them at once exercise and amusement.
A merry-go-round in the grounds suggests a variation
of this scheme. Ghastly suggestion of mirth, with that
stricken host advancing on its aimless journey! As we
stop to see it pass, the plaintive strains of a familiar
song float through a barred window in the gray stone
building. The voice is sweet, but inexpressibly sad:
"Oh, how my heart grows weary, far from——" The
song breaks off suddenly in a low, troubled laugh. She
has forgotten, forgotten——. A woman in the ranks,
whose head has been turned toward the window,
throws up her hands with a scream. The rest stir uneasily. The nurse is by her side in an instant with
words half soothing, half stern. A messenger comes
in haste from the asylum to ask us not to stop.
Strangers may not linger where the patients pass. It
is apt to excite them. As we go in with him the human
file is passing yet, quiet restored. The troubled voice of
the unseen singer still gropes vainly among the lost
memories of the past for the missing key: "Oh! how
my heart grows weary, far from——"

"Who is she, doctor?"

"Hopeless case. She will never see home again."

An average of seventeen hundred women this
asylum harbors; the asylum for men up on Ward's
Island even more. Altogether 1419 patients were admitted to the city asylums for the insane in 1889, and
at the end of the year 4913 remained in them. There
is a constant ominous increase in this class of helpless
unfortunates that are thrown on the city's charity.
Quite two hundred are added year by year, and the
asylums were long since so overcrowded that a great

"farm" had to be established on Long Island to receive the surplus. The strain of our hurried, overworked life has something to do with this. Poverty has more. For these are all of the poor. It is the harvest of sixty and a hundred-fold, the "fearful rolling up and rolling down from generation to generation, through all the ages, of the weakness, vice, and moral darkness of the past."* The curse of the island haunts all that come once within its reach. "No man or woman," says Dr. Louis L. Seaman, who speaks from many years' experience in a position that gave him full opportunity to observe the facts, "who is 'sent up' to these colonies ever returns to the city scot-free. There is a lien, visible or hidden, upon his or her present or future, which too often proves stronger than the best purposes and fairest opportunities of social rehabilitation. The underworld holds in rigorous bondage every unfortunate or miscreant who has once 'served time.' There is often tragic interest in the struggles of the ensnared wretches to break away from the meshes spun about them. But the maelstrom has no bowels of mercy; and the would-be fugitives are flung back again and again into the devouring whirlpool of crime and poverty, until the end is reached on the dissecting table, or in the potter's field. What can the moralist or scientist do by way of resuscitation? Very little at best. The flotsam and jetsam are mere shreds and fragments of wasted lives. Such a ministry must begin at the sources —is necessarily prophylactic, nutritive, educational. On these islands there are no flexible twigs, only gnarled, blasted, blighted trunks, insensible to moral or social influences."

Sad words, but true. The commonest keeper soon learns to pick out almost at sight the "cases" that will

---

* Dr. Louis L. Seaman, late chief of staff of the Blackwell's Island hospitals: "Social Waste of a Great City," read before the American Association for the Advancement of Science, 1886.

leave the penitentiary, the workhouse, the almshouse, only to return again and again, each time more hopeless, to spend their wasted lives in the bondage of the island.

The alcoholic cells in Bellevue Hospital are a way station for a goodly share of them on their journeys back and forth across the East River. Last year they held altogether 3694 prisoners, considerably more than one-fourth of the whole number of 13,813 patients that went in through the hospital gates. The daily average of "cases" in this, the hospital of the poor, is over six hundred. The average daily census of all the prisons, hospitals, workhouses, and asylums in the charge of the Department of Charities and Correction last year was about 14,000, and about one employee was required for every ten of this army to keep its machinery running smoothly. The total number admitted in 1889 to all the jails and institutions in the city and on the islands was 138,332. To the almshouse alone 38,600 were admitted; 9765 were there to start the new year with, and 553 were born with the dark shadow of the poorhouse overhanging their lives, making a total of 48,918. In the care of all their wards the commissioners expended $2,343,372. The appropriation for the police force in 1889 was $4,409,550.94, and for the criminal courts and their machinery $403,190. Thus the first cost of maintaining our standing army of paupers, criminals, and sick poor, by direct taxation, was last year $7,156,112.94.

HOW THE CASE
STANDS

———

What, then, are the bald facts with which we have to deal in New York?

I. That we have a tremendous, ever-swelling crowd of wage earners which it is our business to house decently.

II. That it is not housed decently.

III. That it must be so housed *here* for the present, and for a long time to come, all schemes of suburban relief being as yet utopian, impracticable.

IV. That it pays high enough rents to entitle it to be so housed, as a right.

V. That nothing but our own slothfulness is in the way of so housing it, since "the condition of the tenants is in advance of the condition of the houses which they occupy" (Report of Tenement-House Commission).

VI. That the security of the one no less than of the other half demands, on sanitary, moral, and economic grounds, that it be decently housed.

VII. That it will pay to do it. As an investment, I mean, and in hard cash. This I shall immediately proceed to prove.

VIII. That the tenement has come to stay, and must itself be the solution of the problem with which it confronts us.

This is the fact from which we cannot get away, however we may deplore it. Doubtless the best would be to get rid of it altogether; but as we cannot, all argument on that score may at this time be dismissed as idle. The practical question is what to do with the tenement. I watched a Mott Street landlord, the owner of a row of barracks that have made no end of trouble for the health authorities for twenty years, solve that question for himself the other day. His way was to give the wretched pile a coat of paint, and put a gorgeous tin cornice on with the year 1890 in letters a yard long. From where I stood watching the operation, I looked down upon the same dirty crowds camping on the roof, foremost among them an Italian mother with two stark-naked children who had apparently never made the acquaintance of a wash tub. That was a landlord's way, and will not get us out of the mire.

The "flat" is another way that does not solve the problem. Rather, it extends it. The flat is not a model, though it is a modern, tenement. It gets rid of some of the nuisances of the low tenement, and of the worst of them, the overcrowding—if it gets rid of them at all—at a cost that takes it at once out of the catalogue of "homes for the poor," while imposing some of the evils from which they suffer upon those who ought to escape from them.

There are three effective ways of dealing with the tenements in New York:

I. By law.

II. By remodeling and making the most out of the old houses.

III. By building new, model tenements.

Private enterprise—conscience, to put it in the category of duties, where it belongs—must do the lion's share under these last two heads. Of what the law has effected I have spoken already. The drastic measures adopted in Paris, in Glasgow, and in London are not practicable here on anything like as large a scale. Still it can, under strong pressure of public opinion, rid us of the worst plague spots. The Mulberry Street Bend will go the way of the Five Points when all the red tape that binds the hands of municipal effort has

been unwound. Prizes were offered in public competition, some years ago, for the best plans of modern
tenement houses. It may be that we shall see the day
when the building of model tenements will be encouraged by subsidies in the way of a rebate of taxes.
Meanwhile the arrest and summary punishment of
landlords, or their agents, who persistently violate law
and decency, will have a salutary effect. If a few of
the wealthy absentee landlords, who are the worst
offenders, could be got within the jurisdiction of the
city, and by arrest be compelled to employ proper
overseers, it would be a proud day for New York. To
remedy the overcrowding, with which the night in-
spections of the sanitary police cannot keep step, tenements may eventually have to be licensed, as now
the lodginghouses, to hold so many tenants, and no
more; or the State may have to bring down the rents
that cause the crowding, by assuming the right to
regulate them as it regulates the fares on the elevated
roads. I throw out the suggestion, knowing quite well
that it is open to attack. It emanated originally from
one of the brightest minds that have had to struggle
officially with this tenement-house question in the last
ten years. In any event, to succeed, reform by law
must aim at making it unprofitable to own a bad
tenement. At best, it is apt to travel at a snail's pace,
while the enemy it pursues is putting the best foot
foremost.

In this matter of profit the law ought to have its
strongest ally in the landlord himself, though the reverse is the case. This condition of things I believe
to rest on a monstrous error. It cannot be that tenement property that is worth preserving at all can
continue to yield larger returns, if allowed to run
down, than if properly cared for and kept in good
repair. The point must be reached, and soon, where
the cost of repairs, necessary with a house full of the
lowest, most ignorant tenants, must overbalance the
saving of the first few years of neglect; for this class is

everywhere the most destructive, as well as the poorest paying. I have the experience of owners, who have found this out to their cost, to back me up in the assertion, even if it were not the statement of a plain business fact that proves itself. I do not include tenement property that is deliberately allowed to fall into decay because at some future time the ground will be valuable for business or other purposes. There is unfortunately enough of that kind in New York, often leasehold property owned by wealthy estates or soulless corporations that oppose all their great influence to the efforts of the law in behalf of their tenants.

There is abundant evidence, on the other hand, that it can be made to pay to improve and make the most of the worst tenement property, even in the most wretched locality. The example set by Miss Ellen Collins in her Water Street houses will always stand as a decisive answer to all doubts on this point. It is quite ten years since she bought three old tenements at the corner of Water and Roosevelt Streets, then as now one of the lowest localities in the city. Since then she has leased three more adjoining her purchase, and so much of Water Street has at all events been purified. Her first effort was to let in the light in the hallways, and with the darkness disappeared, as if by magic, the heaps of refuse that used to be piled up beside the sinks. A few of the most refractory tenants disappeared with them, but a very considerable proportion stayed, conforming readily to the new rules, and are there yet. It should here be stated that Miss Collins's tenants are distinctly of the poorest. Her purpose was to experiment with this class, and her experiment has been more than satisfactory. Her plan was, as she puts it herself, fair play between tenant and landlord. To this end the rents were put as low as consistent with the idea of a business investment that must return a reasonable interest to be successful. The houses were thoroughly refitted with proper plumbing. A competent janitor was put in charge to see that the rules were observed by the tenants, when Miss Collins herself was not there. Of late years she has had to give very little time to personal superintendence, and the caretaker told me only the other day that very little was needed. The houses seemed to run themselves in the groove once laid down. Once the reputed haunt of thieves, they have become the most orderly in the neighborhood. Clothes are left hanging on the lines all night with impunity, and the pretty flower beds in the yard where the children not only from the six houses, but of the whole block, play, skip, and swing, are undisturbed. The tenants, by the way, provide the flowers themselves in the spring, and take all the more pride in them because they are their own. The six houses contain forty-five families, and there "has never been any need of putting up a bill." As to the income from the property, Miss Collins said to me last August: "I have had six and even six and three-quarters per cent on the capital invested; on the whole, you may safely say five and a half per cent. This I regard as entirely satisfactory." It should be added that she has persistently refused to let the corner store, now occupied by a butcher, as a saloon; or her income from it might have been considerably increased.

Miss Collins's experience is of value chiefly as showing what can be accomplished with the worst possible material, by the sort of personal interest in the poor that alone will meet their real needs. All the charity in the world, scattered with the most lavish hand, will not take its place. "Fair play" between landlord and tenant is the key, too long mislaid, that unlocks the door to success everywhere as it did for Miss Collins. She has not lacked imitators whose experience has been akin to her own. The case of Gotham Court has been already cited. On the other hand, instances are not wanting of landlords who have undertaken the task, but have tired of it or sold their property before it had been fully redeemed, with the result that it relapsed into its former bad condition faster than it had improved, and the tenants with it. I am inclined to think that such houses are liable to fall even below the average level. Backsliding in brick and mortar does not greatly differ from similar performances in flesh and blood.

Backed by a strong and steady sentiment, such as these pioneers have evinced, that would make it the personal business of wealthy owners with time to spare to look after their tenants, the law would be able in a very short time to work a salutary transformation in the worst quarters, to the lasting advantage, I am well persuaded, of the landlord no less than the tenant. Unfortunately, it is in this quality of personal effort that the sentiment of interest in the poor, upon which we have to depend, is too often lacking. People who are willing to give money feel that that ought to be enough. It is not. The money thus given is too apt to be wasted along with the sentiment that prompted the gift.

Even when it comes to the third of the ways I spoke of as effective in dealing with the tenement-house problem, the building of model structures, the personal interest in the matter must form a large share of the capital invested, if it is to yield full returns. Where that is the case, there is even less doubt about its paying, with ordinary business management, than in the case of reclaiming an old building, which is, like putting life into a defunct newspaper, pretty apt to be uphill work. Model tenement building has not been attempted in New York on anything like as large a scale as in many other great cities, and it is perhaps owing to this, in a measure, that a belief prevails that it cannot succeed here. This is a wrong notion entirely. The various undertakings of that sort that have been made here under intelligent management have, as far as I know, all been successful.

From the managers of the two best-known experiments in model tenement building in the city, the Improved Dwellings Association and the Tenement-House Building Company, I have letters dated last August, declaring their enterprises eminently successful. There is no reason why their experience should not be conclusive. That the Philadelphia plan is not practicable in New York is not a good reason why our own plan, which is precisely the reverse of our neighbor's, should not be. In fact it is an argument for its success. The very reason why we cannot house our working masses in cottages, as has been done in Philadelphia—viz., that they must live on Manhattan Island, where the land is too costly for small houses—is the best guarantee of the success of the model tenement house, properly located and managed. The drift in tenement building, as in everything else, is toward concentration, and helps smooth the way. Four families on the floor, twenty in the house, is the rule of today. As the crowds increase, the need of guiding this drift into safe channels becomes more urgent. The larger the scale upon which the model tenement is planned, the more certain the promise of success. The utmost ingenuity cannot build a house for sixteen or twenty families on a lot 25 × 100 feet in the middle of a block like it, that shall give them the amount of air and sunlight to be had by the erection of a dozen or twenty houses on a common plan around a central yard. This was the view of the committee that awarded the prizes for the best plan for the conventional tenement, ten years ago. It coupled its verdict with the emphatic declaration that, in its view, it was "impossible to secure the requirements of physical and moral health within these narrow and arbitrary limits." Houses have been built since on better plans than any the committee saw, but its judgment stands unimpaired. A point, too, that is not to be overlooked, is the reduced cost of expert superintendence—the first condition of successful management—in the larger buildings.

The Improved Dwellings Association put up its block of thirteen houses in East Seventy-second Street nine years ago. Their cost, estimated at about $240,000 with the land, was increased to $285,000 by troubles with the contractor engaged to build them. Thus the Association's task did not begin under the happiest auspices. Unexpected expenses came to deplete its treasury. The neighborhood was new and not crowded at the start. No expense was spared, and the benefit of all the best and most recent experience in tenement building was given to the tenants. The families were provided with from two to four rooms, all "outer" rooms, of course, at rents ranging from $14 per month for the four on the ground floor, to $6.25 for two rooms on the top floor. Coal lifts, ash chutes, common laundries in the basement, and free baths, are features of these buildings that were then new enough to be looked upon with suspicion by the doubting Thomases who predicted disaster. There are rooms in the block for 218 families, and when I looked in recently all but nine of the apartments were let. One of the nine was rented while I was in the building. The superintendent told me that he had little trouble with disorderly tenants, though the buildings shelter all sorts of people. Mr. W. Bayard Cutting, the President of the Association, writes to me:

"By the terms of subscription to the stock before incorporation, dividends were limited to five per cent on the stock of the Improved Dwellings Association. These dividends have been paid (two per cent each six months) ever since the expiration of the first six months of the buildings operation. All surplus has been expended upon the buildings. New and expensive roofs have been put on for the comfort of such tenants as might choose to use them. The buildings have been completely painted inside and out in a manner not contemplated at the outset. An expensive set of fire escapes has been put on at the command of the Fire Department, and a considerable number of other im-

provements made. *I regard the experiment as eminently successful and satisfactory,* particularly when it
is considered that the buildings were the first erected
in this city upon anything like a large scale, where it
was proposed to meet the architectural difficulties that
present themselves in the tenement-house problem. I
have no doubt that the experiment could be tried today with the improved knowledge which has come
with time, and a much larger return be shown upon
the investment. The results referred to have been attained in spite of the provision which prevents the
selling of liquor upon the Association's premises. You
are aware, of course, how much larger rent can be
obtained for a liquor saloon than for an ordinary store.
An investment at five per cent net upon real estate
security worth more than the principal sum ought to
be considered desirable."

The Tenement House Building Company made its
"experiment" in a much more difficult neighborhood,
Cherry Street, some six years later. Its houses shelter
many Russian Jews, and the difficulty of keeping them
in order is correspondingly increased, particularly as
there are no ash chutes in the houses. It has been
necessary even to shut the children out of the yards
upon which the kitchen windows give, lest they be
struck by something thrown out by the tenants, and
killed. It is the Cherry Street style, not easily got rid of.
Nevertheless, the houses are well kept. Of the one
hundred and six "apartments," only four were vacant in August. Professor Edwin R. A. Seligman, the
secretary of the company, writes to me: "The tenements are now a decided success." In the three years
since they were built, they have returned an interest
of from five to five and a half per cent on the capital
invested. The original intention of making the tenants
profit sharers on a plan of rent insurance, under which
all earnings above four per cent would be put to the
credit of the tenants, has not yet been carried out.

A scheme of dividends to tenants on a somewhat

similar plan has been carried out by a Brooklyn builder, Mr. A. T. White, who has devoted a life of beneficent activity to tenement building, and whose experience, though it has been altogether across the East River, I regard as justly applying to New York as well. He so regards it himself. Discussing the cost of building, he says: "There is not the slightest reason to doubt that the financial result of a similar undertaking in any tenement-house district of New York City would be equally good. . . . High cost of land is no detriment, provided the value is made by the pressure of people seeking residence there. Rents in New York City bear a higher ratio to Brooklyn rents than would the cost of land and building in the one city to that in the other." The assertion that Brooklyn furnishes a better class of tenants than the tenement districts in New York would not be worth discussing seriously, even if Mr. White did not meet it himself with the statement that the proportion of day laborers and sewing women in his houses is greater than in any of the London model tenements, showing that they reach the humblest classes.

Mr. White has built homes for five hundred poor families since he began his work, and has made it pay well enough to allow good tenants a share in the profits, averaging nearly one month's rent out of the twelve, as a premium upon promptness and order. The plan of his last tenements may be justly regarded as the beau ideal of the model tenement for a great city like New York. It embodies all the good features of Sir Sydney Waterlow's London plan, with improvements suggested by the builder's own experience. Its chief merit is that it gathers three hundred real homes, not simply three hundred familes, under one roof. Three tenants, it will be seen, use each entrance hall. Of the rest of the three hundred they may never know, rarely see, one. Each has his private front door. The common hall, with all that it stands for, has disappeared. The fireproof stairs are outside the house, a

perfect fire escape. Each tenant has his own scullery
and ash flue. There are no air shafts, for they are not
needed. Every room, under the admirable arrangement
of the plan, looks out either upon the street or the
yard, which is nothing less than a great park with a
playground set apart for the children, where they may
dig in the sand to their heart's content. Weekly con-
certs are given in the park by a brass band. The drying
of clothes is done on the roof, where racks are fitted
up for the purpose. The outside stairways end in turrets
that give the buildings a very smart appearance. Mr.
White never has any trouble with his tenants, though
he gathers in the poorest; nor do his tenements have
anything of the "institution character" that occasionally attaches to ventures of this sort, to their damage.
They are like a big village of contented people, who
live in peace with one another because they have
elbowroom even under one big roof.

Enough has been said to show that model tenements
can be built successfully and made to pay in New
York, if the owner will be content with the five or six
per cent he does not even dream of when investing
his funds in "governments" at three or four. It is true
that in the latter case he has only to cut off his cou-
pons and cash them. But the extra trouble of looking
after his tenement property, that is the condition of
his highest and lasting success, is the penalty exacted
for the sins of our fathers that "shall be visited upon
the children, unto the third and fourth generation."
We shall indeed be well off, if it stop there. I fear there
is too much reason to believe that our own iniquities
must be added to transmit the curse still further. And
yet, such is the leavening influence of a good deed in
that dreary desert of sin and suffering, that the erection
of a single good tenement has the power to change,
gradually but surely, the character of a whole bad
block. It sets up a standard to which the neighborhood
must rise, if it cannot succeed in dragging it down to
its own low level.

And so this task, too, has come to an end. Whatsoever a man soweth, that shall he also reap. I have aimed to tell the truth as I saw it. If this book shall have borne ever so feeble a hand in garnering a harvest of justice, it has served its purpose. While I was writing these lines I went down to the sea, where thousands from the city were enjoying their summer rest. The ocean slumbered under a cloudless sky. Gentle waves washed lazily over the white sand, where children fled before them with screams of laughter. Standing there and watching their play, I was told that during the fierce storms of winter it happened that this sea, now so calm, rose in rage and beat down, broke over the bluff, sweeping all before it. No barrier built by human hands had power to stay it then. The sea of a mighty population, held in galling fetters, heaves uneasily in the tenements. Once already our city, to which have come the duties and responsibilities of metropolitan greatness before it was able to fairly measure its task, has felt the swell of its resistless flood. If it rise once more, no human power may avail to check it. The gap between the classes in which it surges, unseen, unsuspected by the thoughtless, is widening day by day. No tardy enactment of law, no political expedient, can close it. Against all other dangers our system of government may offer defense and shelter; against this not. I know of but one bridge that will carry us over safe, a bridge founded upon justice and built of human hearts. I believe that the danger of such conditions as are fast growing up around us is greater for the very freedom which they mock. The words of the poet, with whose lines I prefaced this book, are truer today, have far deeper meaning to us, than when they were penned forty years ago:

"—Think ye that building shall endure
  Which shelters the noble and crushes the poor?"

APPENDIX

Statistics of population were left out of the text in the hope that the results of this year's census would be available as a basis for calculation before the book went to press. They are now at hand, but their correctness is disputed. The statisticians of the Health Department claim that New York's population has been underestimated a hundred thousand at least, and they appear to have the best of the argument. A recount is called for, and the printer will not wait. Such statistics as follow have been based on the Health Department estimates, except where the census source is given. The extent of the quarrel of official figures may be judged from this one fact, that the ordinarily conservative and careful calculations of the Sanitary Bureau make the death rate of New York, in 1889, 25.19 for the thousand of a population of 1,575,073, while the census would make it 26.76 in a population of 1,482,273.

Population of	New York, 1880	(census)	1,206,299
"	London, 1881	"	3,816,483
"	Philadelphia, 1880	"	846,980
"	Brooklyn, 1880	"	566,689
"	Boston, 1880	"	362,535
"	New York, 1889	(estimated)	1,575,073
"	London, 1889	"	4,351,738
"	Philadelphia, 1889	"	1,040,245

Population of Brooklyn, 1889 (estimated)	814,505
" Boston, " "	420,000
" New York under five years of age, in 1880	140,327
" New York under five years of age, in 1889 (estimated)	182,770
Population of tenements in New York in 1869* (census)	468,492
Population of tenements in New York in 1888† (census)	1,093,701
Population of tenements in New York in 1888 under five years of age	143,243
Population of New York in 1880 (census)	1,206,299
" Manhattan Island in 1880 (census)	1,164,673
" Tenth Ward in 1880 (census)	47,554
" Eleventh Ward " "	68,778
" Thirteenth Ward in 1880 (census)	37,797
" New York in 1890 (census)	1,513,501
" Manhattan Island in 1890 (census)	1,440,101
" Tenth Ward in 1890 (census)	57,514
" Eleventh Ward " "	75,708
" Thirteenth Ward in 1890 (census)	45,882
Number of acres in New York City	24,890
" " Manhattan Island	12,673
" " Tenth Ward	110
" " Eleventh Ward	196
" " Thirteenth Ward	107
Density of population per acre in 1880, New York City	48.4

* In 1869 a tenement was a house occupied by four families or more.

† In 1888, a tenement was a house occupied by three families or more.

Density of population per acre in 1880, Manhattan Island	92.6
Density of population per acre in 1880, Tenth Ward	432.3
Density of population per acre in 1880, Eleventh Ward	350.9
Density of population per acre in 1880, Thirteenth Ward	353.2
Density of population per acre in 1890, New York City (census)	60.08
Density of population per acre in 1890, Manhattan Island (census)	114.53
Density of population per acre in 1890, Tenth Ward (census)	522.00
Density of population per acre in 1890, Eleventh Ward (census)	386.00
Density of population per acre in 1890, Thirteenth Ward (census)	428.8
Density of population to the square mile in 1880, New York City (census)	30,976
Density of population to the square mile in 1880, Manhattan Island (census)	41,264
Density of population to the square mile in 1880, Tenth Ward (census)	276,672
Density of population to the square mile in 1880, Eleventh Ward (census)	224,576
Density of population to the square mile in 1880, Thirteenth Ward (census)	226,048
Density of population to the square mile in 1890, New York City (census)	38,451
Density of population to the square mile in 1890, Manhattan Island (census)	73,299
Density of population to the square mile in 1890, Tenth Ward (census)	334,080
Density of population to the square mile in 1890, Eleventh Ward (census)	246,040
Density of population to the square mile in 1890, Thirteenth Ward (census)	274,432

Number of persons to a dwelling in New York, 1880 (census)			16.37
Number of persons to a dwelling in London, 1881 (census)			7.9
Number of persons to a dwelling in Philadelphia, 1880 (census)			5.79
Number of persons to a dwelling in Brooklyn, 1880 (census)			9.11
Number of persons to a dwelling in Boston, 1880 (census)			8.26
Number of deaths in New York, 1880			31,937
"	"	London, 1881	81,431
"	"	Philadelphia, 1880	17,711
"	"	Brooklyn, 1880	13,222
"	"	Boston, 1880	8,612
Death rate of New York, 1880			26.47
"	London, 1881		21.3
"	Philadelphia, 1880		20.91
"	Brooklyn, 1880		23.33
"	Boston, 1880		23.75
Number of deaths in New York, 1889			39,679
"	"	London, 1889	75,683
"	"	Philadelphia, 1889	20,536
"	"	Brooklyn, 1889	18,288
"	"	Boston, 1889	10,259
Death rate of New York, 1889			25.19
"	London, 1889		17.4
"	Philadelphia, 1889		19.7
"	Brooklyn, 1889		22.5
"	Boston, 1889		24.42

For every person who dies there are always two disabled by illness, so that there was a regular average of 79,358 New Yorkers on the sick list at any moment last year. It is usual to count 28 cases of sickness the year round for every death, and this would give a total for the year 1889 of 1,111,082 of illness of all sorts.

Number of deaths in tenements in New York, 1869   13,285

Number of deaths in tenements in New York, 1888   24,842

Death rate in tenements in New York, 1869   28.35

"   "   "   "   "   1888   22.71

This is exclusive of deaths in institutions, properly referable to the tenements in most cases. The adult death rate is found to decrease in the larger tenements of newer construction. The child mortality increases, reaching 114.04 per cent of 1000 living in houses containing between 60 and 80 tenants. From this point it decreases with the adult death rate.

Number of deaths in prisons, New York, 1889   85

"   "   hospitals, New York, 1889   6,102

"   "   lunatic asylums, New York, 1889   448

"   "   institutions for children, New York, 1889   522

"   "   homes for aged, New York, 1889   238

"   "   almshouse, New York, 1889   424

"   "   other institutions, New York, 1889   162

Number of burials in city cemetery (paupers), New York, 1889   3,815

Percentage of such burials on total   9.64

Number of tenants weeded out of overcrowded tenements, New York, 1889   1,246

Number of tenants weeded out of overcrowded tenements, in first half of 1890*   1,068

Number of sick poor visited by summer corps of doctors, New York, 1890   16,501

* These figures represent less than two hundred of the worst tenements below Houston Street.

POLICE STATISTICS

	Males	Females
Arrests made by the police in 1889	62,274	19,926
Number of arrests for drunkenness and disorderly conduct	20,253	8,981
Number of arrests for disorderly conduct	10,953	7,477
"　　　"　　　assault and battery	4,534	497
"　　　"　　　theft	4,399	721
"　　　"　　　robbery	247	10
"　　　"　　　vagrancy	1,686	947
Prisoners unable to read or write	2,399	1,281

Number of lost children found in the streets, 1889	2,968
"　　sick and destitute cared for, 1889	2,753
Found sick in the streets	1,211
Number of pawnshops in city, 1889	110
"　　cheap lodginghouses, 1889	270
"　　saloons, 1889	7,884

IMMIGRATION

Immigrants landed at Castle Garden in 20 years, ending with 1889	5,335,396
Immigrants landed at Castle Garden in 1889	349,233
Immigrants from England landed at Castle Garden in 1889	46,214
Immigrants from Scotland landed at Castle Garden in 1889	11,415
Immigrants from Ireland landed at Castle Garden in 1889	43,090
Immigrants from Germany landed at Castle Garden in 1889	75,458

	1883	1884	1885	1886	1887	1888	1889
Italy	25,485	14,076	16,033	29,312	44,274	43,927	28,810
Russia Poland	7,577	12,432	16,578	23,987	33,203	33,052	31,329
Hungary	13,160	15,797	11,129	18,135	17,719	12,905	15,678
Bohemia	4,877	7,093	6,697	4,222	6,449	3,982	5,412

TENEMENTS

Number of tenements in New York, December 1, 1888	32,390
Number built from June 1, 1888, to August 1, 1890	3,733
Rear tenements in existence, August 1, 1890	2,630
Total number of tenements, August 1, 1890	37,316
Estimated population of tenements, August 1, 1890	1,250,000
Estimated number of children under five years in tenements, 1890	163,712

Corner tenements may cover all of the lot, except 4 feet at the rear. Tenements in the block may only cover seventy-eight per cent of the lot. They must have a rear yard 10 feet wide, and air shafts or open courts equal to twelve per cent of the lot.

Tenements or apartment houses must not be built over 70 feet high in streets 60 feet wide.

Tenements or apartment houses must not be built over 80 feet high in streets wider than 60 feet.

II

—

THE CHILDREN
OF THE POOR

—

THE PROBLEM
OF THE CHILDREN

The problem of the children is the problem of the State. As we mold the children of the toiling masses in our cities, so we shape the destiny of the State which they will rule in their turn, taking the reins from our hands. In proportion as we neglect or pass them by, the blame for bad government to come rests upon us. The cities long since held the balance of power; their dominion will be absolute soon unless the near future finds some way of scattering the population which the era of steam power and industrial development has crowded together in the great centers of that energy. At the beginning of the century the urban population of the United States was 3.97 per cent of the whole, or not quite one in twenty-five. Today it is 29.12 per cent, or nearly one in three. In the lifetime of those who were babies in arms when the first gun was fired upon Fort Sumter it has all but doubled. A million and a quarter live today in the tenements of the American metropolis. Clearly, there is reason for the sharp attention given at last to the life and the doings of the other half, too long unconsidered. Philanthropy we call it sometimes with patronizing airs. Better call it self-defense.

In New York there is all the more reason because it is the open door through which pours in a practically unrestricted immigration, unfamiliar with and unattuned to our institutions; the dumping ground where it rids itself of its burden of helplessness and incapacity, leaving the procession of the strong and the able free to move on. This sediment forms the body of our poor, the contingent that lives always from hand to mouth, with no provision and no means of providing for the morrow. In the first generation it pre-empts our slums;* in the second, its worst elements, reinforced by the influences that prevail there, develop the tough, who confronts society with the claim that the world owes him a living and that he will collect it in his own way. His plan is a practical application of the spirit of our free institutions as his opportunities have enabled him to grasp it.

Thus it comes about that here in New York to seek the children of the poor one must go among those who, if they did not themselves come over the sea, can rarely count back another generation born on American soil. Not that there is far to go. Any tenement district will furnish its own tribe, or medley of many tribes. Nor is it by any means certain that the children when found will own their alien descent. Indeed, as a preliminary to gaining their confidence, to hint at such a thing would be a bad blunder. The ragged Avenue B boy, whose father at his age had barely heard, in his corner of the Fatherland, of America as a place where the streets were paved with nuggets of gold and roast pigeons flew into mouths opening wide with wonder, would, it is safe to bet, be as prompt to resent the insinuation that he was a "Dutchman," as would the little "Mick" the Teuton's sore taunt. Even the son of the immigrant Jew in his virtual isolation strains impatiently at the fetters of race and faith, while the

---

* It is, nevertheless, true that while immigration peoples our slums, it also keeps them from stagnation. The working of the strong instinct to better themselves, that brought the crowds here, forces layer after layer of this population up to make room for the new crowds coming in at the bottom, and thus a circulation is kept up that does more than any sanitary law to render the slums harmless. Even the useless sediment is kept from rotting by being constantly stirred.

Italian takes abuse philosophically only when in the minority and bides his time until he too shall be able to prove his title by calling those who came after him names. However, to quarrel with the one or the other on that ground would be useless. It is the logic of the lad's evolution, the way of patriotism in the slums. His sincerity need not be questioned.

Many other things about him may be, and justly are, but not that. It is perfectly transparent. His badness is as spontaneous as his goodness, and for the moment all there is of the child. Whichever streak happens to prevail, it is in full possession; if the bad is on top more frequently than the other, it is his misfortune rather than his design. He is as ready to give his only cent to a hungrier boy than he if it is settled that he can "lick" him, and that he is therefore not a rival, as he is to join him in torturing an unoffending cat for the common cheer. The penny and the cat, the charity and the cruelty, are both pregnant facts in the life that surrounds him, and of which he is to be the coming exponent. In after years, when he is arrested by the officers of the Society for the Prevention of Cruelty to Animals for beating his horse, the episode adds but to his confusion of mind in which a single impression stands out clear and lasting, viz., that somehow he got the worst of it as usual. But for the punishment, the whole proceeding must seem ludicrous to him. As it is he submits without comprehending. *He* had to take the hard knocks always; why should not his horse?

In other words, the child is a creature of environment, of opportunity, as children are everywhere. And the environment here has been bad, as it was and is in the lands across the sea that sent him to us. Our slums have fairly rivaled, and in some respects outdone, the older ones after which they patterned. Still, there is a difference, the difference between the old slum and the new. The hopelessness, the sullen submission of life in East London as we have seen it portrayed, has no counterpart here; neither has the child born in the gutter and predestined by the order of society, from which there is no appeal, to die there. We have our Lost Tenth to fill the trench in the potter's field; quite as many wrecks at the finish, perhaps, but the start seems fairer in the promise. Even on the slums the doctrine of liberty has set its stamp. To be sure, for the want of the schooling to decipher it properly, they spell it license there, and the slip makes trouble. The tough and his scheme of levying tribute are the result. But the police settle that with him, and when it comes to a choice, the tough is to be preferred to the born pauper any day. The one has the making of something in him, unpromising as he looks; seen in a certain light he may even be considered a hopeful symptom. The other is just so much dead loss. The tough is not born: he is made. The all-important point is the one at which the manufacture can be stopped.

So rapid and great are the changes in American cities, that no slum has yet had a chance here to grow old enough to distill its deadliest poison. New York has been no exception. But we cannot always go at so fast a pace. There is evidence enough in the crystallization of the varying elements of the population along certain lines, no longer as uncertain as they were, that we are slowing up already. Any observer of the poor in this city is familiar with the appearance among them of that most distressing and most dangerous symptom, the home feeling for the slum that opposes all efforts at betterment with dull indifference. Pauperism seems to have grown faster of late than even the efforts put forth to check it. We have witnessed this past winter a dozen times the spectacle of beggars extorting money by threats or violence without the excuse which a season of exceptional distress or hardship might have furnished. Further, the raid in the last legislature upon the structure of law built up in a generation to regulate and keep the tenements within safe limits, shows that fresh danger threatens in the alliance of the slum with politics. Only the strongest public sentiment, kept always up to the point of prompt action, avails to ward off this peril. But public sentiment soon wearies of such watch duty, as instanced on this occasion, when several bills radically remodeling the tenement-house law and repealing some of its most beneficent provisions had passed both houses and were in the hands of the Governor before a voice was raised against them, or anyone beside the politicians and their backers seemed even to have heard of them. And this hardly five years after a special commission of distinguished citizens had sat an entire winter under authority of the State considering the tenement-house problem, and as the result of its labors had secured as vital the enactment of the very law against which the raid seemed to be chiefly directed!

The tenement and the saloon, with the street that does not always divide them, form the environment that is to make or unmake the child. The influence of each of the three is bad. Together they have power to overcome the strongest resistance. But the child born under their evil spell has none such to offer. The testimony of all to whom has fallen the task of undoing as much of the harm done by them as may be, from the priest of the parish school to the chaplain of the penitentiary, agrees upon this point, that even the tough, with all his desperation, is weak rather than vicious. He promises well, he even means well; he is as downright sincere in his repentance as he was in his wrongdoing; but it doesn't prevent him from doing the very same evil deed over again the minute he is rid of restraint. He would rather be a saint than a sinner; but somehow he doesn't keep in the role of saint, while the police help perpetuate the memory of his wickedness. After all, he is not so very different from the rest of us. Perhaps that, with a remorseful review of the chances he has had, may help to make a fellow-feeling for him in us.

That is what he needs. The facts clearly indicate

that from the environment little improvement in the child is to be expected. There has been progress in the way of building the tenements of late years, but they swarm with greater crowds than ever—good reason why they challenge the pernicious activity of the politician; and the old rookeries disappear slowly. In the relation of the saloon to the child there has been no visible improvement, and the street is still his refuge. It is, then, his opportunities outside that must be improved if relief is to come. We have the choice of hailing him man and brother or of being slugged and robbed by him. It ought not to be a hard choice, despite the tatters and the dirt, for which our past neglect is in great part to blame. Plenty of evidence will be found in these pages to show that it has been made in the right spirit already, and that it has proved a wise choice. No investment gives a better return today on the capital put out than work among the children of the poor.

A single fact will show what is meant by that. Within the lifetime of the Children's Aid Society, in the thirty years between 1860 and 1890, while the population of this city was doubled, the commitments of girls and women for vagrancy fell off from 5880 to 1980, while the commitments of girl thieves fell between 1865 and 1890 from 1 in 743 to 1 in 7500.* Stealing and vagrancy among boys has decreased too; if not so fast, yet at a gratifying rate.

Enough has been written and said about the children of the poor and their sufferings to make many a bigger book than this. From some of it one might almost be led to believe that one-half of the children are worked like slaves from toddling infancy, while the other half wander homeless and helpless about the streets. Their miseries are great enough without inventing any that do not exist. There is no such host

* Report of committing magistrates. See Annual Report of Children's Aid Society, 1891.

of child outcasts in New York as that. Thanks to the unwearied efforts of the children's societies in the last generation, what there is is decreasing, if anything. As for the little toilers, they will receive attention further on. There are enough of them, but as a whole they are anything but a repining lot. They suffer less, to their own knowledge, from their wretched life than the community suffers for letting them live it, though it, too, sees the truth but in glimpses. If the question were put to a vote of the children tomorrow, whether they would take the old life with its drawbacks, its occasional starvation, and its everyday kicks and hard knocks; or the good clothes, the plentiful grub, and warm bed, with all the restraints of civilized society and the "Sunday-school racket" of the other boy thrown in, I have as little doubt that the street would carry the day by a practically unanimous vote as I have that there are people still to be found—too many of them —who would endorse the choice with a sigh of relief and dismiss the subject, if it could be dismissed that way; which, happily, it cannot.

The immediate duty which the community has to perform for its own protection is to school the children first of all into good Americans, and next into useful citizens. As a community it has not attended to this duty as it should; but private effort has stepped in and is making up for its neglect with encouraging success. The outlook that was gloomy from the point of view of the tenement, brightens when seen from this angle, however toilsome the road yet ahead. The inpouring of alien races no longer darkens it. The problems that seemed so perplexing in the light of freshly formed prejudices against this or that immigrant, yield to this simple solution that discovers all alarm to have been groundless. Yesterday it was the swarthy Italian, today the Russian Jew, that excited our distrust. Tomorrow it may be the Arab or the Greek. All alike they have taken, or are taking, their places in the ranks of our social phalanx, pushing upward from the bottom with steady effort, as I believe they will continue to do unless failure to provide them with proper homes arrests the process. And in the general advance the children, thus firmly grasped, are seen to be a powerful moving force. The one immigrant who does not keep step, who, having fallen out of the ranks, has been ordered to the rear, is the Chinaman, who brought neither wife nor children to push him ahead. He left them behind that he might not become an American, and by the standard he himself set up he has been judged.

THE ITALIAN
SLUM CHILDREN

———

Who and where are the slum children of New York today? That depends on what is understood by the term. The moralist might seek them in Hell's Kitchen, in Battle Row, and in the tenements, east and west, where the descendants of the poorest Irish immigrants live. They are the ones, as I have before tried to show, upon whom the tenement and the saloon set their stamp soonest and deepest. The observer of physical facts merely would doubtless pick out the Italian ragamuffins first, and from his standpoint he would be right. Irish poverty is not picturesque in the New World, whatever it may have been in the Old. Italian poverty is. The worst old rookeries fall everywhere in this city to the share of the immigrants from Southern Italy, who are content to occupy them, partly, perhaps, because they are no worse than the hovels they left behind, but mainly because they are tricked or bullied into putting up with them by their smarter countrymen who turn their helplessness and ignorance to good account. Wherever the invasion of some old home section by the tide of business has left ramshackle tenements falling into hopeless decay, as in the old "Africa," in the Bend, and in many other places in the downtown wards, the Italian sweater landlord is ready with his offer of a lease to bridge over the interregnum, a lease that takes no account of repairs or of the improvements the owner sought to avoid. The crowds to make it profitable to him are never wanting. The bait he holds out is a job at the ash dump with which he connects at the other end of the line. The house, the job, and the man as he comes to them fit in well together, and the copartnership has given the Italian a character which, I am satisfied from close observation of him, he does not wholly deserve. At all events, his wife does not. Dirty as *he* seems and is in the old rags that harmonize so well with his surroundings, there is that about her which suggests not only the capacity for better things, but a willingness to be clean and to look decent, if cause can be shown. It may be a bright kerchief, a bit of old-fashioned jewelry, or the neatly smoothed and braided hair of the wrinkled old hag who presides over the stale bread counter. Even in the worst dens occupied by these people, provided that they had not occupied them too long, I have found this trait crop out in the careful scrubbing of some piece of oilcloth rescued from the dump and laid as a mat in front of the family bed; or in a bit of fringe on the sheet or quilt, ragged and black with age though it was, that showed what a fruitful soil proper training and decent housing would have found there.

I have in mind one Italian "flat" among many, a half underground hole in a South Fifth Avenue yard, reached by odd passageways through a tumbledown tenement that was always full of bad smells and scooting rats. Across the foul and slippery yard, down three steps made of charred timbers from some worse wreck, was this "flat," where five children slept with their elders. How many of those there were I never knew. There were three big family beds, and they nearly filled the room, leaving only patches of the mud floor visible. The walls were absolutely black with age and smoke. The plaster had fallen off in patches and there was green mold on the ceiling. And yet, with it all, with the swarm of squirming youngsters that were as black as the floor they rolled upon, there was evidence of a desperate, if hopeless, groping after order, even neatness. The beds were made up as nicely as they could be with the old quilts and pieces of carpet that served for covering. In Poverty Gap, where an Italian would be stoned as likely as not, there would have been a heap of dirty straw instead of beds, and the artistic arrangement of tallow dips stuck in the necks of bottles about the newspaper cut of a saint on the corner shelf would have been missing altogether, fervent though the personal regard might be of Poverty Gap for the saint. The bottles would have been the only part of the exhibition sure to be seen there.

I am satisfied that this instinct inhabits not only the more aristocratic Genoese, but his fellow countryman from the southern hills as well, little as they resemble each other or agree in most things. But the Neapolitan especially does not often get a chance to prove it. He is so altogether uninviting an object when he presents himself, fresh from the steamer, that he falls naturally the victim of the slum tenement, which in his keep becomes, despite the vigilance of the sanitary police, easily enough the convenient depot and halfway house between the garbage dump and the bone factory. Starting thus below the bottom, as it were, he has an uphill journey before him if he is to work out of the slums, and the promise, to put it mildly, is not good. He does it all the same, or, if not he, his boy. It is not an Italian sediment that breeds the tough. Parental authority has a strong enough grip on the lad in Mulberry Street to make him work, and that is his salvation. "In seventeen years," said the teacher of the oldest Italian ragged school in the city that, day and night, takes in quite six hundred, "I have seen my boys work up into decent mechanics and useful citizens almost to a man, and of my girls only two I know of have gone astray." I had observed the process often enough myself to know that she was right. It is to be remembered, furthermore, that her school is in the very heart of the Five Points district, and takes in always the worst and the dirtiest crowds of children.

Within a year there has been, through some caprice of immigration, a distinct descent in the quality of the children, viewed from even the standard of cleanliness that prevails at the Five Points. Perhaps the exodus from Italy has worked farther south, where there seems to be an unusual supply of mud. Perhaps the rivalry of steamship lines has brought it about. At any rate, the testimony is positive that the children that came to the schools after last vacation, and have kept coming since, were the worst seen here since the influx began. I have watched with satisfaction, since this became apparent, some of the bad old tenements, which the newcomers always sought in droves, disappear to make room for great factory buildings. But there are enough left. The cleaning out of a Mulberry Street block left one lopsided old rear tenement that had long since been shut in on three sides by buildings four stories higher than itself, and forgotten by all the world save the miserable wretches who burrowed in that dark and dismal pit at the bottom of a narrow alley. Now, when the fourth structure goes up against its very windows, it will stand there in the heart of the block, a survival of the unfittest, that, in all its disheartening dreariness, bears testimony, nevertheless, to the beneficent activity of the best Board of Health New York has ever had—the onward sweep of business. It will wipe that last remnant out also, even if the law lack the power to reach it.

Shoals of Italian children lived in that rookery, and in those the workmen tore down, in the actual physical atmosphere of the dump. Not a gunshot away there is a block of tenements, known as the Mott Street Barracks, in which still greater shoals are—I was going to say housed, but that would have been a mistake. Happily they are that very rarely, except when they are asleep, and not then if they can help it. Out on the street they may be found tumbling in the dirt, or up on the roof lying stark-naked, blinking in the sun—content with life as they find it. If they are not a very cleanly crew, they are at least as clean as the frame they are set in, though it must be allowed that something has been done of late years to redeem the buildings from the reproach of a bad past. The combination of a Jew for a landlord and a saloonkeeper—Italian, of course—for a lessee, was not propitious; but the buildings happen to be directly under the windows of the Health Board, and something, I suppose, was due to appearances. The authorities did all that could be done, short of tearing down the tenement, but though comparatively clean, and not nearly as crowded as it was, it is still the old slum. It is an instructive instance of what can and cannot be done with the tenements into which we invite these dirty strangers to teach them American ways and the self-respect of future citizens and voters. There are five buildings—that is, five front and four rear houses, the latter a story higher than those on the street; that is because the rear houses were built last, to "accommodate" this very Italian immigration that could be made to pay for anything. Chiefly Irish had lived there before, but they moved out then. There were 360 tenants in the Barracks when the police census was taken in 1888, and 40 of them were babies. How many were romping children I do not know. The "yard" they had to play in is just 5 feet 10 inches wide, and a dozen steps below the street level. The closets of all the buildings are in the cellar of the rear houses and open upon this "yard," where it is always dark and damp as in a dungeon. Its foul stenches reach even the top floor, but so also does the sun at midday, and that is a luxury that counts as an extra in the contract with the landlord. The rent is nearly one-half higher near the top than it is on the street level. Nine dollars above, six and a half below, for one room with windows, two without, and with barely space for a bed in each. But water pipes have been put in lately, under orders from the Health Department, and the rents have doubtless been raised. "No windows" means no ventilation. The rear building backs up against the tenement on the next street; a space a foot wide separates them, but an attempt to ventilate the bedrooms by windows on that was a failure.

When the health officers got through with the Barracks in time for the police census of 1891, the 360 tenants had been whittled down to 238, of whom 47 were babies under five years. Persistent effort had succeeded in establishing a standard of cleanliness that was a very great improvement upon the condition prevailing in 1888. But still, as I have said, the slum remained and will remain as long as that rear tenement stands. In the four years fifty-one funerals had gone out from the Barracks. The white hearse alone had made thirty-five trips carrying baby coffins. This was the way the two standards showed up in the death returns at the Bureau of Vital Statistics: in 1888 the adult death rate, in a population of 320 over five years old, was 15.62 per 1000; the baby death rate, 325.00 per 1000, or nearly one-third in a total of 40. As a matter of fact 13 of the 40 had died that year. The adult death rate for the entire tenement population of more than a million souls was that year 12.81, and the baby death rate 88.38. Last year, in 1891, the case stood thus: Total population, 238, including 47 babies. Adult death rate per 1000, 20.94; child death rate (under five years) per 1000, 106.38. General adult death rate for 1891 in the tenements, 14.25; general child death rate for 1891 in the tenements, 86.67. It should be added that the reduced baby death rate of the Barracks, high as it was, was probably much lower than it can be successfully maintained. The year before, in 1890, when practically the same improved conditions prevailed, it was twice as high. Twice as many babies died.

I have referred to some of the typical Italian tenements at some length to illustrate the conditions under which their children grow up and absorb the impressions that are to shape their lives as men and women.

Is it to be marveled at, if the first impression of them is sometimes not favorable? I recall, not without amusement, one of the early experiences of a committee with which I was trying to relieve some of the child misery in the East Side tenements by providing an outing for the very poorest of the little ones, who might otherwise have been overlooked. In our anxiety to make our little charges as presentable as possible, it seems we had succeeded so well as to arouse a suspicion in our friends at the other end of the line that something was wrong, either with us or with the poor of which the patrician youngsters in new frocks and with clean faces, that came to them, were representatives. They wrote to us that they were in the field for the "slum children," and slum children they wanted. It happened that their letter came just as we had before us two little lads from the Mulberry Street Bend, ragged, dirty, unkempt, and altogether a sight to see. Our wardrobe was running low, and we were at our wits' end how to make these come up to our standard. We sat looking at each other after we had heard the letter read, all thinking the same thing, until the most courageous said it: "Send them as they are." Well, we did, and waited rather breathlessly for the verdict. It came, with the children, in a note by return train, that said: "Not *that* kind, please!" And after that we were allowed to have things our own way.

The two little fellows were Italians. In justice to our frightened friends, it should be said that it was not their nationality, but their rags, to which they objected; but not very many seasons have passed since the crowding of the black-eyed brigade of "Guineas," as they were contemptuously dubbed, in ever-increasing numbers, into the ragged schools and the kindergartens, was watched with regret and alarm by the teachers, as by many others who had no better cause. The event proved that the children were the real teachers. They had a more valuable lesson to impart than they came to learn, and it has been a salu-

tary one. Today they are gladly welcomed. Their
sunny temper, which no hovel is dreary enough, no
hardship has power to cloud, has made them universal
favorites, and the discovery has been made by their
teachers that as the crowds pressed harder their schoolrooms have marvelously expanded, until they embrace
within their walls an unsuspected multitude, even
many a slum tenement itself, cellar, "stoop," attic, and
all. Every lesson of cleanliness, of order, and of English
taught at the school is reflected into some wretched
home, and rehearsed there as far as the limited opportunities will allow. No demonstration with soap and
water upon a dirty little face but widens the sphere
of these chief promoters of education in the slums.
"By 'm by," said poor crippled Pietro to me, with a
sober look, as he labored away on his writing lesson,
holding down the paper with his maimed hand, "I
learn t' make an Englis' letter; maybe my fadder he
learn too." I had my doubts of the father. He sat
watching Pietro with a pride in the achievement that
was clearly proportionate to the struggle it cost, and
mirrored in his own face every grimace and contor-
tion the progress of education caused the boy. "Si! si!"
he nodded, eagerly. "Pietro he good a boy; make
Englis', Englis'!" and he made a flourish with his clay
pipe, as if he too were making the English letter that
was the object of their common veneration.

Perhaps it is as much his growing and well-founded
distrust of the middleman, whose unresisting victim he
has heretofore been, and his need of some other joint
to connect him with the English-speaking world that
surrounds him, as any personal interest in book learning, that impels the illiterate Italian to bring his boy to
school early and see that he attends it. Greed has something to do with it too. In their anxiety to lay hold
of the child, the charity schools have fallen into
a way of bidding for him with clothes, shoes, and
other bait that is never lost on Mulberry Street. Even
sectarian scruples yield to such an argument, and the

parochial school, where they get nothing but on the contrary are expected to contribute, gets left.

In a few charity schools where the children are boarded they have discovered this, and frown upon Italian children unless there is the best of evidence that the father is really unable to pay for their keep and not simply unwilling. But whatever his motive, the effect is to demonstrate in a striking way the truth of the observation that real reform of poverty and ignorance must begin with the children. In his case, at all events, the seed thus sown bears some fruit in the present as well as in the coming generation of toilers. The little ones, with their new standards and new ambitions, become in a very real sense missionaries of the slums, whose work of regeneration begins with their parents. They are continually fetched away from school by the mother or father to act as interpreters or go-betweens in all the affairs of daily life, to be conscientiously returned within the hour stipulated by the teacher, who offers no objection to this sort of interruption, knowing it to be the best condition of her own success. One cannot help the hope that the office of trust with which the children are thus invested may, in some measure, help to mitigate their home hardships. From their birth they have little else, though Italian parents are rarely cruel in the sense of abusing their offspring.

It is the home itself that constitutes their chief hardship. It is only when his years offer the boy an opportunity of escape to the street that a ray of sunlight falls into his life. In his backyard or in his alley it seldom finds him out. Thenceforward most of his time is spent there, until the school and the shop claim him, but not in idleness. His mother toiled, while she bore him at her breast, under burdens heavy enough to break a man's back. She lets him out of her arms only to share her labor. How well he does it anyone may see for himself by watching the children that swarm where an old house is being torn down, lugging upon their heads loads of kindling wood twice their own size and sometimes larger than that. They come, as crows scenting carrion, from every side at the first blow of the ax. Their odd old-mannish or old-womanish appearance, due more to their grotesque rags than to anything in the children themselves, betrays their race even without their chatter. Be there ever so many children of other nationalities nearer by —the wood gatherers are nearly all Italians. There are still a lot of girls among them who drag as big loads as their brothers, but since the sewing machine found its way, with the sweater's mortgage, into the Italian slums also, little Antonia has been robbed to a large extent even of this poor freedom, and has taken her place among the wage earners when not on the school bench. Once taken, the place is hers to keep for good. Sickness, unless it be mortal, is no excuse from the drudgery of the tenement. When, recently, one little Italian girl, hardly yet in her teens, stayed away from her class in the Mott Street Industrial School so long that her teacher went to her home to look her up, she found the child in a high fever, in bed, sewing on coats, with swollen eyes, though barely able to sit up.

But neither poverty nor hard knocks has power to discourage the child of Italy. His nickname he pockets with a grin that has in it no thought of the dagger and the revenge that come to solace his after years. Only the prospect of immediate punishment eclipses his spirits for the moment. While the teacher of the sick little girl was telling me her pitiful story in the Mott Street school, a characteristic group appeared on the stairway. Three little Italian culprits in the grasp of Nellie, the tall and slender Irish girl who was the mentor of her class for the day. They had been arrested "fur fightin'" she briefly explained as she dragged them by the collar toward the principal, who just then appeared to inquire the cause of the rumpus, and thrust them forward to receive sentence. The three, none of whom was over eight years old, evidently felt that they were in the power of an enemy from whom no mercy was to be expected, and made no appeal for any. One scowled defiance. He was evidently the injured party.

"He hit-a me a clip on de jaw," he said in his defense, in the dialect of Mott Street with a slight touch of "the Bend." The aggressor, a heavy-browed little ruffian, hung back with a dreary howl, knuckling his eyes with a pair of fists that were nearly black. The third and youngest was in a state of bewilderment that was most ludicrous. He only knew that he had received a kick on the back and had struck out in self-defense, when he was seized and dragged away a prisoner. He was so dirty—school had only just begun and there had been no time for the regular inspection —that he was sentenced on the spot to be taken down and washed, while the other two were led away to the principal's desk. All three went out howling.

I said that the Italians do not often abuse their children downright. The padrone has had his day; the last was convicted seven years ago, and an end has been put to the business of selling children into a slavery that meant outrage, starvation, and death; but poverty and ignorance are fearful allies in the homes of the poor against defenseless childhood, even without the child-beating fiend. Two cases which I encountered in the East Side tenements, in the summer of 1891, show how the combination works at its worst. Without a doubt they are typical of very many, though I hope that few come quite up to their standard. The one was the case of little Carmen, who last March died in the New York Hospital, where she had lain five long months, the special care of the Society for the Prevention of Cruelty to Children. One of the summer corps doctors found her in a Mott Street tenement, within stone's throw of the Health Department office, suffering from a wasting disease that could only be combated by the most careful nursing. He put her case into the hands of the King's Daughters' Committee that followed in the steps of the doctor, and it was then that I saw her. She lay in a little back room, two flights and giving upon a narrow yard where it was always twilight. The room was filthy and close, and entirely devoid of furniture, with the exception of a rickety stool, a slop pail, and a rusty old stove, one end of which was propped up with bricks. Carmen's bed was a board laid across the top of a barrel and a trunk set on end. I could not describe, if I would, the condition of the child when she was raised from the mess of straw and rags in which she lay. The sight unnerved even the nurse, who had seen little else than such scenes all summer. Loathsome bedsores had attacked the wasted little body, and in truth Carmen was more dead than alive. But when, shocked and disgusted, we made preparations for her removal with all speed to the hospital, the parents objected and refused to let us take her away. They had to be taken into court and forced to surrender the child under warrant of law, though it was clearly the little sufferer's only chance for life, and only the slenderest of chances at that.

Carmen was the victim of the stubborn ignorance that dreads the hospital and the doctor above the discomfort of the dirt and darkness and suffering that are its everyday attendants. Her parents were no worse than the Monroe Street mother who refused to let the health officer vaccinate her baby, because her crippled boy, with one leg an inch shorter than the other, had "caught it"—the lame leg, that is to say —from his vaccination. She knew it was so, and with ignorance of that stamp there is no other argument than force. But another element entered into the case of a sick Essex Street baby. The tenement would not let it recover from a bad attack of scarlet fever, and the parents would not let it be taken to the country or to the seashore, despite all efforts and entreaties. When their motive came out at last, it proved to be a mercenary one. They were behind with the rent, and as long as they had a sick child in the house the landlord could not put them out. Sick, the baby was to them a source of income, at all events a bar to expense, and in that way so much capital. Well, or away, it would put them at the mercy of the rent collector at once. So they chose to let it suffer. The parents were Jews, a fact that emphasizes the share borne by desperate poverty in the transaction, for the family tie is notoriously strong among their people.

No doubt Mott Street echoed with the blare of brass bands when poor little Carmen was carried from her bed of long suffering to her grave in Calvary. Scarce a day passes now in these tenements that does not see some little child, not rarely a newborn babe, carried to the grave in solemn state, preceded by a band playing mournful dirges and followed by a host with trailing banners, from some wretched home that barely sheltered it alive. No suspicion of the ludicrous incongruity of the show disturbs the paraders. It seems as if, but one remove from the dump, an insane passion for pomp and display, perhaps a natural reaction from the ash barrel, lies in wait for this Italian, to which he falls a helpless victim. Not content with his own national and religious holidays and those he finds awaiting him here, he has invented or introduced a system of his own, a sort of communal celebration of proprietary saints, as it were, that has taken Mulberry Street by storm. As I understand it, the townsmen of some Italian village, when there is a sufficient number of them within reach, club together to celebrate its patron saint, and hire a band and set up a gorgeous altar in a convenient backyard. The fire escapes overlooking it are draped with flags and transformed into reserved seat galleries with the taste these people display under the most adverse circumstances. Crowds come and go, parading at intervals in gorgeous uniforms around the block. Admission is by the saloon door, which nearly always holds the key to the situation, the saloonist who prompts the sudden attack of devotion being frequently a namesake of the saint and willing to go shares on the principle that he takes the profit and the saint the glory.

The partnership lasts as long as there is any profit in it, sometimes the better part of the week, during which time all work stops. If the feast panned out well, the next block is liable to be the scene of a rival celebration before the first is fairly ended. As the supply of Italian villages represented in New York is practically as inexhaustible as that of the saloons, there is no reason why Mulberry Street may not become a perennial picnic ground long before the scheme to make a park of one end of it gets under way. From the standpoint of the children there can be no objection to this, but from that of the police there is. They found themselves called upon to interfere in such a four days' celebration of St. Rocco last year, when his votaries strung cannon firecrackers along the street the whole length of the block and set them all off at once. It was at just such a feast, in honor of the same saint, that a dozen Italians were killed a week later at Newark in the explosion of their fireworks.

It goes without saying that the children enter into this sort of thing with all the enthusiasm of their little souls. The politician watches it attentively, alert for some handle to catch his new allies by and effect their "organization." If it is a new experience for him to find the saloon put to such use, he betrays no surprise. It is his vantage ground, and whether it serve as the political bait for the Irishman, or as the religious initiative of the Italian, is of less account than that its patrons, young and old, in the end fall into his trap. Conclusive proof that the Italian has been led into camp came to me on last St. Patrick's Day through the assurance of a certain popular clergyman, that he had observed, on a walk through the city, a number of hand organs draped in green, evidently for the occasion.

This dump of which I have spoken as furnishing the background of the social life of Mulberry Street has lately challenged attention as a slum annex to the Bend, with fresh horrors in store for defenseless childhood. To satisfy myself upon this point I made a personal inspection of the dumps along both rivers last winter and found the Italian crews at work there making their home in every instance among the refuse they picked from the scows. The dumps are wooden bridges raised above the level of the piers upon which they are built to allow the discharge of the carts directly into the scows moored under them. Under each bridge a cabin had been built of old boards, oilcloth, and the like, that had found its way down on the carts; an old milk can had been made into a fireplace without the ceremony of providing stovepipe or draught, and here, flanked by mountains of refuse, slept the crews of from half a dozen to three times that number of men, secure from the police, who had grown tired of driving them from dump to dump and had finally let them alone. There were women at some of them, and at four dumps, three on the North River and one on the East Side, I found boys who ought to have been at school, picking bones and sorting rags. They said that they slept there, and as the men did, why should they not? It was their home. They were children of the dump, literally. All of them except one were Italians. That one was a little homeless Jew who had drifted down at first to pick cinders. Now that his mother was dead and his father in a hospital, he had become a sort of fixture there, it seemed, having made the acquaintance of the other lads.

Two boys whom I found at the West Nineteenth Street dumps sorting bones were as bright lads as I had seen anywhere. One was nine years old and the other twelve. Filthy and ragged, they fitted well into their environment—even the pig I had encountered at one of the East River dumps was much the more respectable, as to appearance, of the lot—but were entirely undaunted by it. They scarcely remembered anything but the dump. Neither could read, of course. Further down the river I came upon one seemingly not over fifteen, who assured me that he was twenty-one. I thought it possible when I took a closer look at him. The dump had stunted him. He did not even know what a letter was. He had been there five years, and garbage limited his mental as well as his physical horizon.

Enough has been said to show that the lot of the poor child of the Mulberry Street Bend, or of Little Italy, is not a happy one, courageously and uncomplainingly, even joyously, though it be borne. The stories of two little lads from the region of Crosby Street always stand to me as typical of their kind. One I knew all about from personal observation and acquaintance; the other I give as I have it from his teachers in the Mott Street Industrial School, where he was a pupil in spells. It was the death of little Giuseppe that brought me to his home, a dismal den in a rear tenement down a dark and forbidding alley. I have seldom seen a worse place. There was no trace there of a striving for better things—the tenement had stamped that out—nothing but darkness and filth and misery. From this hole Giuseppe had come to the school a mass of rags, but with that jovial gleam in his brown eyes that made him an instant favorite with the teachers as well as with the boys. One of them especially, little Mike, became attached to him, and a year after his cruel death shed tears yet, when reminded of it. Giuseppe had not been long at the school when he was sent to an Elizabeth Street tenement for a little absentee. He brought her, shivering in even worse rags than his own; it was a cold winter day.

"This girl is very poor," he said, presenting her to the teacher, with a pitying look. It was only then that he learned that she had no mother. His own had often stood between the harsh father and him when he came home with unsold evening papers. Giuseppe fished his only penny out of his pocket—his capital for the afternoon's trade. "I would like to give her that," he said. After that he brought her pennies regularly from his day's sale, and took many a thrashing for it. He undertook the general supervision of the child's education, and saw to it that she came to school every day. Giuseppe was twelve years old.

There came an evening when business had been very bad, so bad that he thought a bed in the street healthier for him than the Crosby Street alley. With three other lads in similar straits he crawled into the iron chute that ventilated the basement of the post office on the Mail Street side and snuggled down on the grating. They were all asleep, when fire broke out in the cellar. The three climbed out, but Giuseppe, whose feet were wrapped in a mailbag, was too late. He was burned to death.

The little girl still goes to the Mott Street school. She is too young to understand, and marvels why Giuseppe comes no more with his pennies. Mike cries for his friend. When, some months ago, I found myself in the Crosby Street alley, and went up to talk to Giuseppe's parents, they would answer no questions before I had replied to one of theirs. It was thus interpreted to me by a girl from the basement, who had come in out of curiosity: "Are youse goin' to give us any money?" Poor Giuseppe!

My other little friend was Pietro, of whom I spoke before. Perhaps of all the little life stories of poor Italian children I have come across in the course of years —and they are many and sad, most of them—none comes nearer to the hard everyday fact of those dreary tenements than his, exceptional as was his own heavy misfortune and its effect upon the boy. I met him first in the Mulberry Street police station, where he was interpreting the defense in a shooting case, having come in with the crowd from Jersey Street, where the thing had happened at his own door. With his rags, his dirty bare feet, and his shock of tousled hair, he seemed to fit in so entirely there of all places, and took so naturally to the ways of the police station, that he might have escaped my notice altogether but for his maimed hand and his oddly grave yet eager face, which no smile ever crossed despite his thirteen years. Of both, his story, when I afterward came to know it, gave me full explanation. He was the oldest son of a laborer, not "borned here" as the rest of his sisters and brothers. There were four of them, six in the family besides himself, as he put it: "two sisters, two broders, one fader, one modder," subsisting on an unsteady maximum income of $9 a week, the rent taking always the earnings of one week in four. The home thus dearly paid for was a wretched room with a dark alcove for a bedchamber, in one of the vile old barracks that until very recently preserved to Jersey Street the memory of its former bad eminence as among the worst of the city's slums. Pietro had gone to the Sisters' school, blacking boots in a haphazard sort of way in his off-hours, until the year before, upon his mastering the alphabet, his education was considered to have sufficiently advanced to warrant his graduating into the ranks of the family wage earners, that were sadly in need of recruiting. A steady job of "shinin'" was found for him in an Eighth Ward saloon, and that afternoon, just before Christmas, he came home from school and putting his books away on the shelf for the next in order to use, ran across Broadway full of joyous anticipation of his new dignity in an independent job. He did not see the streetcar until it was fairly upon him, and then it was too late. They thought he was killed, but he was only crippled for life. When, after many months, he came out of the hospital, where the company had paid his board and posed as doing a generous thing, his bright smile was gone; his "shining" was at an end, and with it his career as it had been marked out for him. He must needs take up something new, and he was bending all his energies, when I met him, toward learning to make the "Englis' letter" with a degree of proficiency that would justify the hope of his doing something somewhere at sometime to make up for what he had lost. It was a far-off possibility yet. With the same end in view, probably, he was taking nightly writing lessons in his mother tongue from one of the perambulating schoolmasters who circulate in the Italian colony, peddling education cheap in lots to suit. In his sober, submissive way he was content with the prospect. It had its compensations. The boys who used to worry him, now let him alone. "When they see this," he said, holding up his scarred and misshapen arm, "they don't strike me no more." Then there was his fourteen-month-old baby brother who was beginning to walk, and could almost "make a letter." Pietro was much concerned about his education, anxious evidently that he should one day take his place. "I take him to school sometime," he said, piloting him across the floor and talking softly to the child in his own melodious Italian. I watched his grave, unchanging face.

"Pietro," I said, with a sudden yearning to know, "did you ever laugh?"

The boy glanced from the baby to me with a wistful look.

"I did wonst," he said, quietly, and went on his way. And I would gladly have forgotten that I ever asked the question; even as Pietro had forgotten his laugh.

TONY
AND HIS TRIBE

———

I have a little friend somewhere in Mott Street whose picture comes up before me. I wish I could show it to the reader, but to photograph Tony is one of the unattained ambitions of my life. He is one of the whimsical birds one sees when one hasn't got a gun, and then never long enough in one place to give one a chance to get it. A ragged coat three sizes at least too large for the boy, though it has evidently been cropped to meet his case, hitched by its one button across a bare brown breast; one sleeve patched on the under side with a piece of sole leather that sticks out straight, refusing to be reconciled; trousers that boasted a seat once, but probably not while Tony has worn them; two left boots tied on with packing twine, bare legs in them the color of the leather, heel and toe showing through; a shock of sunburnt hair struggling through the rent in the old straw hat; two frank, laughing eyes under its broken brim—that is Tony.

He stood over the gutter the day I met him, reaching for a handful of mud with which to "paste" another hoodlum who was shouting defiance from across the street. He did not see me, and when my hand touched his shoulder his whole little body shrank with a convulsive shudder, as from an expected blow. Quick as a flash he dodged, and turning, out of reach, confronted the unknown enemy, gripping tight his handful of mud. I had a bunch of white pinks which a young lady had given me half an hour before for one of my little

friends. "They are yours," I said, and held them out to
him, "take them."

Doubt, delight, and utter bewilderment struggled in
the boy's face. He said not one word, but when he
had brought his mind to believe that it really was so,
clutched the flowers with one eager, grimy fist, held
them close against his bare breast, and, shielding
them with the other, ran as fast as his legs could carry
him down the street. Not far; fifty feet away he stopped
short, looked back, hesitated a moment, then turned
on his track as fast as he had come. He brought up
directly in front of me, a picture a painter would have
loved, ragamuffin that he was, with the flowers held
so tightly against his brown skin, scraped out with one
foot and made one of the funniest little bows.

"Thank you," he said. Then he was off. Down the
street I saw squads of children like himself running
out to meet him. He darted past and through them
all, never stopping, but pointing back my way, and in
a minute there bore down upon me a crowd of little
ones, running breathless with desperate entreaty:
"Oh, mister! give *me* a flower." Hot tears of grief and
envy—human passions are much the same in rags and
in silks—fell when they saw I had no more. But by that
time Tony was safe.

And where did he run so fast? For whom did he
shield the "posy" so eagerly, so faithfully, that ragged
little wretch that was all mud and patches? I found out
afterward when I met him giving his sister a ride in a
dismantled tomato crate likely enough "hooked" at the
grocer's. It was for his mother. In the dark hovel he
called home, to the level of which all it sheltered had
long since sunk through the brutal indifference of a
drunken father, my lady's pinks blossomed, and, long
after they were withered and yellow, still stood in their
cracked jar, visible token of something that had
entered Tony's life and tenement with sweetening
touch that day for the first time. Alas! for the last,
too, perhaps. I saw Tony off and on for a while and

then he was as suddenly lost as he was found, with all that belonged to him. Moved away—put out, probably —and, except the assurance that they were still somewhere in Mott Street, even the saloon could give me no clue to them.

I gained Tony's confidence, almost, in the time I knew him. There was a little misunderstanding between us that had still left a trace of embarrassment when Tony disappeared. It was when I asked him one day, while we were not yet "solid," if he ever went to school. He said "sometimes," and backed off. I am afraid Tony lied that time. The evidence was against him. It was different with little Katie, my nine-year-old housekeeper of the sober look. Her I met in the Fifty-second Street Industrial School, where she picked up such crumbs of learning as were for her in the intervals of her housework. The serious responsibilities of life had come early to Katie. On the top floor of a tenement in West Forty-ninth Street she was keeping house for her older sister and two brothers, all of whom worked in the hammock factory, earning from $4.50 to $1.50 a week. They had moved together when their mother died and the father brought home another wife. Their combined income was something like $9.50 a week, and the simple furniture was bought on installments. But it was all clean, if poor. Katie did the cleaning and the cooking of the plain kind. They did not run much to fancy cooking, I guess. She scrubbed and swept and went to school, all as a matter of course, and ran the house generally, with an occasional lift from the neighbors in the tenement, who were, if anything, poorer than they. . . . She was a sober, patient, sturdy little thing . . . , with that dull life wearing on her day by day. At the school they loved her for her quiet, gentle ways. She got right up when asked and stood for her picture without a question and without a smile.

"What kind of work do you do?" I asked, thinking to interest her while I made ready.

"I scrubs," she replied, promptly, and her look guaranteed that what she scrubbed came out clean.

Katie was one of the little mothers whose work never ends. Very early the cross of her sex had been laid upon the little shoulders that bore it so stoutly. Tony's, as likely as not, would never begin. There were earmarks upon the boy that warranted the suspicion. They were the earmarks of the street to which his care and education had been left. The only work of which it heartily approves is that done by other people. I came upon Tony once under circumstances that foreshadowed his career with tolerable distinctness. He was at the head of a gang of little shavers like himself, none over eight or nine, who were swaggering around in a ring, in the middle of the street, rigged out in war paint and hen feathers, shouting as they went: "Whoop! We are the Houston Streeters." They meant no harm and they were not doing any just then. It was all in the future, but it *was* there, and no mistake. The game which they were then rehearsing was one in which the policeman who stood idly swinging his club on the corner would one day take a hand, and not always the winning one.

The fortunes of Tony and Katie, simple and soon told as they are, encompass as between the covers of a book the whole story of the children of the poor, the story of the bad their lives struggle vainly to conquer, and the story of the good that crops out in spite of it. Sickness, that always finds the poor unprepared and soon leaves them the choice of beggary or starvation, hard times, the death of the bread winner, or the part played by the growler in the poverty of the home, may vary the theme for the elders; for the children it is the same sad story, with little variation, and that rarely of a kind to improve. Happily for their peace of mind, they are the least concerned about it. In New York, at least, the poor children are not the stunted, repining lot we have heard of as being hatched in cities abroad. Stunted in body perhaps. It was said of

Napoleon that he shortened the average stature of the Frenchman one inch by getting all the tall men killed in his wars. The tenement has done that for New York. Only the other day one of the best-known clergymen in the city, who tries to attract the boys to his church on the East Side by a very practical interest in them, and succeeds admirably in doing it, told me that the drillmaster of his cadet corps was in despair because he could barely find two or three among half a hundred lads verging on manhood over five feet six inches high. It is queer what different ways there are of looking at a thing. My medical friend finds in the fact that poverty stunts the body what he is pleased to call a beautiful provision of nature to prevent unnecessary suffering: there is less for the poverty to pinch then. It is self-defense, he says, and he claims that the consensus of learned professional opinion is with him. Yet, when this shortened sufferer steals a loaf of bread to make the pinching bear less hard on what is left, he is called a thief, thrown into jail, and frowned upon by the community that just now saw in his case a beautiful illustration of the operation of natural laws for the defense of the man.

Stunted morally, yes! It could not well be otherwise. But stunted in spirits—never! As for repining, there is no such word in his vocabulary. He accepts life as it comes to him and gets out of it what he can. If that is not much, he is not justly to blame for not giving back more to the community of which by and by he will be a responsible member. The kind of the soil determines the quality of the crop. The tenement is his soil and it pervades and shapes his young life. It is the tenement that gives up the child to the street in tender years to find there the home it denied him. Its exorbitant rents rob him of the schooling that is his one chance to elude its grasp, by compelling his enrollment in the army of wage earners before he has learned to read. Its alliance with the saloon guides his baby feet along the well-beaten track of the growler that completes

his ruin. Its power to pervert and corrupt has always
to be considered, its point of view always to be taken
to get the perspective in dealing with the poor, or the
cart will seem to be forever getting before the horse
in a way not to be understood. We had a girl once at
our house in the country who left us suddenly after a
brief stay and went back to her old tenement life, because "all the green hurt her eyes so." She meant just
what she said, though she did not know herself what
ailed her. It was the slum that had its fatal grip upon
her. She longed for its noise, its bustle, and its crowds,
and laid it all to the green grass and the trees that
were new to her as steady company.

From this tenement the street offered, until the
kindergarten came not long ago, the one escape, does
yet for the great mass of children—a Hobson's choice,
for it is hard to say which is the most corrupting. The
opportunities rampant in the one are a sad commentary on the sure defilement of the other. What could
be expected of a standard of decency like this one, of
a household of tenants who assured me that Mrs.
M——, at that moment under arrest for half clubbing
her husband to death, was "a very good, a very decent, woman indeed, and if she did get full, he (the
husband) was not much." Or of the rule of good conduct laid down by a young girl, found beaten and
senseless in the street up in the Annexed District last
autumn: "Them was two of the fellers from Frog
Hollow," she said, resentfully, when I asked who
struck her; "them toughs don't know how to behave
theirselves when they see a lady in liquor."

Hers was the standard of the street, the other's that
of the tenement. Together they stamp the child's life
with the vicious touch which is sometimes only the
caricature of the virtues of a better soil. Under the
rough burr lie undeveloped qualities of good and of
usefulness, rather, perhaps, of the capacity for them,
that crop out in constant exhibitions of loyalty, of
gratitude, and trueheartedness, a never-ending source

of encouragement and delight to those who have
made their cause their own and have in their true
sympathy the key to the best that is in the children.
The testimony of a teacher for twenty-five years in
one of the ragged schools, who has seen the shanty
neighborhood that surrounded her at the start give
place to mile-long rows of big tenements, leaves no
room for doubt as to the influence the change has had
upon the children. With the disappearance of the
shanties—homesteads in effect, however humble—and
the coming of the tenement crowds, there has been a
distinct descent in the scale of refinement among the
children, if one may use the term. The crowds and the
loss of home privacy, with the increased importance
of the street as a factor, account for it. The general
tone has been lowered, while at the same time, by
reason of the greater rescue efforts put forward, the
original amount of ignorance has been reduced. The
big loafer of the old day, who could neither read nor
write, has been eliminated to a large extent, and his
loss is our gain. The tough who has taken his place is
able at least to spell his way through "The Bandits'
Cave," the pattern exploits of Jesse James and his
band, and the newspaper accounts of the latest raid
in which he had a hand. Perhaps that explains why he
is more dangerous than the old loafer. The transition
period is always critical, and a little learning is pro-
verbially a dangerous thing. It may be that in the day
to come, when we shall have got the grip of our compulsory school law in good earnest, there will be an
educational standard even for the tough, by which
time he will, I think, have ceased to exist from sheer
disgust, if for no other reason. At present he is in no
immediate danger of extinction from such a source.
It is not how much book learning the boy can get, but
how little he can get along with, and that is very little
indeed. He knows how to make a little go a long way,
however, and to serve on occasion a very practical
purpose; as, for instance, when I read recently on the

wall of the church next to my office in Mulberry Street this observation, chalked in an awkward hand half the length of the wall: "Mary McGee is engagd to the feller in the alley." Quite apt, I should think, to make Mary show her colors and to provoke the fight with the rival "feller" for which the writer was evidently spoiling. I shall get back, farther on, to the question of the children's schooling. It is so beset by lies ordinarily as to be seldom answered as promptly and as honestly as in the case of a little fellow whom I found in front of St. George's Church, engaged in the æsthetic occupation of pelting the Friends' Seminary across the way with mud. There were two of them, and when I asked them the question that estranged Tony, the wicked one dug his fists deep down in the pockets of his blue jeans trousers and shook his head gloomily. He couldn't read; didn't know how; never did.

"He?" said the other, who could, "he? He don't learn nothing. He throws stones." The wicked one nodded. It was the extent of his education.

But if the three R's suffer neglect among the children of the poor, their lessons in the three D's—Dirt, Discomfort, and Disease—that form the striking features of their environment, are early and thorough enough. The two latter, at least, are synonymous terms, if dirt and discomfort are not. Any dispensary doctor knows of scores of cases of ulceration of the eye that are due to the frequent rubbing of dirty faces with dirty little hands. Worse filth diseases than that find a fertile soil in the tenements, as the health officers learn when typhus and smallpox break out. It is not the desperate diet of ignorant mothers, who feed their month-old babies with sausage, beer, and Limburger cheese, that alone accounts for the great infant mortality among the poor in the tenements. The dirt and the darkness in their homes contribute their full share, and the landlord is more to blame than the mother. He holds the key to the situation which her ignorance fails to grasp, and it is he who is responsible for much of the unfounded and unnecessary prejudice against foreigners, who come here willing enough to fall in with the ways of the country that are shown to them. The way he shows them is not the way of decency. I am convinced that the really injurious foreigners in this community, outside of the walking delegate's tribe, are the foreign landlords of two kinds: those who, born in poverty abroad, have come up through tenement-house life to the ownership of tenement property, with all the bad traditions of such a career; and the absentee landlords of native birth who live and spend their rents away from home, without knowing or caring what the condition of their property is, so the income from it suffer no diminution. There are honorable exceptions to the first class, but few enough to the latter to make them hardly worth mentioning.

To a good many of the children, or rather to their parents, this latter statement and the experience that warrants it must have a sadly familiar sound. The Irish element is still an important factor in New York's tenements, though it is yielding one stronghold after another to the Italian foe. It lost its grip on the Five Points and the Bend long ago, and at this writing the time seems not far distant when it must vacate for good also that classic ground of the Kerryman, Cherry Hill. It is Irish only by descent, however; the children are Americans, as they will not fail to convince the doubter. A school census of this district, the Fourth Ward, taken last winter, discovered 2016 children between the ages of five and fourteen years. No less than 1706 of them were put down as native born, but only one-fourth, or 519, had American parents. Of the others 572 had Irish and 536 Italian parents. Uptown, in many of the poor tenement localities, in Poverty Gap, in Battle Row, and in Hell's Kitchen, in short, wherever the gang flourishes, the Celt is still supreme and seasons the lump enough to give it his own peculiar flavor, easily discovered through its "native" guise in the story of the children of the poor.

The case of one Irish family that exhibits a shoal which lies always close to the track of ignorant poverty is even now running in my mind, vainly demanding a practical solution. I may say that I have inherited it from professional philanthropists, who have struggled with it for more than half a dozen years without finding the way out they sought.

There were five children when they began, depending on a mother who had about given up the struggle as useless. The father was a loafer. When I took them the children numbered ten, and the struggle was long since over. The family bore the pauper stamp, and the mother's tears, by a transition imperceptible probably to herself, had become its stock in trade. Two of the children were working, earning all the money that came in; those that were not lay about in the room, watching the charity visitor in a way and with an intentness that betrayed their interest in the mother's appeal. It required very little experience to make the prediction that, shortly, ten pauper families would carry on the campaign of the one against society, if those children lived to grow up. And they were not to blame, of course. I scarcely know which was most to be condemned, when we tried to break the family up by throwing it on the street as a necessary step to getting possession of the children—the politician who tripped us up with his influence in the court, or the landlord who had all those years made the poverty on the second floor pan out a golden interest. It was the outrageous rent for the filthy den that had been the most effective argument with sympathizing visitors. Their pity had represented to him, as nearly as I could make out, for eight long years, a capital of $2600 invested at six per cent, payable monthly. The idea of moving was preposterous; for what other landlord would take in a homeless family with ten children and no income?

Children anywhere suffer little discomfort from mere dirt. As an ingredient of mud pies it may be said to be not unwholesome. Play with the dirt is better than none without it. In the tenements the children and the dirt are sworn and loyal friends. In his early raids upon the established order of society, the gutter backs the boy up to the best of its ability, with more or less exasperating success. In the hot summer days, when he tries to sneak into the free baths with every fresh batch, twenty times a day, wretched little repeater that he is, it comes to his rescue against the policeman at the door. Fresh mud smeared on the face serves as a ticket of admission which no one can refuse. At least so he thinks, but in his anxiety he generally overdoes it and arouses the suspicion of the policeman, who, remembering that he was once a boy himself, feels of his hair and reads his title there. When it is a mission that is to be raided, or a "dutch" grocer's shop, or a parade of the rival gang from the next block, the gutter furnishes ammunition that is always handy. Dirt is a great leveler;* it is no respecter of persons or principles, and neither is the boy where it abounds. In proportion as it accumulates such raids increase, the Fresh Air Funds lose their grip, the saloon flourishes, and turbulence grows. Down from the Fourth Ward, where there is not much else, this wail came recently from a Baptist Mission Church: "The Temple stands in a hard spot and

* Even as I am writing a transformation is being worked in some of the filthiest streets on the East Side by a combination of new asphalt pavements with a greatly improved street-cleaning service, that promises great things. Some of the worst streets have within a few weeks become as clean as I have not seen them in twenty years, and as they probably never were since they were made. The unwonted brightness of the surroundings is already visibly reflected in the persons and dress of the tenants, notably the children. They take to it gladly, giving the lie to the old assertion that they are pigs and would rather live like pigs.

neighborhood. The past week we had to have arrested
two fellows for throwing stones into the house and
causing annoyance. On George Washington's Birthday
we had not put a flag over the door on Henry Street
half an hour before it was stolen. When they neither
respect the house of prayer or the Stars and Stripes
one can feel young America is in a bad state." The
pastor added that it was a comfort to him to know
that the "fellows" were Catholics; but I think he was
hardly quite fair to them there. Religious enthusiasm
very likely had something to do with it, but it was not
the moving cause. The dirt was, in other words, the
slum.

Such diversions are among the few and simple joys
of the street child's life. Not all it affords, but all the
street has to offer. The Fresh Air Funds, the free excursions, and the many charities that year by year
reach farther down among the poor for their children
have done and are doing a great work in setting up
new standards, ideals, and ambitions in the domain of
the street. One result is seen in the effort of the poorest
mothers to make their little ones presentable when
there is anything to arouse their maternal pride. But
all these things must and do come from the outside.
Other resources than the sturdy independence that is
its heritage the street has none. Rightly used, that in
itself is the greatest of all. Chief among its native en-
tertainments is that crowning joy, the parade of the
circus when it comes to town in the spring. For many
hours after that has passed, as after every public show
that costs nothing, the matron's room at Police Headquarters is crowded with youngsters who have followed it miles and miles from home, devouring its
splendors with hungry eyes until the last elephant, the
last soldier, or the last policeman vanished from sight
and the child comes back to earth again and to the
knowledge that he is lost.

If the delights of his life are few, its sorrows do not
sit heavily upon him either. He is in too close and

constant touch with misery, with death itself, to mind it much. To find a family of children living, sleeping, and eating in the room where father or mother lies dead, without seeming to be in any special distress about it, is no unusual experience. But if they do not weigh upon him, the cares of home leave their mark; and it is a bad mark. All the darkness, all the drudgery is there. All the freedom is in the street; all the brightness in the saloon to which he early finds his way. And as he grows in years and wisdom, if not in grace, he gets his first lessons in spelling and in respect for the law from the card behind the bar, with the big black letters: "No liquor sold here to children." His opportunities for studying it while the barkeeper fills his growler are unlimited and unrestricted.

Someone has said that our poor children do not know how to play. He had probably seen a crowd of tenement children dancing in the street to the accompaniment of a hand organ and been struck by their serious mien and painfully formal glide and carriage— if it was not a German neighborhood, where the "proprieties" are less strictly observed—but that was only because it was a ball and it was incumbent on the girls to act as ladies. Only ladies attend balls. "London Bridge is falling down," with as loud a din in the streets of New York, every day, as it has fallen these hundred years and more in every British town, and the children of the Bend march "all around the mulberry bush" as gleefully as if there were a green shrub to be found within a mile of their slum. It is the slum that smudges the game too easily, and the kindergarten work comes in in helping to wipe off the smut. So far from New York children being duller at their play than those of other cities and lands, I believe the reverse to be true. Only in the very worst tenements have I observed the children's play to languish. In such localities two policemen are required to do the work of one. Ordinarily they lack neither spirit nor inventiveness. I watched a crowd of them having a donkey party in the street one night, when those parties were all the rage. The donkey hung in the window of a notion store, and a knot of tenement-house children with tails improvised from a news-paper, and dragged in the gutter to make them stick, were staggering blindly across the sidewalk trying to fix them in place on the pane. They got a heap of fun out of the game, quite as much, it seemed to me, as any crowd of children could have got in a fine parlor, until the storekeeper came out with his club. Every cellar door becomes a toboggan slide where the children are around, unless it is hammered full of envious nails; every block a ball ground when the policeman's back is turned, and every roof a kite field; for that innocent amusement is also forbidden by city ordinance "below Fourteenth Street."

It is rather that their opportunities of mischief are greater than those of harmless amusement; made so, it has sometimes seemed to me, with deliberate purpose to hatch the "tough." Given idleness and the street, and he will grow without other encouragement than an occasional "fanning" of a policeman's club. And the street has to do for a playground. There is no other. Central Park is miles away. The small parks that were ordered for his benefit five years ago exist yet only on paper. Games like kite flying and ball playing, forbidden but not suppressed, as happily they cannot be, become from harmless play a successful challenge of law and order that points the way to later and worse achievements. Every year the police forbid the building of election bonfires and threaten vengeance upon those who disobey the ordinance; and every election night sees the sky made lurid by them from one end of the town to the other, with the police powerless to put them out. Year by year the boys grow bolder in their raids on property when their supply of firewood has given out, until the destruction wrought at the last election became a matter of public scandal. Stoops, wagons, and in one place a showcase containing prop-

erty worth many hundreds of dollars were fed to the
flames. It has happened that an entire frame house
has been carried off piecemeal and burned up election night. The boys, organized in gangs, with the one
condition of membership that all must "give in wood,"
store up enormous piles of fuel for months before, and
though the police find and raid a good many of them,
incidentally laying in supplies of kindling wood for the
winter, the pile grows again in a single night, as the
neighborhood reluctantly contributes its ash barrels to
the cause. The germ of the gangs that terrorize whole
sections of the city at intervals, and feed our courts
and our jails, may without much difficulty be discovered in these early and rather grotesque struggles
of the boys with the police.

Even on the national day of freedom the boy is not
left to the enjoyment of his firecracker without the
ineffectual threat of the law. I am not defending the
firecracker, but arraigning the failure of the law to
carry its point and maintain its dignity. It has robbed
the poor child of the street band, one of his few harmless delights, grudgingly restoring the hand organ, but
not the monkey that lent it its charm. In the band
that, banished from the street, sneaks into the back
yard, horns and bassoons hidden under bulging coats,
the boy hails no longer the innocent purveyor of
amusement, but an ally in the fight with the common
enemy, the policeman. In the Thanksgiving Day and
New Year parades which the latter formally permits
he furnishes them with the very weapon of gang
organization which they afterward turn against him
to his hurt.

And yet this boy who, when taken from his alley
into the country for the first time, cries out in delight
"How blue the sky and what a lot of it there is!"—not
much of it at home in his barrack—has in the very love
of dramatic display that sends him forth to beat a
policeman with his own club or die in the attempt,
in the intense vanity that is only a perverted form of

pride, capable of any achievement, a handle by which he may be most easily grasped and led. It cannot be done by gorging him en masse with apples and ginger-bread at a Christmas party.* It can be done only by individual effort, and by the influence of personal character in direct contact with the child—the great secret of success in all dealings with the poor. Foul as the gutter he comes from, he is open to the re-proach of "bad form" as few of his betters. Greater even than his desire eventually to "down" a police-man, is his ambition to be a "gentleman," as his sister's to be a "lady." The street is responsible for the carica-ture either makes of the character. On a playbill I saw in an East Side street, only the other day, this repertoire set down: "Thursday—The Bowery Tramp; Friday—The Thief." It was a theater I knew news-boys, and the other children of the street who were earning money, to frequent in shoals. The playbill suggested the sort of training they received there.

I wish I might tell the story of some of these very lads whom certain enthusiastic friends of mine tried to reclaim on a plan of their own, in which the gang became a club and its members "Knights," who made and executed their own laws; but I am under heavy bonds of promises made to keep the peace on this point. The fact is, I tried it once, and my well-meant effort made no end of trouble. I had failed to ap-preciate the stride of civilization that under my friends' banner marched about the East Side with seven-league boots. They read the magazines down there and objected, rather illogically, to being "shown up." The incident was a striking revelation of the wide

---

* As a matter of fact, I heard, after the last one that caused so much discussion, in a court that sent seventy-five children to the show, a universal growl of discontent. The effect on the children, even to those who received presents, was bad. They felt that they had been on exhibition, and their greed was aroused. It was as I expected it would be.

gap between the conditions that prevail abroad and those that confront us. Fancy the *Westminster Review* or the *Nineteenth Century* breeding contention among the denizens of East London by any criticism of their ways? Yet even from Hell's Kitchen had I not long before been driven forth with my camera by a band of angry women, who pelted me with brickbats and stones on my retreat, shouting at me never to come back unless I wanted by head broken, or let any other "duck" from the (mentioning a well-known newspaper of which I was unjustly suspected of being an emissary) poke his nose in there. Reform and the magazines had not taken that stronghold of toughdom yet, but their vanguard, the newspapers, had evidently got there.

"It only shows," said one of my missionary friends, commenting upon the East Side incident, "that we are all at sixes and at sevens here." It is our own fault. In our unconscious pride of caste most of us are given to looking too much and too long at the rough outside. These same workers bore cheerful testimony to the "exquisite courtesy" with which they were received every day in the poorest homes; a courtesy that might not always know the ways of polite society, but always tried its best to find them. "In over fifty thousand visits," reports a physician, whose noble life is given early and late to work that has made her name blessed where sorrow and suffering add their sting to bitter poverty, "personal violence has been attempted on but two occasions. In each case children had died from neglect of parents, who, in their drunken rage, would certainly have taken the life of the physician, had she not promptly run away." Patience and kindness prevailed even with these. The doctor did not desert them, even though she had had to run, believing that one of the mothers at least drank because she was poor and unable to find work; and now, after five years of many trials and failures, she reports that the family is at work and happy and grateful in rooms "where the sun beams in." Gratitude, indeed, she found to be their strong point, always seeking an outlet in expression—evidence of a lack of bringing up, certainly. "Once," she says, "the thankful fathers of two of our patients wished to vote for us, as 'the lady doctors have no vote.' Their intention was to vote for General Butler; we have proof that they voted for Cleveland. They have even placed their own lives in danger for us. One man fought a duel with a woman, she having said that women doctors did not know as much as men. After bar tumblers were used as weapons, the question was decided in favor of women doctors by the man. It seemed but proper that 'the lady doctor' was called in to bind up the wounds of her champion, while a 'man doctor' performed the service for the woman."

My friends, in time, by their gentle but firm management, gained the honest esteem and loyal support of the boys whose manners and minds they had set out to improve, and through such means worked wonders. While some of their experiences were exceedingly funny, more were of a kind to show how easily the material could be molded, if the hands were only there to mold it. One of their number, by and by, hung out her shingle in another street with the word "Doctor" over the bell (not the physician above referred to), but her "character" had preceded her, and woe to the urchin who as much as glanced at that when the gang pulled all the other bells in the block and laughed at the wrath of the tenants. One luckless chap forgot himself far enough to yank it one night, and immediately an angry cry went up from the gang, "Who pulled dat bell?" "Mickey did," was the answer, and Mickey's howls announced to the amused doctor the next minute that he had been "slugged" and she avenged. This doctor's account of the first formal call of the gang in the block was highly amusing. It called in a body and showed a desire to please that tried the host's nerves not a little. The boys vied with each other in recounting for her entertainment their encounters with the police enemy, and in exhibiting their intimate knowledge of the wickedness of the slums in minutest detail. One, who was scarcely twelve years old, and had lately moved from Bayard Street, knew all the ins and outs of the Chinatown opium dives, and painted them in glowing colors. The doctor listened with half-amused dismay, and when the boys rose to go, told them she was glad they had called. So were they, they said, and they guessed they would call again the next night.

"Oh! don't come tomorrow," said the doctor, in something of a fright; "come next week!" She was relieved upon hearing the leader of the gang reprove the rest of the fellows for their want of style. He bowed with great precision, and announced that he would call "in about two weeks."

The testimony of these workers agrees with that of most others who reach the girls at an age when they are yet manageable that the most abiding results follow with them, though they are harder to get at. The boys respond more readily, but also more easily fall from grace. The same good and bad traits are found in both; the same trying superficiality—which merely means that they are raw material; the same readiness to lie as the shortest cut out of a scrape; the same generous helpfulness, characteristic of the poor everywhere. Out of the depth of their bitter poverty I saw the children in the West Fifty-second Street Industrial School, last Thanksgiving, bring for the relief of the aged and helpless and those even poorer than they such gifts as they could—a handful of ground coffee in a paper bag, a couple of Irish potatoes, a little sugar or flour, and joyfully offer to carry them home. It was on such a trip I found little Katie. In her person and work she answered the question sometimes asked, why we hear so much about the boys and so little of the girls; because the home and the shop claim their work much earlier and to a much greater extent, while the boys are turned out to shift for themselves, and because, therefore, their miseries are so much more commonplace, and proportionally uninteresting. It is a woman's lot to suffer in silence. If occasionally she makes herself heard in querulous protest; if injustice long borne gives her tongue a sharper edge than the occasion seems to require, it can at least be said in her favor that her bark is much worse than her bite. The missionary who complains that the wife nags her husband to the point of making the saloon his refuge, or the sister her brother until he flees to the street, bears testimony in the same breath to her readiness to sit up all night to mend the clothes of the scamp she so hotly denounces. Sweetness of temper or of speech is not a distinguishing feature of tenement-house life, any more among the children than with their elders. In a party sent out by our committee for a summer vacation on a Jersey farm, last summer was a little knot of six girls from the Seventh Ward. They had not been gone three days before a letter came from one of them to the mother of one of the others. "Mrs. Reilly," it read, "if you have any sinse you will send for your child." That they would all be murdered was the sense the frightened mother made out of it. The six came home posthaste, the youngest in a state of high dudgeon at her sudden translation back to the tenement. The lonesomeness of the farm had frightened the others. She was little more than a baby, and her desire to go back was explained by one of the rescued ones thus: "She sat two mortil hours at the table a stuffin' of herself, till the missus she says, says she, 'Does yer mother lave ye to sit that long at the table, sis?'" The poor thing was where there was enough to eat for once in her life, and she was making the most of her opportunity.

Not rarely does this child of common clay rise to a height of heroism that discovers depths of feeling and character full of unsuspected promise. It was in March a year ago that a midnight fire, started by a fiend in human shape, destroyed a tenement in Hester Street, killing a number of the tenants. On the fourth floor the firemen found one of these penned in with his little girl and helped them to the window. As they were handing out the child, she broke away from them suddenly and stepped back into the smoke to what seemed certain death. The firemen climbing after, groped around shouting for her to come back. Halfway across the room they came upon her, gasping and nearly smothered, dragging a doll's trunk over the floor.

"I could not leave it," she said, thrusting it at the men as they seized her; "my mother——"

They flung the box angrily through the window. It fell crashing on the sidewalk and, breaking open, revealed no doll or finery, but the deed for her dead mother's grave. Little Bessie had not forgotten her, despite her thirteen years.

Yet Bessie might, likely would, have been found in the front row where anything was going on or to be had, crowding with the best of them and thrusting herself and her claim forward regardless of anything or anybody else. It is a quality in the children which, if not admirable, is at least natural. The poor have to take their turn always, and too often it never comes, or, as in the case of the poor young mother, whom one of our committee found riding aimlessly in a streetcar with her dying baby, not knowing where to go or what to do, when it is too late. She took mother and child to the dispensary. It was crowded and they had to wait their turn. When it came, the baby was dead. It is not to be expected that children who have lived the lawless life of the street should patiently put up with such a prospect. That belongs to the discipline of a life of failure and want. The children know generally what they want, and they go for it by the shortest cut. I found that out, whether I had flowers to give or pictures to take. In the latter case they reversed my Hell's Kitchen experience with a vengeance. Their

determination to be "took," the moment the camera
hove in sight, in the most striking pose they could
hastily devise, was always the most formidable bar to
success I met. The recollection of one such occasion
haunts me yet. They were serving a Thanksgiving
dinner free to all comers at a charitable institution in
Mulberry Street, and more than a hundred children
were in line at the door under the eye of a policeman
when I tried to photograph them. Each one of the
forlorn host had been hugging his particular place for
an hour, shivering in the cold as the line slowly advanced toward the door and the promised dinner, and
there had been numberless little spats due to the
anxiety of someone farther back to steal a march on a
neighbor nearer the goal; but the instant the camera
appeared, the line broke and a howling mob swarmed
about me, up to the very eye of the camera, striking
attitudes on the curb, squatting in the mud in alleged
picturesque repose, and shoving and pushing in a
wild struggle to get into the most prominent position.
With immense trouble and labor the policeman and I
made a narrow lane through the crowd from the
camera to the curb, in the hope that the line might
form again. The lane was studded, the moment I
turned my back, with dirty faces that were thrust into
it from both sides in ludicrous anxiety lest they should
be left out, and in the middle of it two frowsy, ill-
favored girls, children of ten or twelve, took position,
hand in hand, flatly refusing to budge from in front of
the camera. Neither jeers nor threats moved them.
They stood their ground with a grim persistence that
said as plainly as words that they were not going to let
this, the supreme opportunity of their lives, pass, cost
what it might. In their rags, barefooted, and in that
disdainful pose in the midst of a veritable bedlam of
shrieks and laughter, they were a most ludicrous
spectacle. The boys fought rather shy of them, of one
they called "Mag" especially, as it afterward appeared
with good reason. A chunk of wood from the outskirts

of the crowd that hit Mag on the ear at length precipitated a fight in which the boys struggled ten deep on the pavement, Mag in the middle of the heap, doing her full share. As a last expedient I bethought myself of a dogfight as the means of scattering the mob, and sent around the corner to organize one. Fatal mistake! At the first suggestive bark the crowd broke and ran in a body. Not only the hangers-on, but the hungry line collapsed too in an instant, and the policeman and I were left alone. As an attraction, the dogfight outranked the dinner.

This unconquerable vanity, if not turned to use for his good, makes a tough of the lad with more muscle than brains in a perfectly natural way. The newspapers tickle it by recording the exploits of his gang with embellishments that fall in exactly with his tastes. Idleness encourages it. The home exercises no restraint. Parental authority is lost. At a certain age young men of all social grades know a heap more than their fathers, or think they do. The young tough has some apparent reason for thinking that way. He has likely learned to read. The old man has not; he probably never learned anything, not even to speak the language that his son knows without being taught. He thinks him "dead slow," of course, and lays it to his foreign birth. All foreigners are "slow." The father works hard. The boy thinks he knows a better plan. The old man has lost his grip on the lad, if he ever had any. That is the reason why the tough appears in the second generation and disappears in the third. By that time father and son are again on equal terms, whatever those terms may be. The exception to this rule is in the poorest Irish settlements where the manufacture of the tough goes right on, aided by the "inflooence" of the police court on one side and the saloon on the other. Between the two the police fall unwillingly into line. I was in the East Thirty-fifth Street police station one night when an officer came in with two young toughs whom he had arrested in a

lumber yard where they were smoking and drinking.
They had threatened to kill him and the watchman,
and loaded revolvers were taken from them. In spite
of this evidence against them, the justice in the police
court discharged them on the following morning with
a scowl at the officer, and they were both jeering at
him before noon. Naturally he let them alone after
that. It was one case of hundreds of like character.
The politician, of course, is behind them. Toughs have
votes just as they have brickbats and brass knuckles;
when the emergency requires, an assortment to suit
of the one as of the other.

The story of the tough's career I told in *How the
Other Half Lives*, and there is no need of repeating it
here. Its end is generally lurid, always dramatic. It is
that even when it comes to him "with his boots off," in
a peaceful sick bed. In his bravado one can sometimes
catch a glimpse of the sturdiest traits in the Celtic
nature, burlesqued and caricatured by the tenement.
One who had been a cutthroat, bruiser, and prize-
fighter all his brief life lay dying from consumption in
his Fourth Ward tenement not long ago. He had made
what he proudly called a stand-up fight against the
disease until now the end had come and he had at last
to give up.

"Maggie," he said, turning to his wife with eyes
growing dim, "Mag! I had an iron heart, but now it is
broke. Watch me die!" And Mag told it proudly at the
wake as proof that Pat died game.

And the girl that has come thus far with him?
Fewer do than one might think. Many more switch
off their lovers to some honest work this side of the
jail, making decent husbands of them as they are loyal
wives, thus proving themselves truly their better
halves. But of her who goes his way with him—it is
not generally a long way for either—what of her
end? . . .

THE LITTLE TOILERS

Poverty and child labor are yoke fellows everywhere. Their union is perpetual, indissoluble. The one begets the other. Need sets the child to work when it should have been at school and its labor breeds low wages, thus increasing the need. Solomon said it three thousand years ago, and it has not been said better since: "The destruction of the poor is their poverty."

It is the business of the State to see to it that its interest in the child as a future citizen is not imperiled by the compact. Here in New York we set about this within the memory of the youngest of us. Today we have compulsory education and a factory law prohibiting the employment of young children. All between eight and fourteen years old must go to school at least fourteen weeks in each year. None may labor in factories under the age of fourteen; not under sixteen unless able to read and write simple sentences in English. These are the barriers thrown up against the inroads of ignorance, poverty's threat. They are barriers of paper. We have the laws, but we do not enforce them.

By that I do not mean to say that we make no attempt to enforce them. We do. We catch a few hundred truants each year and send them to reformatories to herd with thieves and vagabonds worse than they, rather illogically, since there is no pretense that there would have been room for them in the schools had they wanted to go there. We get half a dozen factory inspectors to canvass more than twice

as many thousand workshops and to catechize the
children they find there. Some are turned out and go
back the next day to that or some other shop. The
great mass that are under age lie and stay. And their
lies go on record as evidence that we are advancing
and that child labor is getting to be a thing of the past.
That the horrible cruelty of a former day is [past];
that the children have better treatment and a better
time of it in the shops—often a good enough time to
make one feel that they are better off there learning
habits of industry than running about the streets, so
long as there is no way of *making* them attend school
—I believe from what I have seen. That the law has
had the effect of greatly diminishing the number of
child workers I do not believe. It has had another and
worse effect. It has bred wholesale perjury among
them and their parents. Already they have become so
used to it that it is a matter of sport and a standing
joke among them. The child of eleven at home and
at night school is fifteen in the factory as a matter of
course. Nobody is deceived, but the perjury defeats
the purpose of the law.

More than a year ago, in an effort to get at the truth
of the matter of children's labor, I submitted to the
Board of Health, after consultation with Dr. Felix
Adler, who earned the lasting gratitude of the community by his labors on the Tenement House Commission, certain questions to be asked concerning the
children by the sanitary police, then about to begin a
general census of the tenements. The result was a
surprise, and not least to the health officers. In the
entire mass of nearly a million and a quarter of tenants* only two hundred and forty-nine children under
fourteen years of age were found at work in living
rooms. To anyone acquainted with the ordinary

* The Sanitary census of 1891 gave 37,358 tenements, containing 276,565 families, including 160,708 children under five
years of age; total population of tenements, 1,225,411.

aspect of tenement-house life the statement seemed preposterous, and there are valid reasons for believing that the policemen missed rather more than they found even of those that were confessedly or too evidently under age. They were seeking that which, when found, would furnish proof of lawbreaking against the parent or employer, a fact of which these were fully aware. Hence their coming uniformed and in search of children into a house could scarcely fail to give those a holiday who were not big enough to be palmed off as fourteen at least. Nevertheless, upon reflection, it seemed probable that the policemen were nearer the truth than their critics. Their census took no account of the factory in the backyard, but only of the living rooms, and it was made during the day. Most of the little slaves, as of those older in years, were found in the sweater's district on the East Side, where the homework often only fairly begins after the factory has shut down for the day and the stores released their army of child laborers. Had the policemen gone their rounds after dark they would have found a different state of things. Between the sweatshops and the school, which, as I have shown, is made to reach farther down among the poorest in this Jewish quarter than anywhere else in this city, the children were fairly accounted for in the daytime. The record of school attendance in the district shows that forty-seven attended day school for every one who went to night school.

To settle the matter to my own satisfaction I undertook a census of a number of the most crowded houses, in company with a policeman not in uniform. The outcome proved that, as regards those houses at least, it was as I suspected, and I have no doubt they were a fair sample of the rest. In nine tenements that were filled with homeworkers we found five children at work who owned that they were under fourteen. Two were girls nine years of age. Two boys said they were thirteen. We found thirteen who swore that they were

PLATE 1.
Necktie Workshop in a Division
Street Tenement, 1889–90.

1. PHOTOGRAPH: *Jacob A. Riis, the Jacob A. Riis*
Collection, Museum of the City of New York.

PLATE 2.
Bottle Alley.

2. PHOTOGRAPH: *Jacob A. Riis, the Jacob A. Riis Collection, Museum of the City of New York.*

PLATE 3.
Bohemian Cigarmakers at Work in Tenement.

PLATE 4.
Room in Tenement Flat, 1910.

4. PHOTOGRAPH: *Jacob A. Riis, the Jacob A. Riis Collection, Museum of the City of New York.*

5. PHOTOGRAPH: *Jacob A. Riis, the Jacob A. Riis Collection, Museum of the City of New York.*

PLATE 6.
Ready for the Sabbath Eve in a Coal
Cellar, Ludlow Street, Early 1890s.

6. PHOTOGRAPH: *Jacob A. Riis, the Jacob A. Riis
Collection, Museum of the City of New York.*

PLATE 7.
The Mulberry Bend, About 1888–89.

7. PHOTOGRAPH: *Jacob A. Riis, the Jacob A. Riis Collection, Museum of the City of New York.*

PLATE 8.
Happy Jack's 7¢ Lodginghouse.

8. PHOTOGRAPH: *Jacob A. Riis, the Jacob A. Riis Collection, Museum of the City of New York.*

of age, proof which the policeman as an uninterested census taker would have respected as a matter of course, even though he believed with me that the children lied. On the other hand, in seven backyard factories we found a total of sixty-three children, of whom five admitted being under age, while of the rest forty-five seemed surely so. To the other thirteen we gave the benefit of the doubt, but I do not think they deserved it. All the sixty-three were to my mind certainly under fourteen, judging not only from their size, but from the whole appearance of the children. My subsequent experience confirmed me fully in this belief. Most of them were able to write their names after a fashion. Few spoke English, but that might have been a subterfuge. One of the homeworkers, a marvelously small lad whose arms were black to the shoulder from the dye in the cloth he was sewing, and who said in his broken German, without evincing special interest in the matter, that he had gone to school "e' bische'," referred us to his "mother" for a statement as to his age. The "mother," who proved to be the boss's wife, held a brief consultation with her husband and then came forward with a verdict of sixteen. When we laughed rather incredulously the man offered to prove by his marriage certificate that the boy must be sixteen. The effect of this demonstration was rather marred, however, by the inopportune appearance of another tailor, who, ignorant of the crisis, claimed the boy as his. The situation was dramatic. The tailor with the certificate simply shrugged his shoulders and returned to his work, leaving the boy to his fate.

One girl, who could not have been twelve years old, was hard at work at a sewing machine in a Division Street shirt factory when we came in. She got up and ran the moment she saw us, but we caught her in the next room hiding behind a pile of shirts. She said at once that she was fourteen years old but didn't work there. She "just came in." The boss of the shop was

lost in astonishment at seeing her when we brought
her back. He could not account at all for her presence.
There were three boys at work in the room who said
"sixteen" without waiting to be asked. Not one of them
was fourteen. The habit of saying fourteen or sixteen
—the fashion varies with the shops and with the degree of the child's educational acquirements—soon becomes an unconscious one with the boy. He plumps it
out without knowing it. While occupied with these
investigations I once had my boots blacked by a little
shaver, hardly knee-high, on a North River ferryboat.
While he was shining away, I suddenly asked him
how old he was. "Fourteen, sir!" he replied promptly,
without looking up.

In a Hester Street house we found two little girls
pulling basting thread. They were both Italians and
said that they were nine. In the room in which one of
them worked, thirteen men and two women were
sewing. The child could speak English. She said that
she was earning a dollar a week and worked every
day from seven in the morning till eight in the evening. This sweatshop was one of the kind that comes
under the ban of the new law, passed last winter—
that is, if the factory inspector ever finds it. Where
the crowds are greatest and the pay poorest, the
Italian laborer's wife and child have found their way
in since the strikes among the sweater's Jewish slaves,
outbidding even these in the fierce strife for bread.

Even the crowding, the feverish haste of the half-
naked men and women, and the litter and filth in
which they worked were preferable to the silence and
desolation we encountered in one shop up under the
roof of a Broome Street tenement. The work there had
given out—there had been none these two months,
said the gaunt, hard-faced woman who sat eating a
crust of dry bread and drinking water from a tin pail
at the empty bench. The man sat silent and moody in
a corner; he was sick. The room was bare. The only
machine left was not worth taking to the pawnshop.
Two dirty children, naked but for a torn undershirt

apiece, were fishing over the stair rail with a bent pin on an idle thread. An old rag was their bait.

From among a hundred and forty hands on two big lofts in a Suffolk Street factory we picked seventeen boys and ten girls who were patently under fourteen years of age, but who all had certificates, sworn to by their parents, to the effect that they were sixteen. One of them whom we judged to be between nine and ten, and whose teeth confirmed our diagnosis—the second bicuspids in the lower jaw were just coming out—said that he had worked there "by the year." The boss, deeming his case hopeless, explained that he only "made sleeves and went for beer." Two of the smallest girls represented themselves as sisters, respectively sixteen and seventeen, but when we came to inquire which was the oldest, it turned out that she was the sixteen-year one. Several boys scooted as we came up the stairs. When stopped, they claimed to be visitors. I was told that this sweater had been arrested once by the Factory Inspector, but had successfully barricaded himself behind his pile of certificates. I caught the children laughing and making faces at us behind our backs as often as these were brought out anywhere. In an Attorney Street "pants" factory we counted thirteen boys and girls who could not have been of age, and on a top floor in Ludlow Street, among others, two brothers, sewing coats, who said that they were thirteen and fourteen, but, when told to stand up, looked so ridiculously small as to make even their employer laugh. Neither could read, but the oldest could sign his name and did it thus, from right to left:

It was the full extent of his learning, and all he would probably ever receive.

He was one of many Jewish children we came across who could neither read nor write. Most of them answered that they had never gone to school. They were mostly those of larger growth, bordering on fourteen, whom the charity school managers find it next to impossible to reach, the children of the poorest and most ignorant immigrants, whose work is imperatively needed to make both ends meet at home, the "thousand" the school census failed to account for. To banish them from the shop serves no useful purpose. They are back the next day, if not sooner. One of the Factory Inspectors told me of how recently he found a little boy in a sweatshop and sent him home. He went up through the house after that and stayed up there quite an hour. On his return it occurred to him to look in to see if the boy was gone. He was back and hard at work, and with him were two other boys of his age who, though they claimed to have come in with dinner for some of the hands, were evidently workers there.

So much for the sweatshops. Jewish, Italian, and Bohemian, the story is the same always. In the children that are growing up, to "vote as would their master's dogs if allowed the right of suffrage," the community reaps its reward in due season for allowing such things to exist. It is a kind of interest in the payment of which there is never default. The physician gets another view of it. "Not long ago," says Dr. Annie S. Daniel, in the last report of the out-practice of the Infirmary for Women and Children, "we found in such an apartment five persons making cigars, including the mother. Two children were ill with diphtheria. Both parents attended to the children; they would syringe the nose of each child and, without washing their hands, return to their cigars. We have repeatedly observed the same thing when the work was manufacturing clothing and undergarments, to be bought as well by the rich as the poor. Hand-sewed shoes, made for a fashionable Broadway shoe store, were sewed at

home by a man in whose family were three children
with scarlet fever. And such instances are common.
Only death or lack of work closes tenement-house
manufactories. When reported to the Board of Health,
the inspector at once prohibits further manufacture
during the continuance of the disease, but his back is
scarcely turned before the people return to their work.
When we consider that stopping this work means no
food and no roof over their heads, the fact that the
disease may be carried by their work cannot be expected to impress the people."

And she adds: "Wages have steadily decreased.
Among the women who earned the whole or part of
the income the finishing of pantaloons was the most
common occupation. For this work in 1881 they received ten to fifteen cents per pair; for the same work
in 1891 three to five, at the most ten cents per pair.
When the women have paid the express charges to
and from the factory there is little margin left for
profit. The women doing this work claim that wages
are reduced because of the influx of Italian women."
The rent has not fallen, however, and the need of
every member of the family contributing by his or her
work to its keep is greater than ever. The average total wage of 160 families whom the doctor personally
treated and interrogated during the year was $5.99
per week, while the average rent was $8.62¾. The
list included twenty-three different occupations and
trades. The maximum wage was $19, earned by three
persons in one family; the minimum $1.50, by a
woman finishing pantaloons and living in one room for
which she paid $4 a month rent! In nearly every in-
stance observed by Dr. Daniel, the children's wages,
when there were working children, was the greater
share of the family income. A specimen instance is
that of a woman with a consumptive husband, who is
under her treatment. The wife washes and goes out
by the day, when she can get such work to do. The
three children, aged eleven, seven, and five years, not

counting the baby for a wonder, work at home covering wooden buttons with silk at four cents a gross. The oldest goes to school, but works with the rest evenings and on Saturday and Sunday, when the mother does the finishing. Their combined earnings are from $3 to $6 a week, the children earning two-thirds. The rent is $8 a month.

The doctor's observations throw a bright sidelight upon the economic home conditions that lie at the root of this problem of child labor in the factories. With that I have not done. Taking the Factory Inspector's report for 1890, the last at that time available, I found that in that year his deputies got around to 2147 of the 11,000 workshops (the number given in the report) in the Second District, which is that portion of New York south of Twenty-third Street. In other words, they visited less than one-fifth of them all. They found 1102 boys and 1954 girls under sixteen at work; 3485 boys under eighteen, and 12,701 girls under twenty-one, as nearly as I could make the footings. The figures alone are instructive, as showing the preponderance of girls in the shops. The report, speaking of the State as a whole, congratulates the community upon the alleged fact "that the policy of employing very young children in manufactories has been practically abolished." It states that "since the enactment of the law the sentiment among employers has become nearly unanimous in favor of its stringent enforcement," and that it "has had the further important effect of preventing newly arrived non-English speaking foreigners from forcing their children into factories before they learned the language of the country," these being "now compelled to send their children to school, for a time at least, until they can qualify under the law." Further, "the system of requiring sworn certificates, giving the name, date, and place of birth of all children under sixteen years of age . . . has resulted in causing parents to be very cautious about making untrue statements of the ages of their children." The deputies "are aware of the various subterfuges which have been tried in order to evade the law and put children at labor before the legal time," and the Factory Inspector is "happy to say that they are not often imposed upon by such tactics."

Without wading through nearly seventy pages of small print it was not possible to glean from the report how many of the "under sixteen" workers were really under fourteen, or so adjudged. A summary of what has been accomplished since 1886 showed that 1614 children under fourteen were discharged by the Inspector in the Second District in that time, and that 415 were discharged because they could not read or write simple sentences in the English language. The "number of working children who could not read and write English" was in 1890 alone 252, according to the report, or more than one-half of the whole number discharged in the four years, which does not look as if the law had had much effect in that way, at least in New York City. I determined to see for myself what were the facts.

I visited a number of factories, in a few instances accompanied by the deputy factory inspector, more frequently alone. Where it was difficult to gain admission I watched at the door when the employees were going to or coming from work, finding that on the whole the better plan, as affording a fairer view of the children and a better opportunity to judge of their age than when they sat at their workbenches. I found many shops in which there were scarcely any children, some from which they had been driven, so I was informed by the inspectors. But where manufacturers were willing to employ their labor—and this I believe to be quite generally the case where children's labor can be made to pay—I found the age certificate serving as an excellent protection for the employer, never for the child. I found the law considered as a good joke by some conscienceless men, who hardly took the trouble to see that the certificates were filled out properly; loudly commended by others whom it enabled, at the expense of a little perjury in which they had no hand, to fill up their shops with cheap labor, with perfect security to themselves. The bookkeeper in an establishment of the conscienceless kind told me with glee how a boy who had been bounced there three times in one year, upon his return each time had presented a sworn certificate giving a different age. He was fifteen, sixteen, and seventeen years old upon the records of the shop, until the inspectors caught him one day and proved him only thirteen. I found boys at work, posing as seventeen, who had been so recorded in the same shop three full years, and were thirteen at most. As seventeen-year freaks they could have made more money in a dime museum than at the workbench, only the museum would have required something more convincing than the certificate that satisfied the shop. Some of these boys were working at power presses and doing other work beyond their years. An examination of their teeth often disproved their stories as to their age. It was not always possible to make this test, for the children seemed to see something funny in it, and laughed and giggled so, especially the girls, as to make it difficult to get a good look. Some of the girls, generally those with decayed teeth,* would pout and refuse to show them. These were usually American girls, that is to say, they were born here. The greater number of the child workers I questioned were foreigners, and our birth returns could have given no clue to them. The few natives were alert and on the defensive from the moment

---

* The general impression survives with me that the children's teeth were bad, and those of the native-born the worst. Ignorance and neglect were clearly to blame for most of it, poor and bad food for the rest, I suppose. I give it as a layman's opinion, and leave it to the dentist to account for the bad teeth of the many who are not poor. That is his business.

they divined my purpose. They easily defeated it by giving a false address.

I finally picked out a factory close to my office where Italian girls were employed in large numbers, and made it my business to ascertain the real ages of the children. They seemed to me, going and coming, to average twelve or thirteen years. The year before the factory inspector had reported that nearly a hundred girls "under sixteen" were employed there. She had discharged sixty of them as unable to read or write English. I went to see the manufacturers. They were not disposed to help me and fell back on their certificates—no child was employed by them without one—until I told them that my purpose was not to interfere with their business but to prove that a birth certificate was the only proper warrant for employment of child labor.

"Why," said the manufacturer, in his astonishment forgetting that he had just told me his children were all of age, "my dear sir! would you throw them all out of work?"

It was what I expected. I found out eventually that a number of the children attended the evening classes in the Leonard Street Italian School, and there one rainy night I corralled twenty-three of them, all but one officially certified under oath to be fourteen or sixteen. But for the rain I might have found twice the number. The twenty-three I polled, comparing their sworn age with the entry in the school register, which the teachers knew to be correct. This was the result: one was eleven years old and had worked in the factory a year; one, also eleven, had just been engaged and was going for her certificate that night; three were twelve years old, and had worked in the factory from one month to a year; seven were thirteen, and of them three had worked in the shop two years, the others one; nine were fourteen; one of them had been there three years, four others two years, the rest shorter terms; one was fifteen and had worked in the factory three years; the last and tallest was sixteen and had been employed in the one shop four years. She said with a laugh that she had a "certificate of sixteen" when she first went there. Not one of them all was of legal age when she went to work in the shop, under the warrant of her parents' oath. The majority were not even then legally employed, since of those who had passed fourteen there were several who could not read simple sentences in English intelligibly; yet they had been at work in the factory for months and years. One of the eleven-year workers, who felt insulted somehow, said spitefully that I "needn't bother, there was lots of other girls in the shop younger than she." I have no doubt she was right. I should add that the firm was a highly respectable one, and its members of excellent social standing.

I learned incidentally where the convenient certificates came from, at least those that were current in that school. They were issued, the children said, free of charge, by a benevolent undertaker in the ward. I thought at first that it was a bid for business, or real helpfulness. The neighborhood undertaker is often found figuring suggestively as the nearest friend of the poor in his street, when they are in trouble. But I found out afterward that it was politics combined with business. The undertaker was an Irishman and an active organizer of his district. Unpolitical notaries charged twenty-five cents for each certificate. This one made them out for nothing. All they had to do was to call for them. The girls laughed scornfully at the idea of there being anything wrong in the transaction. Their parents swore in a good cause. They needed the money. The end conveniently justified the means in their case. Besides "they merely had to touch the pen." Evidently, any argument in favor of education could scarcely be expected to have effect upon parents who thus found in their own ignorance a valid defense against an accusing conscience as well as a source of added revenue.

My experience satisfied me that the factory law has had little effect in prohibiting child labor in the factories of New York City, although it may have had some in stimulating attendance at the night schools. The census figures, when they appear, will be able to throw no valuable light on the subject. The certificate lie naturally obstructs the census as it does the factory law. The one thing that is made perfectly clear by even such limited inquiry as I have been able to make is that a birth certificate should be substituted for the present sworn warrant, if it is intended to make a serious business of the prohibition. In the piles upon piles of these which I saw, I never came across one copy of the birth registry. There are two obstacles to such a change. One is that our birth returns are at present incomplete; the other, that most of the children are not born here. Concerning the first, the Registrar of Vital Statistics estimates that he is registering nearly or quite a thousand births a month less than actually occur in New York; but even that is a great improvement upon the record of a few years ago. The registered birth rate is increasing year by year, and experience has shown that a determination on the part of the Board of Health to prosecute doctors and midwives who neglect their duty brings it up with a rush many hundreds in a few weeks. A wholesome strictness at the Health Office on this point would in a short time make it a reliable guide for the Factory Inspector in the enforcement of the law. The other objection is less serious than it appears at first sight. Immigrants might be required to provide birth certificates from their old homes, where their children are sure to be registered under the stringent laws of European governments. But as a matter of fact that would not often be necessary. They all have passports in which the name and ages of their children are set down. The claim that they had purposely registered them as younger to cheapen transportation, which they would be sure to make, need not be considered seriously. One lie is as good and as easy as another.

Another lesson we may learn with advantage from some old-country governments, which we are apt to look down upon as "slow," is to punish the parents for the truancy of their children, whether they are found running in the street or working in a shop when they should have been at school. Greed, the natural child of poverty, often has as much to do with it as real need. In the case of the Italians and the Jewish girls, it is the inevitable marriage portion, without which they would stand little chance of getting a husband, that dictates the sacrifice. One little one of twelve in a class in the Leonard Street School, who had been working on coats in a sweatshop nine months, and had become expert enough to earn three dollars a week, told me that she had $200 in bank, and that her sister, also a worker, was as forehanded. Their teacher supported her story. But often a meaner motive than the desire to put money in bank forges the child's fetters. I came across a little girl in an East Side factory who pleaded so pitifully that she had to work, and looked so poor and wan, that I went to her home to see what it was like. It was on the top floor of a towering tenement. The mother, a decent German woman, was sewing at the window, doing her share, while at the table her husband, a big, lazy lout who weighed two hundred pounds if he weighed one, lolled over a game of checkers with another vagabond like himself. A half-empty beer growler stood between them. The contrast between that pitiful child hard at work in the shop, and the big loafer taking his ease, was enough to make anybody lose patience, and I gave him the piece of my mind he so richly deserved. But it rolled off him as water rolls off a duck. He merely ducked his head, shifted his bare feet under the table, and told his crony to go on with the play.

It is only when the child rebels in desperation against such atrocious cruelty and takes to the street

as his only refuge that his tyrant hands him over to
the justice so long denied him. Then the school comes
as an avenger, not as a friend, to the friendless lad,
and it is scarcely to be wondered at if behind his
prison bars he fails to make sense of the justice of a
world that locks him up and lets his persecutor go free
—likely enough applauds him for his public spirit in
doing what he did. When the child ceases to be a
source of income because he will not work, and has
to be supported, at the odd intervals at least when he
comes back from the street, the father surrenders him
as a truant and incorrigible. A large number of the
children that are every year sent to the Juvenile
Asylum are admitted in that way. The real animus of
it crops out when it is proposed to put the little prisoner in a way of growing up a useful citizen by sending him to a home out of the reach of his grasping
relatives. Then follows a struggle for the possession
of the child that would make the uninitiated onlooker
think a gross outrage was about to be perpetrated on a
fond parent. The experienced Superintendent of the
Asylum, who has fought many such fights to a successful end, knows better. "In a majority of these cases,"
he remarks in his report for last year, "the opposition
is due, not to any special interest in the child's welfare, but to self-interest, the relative wishing to obtain
a situation for the boy in order to get his weekly
wages."

Little Susie, whose picture I took while she was
pasting linen on tin covers for pocket flasks—one of
the hundred odd trades, wholly impossible of classification, one meets with in the tenements of the poor—
with hands so deft and swift that even the flash could
not catch her moving arm, but lost it altogether, is a
type of the tenement-house children whose work begins early and ends late. Her shop is her home. Every
morning she drags down to her Cherry Street court
heavy bundles of the little tin boxes, much too heavy
for her twelve years, and when she has finished run-

ning errands and earning a few pennies that way,
takes her place at the bench and pastes two hundred
before it is time for evening school. Then she has
earned sixty cents—"more than mother," she says with
a smile. "Mother" has been finishing "knee pants" for
a sweater, at a cent and a quarter a pair for turning
up and hemming the bottom and sewing buttons on;
but she cannot make more than two and a half dozen
a day, with the baby to look after besides. The husband, a lazy, good-natured Italian, who "does not love
work well," in the patient language of the housekeeper, had been out of a job, when I last saw him,
three months, and there was no prospect of his getting
one again soon, certainly not so long as the agent did
not press for the rent long due. That was Susie's
doings, too, though he didn't know it. Her sunny smile
made everyone and everything, even in that dark
alley, gentler, more considerate, when she was around.

Of Susie's hundred little companions in the alley—
playmates they could scarcely be called—some made
artificial flowers, some paper boxes, while the boys
earned money at "shinin'" or selling newspapers. The
smaller girls "minded the baby," so leaving the mother
free to work. Most of them did something toward
earning the family living, young as they were. The
rest did all the mischief. The occupations that claim
children's labor in and out of the shop are almost as
numberless as the youngsters that swarm in tenement
neighborhoods. The poorer the tenements the more of
them always. In an evening school class of nineteen
boys and nine girls which I polled once I found twelve
boys who "shined," five who sold papers, one of thirteen years who by day was the devil in a printing
office, and one of twelve who worked in a wood yard.
Of the girls, one was thirteen and worked in a paper-
box factory, two of twelve made paper lanterns, one
twelve-year-old girl sewed coats in a sweatshop, and
one of the same age minded a pushcart every day.
The four smallest girls were ten years old, and of

them one worked for a sweater and "finished twenty-five coats yesterday," she said with pride. She looked quite able to do a woman's work. The three others minded the baby at home; one of them found time to help her mother sew coats when baby slept.

I have heard it said that the factory law has resulted in crowding the children under age into the stores, where they find employment as "cash" girls and boys, and have to fear only the truant officer, whose calls are as rare as angels' visits. I do not believe this is true to any great extent. The more general employment of automatic carriers and other mechanical devices for doing the work once done by the children would alone tend to check such a movement, if it existed. The Secretary of the Working Women's Society, who has made a study of the subject, estimates that there are five thousand children under fourteen years so employed all the year round. In the holiday season their number is much larger. Native-born children especially prefer this work, as the more genteel and less laborious than work in the factories. As a matter of fact it is, I think, much the harder and the more objectionable of the two kinds, and not, as a rule, nearly as well paid. If the factory law does not drive the children from the workshops, it can at least punish the employer who exacts more than ten hours a day of them there, or denies them their legal dinner hour. In the store there is nothing to prevent their being worked fifteen and sixteen hours during the busy season. Few firms allow more than half an hour for lunch, some even less. The children cannot sit down when tired, and their miserable salaries of a dollar and a half or two dollars a week are frequently so reduced by fines for tardiness as to leave them little or nothing. The sanitary surroundings are often most wretched. At best the dust-laden atmosphere of a large store, with the hundreds of feet tramping through it and the many pairs of lungs breathing the air over and over again, is most exhausting to a tender child. An hour spent in going through such a store tires many grown persons more than a whole day's work at their accustomed tasks. These children spend their whole time there at the period when the growth of the body taxes all their strength.

An effort was made last year to extend the prohibition of the factory law to the stores, but it failed. It ought not to fail this winter, but if it is to be coupled with the sworn certificate, it were better to leave things as they are. The five thousand children under age are there now in defiance of one law that requires them to go to school. They lied to get their places. They will not hesitate to lie to keep them. The royal road is provided by the certificate plan. Beneficent undertakers will not be wanting to smooth the way for them.

There is still another kind of employment that absorbs many of the boys and ought to be prohibited with the utmost rigor of the law. I refer to the messenger service of the District Telegraph Companies especially. Anyone can see for himself how old some of these boys are who carry messages about the streets every day; but everybody cannot see the kind of houses they have to go to, the kind of people they meet, or the sort of influences that beset them hourly at an age when they are most easily impressed for good or bad. If that were possible, the line would be drawn against their employment rather at eighteen than at sixteen or fourteen. At present there is none except the fanciful line drawn against truancy, which, to a boy who has learned the tricks of the telegraph messenger, is very elastic indeed.

To send the boys to school and see that they stay there until they have learned enough to at least vote intelligently when they grow up is the bounden duty of the State—celebrated in theory but neglected in practice. If it did its duty, much would have been gained, but even then the real kernel of this question of child labor would remain untouched. The trouble is not so much that the children have to work early as with the sort of work they have to do. It is, all of it, of a kind that leaves them, grown to manhood and womanhood, just where it found them, knowing no more, and therefore less, than when they began, and with the years that should have prepared them for life's work gone in hopeless and profitless drudgery. How large a share of the responsibility for this failure is borne by the senseless and wicked tyranny of so-called organized labor, in denying to our own children a fair chance to learn honest trades, while letting foreign workmen in in shoals to crowd our market under the plea of the "solidarity of labor"—a policy that is in a fair way of losing to labor all the respect due it from our growing youth, I shall not here discuss. The general result was well put by a tireless worker in the cause of improving the condition of the poor, who said to me, "They are down on the scrub level; there you find them and have to put them to such use as you can. They don't know anything else, and that is what makes it so hard to find work for them. Even when they go into a shop to sew, they come out mere machines, able to do only one thing, which is a small part of the whole they do not grasp. And thus, without the slightest training for the responsibilities of life, they marry and transmit their incapacity to another generation that is so much worse to start off with." She spoke of the girls, but what she said fitted the boys just as well. The incapacity of the mother is no greater than the ignorance of the father in the mass of such unions. Ignorance and poverty are the natural heritage of the children.

I have in mind a typical family of that sort which our relief committee wrestled with a whole summer, in Poverty Gap. Suggestive location! The man found his natural level on the island, where we sent him first thing. The woman was decent and willing to work, and the girls young enough to train. But Mrs. Murphy did not get on. "She can't even hold a flatiron in her hand," reported her first employer, indignantly.

The children were sent to good places in the country, and repaid the kindness shown them by stealing and lying to cover up their thefts. They were not depraved; they were simply exhibiting the fruit of the only training they had ever received—that of the street. It was like undertaking a job of original creation to try to make anything decent or useful out of them.

I confess I had always laid the blame for this discouraging feature of the problem upon our general industrial development in a more or less vague way— steam, machinery, and all that sort of thing—until the other day I met a man who gave me another view of it altogether. He was a manufacturer of cheap clothing, a very intelligent and successful one at that; a large employer of cheap Hebrew labor and, heaven save the mark!—a Christian. His sincerity was unquestionable. He had no secrets to keep from me. He was in the business to make money, he said with perfect frankness, and one condition of his making money was, as he had had occasion to learn when he was himself a wage worker and a union man, to keep his workmen where they were at his mercy. He had some four hundred hands, all Jewish immigrants, all working for the lowest wages for which he could hire them. Among them all there was not one tailor capable of making a whole garment. His policy was to keep them from learning. He saw to it that each one was kept at just one thing—sleeves, pockets, buttonholes—some small part of one garment, and never learned anything else.

"This I do," he explained, "to prevent them from going on strike with the hope of getting a job anywhere else. They can't. They don't know enough. Not only do we limit them so that a man who has worked three months in my shop and never held a needle before is just as valuable to me as one I have had five years, but we make the different parts of the suit in different places and keep Christians over the hands as cutters so that they shall have no chance to learn."

Where we stood in his shop, a little boy was stacking some coats for removal. The manufacturer pointed him out. "Now," he said, "this boy is not fourteen years old, as you can see as well as I. His father works here and when the Inspector comes I just call him up. He swears that the boy is old enough to work, and there the matter ends. What would you? Is it not better that he should be here than on the street? Bah!" And this successful Christian manufacturer turned upon his heel with a vexed air. It was curious to hear him, before I left, deliver a homily on the "immorality" of the sweatshops, arraigning them severely as "a blot on humanity."

THE TRUANTS
OF OUR STREETS

On my way to the office the other day, I came upon three boys sitting on a beer keg in the mouth of a narrow alley intent upon a game of cards. They were dirty and "tough." The bare feet of the smallest lad were nearly black with dried mud. His hair bristled, unrestrained by cap or covering of any kind. They paid no attention to me when I stopped to look at them. It was an hour before noon.

"Why are you not in school?" I asked of the oldest rascal. He might have been thirteen.

"'Cause," he retorted calmly, without taking his eye off his neighbor's cards, "'cause I don't believe in it. Go on, Jim!"

I caught the black-footed one by the collar. "And you," I said, "why don't you go to school? Don't you know you have to?"

The boy thrust one of his bare feet out at me as an argument there was no refuting. "They don't want me; I aint got no shoes." And he took the trick.

I had heard his defense put in a different way to the same purpose more than once on my rounds through the sweatshops. Every now and then some father whose boy was working under age would object, "We send the child to school, as the Inspector says, and there is no room for him. What shall we do?" He spoke the whole truth, likely enough; the boy only half of it. There was a charity school around the corner from where he sat struggling manfully with his disappointment where they would have taken him and fitted him out with shoes in the bargain, if the public school rejected him. If anything worried him, it was probably the fear that I might know of it and drag him around there. I had seen the same thought working in the tailor's mind. Neither had any use for the school; the one that his boy might work, the other that he might loaf and play hookey.

Each had found his own flaw in our compulsory education law and succeeded. The boy was safe in the street because no truant officer had the right to arrest him at sight for loitering there in school hours. His only risk was the chance of that functionary's finding him at home, and he was trying to provide against that. The tailor's defense was valid. With a law requiring—compelling is the word, but the compulsion is on the wrong tack—all children between the ages of eight and fourteen years to go to school at least one-fourth of the year or a little more; with a costly machinery to enforce it, even more costly to the child who falls under the ban as a truant than to the citizens who foot the bills, we should most illogically be compelled to exclude, by force if they insisted, more than fifty thousand of the children, did they all take it into their heads to obey the law. We have neither schools enough nor seats enough in them. As it is, we are spared that embarrassment. They don't obey it.

This is the way the case stands: Computing the school population upon the basis of the federal census of 1880 and the state census of 1892, we had in New York, in the summer of 1891, 351,330 children between five and fourteen* years. I select these limits because children are admitted to the public schools under the law at the age of five years, and the statistics of the Board of Education show that the average age of the pupils entering the lowest primary grade is six years and five months. The whole number of different pupils

---

* The fourteenth year is included. The census phrase means "up to 15."

taught in that year was 196,307.* The Catholic schools, parochial and select, reported a total of 35,055; the corporate schools (Children's Aid Society's, Orphan Asylums, American Female Guardian Society's, etc.), 23,276; evening schools, 29,165; Nautical School, 111; all other private schools (as estimated by Superintendent of Schools Jasper), 15,000; total, 298,914; any possible omissions in this list being more than made up for by the thousands over fourteen who are included. So that by deducting the number of pupils from the school population as given above, more than 50,000 children between the ages of five and fourteen are shown to have received no schooling whatever last year. As the public schools had seats for only 195,-592, while the registered attendance exceeded that number, it follows that there was no room for the fifty thousand had they chosen to apply. In fact, the year before, 3783 children had been refused admission at the opening of the schools after the summer vacation because there were no seats for them. To be told in the same breath that there were more than twenty thousand unoccupied seats in the schools at that time is like adding insult to injury. Though vacant and inviting pupils, they were worthless, for they were in the wrong schools. Where the crowding of the growing population was greatest and the need of schooling for the children most urgent, every seat was taken. Those who could not travel far from home—the poor never can—in search of an education had to go without.

The Department of Education employs twelve truant officers, who in 1891 "found and returned to school" 2701 truants. There is a timid sort of pretense that this was "enforcing the compulsory education law," though it is coupled with the statement that at least eight more officers are needed to do it properly, and that they should have power to seize the culprits

---

* The average attendance was only 136,413, so that there were 60,000 who were taught only a small part of the time.

wherever found. Superintendent Jasper tells me that he thinks there are only about 8000 children in New York who do not go to school at all. But the department's own records furnish convincing proof that he is wrong, and that the 50,000 estimate is right. That number is just about one-seventh of the whole number of children between five and fourteen years, as stated above. In January of this year a school census of the Fourth and Fifteenth wards,* two widely separated localities, differing greatly as to character of population, gave the following result: Fourth Ward, total number of children between five and fourteen years, 2016;† of whom 297 did not go to school. Fifteenth Ward, total number of children, 2276; number of non-attendants, 339. In each case the proportion of non-attendants was nearly one-seventh, curiously corroborating the estimate made by me for the whole city.

Testimony to the same effect is borne by a different set of records, those of the reformatories that receive the truants of the city. The Juvenile Asylum, which takes most of those of the Protestant faith, reports that of 28,745 children of school age committed to its care in thirty-nine years 32 per cent could not read when received. The proportion during the last five years was 23 per cent. At the Catholic Protectory, of 3123 boys and girls cared for during the year 1891, 689 were utterly illiterate at the time of their reception and the education of the other 2434 was classified in various degrees between illiterate and "able to read and write" only.‡ The moral status of these last children may be inferred from the statement that 739 of them possessed no religious instruction at all when admitted. The analysis might be extended, doubtless with the same result as to illiteracy, throughout the

* See Minutes of Stated Session of the Board of Education, February 3, 1892.

† Meaning evidently in this case "up to fourteen."

‡ Report of New York Catholic Protectory, 1892.

institutions that harbor the city's dependent children,
to the State Reformatory, where the final product is
set down in 75 per cent of "grossly ignorant" inmates,
in spite of the fact that more than that proportion is
recorded as being of "average natural mental capacity." In other words, they could have learned, had they
been taught.

How much of this bad showing is due to the system,
or the lack of system, of compulsory education, as we
know it in New York, I shall not venture to say. In
such a system a truant school or home would seem to
be a logical necessity. Because a boy does not like to
go to school, he is not necessarily bad. It may be the
fault of the school and of the teacher as much as of
the boy. Indeed, a good many people of sense hold
that the boy who has never planned to run away from
home or school does not amount to much. At all events,
the boy ought not to be classed with thieves and
vagabonds. But that is what New York does. It has no
truant home. Its method of dealing with the truant
is little less than downright savagery. It is thus set
forth in a report of a special committee of the Board
of Education, made to that body on November 18,
1891. "Under the law the truant agents act upon reports received from the principals of the schools. After
exhausting the persuasion that they may be able to
exercise to compel the attendance of truant children,
and in cases which seem to call for the enforcement
of the law, the agent procures the endorsement of the
President of the Board of Education and the Superintendent of Schools upon his requisition for a warrant
for the arrest of the truant, which warrant, under the
provisions of the law, is then issued by a Police Justice. A policeman is then detailed to make the arrest,
and when apprehended, the truant is brought to the
Police Court, where his parents or guardians are
obliged to attend. Should it happen that the latter
are not present, the boy is put in a cell to await their
appearance. It has sometimes happened that a public-

school boy, whose only offense against the law was his
refusal to attend school, has been kept in a cell two or
three days with old criminals pending the appearance
of his parents or guardians.* While we fully realize
the importance of enforcing the laws relating to compulsory education, we believe that bringing the boys
into associations with criminals in this way and making it necessary for parents to be present under such
circumstances is unjust and improper, and that criminal associations of this kind in connection with the
administration of the truancy laws should not be allowed to continue. The Justice may, after hearing the
facts, commit the child, who, in a majority of cases,
is between eight and eleven years old, to one of the
institutions designated by law. We do not think that
the enforcement of the laws relating to compulsory
education should at any time enforce association with
criminal classes."

But it does, all the way through. The "institutions
designated by law" for the reception of truants are
chiefly the Protectory and the Juvenile Asylum. In the
thirty-nine years of its existence the latter has harbored 11,636 children committed to it for disobedi-
ence and truancy. And this was the company they
mingled with there on a common footing: "Unfortunate children," 8806; young thieves, 3097; vagrants,
3173; generally bad boys and girls, 1390; beggars, 542;
children committed for peddling, 51; as witnesses, 50.
Of the whole lot barely a hundred, comprised within
the last two items, might be supposed to be harmless,
though there is no assurance that they were. Of the
Protectory children I have already spoken. It will serve
further to place them to say that nearly one-third of
the 941 received last year were homeless, while fully
35 per cent of all the boys suffered when entering
from the contagious eye disease that is the scourge of

* If this were not the sober statement of public officials of
high repute it would seem fairly incredible.

the poorest tenements as of the public institutions that admit their children. I do not here take into account the House of Refuge, though that is also one of the institutions designated by law for the reception of truants, for the reason that only about one-fifth of those admitted to it last year came from New York City. Their number was 55. The rest came from other counties in the State. But even there the percentage of truants to those committed for stealing or other crimes was as 53 to 47.

This is the "system," or one end of it—the one where the waste goes on. The Committee spoken of reported that the city paid in 1890, $63,690 for the maintenance of the truants committed by magistrates, at the rate of $110 for every child, and that two truant schools and a home for incorrigible truants could be established and maintained at less cost, since it would probably not be necessary to send to the home for incorrigibles more than 25 per cent of all. It further advised the creation of the special office of Truant Commissioner to avoid dragging the children into the police courts. In his report for the present year Superintendent Jasper renews in substance these recommendations. But nothing has been done.

The situation is this, then, that a vast horde of fifty thousand children is growing up in this city whom our public school does not and cannot reach; if it reaches them at all it is with the threat of the jail. The mass of them is no doubt to be found in the shops and factories, as I have shown. A large number peddle newspapers or black boots. Still another contingent, much too large, does nothing but idle, in training for the penitentiary. I stopped one of that kind at the corner of Baxter and Grand Streets one day to catechize him. It was in the middle of the afternoon when the schools were in session, but while I purposely detained him with a long talk to give the neighborhood time to turn out, thirteen other lads of his age, all of them under fourteen, gathered to listen to my business with Grac-

cho. When they had become convinced that I was not
an officer, they frankly owned that they were all playing hookey. All of them lived in the block. How many
more of their kind it sheltered I do not know. They
were not exactly a nice lot, but not one of them would
I have committed to the chance of contact with
thieves with a clear conscience. I should have feared
especial danger from such contact in their case.

As a matter of fact, the record of average attendance (136,413) shows that the public school per se
reaches little more than a third of all the children.
And even those, it does not hold long enough to do
them the good that was intended. The Superintendent
of Schools declares that the average age at which the
children leave school is twelve or a little over. It must
needs be, then, that very many quit much earlier, and
the statement that in New York, as in Chicago, St.
Louis, Brooklyn, New Orleans, and other American
cities, half or more than half the schoolboys leave
school at the age of eleven (the source of the statement is unknown to me) seems credible enough. I
am not going to discuss here the value of school education as a preventive of crime. That it is, so far as it
goes, a positive influence for good I suppose few thinking people doubt nowadays. Dr. William T. Harris,
Federal Commissioner of Education, in an address
delivered before the National Prison Association in
1890, stated that an investigation of the returns of
seventeen states that kept a record of the educational status of their criminals showed the number of
criminals to be eight times as large from the illiterate
stratum as from an equal number of the population
that could read and write. That census was taken in
1870. Ten years later a canvass of the jails of Michigan,
a state that had an illiterate population of less than
five per cent, showed exactly the same ratio, so that I
presume that may safely be accepted.

In view of these facts it does not seem that the
showing the public school is making in New York is

either creditable or safe. It is not creditable, because
the city's wealth grows even faster than its population,* and there is no lack of means with which to
provide schools enough and the machinery to enforce
the law and fill them. Not to enforce it because it
would cost a great deal of money is wicked waste and
folly. It is not safe, because the school is our chief defense against the tenement and the flood of ignorance
with which it would swamp us. Prohibition of child
labor without compelling the attendance at school of
the freed slaves is a mockery. The children are better
off working than idling, any day. The physical objec-
tions to the one alternative are vastly outweighed by
the moral iniquities of the other.

I have tried to set forth the facts. They carry their
own lesson. The then State Superintendent of Education, Andrew Draper, read it aright when, in his report for 1889, he said about the compulsory education
law:

"It does not go far enough and is without an execu-
tor. It is barren of results. . . . It may be safely said
that no system will be effectual in bringing the unfortunate children of the streets into the schools which
at least does not definitely fix the age within which
children must attend the schools, which does not determine the period of the year within which all must
be there, which does not determine the method for
gathering all needed information, which does not provide especial schools for incorrigible cases, which does
not punish people charged with the care of children
for neglecting their education, and which does not
provide the machinery and officials for executing the
system."

* Between 1880 and 1890 the increase in assessed value of
the real and personal property in this city was 48.36 per cent,
while the population increased 41.06 per cent.

WHAT IT IS THAT
MAKES BOYS BAD

—

I am reminded, in trying to show up the causes that go to make children bad, of the experience of a certain sanitary inspector who was laboring with the proprietor of a seven-cent lodginghouse to make him whitewash and clean up. The man had reluctantly given in to several of the inspector's demands; but, as they kept piling up, his irritation grew, until at the mention of clean sheets he lost all patience and said, with bitter contempt, "Well! you needn't tink dem's angels!"

They were not—those lodgers of his—they were tramps. Neither are the children of the street angels. If, once in a while, they act more like little devils, the opportunities we have afforded them, as I have tried to show, hardly give us the right to reproach them. They are not the kind of opportunities to make angels. And yet, looking the hundreds of boys in the Juvenile Asylum over, all of whom were supposed to be there because they were bad (though, as I had occasion to ascertain, that was a mistake—it was the parents that were bad in some cases), I was struck by the fact that they were anything but a depraved lot. Except as to their clothes and their manners, which were the manners of the street, they did not seem to be very different in looks from a like number of boys in any public school. Fourth of July was just then at hand, and when I asked the official who accompanied me how they proposed to celebrate it, he said that they were in the habit of marching in procession up Eleventh Avenue to Fort George, across to Washington Bridge, and all about the neighborhood, to a grove where speeches were made. Remembering the iron bars and high fences I had seen, I said something about it being unsafe to let a thousand young prisoners go at large in that way. The man looked at me in some bewilderment before he understood.

"Bless you, no!" he said, when my meaning dawned upon him. "If any one of them was to run away that day he would be in eternal disgrace with all the rest. It is a point of honor with them to deserve it when they are trusted. Often we put a boy on duty outside, when he could walk off, if he chose, just as well as not; but he will come in in the evening, as straight as a string, only, perhaps, to twist his bedclothes into a rope that very night and let himself down from a third-story window, at the risk of breaking his neck. Boys will be boys, you know."

But it struck me that boys whose honor could be successfully appealed to in that way were rather the victims than the doers of a grievous wrong, being in that place, no matter if they *had* stolen. It was a case of misdirection, or no direction at all, of their youthful energies. There was one little fellow in the Asylum band who was a living illustration of this. I watched him blow his horn with a supreme effort to be heard above the rest, growing redder and redder in the face, until the perspiration rolled off him in perfect sheets, the veins stood out swollen and blue and it seemed as if he must burst the next minute. He was a tremendous trumpeter. I was glad when it was over, and patted him on the head, telling him that if he put as much vim into all he had to do, as he did into his horn, he would come to something great yet. Then it occurred to me to ask him what he was there for.

"'Cause I was lazy and played hookey," he said, and joined in the laugh his answer raised. The idea of that little body, that fairly throbbed with energy, being sent to prison for laziness was too absurd for anything.

The report that comes from the Western Agency of the Asylum, through which the boys are placed out on farms, that the proportion of troublesome children is growing larger does not agree with the idea of laziness either, but well enough with the idleness of the street, which is what sends nine-tenths of the boys to the Asylum. Satan finds plenty of mischief for the idle hands of these lads to do. The one great point is to give them something to do—something they can see the end of, yet that will keep them busy right along. The more ignorant the child, the more urgent this rule, the shorter and simpler the lesson must be. Over in the Catholic Protectory, where they get the most ignorant boys, they appreciate this to the extent of encouraging the boys to a game of Sunday baseball rather than see them idle even for the briefest spell. Of the practical wisdom of their course there can be no question.

"I have come to the conclusion," said a well-known educator on a recent occasion, "that much of crime is a question of athletics." From over the sea the Earl of Meath adds his testimony: "Three-fourths of the youthful rowdyism of large towns is owing to the stupidity, and, I may add, cruelty, of the ruling powers in not finding some safety valve for the exuberant energies of the boys and girls of their respective cities." For our neglect to do so in New York we are paying heavily in the maintenance of these costly reform schools. I spoke of the chance for romping and play where the poor children crowd. In a Cherry Street hallway I came across this sign in letters a foot long: "No ball playing, dancing, card playing, and no persons but tenants allowed in the yard." It was a five-story tenement, swarming with children, and there was another just as big across that yard. Out in the street the policeman saw to it that the ball playing at least was stopped, and as for the dancing, that, of course, was bound to collect a crowd, the most heinous offense known to him as a preserver of the peace. How the peace was preserved by such means I saw on the occasion of my discovering that sign. The business that took me down there was a murder in another tenement just like it. A young man, hardly more than a boy, was killed in the course of a midnight "can racket" on the roof, in which half the young people in the block had a hand night after night. It was *their* outlet for the "exuberant energies" of their natures. The safety valve was shut, with the landlord and the policeman holding it down.

It is when the wrong outlet has thus been forced that the right and natural one has to be reopened with an effort as the first condition of reclaiming the boy. The play in him has all run to "toughness," and has first to be restored. "We have no great hope of a boy's reformation," writes Mr. William F. Round, of the Burnham Industrial Farm, to a friend who has shown me his letter, "till he takes an active part and interest in outdoor amusements. Plead with all your might for playgrounds for the city waifs and school children. When the lungs are freely expanded, the blood coursing with a bound through all veins and arteries, the whole mind and body in a state of high emulation in wholesome play, there is no time or place for wicked thought or consequent wicked action and the body is growing every moment more able to help in the battle against temptation when it shall come at other times and places. Next time another transit company asks a franchise, make them furnish tickets to the parks and suburbs to all school children on all holidays and Saturdays, the same to be given out in school for regular attendance, as a method of health promotion and a preventive of truancy." Excellent scheme! If we could only make them. It is five years and over now since we made them pass a law at Albany appropriating a million dollars a year for the laying out of small parks in the most crowded tenement districts, in the Mulberry Street Bend for instance, and practically we stand today where we stood then. The Mulberry Street

Bend is still there, with no sign of a park or play-ground other than in the gutter. When I asked, a year ago, why this was so, I was told by the Counsel to the Corporation that it was because "not much interest had been taken" by the previous administration in the matter. Is it likely that a corporation that runs a rail-road to make money could be prevailed upon to take more interest in a proposition to make it surrender part of its profits than the city's sworn officers in their bounden duty? Yet let anyone go and see for himself what effect such a park has in a crowded tenement district. Let him look at Tompkins Square Park as it is today and compare the children that skip among the trees and lawns and around the bandstand with those that root in the gutters only a few blocks off. That was the way they looked in Tompkins Square twenty years ago when the square was a sandlot given up to riot-ing and disorder. The police had their hands full then. I remember being present when they had to take the square by storm more than once, and there is at least one captain on the force today who owes his promo-tion to the part he took and the injuries he suffered in one of those battles. Today it is as quiet and orderly a neighborhood as any in the city. Not a squeak has been heard about "bread or blood" since those trees were planted and the lawns and flower beds laid out. It is not all the work of the missions, the kindergartens, and boys' clubs and lodginghouses, of which more anon; nor even the larger share. The park did it, ex-actly as the managers of the Juvenile Asylum ap-pealed to the sense of honor in their prisoners. It ap-pealed with its trees and its grass and its birds to the sense of decency and of beauty, undeveloped but not smothered, in the children, and the whole neighbor-hood responded. One can go around the whole square that covers two big blocks, nowadays, and not come upon a single fight. I should like to see anyone walk that distance in Mulberry Street without running across half a dozen.

Thus far the street and its idleness as factors in making criminals of the boys. Of the factory I have spoken. Certainly it is to be preferred to the street, if the choice must be between the two. Its offense is that it makes a liar of the boy and keeps him in ignorance, even of a useful trade, thus blazing a wide path for him straight to the prison gate. The school does not come to the rescue; the child must come to the school, and even then is not sure of a welcome. The trade unions do their worst for the boy by robbing him of the slim chance to learn a trade which the factory left him. Of the tenement I have said enough. Apart from all other considerations and influences, as the destroyer of character and individuality everywhere, it is the wickedest of all the forces that attack the defenseless child. The tenements are increasing in number, and so is "the element that becomes criminal because of lack of individuality and the self-respect that comes with it."*

I am always made to think in connection with this subject of a story told me by a bright little woman of her friend's kittens. There was a litter of them in the house and a jealous terrier dog to boot, whose one aim in life was to get rid of its mewing rivals. Out in the garden where the children played there was a sand heap and the terrier's trick was to bury alive in the sand any kitten it caught unawares. The children were constantly rushing to the rescue and unearthing their pets; on the day when my friend was there on a visit they were too late. The first warning of the tragedy in the garden came to the ladies when one of the children rushed in, all red and excited, with bulging eyes. "There," she said, dropping the dead kitten out of her apron before them, "a perfectly good cat spoiled!"

Perfectly good children, as good as any on the Avenue, are spoiled every day by the tenement; only we

* Philosophy of Crime and Punishment, by Dr. William T. Harris, Federal Commissioner of Education.

have not done with them then, as the terrier had with the kitten. There is still posterity to reckon with.

What this question of heredity amounts to, whether in the past or in the future, I do not know. I have not had opportunity enough of observing. No one has that I know of. Those who have had the most disagree in their conclusions, or have come to none. I have known numerous instances of criminality, running apparently in families for generations, but there was always the desperate environment as the unknown factor in the make-up. Whether that bore the greatest share of the blame, or whether the reformation of the criminal to be effective should have begun with his grandfather, I could not tell. Besides, there was always the chance that the great-grandfather, or someone still farther back, of whom all trace was lost, might have been a paragon of virtue, even if his descendant was a thief, and so there was no telling just where to begin. In general I am inclined to think with such practical philanthropists as Superintendent Barnard, of the Five Points House of Industry, the Manager of the Children's Aid Society, Superintendent E. Fellows Jenkins, of the Society for the Prevention of Cruelty to Children, and Mr. Israel C. Jones, who for more than thirty years was in charge of the House of Refuge, that the bugbear of heredity is not nearly as formidable as we have half taught ourselves to think. It is rather a question of getting hold of the child early enough before the evil influences surrounding him have got a firm grip on him. Among a mass of evidence quoted in support of this belief, perhaps this instance, related by Superintendent Jones in *The Independent* last March, is as convincing as any:

Thirty years ago there was a depraved family living adjacent to what is now a part of the city of New York. The mother was not only dishonest, but exceedingly intemperate, wholly neglectful of her duties as a mother, and frequently served terms in jail until she finally died. The father was also dissipated and neglectful. It was a miserable existence for the children.

Two of the little boys, in connection with two other boys in the neighborhood, were arrested, tried, and found guilty of entering a house in the daytime and stealing. In course of time both of these boys were indentured. One remained in his place and the other left for another part of the country, where he died. He was a reputable lad.

The first boy, in one way and another, got a few pennies together with which he purchased books. After a time he proposed to his master that he be allowed to present himself for examination as a teacher. The necessary consent was given, he presented himself, and was awarded a "grade A" certificate.

Two years from that time he came to the House of Refuge, as proud as a man could be, and exhibited to me his certificate. He then entered a law office, diligently pursued his studies, and was admitted to the bar. He was made a judge, and is now chief magistrate of the court in the city where he lives.

His sister, a little girl, used to come to the Refuge with her mother, wearing nothing but a thin cloak in very cold weather, almost perishing with the cold. As soon as this young man got on his feet he rescued the little girl. He placed her in a school; she finally graduated from the Normal School, and today holds an excellent position in the schools in the state where she lives.

The records of the three reformatory institutions before mentioned throw their own light upon the question of what makes criminals of the young. At the Elmira Reformatory, of more than five thousand prisoners only a little over one per cent were shown to have kept good company prior to their coming there.

One and a half per cent are put down under this head as "doubtful," while the character of association is recorded for 41.2 per cent as "not good," and for 55.9 per cent as "positively bad." Three-fourths possessed no culture or only the slightest. As to moral sense, 42.6 per cent had absolutely none, 35 per cent "possibly some." Only 7.6 per cent came from good homes. Of the rest 39.8 per cent had homes that are recorded as "fair only," and 52.6 per cent downright bad homes; 4.8 per cent had pauper, and 76.8 per cent poor parents; 38.4 per cent of the prisoners had drunken parents, and 13 per cent parents of doubtful sobriety. Of more than twenty-two thousand inmates of the Juvenile Asylum in thirty-nine years one-fourth had either a drunken father or mother, or both. At the Protectory the percentage of drunkenness in parents was not quite one-fifth among over three thousand children cared for in the institution last year.

There is never any lack of trashy novels and cheap shows in New York, and the children who earn money selling newspapers or otherwise take to them as ducks do to water. They fall in well with the ways of the street that are showy always, however threadbare may be the cloth. As for that, it is simply the cheap side of our national extravagance.

The cigarette, if not a cause, is at least the mean accessory of half the mischief of the street. And I am not sure it is not a cause too. It is an inexorable creditor that has goaded many a boy to stealing; for cigarettes cost money, and they do not encourage industry. Of course there is a law against the cigarette, or rather against the boy smoking it who is not old enough to work—there is law in plenty, usually, if that would only make people good. It doesn't in the matter of the cigarette. It helps make the boy bad by adding the relish of lawbreaking to his enjoyment of the smoke. Nobody stops him.

The mania for gambling is all but universal. Every street child is a born gambler; he has nothing to lose and all to win. He begins by "shooting craps" in the street and ends by "chucking dice" in the saloon, two names for the same thing, sure to lead to the same goal. By the time he has acquired individual standing in the saloon, his long apprenticeship has left little or nothing for him to learn of the bad it has to teach. Never for his own sake is he turned away with the growler when he comes to have it filled; once in a while for the saloonkeeper's, if that worthy suspects in him a decoy and a "job." Just for the sake of the experiment, not because I expected it to develop anything new, I chose at random, while writing this chapter, a saloon in a tenement-house district on the East Side and posted a man, whom I could trust implicitly, at the door with orders to count the children under age who went out and in with beer jugs in open defiance of law. Neither he nor I had ever been in or even seen the saloon before. He reported as the result of three and a half hours' watch at noon and in the evening a total of fourteen—ten boys and a girl under ten years of age, and three girls between ten and fourteen years, not counting a little boy who bought a bottle of ginger. It was a cool, damp day; not a thirsty day, or the number would probably have been twice as great. There was not the least concealment about the transaction in any of the fourteen cases. The children were evidently old customers.

The law that failed to save the boy while there was time yet to make a useful citizen of him provides the means of catching him when his training begins to bear fruit that threatens the public peace. Then it is with the same blundering disregard of common sense and common decency that marked his prosecution as a truant that the half-grown lad is dragged into a police court and thrust into a prison pen with hardened thieves and criminals to learn the lessons they have to teach him. The one thing New York needs most after a truant home is a special court for the trial of youthful offenders only. I am glad to say that this want

seems at last in a way to be supplied. The last legislature authorized the establishment of such a court,
and it may be that even as these pages see the light
this blot upon our city is about to be wiped out.

Lastly, but not least, the Church is to blame for deserting the poor in their need. It is an old story that
the churches have moved uptown with the wealth and
fashion, leaving the poor crowds to find their way to
heaven as best they could, and that the crowds have
paid them back in their own coin by denying that they,
the churches, knew the way at all. The Church has
something to answer for; but it is a healthy sign at
least that it is accepting the responsibility and profess-
ing anxiety to meet it. In much of the best work done
among the poor and for the poor it has lately taken the
lead, and it is not likely that any more of the churches
will desert the downtown field, with the approval of
Christian men and women at least.

Little enough of the light I promised in the opening
chapter has struggled through these pages so far. We
have looked upon the dark side of the picture; but
there is a brighter. If the battle with ignorance, with
misery, and with vice has but just begun, if the army
that confronts us is strong, too strong, in numbers still
and in malice—the gauntlet has been thrown down,
the war waged, and blows struck that tell. They augur
victory, for we have cut off the enemy's supplies and
turned his flank. As I showed in the case of the immigrant Jews and the Italians, we have captured his
recruits. With a firm grip on these, we may hope to
win, for the rest of the problem ought to be and *can*
be solved. With our own we should be able to settle, if
there is any virtue in our school and our system of government. In this, as in all things, the public conscience
must be stirred before the community's machinery for
securing justice can move. That it has been stirred,
profoundly and to useful purpose, the multiplication
in our day of charities for attaining the ends the law

has failed to reach, gives evidence. Their number is so great that mention can be made here merely of a few of the most important and typical efforts along the line. A register of all those that deal with the children especially, as compiled by the Charity Organization Society, will be found in an appendix to this book. Before we proceed to look at the results achieved through endeavors to stop the waste down at the bottom by private reinforcement of the public school, we will glance briefly at two of the charities that have a plainer purpose—if I may so put it without disparagement to the rest—that look upon the child merely as a child worth saving for its own sake, because it is helpless and poor and wretched. Both of them represent distinct departures in charitable work. Both, to the everlasting credit of our city be it said, had their birth here, and in this generation, and from New York their blessings have been carried to the farthest lands. One is the Society for the Prevention of Cruelty to Children, known far and near now as the Children's Society, whose strong and beneficent plan has been embodied in the structure of law of half the civilized nations of the world. The other, always spoken of as the "Fresh Air Fund," never had law or structural organization of any kind, save the law of love, laid down on the Mount for all time; but the life of that divine command throbs in it and has touched the heart of mankind wherever its story has been told.

PLATE 9.
Slept in That Cellar Four Years,
About 1890.

9. PHOTOGRAPH: *Jacob A. Riis, the Jacob A. Riis Collection, Museum of the City of New York.*

PLATE 10.
Talmud School on Hester Street.

10. PHOTOGRAPH: *Jacob A. Riis, the Jacob A. Riis
Collection, Museum of the City of New York.*

PLATE 11.
Baxter Street Court, 22 Baxter Street.

11. PHOTOGRAPH: *Jacob A. Riis, the Jacob A. Riis Collection, Museum of the City of New York.*

PLATE 12.
A Class in the Condemned Essex
Market School, Early 1890s.

12. PHOTOGRAPH: *Jacob A. Riis, the Jacob A. Riis
Collection, Museum of the City of New York.*

PLATE 13.
Bathtub in Airshaft.

13. PHOTOGRAPH: *Jacob A. Riis, the Jacob A. Riis Collection, Museum of the City of New York.*

PLATE 14.
Street Arabs in the Area of Mulberry
Street.

*14. PHOTOGRAPH: Jacob A. Riis, the Jacob A. Riis
Collection, Museum of the City of New York.*

PLATE 15.
Lost Child at Police Headquarters,
About 1890.

15. PHOTOGRAPH: *Jacob A. Riis, the Jacob A. Riis Collection, Museum of the City of New York.*

PLATE 16.
Child of the Tenement.

16. PHOTOGRAPH: *Jacob A. Riis, the Jacob A. Riis Collection, Museum of the City of New York.*

THE KINDERGARTENS
AND NURSERIES

If the influence of an annual cleaning up is thus distinctly traced in the lives of the children, what must be the effect of the daily teaching of the kindergarten, in which soap is always the moral agent that leads all the rest? I have before me the inventory of purchases for a single school of this kind that was started a year ago in a third loft of a Suffolk Street tenement. It included several boxes of soap and soap dishes, 200 feet of rope, 10 beanbags, 24 tops, 200 marbles, a box of chalk, a baseball outfit for indoor use, a supply of tiddledy-winks and "sliced animals," and 20 clay pipes. The pipes were not for lessons in smoking, but to smooth the way for a closer acquaintance with the soap by the friendly intervention of the soap bubble. There were other games and no end of colored paper to cut up, the dear delight of childhood, but made in the hands and under the eyes of the teacher to train eye and hand while gently but firmly cementing the friendship ushered in by the gorgeous bubble. No wonder, with such a stock, a mother complained that she had to whip her Jimmie to keep him home.

Without a doubt the kindergarten is one of the longest steps forward that has yet been taken in the race with poverty; for in gathering in the children it is gradually, but surely, conquering also the street with its power for mischief. There is only one force that, to my mind, exerts an even stronger influence upon the boys' lives especially; I mean the club, of which I shall speak presently. But that comes at a later stage. The kindergarten begins at the very beginning, and in the best of all ways, with the children's play. What it does, counts at both ends on that tack. Very soon it makes itself felt in the street and in what goes on there, as anyone can see for himself by observing the children's play in a tenement neighborhood where there is a kindergarten and again where there is none, while by imperceptibly turning the play into work that teaches habits of observation and of industry that stick, it builds a strong barrier against the doctrine of the slum that the world owes one a living, which lies in ambush for the lad on every grog-shop corner. And all corners in the tenement districts are grog-shop corners. Beyond all other considerations, beyond its now admitted function as the right beginning of all education, whether of rich or poor, its war upon the street stands to me as the true office of the kindergarten in a city like New York, with a tenement-house population of a million and a quarter souls.* The street itself owns it, with virtual surrender. Hostile as its normal attitude is to every new agency of reform, the best with the worst, I have yet to hear of the first instance in which a kindergarten has been molested by the toughest neighborhood, or has started a single dead cat on a post-mortem career of window smashing, whether it sprang from Christian, Jewish, or heathen humanity. There is scarce a mission or a boy's club in the city that can say as much.

The kindergarten is no longer an experiment in New York. Probably as many as a hundred are today in operation, or will be when the recently expressed purpose of the Board of Education to make the kindergarten a part of the public school system has been fully carried out. The Children's Aid Society alone conducts a dozen in connection with its industrial schools,

* The Superintendent of the House of Refuge for thirty years wrote recently: "It is essential to have the plays of the children more carefully watched than their work."

and the New York Kindergarten Association nine, if its intention of opening two new schools by the time this book is in the printer's hands is realized. There is no theology, though there is a heap of religion in most of them. Protestants, Catholics, Jews, Theosophists, and Ethical Culturists, if I may so call them, men of one or of various opinions, or of none, concerning the hereafter, alike make use of the kindergarten as a means of reaching and saving the shipwrecked of the present. Sometimes the Sunday School is made to serve as a feeder for the kindergarten, or the kindergarten for the Sunday School. Sometimes the wisdom that wrests success from doubt and perplexity is expressed in the fundamental resolution that the kindergarten "shall not be a Sunday School." The system is the same in all cases with very little change. "We have tried it and seen it tried with various kinks and variations," said one of the old managers of the Children's Aid Society to me, "but after all there is only one way, the way of the great kindergartner who said, 'We learn by doing.'"

A clean face is the ticket of admission to the kindergarten. A clean or whole frock is wisely not insisted upon too firmly at the start; torn or dirty clothes are not so easily mended as a smudged face, but the kindergarten reaches that too in the end, and by the same road as the Fresh Air scrubbing—the home. Once he is let in, the child is in for a general good time that has little of school or visible discipline to frighten him. He joins in the ring for the familiar games, delighted to find that the teacher knows them too, and can be "It" and his "fair lady" in her turn. He does not notice the little changes the game has undergone, the kindergarten touch here and there that lifts it out of the mud; but the street does presently, when the new version is transferred to it, and is the better for it. After the game there are a hundred things for him to do that do not seem like work in the least. Between threading colored beads, cutting and folding pink and green papers in all sorts of odd ways, as boats and butterflies and fancy baskets; molding, pasting, drawing, weaving and blowing soap bubbles when all the rest has ceased to hold his attention, the day slips by like a beautiful dream, and he flatly refuses to believe that it is gone when the tenement home claims him again. Not infrequently he goes home howling, to be found the next morning waiting at the door an hour before the teacher comes. Little Jimmie's mother says that he gets up at six o'clock to go to the Fifty-first Street kindergarten, and that she has to whip him to make him wait until nine.

The hours pass with happy play that slowly but surely molds head, hand, and heart together. The utmost freedom is allowed, but it stops short of the license of the street. Its law of violence is replaced by the law of love. The child learns to govern himself. Not at once; I observed two or three black eyes during a tour of a half-score kindergartens, last June, that showed that the street yielded its reign reluctantly. During my visit to the East Sixty-third Street school I became interested in a little fellow who was its special pet and the ward of the alumnæ of the normal college, who through the New York Kindergarten Association had established and maintained the school. Johnny was a sweet little fellow, one of eight children from a wretched tenement home down the street into which the kindergartner had found her way. The youngest of the eight was a baby that was getting so big and heavy that it half killed the mother to drag it around when she went out working, and the father, with a consideration for her that was generously tempered with laziness, was considering the advisability of staying home to take care of it himself, "so as to give her a show." There was a refinement of look and manner, if not of dress, about little Johnny after he was washed clean, that made the tenement setting seem entirely too plebeian for him, and his rescuers had high hopes of his future. I regret to say that I saw the pet, before I left, deliberately knock the smallest baby in the school down, and when he was banished from the ring in consequence and condemned to take his howling playmate over in the corner and show her pictures until he repented, take an unworthy revenge by pinching her surreptitiously until she howled louder. Worse than that, when the baby had finally been comforted with a headless but squeaking toy sheep, he secretly pulled the insides and the ba-a out of the lambkin through its broken neck, when no one was looking. I was told that Johnny was believed to have the making of a diplomat in his little five-year-old body, and I think it very likely—of a politician anyway.

While this was going on, another boy, twice as large as Johnny, had been temporarily exiled from the ring for clumsiness. It was even more hopelessly constitutional, to all appearances, than Johnny's Machiavelian cunning. In the game he had persistently stumbled over his own feet. Made to take a seat at the long table, he fell off his chair twice in one minute from sheer embarrassment. In luminous contrast to his awkwardness was the desperate agility of a little Irishman I had just left in another kindergarten. Each time he was told to take his seat, which was about every ten seconds, he would perform the feat with great readiness by climbing over the back of the chair as a dog climbs over a fence, to the consternation of the teacher, whose reproachful "O Alexander!" he disarmed with a cheerful "I'm all right, Miss Brown," and an offer to shake hands.

Let it not be inferred from this that the kindergarten is the home of disorder. Just the reverse. Order and prompt obedience are the cardinal virtues taught there, but taught in such a way as to make the lesson seem all fun and play to the child. It sticks all the better. It is the province of the kindergarten to rediscover, as it were, the natural feelings the tenement had smothered. But for its appeal, the love of the beautiful might slumber in those children forever. In their

homes there is nothing to call it into life. The ideal of
the street is caricature, burlesque, if nothing worse.
Under the gentle training of the kindergartner the
slumbering instinct blossoms forth in a hundred different ways, from the day the little one first learns the difference between green and red by stringing colored
beads for a necklace "for teacher," until later on he is
taught to make really pretty things of pasteboard and
chips to take home for papa and mamma to keep. And
they do keep them, proud of the child—who would
not?—and their influence is felt where mayhap there
was darkness and dirt only before. So the kindergarten
reaches directly into the home, too, and thither follows
the teacher, if she is the right kind, with encouragement and advice that is not lost either. No door is
barred against her who comes in the children's name.
In the truest and best sense she is a missionary to the
poor.

Nearly all the kindergartens in this city are crowded.
Many have scores of applicants upon the register
whom they cannot receive. There are no truants
among their pupils. All of the New York Kindergarten
Association's schools are crowded, and new are added
as fast as the necessary funds are contributed. The Association was organized in the fall of 1889 with
the avowed purpose of engrafting the kindergarten
upon the public school system of the city, through persistent agitation. There had been no official recognition of it up till that time. The normal-school kindergarten was an experiment not countenanced by the
School Board. The Association has now accomplished
its purpose, but its work, far from being ended, has but
just begun. It is doubtful if all the kindergartens in the
city, including those now in the public schools, accommodate much more than five or six thousand children,
if that number. The last sanitary census showed that
there were 160,708 children under five years old in the
tenements. At least half of these are old enough to be
in a kindergarten, and ought to be, seeing how little

schooling they will get after they outgrow it. That leaves in round numbers 75,000 children yet to be so provided for in New York's tenements. There is no danger that the kindergarten will become too "common" in this city for a while yet. As an adjunct to the public school in preparing the young minds for more serious tasks, it is admitted by teachers to be most valuable. But its greatest success is as a jail deliverer. "The more kindergartens the fewer prisons" is a saying the truth of which the generation that comes after us will be better able to grasp than we.

The kindergarten is the city's best truant officer. Not only has it no truants itself, but it ferrets out a lot who are truants from necessity, not from choice, and delivers them over to the public school. There are lots of children who are kept at home because someone has to mind the baby while father and mother earn the bread for the little mouths. The kindergarten steps in and releases these little prisoners. If the baby is old enough to hop around with the rest, the kindergarten takes it. If it can only crawl and coo, there is the nursery annex. Sometimes it is an independent concern. Almost every church or charity that comes into direct touch with the poor has nowadays its nursery where poor mothers may leave their children to be cared for while they are out working. Relief more practical could not be devised. A small fee, usually five cents, is charged as a rule for each baby. Pairs come cheaper, and three go for ten cents at the nursery in the Wilson mission. Over 50,000 babies were registered there last year, which meant, if not 5000 separate children, at least 5000 days' work and wages to poor mothers in dire need of both, and a good, clean, healthy start for the infants, a better [one] than the tenement could have given them. To keep them busy, when the rocking horse and the picture book have lost their charm, the kindergarten grows naturally out of the nursery, where that was the beginning, just as the nursery stepped in to supplement the kindergarten where that had the lead. The two go hand in hand. The soap cure is even more potent in the nursery than in the kindergarten, as a silent rebuke to the mother, who rarely fails to take the hint. At the Five Points House of Industry the children who come in for the day receive a general scrubbing twice a week, and the whole neighborhood has a cleaner look after it. The establishment has come to be known among the ragamuffins of Paradise Park as "the school where dey washes 'em." Its value as a moral agent may be judged from the statements of the Superintendent that some of the children "cried at the sight of a wash tub," as if it were some new and hideous instrument of torture for their oppression.

Private benevolence in this, as in all measures for the relief of the poor, has been a long way ahead of public action; properly so, though it has seemed sometimes that we might as a body make a little more haste and try to catch up. It has lately, by the establishment of children's playgrounds in certain tenement districts, west and east, provided a kind of open-air kindergarten that has hit the street in a vital spot. These playgrounds do not take the place of the small parks which the city has neglected to provide, but they show what a boon these will be some day. There are at present, as far as I know, three of them, not counting the backyard "beaches" and "Coney Islands," that have made the practical missionaries of the College Settlement, the King's Daughters' Tenement Chapter, and like helpers of the poor solid with their little friends. One of them, the largest, is in Ninety-second Street, on the East Side, another at the foot of West Fiftieth Street, and still another in West Twenty-eighth Street, between Tenth and Eleventh Avenues, the block long since well named Poverty Gap. Two, three, or half a dozen vacant lots, borrowed or leased of the owner, have been leveled out, a few loads of sand dumped in them for the children to dig in; scups, swings, and seesaws, built of rough timber; a hydrant in the corner;

little wheelbarrows, toy spades and pails to go round, and the outfit is complete. Two at least of the three are supported each by a single generous woman, who pays the salaries of a man janitor and of two women "teachers" who join in the children's play, strike up "America" and the "Star Spangled Banner" when they tire of "Sally in our Alley" and "Ta-ra-ra-boom-de-ay," and by generally taking a hand in what goes on manage to steer it into safe and mannerly ways.

More than two hundred children were digging, swinging, seesawing, and cavorting about the Poverty Gap playground when I looked in on a hot Saturday afternoon last July. Long files of eager girls, whose shrill voices used to make the echoes of the Gap ring with angry clamor, awaited their turn at the scups, quiet as mice and without an ill word when they trod upon each other's toes. The street that used to swarm with mischievous imps was as quiet as a church. The policeman on the beat stood swinging his club idly in the gate. It was within sight of this spot that the Alley Gang beat one of his comrades half to death for telling them to go home and let decent people pass; the same gang which afterward murdered young Healey for the offense of being a decent, hard-working lad, who was trying to support his aged father and mother by his work. The Healeys lived in one of the rear houses that stood where the children now skip at their play, and the murder was done on his doorstep. The next morning I found the gang camping on a vacant floor in the adjoining den, as if nothing had happened. The tenants knew the toughs were there, but were afraid of betraying them. All that was only a couple of years ago; but a marvelous transformation had been wrought in the Gap. The toughs were gone, with the old tenements that harbored them. Poverty Gap itself was gone. A decent flat had taken the place of the shanty across the street where a longshoreman kicked his wife to death in drunken rage. And this playground, with its swarms of happy children who a year ago

would have pelted the stranger with mud from behind the nearest truck—that was the greatest change
of all. The retiring toughs have dubbed it "Holy Terror
Park" in memory of what it was, not of what it is. Poverty Park the policeman called it, with more reason.
It was not exactly an attractive place. A single stunted
ailanthus tree struggled over the fence of the adjoining
yard, the one green spot between ugly and ragged
brick walls. The "sand" was as yet all mud and dirt,
and the dust the many little feet kicked up was smothering. But the children thought it lovely, and lovely it
was for Poverty Gap, if not for Fifth Avenue.

I came back to my office to find a letter there from a
rich man who lives on the Avenue, offering to make
another Poverty Park for the tenement-house children
of another street if he had to buy the lots. I told him
the story of Poverty Gap and bade him go and see for
himself if he could spend his money to better purpose.
There are no playgrounds yet below Fourteenth Street
and room and need for fifty. The Alley and the Avenue
could not meet on a plane that argues better for the
understanding between the two that has been too long
and needlessly delayed.

THE INDUSTRIAL
SCHOOLS

That "dirt is a disease," and their mission to cure it, was the new gospel which the managers of the Children's Aid Society carried to the slums a generation ago. In practice they have not departed from their profession. Their pill is the industrial school, their plaster a western farm and a living chance in exchange for the tenement and the city slum. The wonder cures they have wrought by such simple treatment have been many. In the executive chair of a sovereign State sits today a young man who remembers with gratitude and pride the day they took him in hand and, of the material the street would have molded into a tough, made an honorable man and a governor. And from among the men whose careers of usefulness began in the Society's schools, and who today, as teachers, ministers, lawyers, and editors, are conspicuous ornaments of the communities, far and near, in which they have made their homes, he would have no difficulty in choosing a cabinet that would do credit and honor to his government. Prouder monument could be erected to no man's memory than this record at the grave of the late Charles Loring Brace, the founder of the Children's Aid Society.

The industrial school plants itself squarely in the gap between the tenement and the public school. If it does not fill it, it at least spreads itself over as much of it as it can, and in that position demonstrates that this land of lost or missing opportunities is not the barren ground once supposed, but of all soil the most fruitful, if properly tilled. Wherever the greatest and the poorest crowds are, there also is the industrial school. The Children's Aid Society maintains twenty-one in seventeen of the city's twenty-four wards, not counting twelve evening schools, five of which are in the Society's lodginghouses. It is not alone in the field. The American Female Guardian Society conducts twelve such day schools, and individual efforts in the same direction are not wanting. The two societies' schools last year reached a total enrollment of nearly fifteen thousand children, and an average attendance of almost half that number. Slum children, all of them. Only such are sought and admitted. The purpose of the schools, in the language of the last report of the Children's Aid Society, whose work, still carried on with the aggressive enthusiasn that characterized its founder, may well be taken as typical and representative in this field, "is to receive and educate children who cannot be accepted by the public schools, either by reason of their ragged and dirty condition, or owing to the fact that they can attend but part of the time, because they are obliged to sell papers or to stay at home to help their parents. The children at our schools belong to the lowest and poorest class of people in the city." They are children, therefore, who to a very large extent speak another language at home than the one they come to school to learn, and often have to work their way in by pantomime. It is encouraging to know that these schools are almost always crowded to their utmost capacity.

A census of the Society's twenty-one day schools, that was taken last April, showed that they contained that day 5132 pupils, of whom 198 were kindergarten children under five years of age, 2347 between five and seven, and 2587 between eight and fourteen years of age. Considerably more than ten per cent—the exact number was 571—did not understand questions put to them in English. They were there waiting to "catch on," silent but attentive observers of what was going on, until such time as they should be ready to take a hand in it themselves. Divided according to nativity, 2082 of the children were found to be of foreign birth. They hailed from twenty-two different countries; 3050 were born in this country, but they were able to show only 1009 native parents out of 6991 whose pedigrees could be obtained. The other 5176 were foreign born, and only 810 of them claimed English as their mother tongue. This was the showing the chief nationalities made in the census:

Born in	Children	Parents
United States	3050	1009
Italy	1066	2354
Germany	460	1819
Bohemia	198	720
Ireland	98	583

At that time the Jewish children were crowding into the Monroe Street and some other schools, at a rate that promised to put them in complete possession before long. Upon this lowest level, as upon every other where they come into competition with the children of Christian parents, they distanced them easily, taking all the prizes that were to be had for regular attendance, proficiency in studies, and good conduct generally. Generally these prizes consisted of shoes or much-needed clothing. Often, as in the Monroe Street School, the bitter poverty of the homes that gave up the children to the school because there they would receive the one square meal of the day, made a loaf of bread the most acceptable reward, and the teachers gladly took advantage of it as the means of forging another link in the chain to bind home and school, parents, children, and teachers firmly together.

This "square meal" is a chief element in the educational plan of most of the schools, because very often it is the one hot meal the little ones receive—not infrequently, as I have said, the only one of the day that is worthy of the name. It is not an elaborate or expensive affair, though substantial and plentiful. At the West Side Industrial School, on Seventh Avenue, where one day not long ago I watched a file of youngsters crowding into the dining room with glistening eyes and happy faces, the cost of the dinners averaged 2½ cents last year. In a specimen month they served there 4080 meals and compared this showing gleefully with the record of the old School in Twenty-ninth Street, nine years before. The largest number of dinners served there in any one month, was 2666. It is perhaps a somewhat novel way of measuring the progress of a school: by the amount of eating done on the premises. But it is a very practical one, as the teachers have found out. Yet it is not used as a bait. Care is taken that only those are fed who would otherwise go without their dinner, and it is served only in winter, when the need of "something warm" is imperative. In the West Side School, as in most of the others, the dinners are furnished by some one or more practical philanthropists, whose pockets as well as their hearts are in the work. The schools themselves, like the Society's lodginghouses for homeless children, stand as lasting monuments to a Christian charity that asks no other reward than the consciousness of having done good where the need was great. Sometimes the very name of the generous giver is unknown to all the world save the men who built as he or she directed. The benefactor is quite as often a devoted woman as a rich and charitable man, who hides his munificence under a modesty unsuspected by a community that applauds and envies his shrewd and successful business ventures, but never hears of the investment that paid him and it best of all.

According to its location, the school is distinctively Italian, Bohemian, Hebrew or mixed; the German, Irish, and colored children coming in under this head, and mingling usually without the least friction. The

Leonard Street School and the West Side Italian School in Sullivan Street are devoted wholly to the little swarthy Southerners. In the Leonard Street School alone there were between five and six hundred Italian children on the register last year; but in the Beach Street School, and in the Astor Memorial School in Mott Street they are fast crowding the Irish element, that used to possess the land, to the wall. So, in Monroe Street and East Broadway are the Jewish children. Neither the teachers nor the Society's managers are in any danger of falling into sleepy routine ways. The conditions with which they have to deal are constantly changing; new problems are given them to solve before the old are fairly worked out, old prejudices to be forgotten or worked over into a new and helpful interest. And they do it bravely, and are more than repaid for their devotion by the real influence they find themselves exerting upon the young lives which had never before felt the touch of genuine humane sympathy, or been awakened to the knowledge that somebody cared for them outside of their own dark slum.

All the children are not as tractable as the Russian Jews or the Italians. The little Irishman, brimful of mischief, is, like his father, in the school and in the street, "agin' the government" on general principles, though in a jovial way that often makes it hard to sit in judgment on his tricks with serious mien. He feels, too, that to a certain extent he has the sympathy of his father in his unregenerate state, and is the more to be commended if he subdues the old Adam in himself and allows the instruction to proceed. The hardest of them all to deal with, until he has been won over as a friend and ally, is perhaps the Bohemian child. He inherits, with some of his father's obstinacy, all of his hardships, his bitter poverty and grinding work. School to him is merely a change of tasks in an unceasing round that leaves no room for play. If he lingers on the way home to take a hand in a stolen game of ball, the mother is speedily on his track. Her instruction to the teacher is not to let the child stay "a minute after three o'clock." He is wanted at home to roll cigars or strip tobacco leaves for his father, while the mother gets the evening meal ready. The Bohemian has his own cause for the reserve that keeps him a stranger in a strange land after living half his life among us; his reception has not been altogether hospitable, and it is not only his hard language and his sullen moods that are to blame. All the better he knows the value of the privilege that is offered his child, and will "drive him to school with sticks" if need be; an introduction that might be held to account for a good deal of reasonable reluctance, even hostility to the school, in the pupil. The teacher has only to threaten the intractable ones with being sent home to bring them round. And yet, it is not that they are often cruelly treated there. On the contrary, the Bohemian is an exceptionally tender and loving father, perhaps because his whole life is lived with his family at home, in the tenement that is his shop and his world. He simply proposes that his child shall enjoy the advantages that are denied him—denied partly perhaps because of his refusal to accept them, but still from his point of view denied. And he takes a shortcut to that goal by sending the child to school. The result is that the old Bohemian disappears in the first generation born upon our soil. His temper remains to some extent, it is true. He still has his surly streaks, refuses to sing or recite in school when the teacher or something else does not suit him, and can never be driven where yet he is easily led; but as he graduates into the public school and is thrown more into contact with the children of more lighthearted nationalities, he grows into that which his father would have long since become, had he not got a wrong start: a loyal American, proud of his country, and a useful citizen.

In the school in East Seventy-third Street of which I am thinking, there was last winter, besides the day school of some four hundred pupils, an evening class of big factory girls, most of them women grown, that vividly illustrated the difficulties that beset teaching in the Bohemian quarter. It had been got together with much difficulty by the principal and one of the officers of the Society, who gave up his nights and his own home life to the work of instructing the school. On the night when it opened, he was annoyed by a smell of tobacco in the hallways and took the janitor to task for smoking in the building. The man denied the charge, and Mr. H—— went hunting through the house for the offender with growing indignation, as he found the teachers in the classrooms sneezing and sniffing the air to locate the source of the infliction. It was not until later in the evening, when the sneezing fit took him, too, as he was bending over a group of the girls to examine their slates, that he discovered it to be a feature of the new enterprise. The perfume was part of the school. Without it, it could not go on. The girls were all cigar makers; so were their parents at home. The shop and the tenement were organized on the tobacco plan, and the school must needs adopt it with what patience it could, if its business were to proceed.

It did, and got on fairly well until a reporter found his way into it and roused the resentment of the girls by some inconsiderate, if well-meant, criticisms of their ways. The rebellion he caused was quelled with difficulty by Mr. H——, who re-established his influence over them at this point and gained their confidence by going to live among them in the schoolhouse with his family. Still the sullen moods, the nightly ructions. The girls were as ready to fight as to write, in their fits of angry spite, until my friend was almost ready to declare with the angry Irishman, that he would have peace in the house if he had to whip all hands to get it. Christmas was at hand with its message of peace and good will, but the school was more than usually unruly, when one night, in despair, he started to read a story to them to lay the storm. It was Hans Christian Andersen's story of the little girl who sold matches and lighted her way to mother and heaven with them as she sat lonely and starved, freezing to death in the street on New Year's Eve. As match after match went out with the pictures of home, of warmth and brightness it had shown the child, and her trembling fingers fumbled eagerly with the bunch to call them back, a breathless hush fell upon the class, and when the story was ended, and Mr. H—— looked up with misty eyes, he found the whole class in tears. The picture of friendless poverty, more bitterly desolate than any even they had known, had gone to their hearts and melted them. The crisis was passed and peace restored.

A crisis of another kind came later, when the pupils' "young men" got into the habit of coming to see the girls home. They waited outside until school was dismissed, and night after night Mr. H—— found a ball in progress on the sidewalk when the girls should long have been home. The mothers complained and the success of the class was imperiled. Their passion for dancing was not to be overcome. They would give up the school first. Mr. H—— thought the matter out and took a long step—a perilous one. He started a dancing class, and on certain nights in the week taught the girls the lanciers instead of writing and spelling. Simultaneously he wrote to every mother that the school was not to be blamed if the girls were not home at ten minutes after nine o'clock; it was dismissed at 8.55 sharp every night. The thing took tremendously. The class filled right up, complaints ceased, and everything was lovely when examination day approached with the annual visit of friends and patrons. My friend awaited its coming with fear and trembling. There was no telling what the committee might say to the innovation. The educational plan of the Society is most liberal, but the lanciers was a step even the broadest of its pedagogues had not yet ventured upon.

The evil day came at last, and, full of forebodings, Mr. H—— had the girls soothe their guests with cakes and lemonade of their own brewing until they were in a most amiable mood. Then, when they expected the reading to begin, with a sinking heart he bade them dance. The visitors stared in momentary amazement, but at the sight of the happy faces in the quadrilles, and the enthusiasm of the girls, they caught the spirit of the thing and applauded to the echo. The dancing class was a success, and so has the school been ever since.

As far as I know, this is the only instance in which the quadrille has been made one of the regular English branches taught in the industrial schools. But cake and lemonade have more than once smoothed the way to a hearty acceptance of the three R's with their useful concomitants, as taught there. One of the excellent features of the system is the "kitchen garden," for the little ones, a kind of play housekeeping that covers the whole range of housework, and the cooking class for the larger girls that gives many of them a taste for housekeeping which helps to overcome their prejudice against domestic service, and so to solve one of the most perplexing questions of the day—no less serious to the children of the poor than to the wives of the rich, if they only knew or would believe it. It is the custom of the wise teachers, when the class has become proficient, to invite the mothers to a luncheon gotten up by their children. "I never," reports the teacher of the Eighteenth Ward Industrial School after such a session, "saw women so thoroughly interested." And it was not only the mother who was thus won over in the pride over her daughter's achievement. It was the home itself that was invaded with influences that had been strangers to it heretofore. For the mother learned something she would not be apt to forget, by seeing her child do intelligently and economically what she had herself done ignorantly and wastefully before. Poverty and waste go always hand in hand. The girls are taught, with the doing of a thing, enough also of the chemistry of cooking to enable them to understand the "why" of it. The influence of that sort of teaching in the tenement of the poor no man can measure. I am well persuaded that half of the drunkenness that makes so many homes miserable is at least encouraged, if not directly caused, by the mismanagement and bad cooking at home. All the wife and mother knows about housekeeping she has picked up in the tenement since she was married, among those who never knew how to cook a decent meal or set a clean table; while the saloonkeeper hires the best cook he can get for money, and serves his hot lunch free to her husband in a tidy and cheerful room, where no tired women—tired of the trials and squabbles of the day—no cross looks, and no dirty, fighting children come to spoil his appetite and his hour of rest.

Here, as everywhere, it is the personal influence of the teacher that counts for most in dealing with the child. It follows it into the home, and often through life to the second and third generation, smoothing the way of trouble and sorrow and hardship with counsel and aid in a hundred ways. "Sometimes," says one of the teachers, who has seen the children of her first pupils go from her school into their own homes to take up the battle of life, "sometimes a teacher, while conducting a class, is also fashioning, from some soft white material, a shroud for some little one whose parents can provide none themselves. When a child dies of a disease that is not contagious, its classmates gather around the coffin and sing in German or English, 'I am Jesus's little lamb.' Sometimes the children's hymn and the Lord's Prayer are the only service." Her life work has been among the poorest Germans on the East Side. "Among our young men," she reports, "I know of only three who have become drunkards, and many are stanch temperance men. I have never known of one of our girls drinking to excess. I have looked carefully over our records, and can truly say that, so far as I can learn, not one girl who remained with us until over seventeen lived a life of shame."

What teaching meant to this woman the statement that follows gives an idea of: "Shrove Tuesday evening is a time when all Germans plan for a frolic; they call it 'Fastnacht.' Twenty years ago I gave the young people of the evening school a party on that evening, and at the suggestion of one of the girls decided to have a reunion every year at that time. So each year our married girls and boys, and those still unmarried, who have grown beyond us in other ways, come 'home.' We sing the old songs, talk over old times, play games, drink coffee and eat doughnuts, and always end the evening with 'Auld Lang Syne.' Last spring, two of the young men stood at the stairway and counted the guests as they went to the supper room: they reported over four hundred. Letters came from Boston, Chicago, Philadelphia, Washington, Texas, Idaho, and Wyoming from those who would gladly have been with us. All who live within a radius of fifty miles try to be here."

"Among our grown girls," she adds, "we have teachers, governesses, dressmakers, milliners, trained nurses, machine operators, hand sewers, embroiderers, designers for embroidering, servants in families, saleswomen, bookkeepers, typewriters [sic], candy packers, bric-a-brac packers, bank-note printers, silk winders, button makers, box makers, hairdressers, and fur sewers. Among our boys are bookkeepers, workers in stained glass, painters, printers, lithographers, salesmen in wholesale houses, as well as in many of our largest retail stores, typewriters, stenographers, commission merchants, farmers, electricians, ship carpenters, foremen in factories, grocers, carpet designers, silver engravers, metal burnishers, carpenters, masons, carpet weavers, plumbers, stone workers, cigar makers, and cigar packers. Only one of our boys, so far as we can learn, ever sold liquor, and he has given it up."

Not a few of these, without a doubt, got the first inkling of their trade in the class where they learned to read. The curriculum of the industrial schools is comprehensive. The nationality of the pupils makes little or no difference in it. The start, as often as is necessary, is made with an object lesson—soap and water being the elements, and the child the object. As in the kindergarten, the alphabet comes second on the list. Then follow lessons in sewing, cooking, darning, mat weaving, pasting, and dressmaking for the girls, and in carpentry, wood carving, drawing, printing, and like practical "branches" for the boys, not a few of whom develop surprising cleverness at this or that kind of work. The system is continually expanding. There are schools yet that have not the necessary facilities for classes in manual training, but as the importance of the subject is getting to be more clearly understood, and interest in the subject grows, new "shops" are being constantly opened and other occupations found for the children. Even where the school quarters are most pinched and inadequate, a shift is made to give the children work to do that will teach them habits of industry and precision as the all-important lesson to be learned there. In some of the industrial schools the boys learn to cook with the girls, and in the West Side Italian School an attempt to teach them to patch and sew buttons on their own jackets resulted last year in their making their own shirts, and making them well, too. Perhaps the possession of the shirt as a reward for making it acted as a stimulus. The teacher thought so, and she was probably right, for more than one of them had never owned a whole shirt before, let alone a clean one. A heap can be done with the children by appealing to their proper pride—much more than many might think, judging hastily from their rags. Call it vanity—if it is a kind of vanity that can be made a stepping-stone to the rescue of the child, it is worth laying hold of. It was distinct evidence that civilization and the nineteenth century had invaded Lewis Street, when a class of Hungarian boys in the American Female Guardian Society's school in that thoroughfare earned the name of the "necktie class" by adopting that article of apparel in a body. None of them had ever known collar or necktie before.

It is the practice to let the girls have what garments they make, from material, old or new, furnished by the school, and thus a good many of the pupils in the industrial schools are supplied with decent clothing. In the winter especially, some of them need it sadly. In the Italian school of which I just spoke, one of the teachers found a little girl of six years crying softly in her seat on a bitter cold day. She had just come in from the street. In answer to the question what ailed her, she sobbed out, "I'se so cold." And no wonder. Beside a worn old undergarment, all the clothing upon her shivering little body was a thin calico dress. The soles were worn off her shoes, and toes and heels stuck out. It seemed a marvel that she had come through the snow and ice as she had, without having her feet frozen.

Naturally the teacher would follow such a child into her home and there endeavor to clinch the efforts begun for its reclamation in the school. It is the very core and kernel of the Society's purpose not to let go of the children of whom once it has laid hold, and to this end it employs its own physicians to treat those who are sick, and to canvass the poorest tenements in the summer months, on the plan pursued by the Health Department. Last year these doctors, ten in number, treated 1578 sick children and 174 mothers. Into every sickroom and many wretched hovels, daily bouquets of sweet flowers found their way too, visible tokens of a sympathy and love in the world beyond— seemingly so far beyond the poverty and misery of the slum—that had thought and care even for such as they. Perhaps in the final reckoning these flowers, which came from friends far and near, will have a story to tell that will outweigh all the rest. It may be an "impracticable notion," as I have sometimes been told by hardheaded men of business; but it is not always the hard head that scores in work among the poor. The language of the heart is a tongue that is understood in the poorest tenements where the English speech is scarcely comprehended and rated little above the hovels in which the immigrants are receiving their first lessons in the dignity of American citizenship.

Very lately a unique exercise has been added to the course in these schools that lays hold of the very marrow of the problem with which they deal. It is called "saluting the flag," and originated with Colonel George T. Balch, of the Board of Education, who conceived the idea of instilling patriotism into the little future citizens of the Republic in doses to suit their childish minds. To talk about the Union, of which most of them had but the vaguest notion, or of the duty of the citizen, of which they had no notion at all, was nonsense. In the flag it was all found embodied in a central idea which they could grasp. In the morning the star-spangled banner was brought into the school, and the children were taught to salute it with patriotic words. Then the best scholar of the day before was called out of the ranks, and it was given to him or her to keep for the day. The thing took at once and was a tremendous success.

Then was evolved the plan of letting the children decide for themselves whether or not they would so salute the flag as a voluntary offering, while incidentally instructing them in the duties of the voter at a time when voting was the one topic of general interest. Ballot boxes were set up in the schools on the day before the last general election (1891). The children had been furnished with ballots for and against the flag the week before, and told to take them home to their parents and talk it over with them, a very apt reminder to those who were naturalized citizens of their own duties, then pressing. On the face of the ballot was the question to be decided: "Shall the school salute the nation's flag every day at the morning exercises?" with a Yes and a No, to be crossed out as the voter wished. On its back was printed a Voter's A, B, C, in large plain type, easy to read:

"This country in which I live, and which is *my* country, is called a *republic*. In a republic, *the people govern*. The people who govern are called *citizens*. I am one of the people and *a little citizen*.

"The way the citizens govern is either by voting for the person whom they want to represent them or who will say what the people want him to say—or by voting *for* that thing they would like to do, or *against* that thing which they do not want to do.

"The citizen who votes is called a *voter* or an *elector*, and the right of voting is called the *suffrage*. The voter puts on a piece of paper what he wants. The piece of paper is called a *ballot*. THIS PIECE OF PAPER IS MY BALLOT.

"The right of a citizen to vote; the right to say what the citizen thinks is best for himself and all the rest of the people; the right to say who shall govern us and make laws for us, is A GREAT PRIVILEGE, A SACRED TRUST, A VERY GREAT RESPONSIBILITY, which I must learn to exercise conscientiously, and to the best of my knowledge and ability, as a little citizen of this great AMERICAN REPUBLIC."

On Monday the children cast their votes in the Society's twenty-one industrial schools, with all the solemnity of a regular election and with as much of its simple machinery as was practicable. Eighty-two per cent of the whole number of enrolled scholars turned out for the occasion, and of the 4306 votes cast, 88, not quite two per cent, voted against the flag. Some of these, probably the majority, voted No under a misapprehension, but there were a few exceptions.

One little Irishman, in the Mott Street school, came without his ballot. "The old man tored it up," he reported. In the East Seventy-third Street school five Bohemians of tender years set themselves down as opposed to the scheme of making Americans of them. Only one, a little girl, gave her reason. She brought her own flag to school: "I vote for that," she said, sturdily, and the teacher wisely recorded her vote and let her keep the banner.

I happened to witness the election in the Beach Street school, where the children are nearly all Italians. The minority elements were, however, represented on the board of election inspectors by a colored girl and a little Irish miss, who did not seem in the least abashed by the fact that they were nearly the only representatives of their people in the school. The tremendous show of dignity with which they took their seats at the poll was most impressive. As a lesson in practical politics, the occasion had its own humor. It was clear that the negress was most impressed with the solemnity of the occasion, and the Irish girl with its practical opportunities. The Italian's [sic] disposition to grin and frolic, even in her new and solemn character, betrayed the ease with which she would, were it real politics, become the game of her Celtic colleague. When it was all over they canvassed the vote with all the solemnity befitting the occasion, signed together a certificate stating the result, and handed it over to the principal sealed in a manner to defeat any attempt at fraud. Then the school sang Santa Lucia, a sweet Neapolitan ballad. It was amusing to hear the colored girl and the half-dozen little Irish children sing right along with the rest the Italian words, of which they did not understand one. They had learned them from hearing them sung by the others, and rolled them out just as loudly, if not as sweetly, as they.

The first patriotic election in the Fifth Ward Industrial School was held on historic ground. The house it occupies was John Ericsson's until his death, and there he planned nearly all his great inventions, among them one that helped save the flag for which the children voted that day. The children have lived faithfully up to their pledge. Every morning sees the flag carried to the principal's desk and all the little ones, rising at the stroke of the bell, say with one voice: "We turn to our flag as the sunflower turns to the sun!" One bell, and every brown right fist is raised to the brow, as in military salute: "We give our heads!" Another stroke, and the grimy little hands are laid on as many hearts: "and our hearts!" Then with a shout that can be heard around the corner: "—— to our country! One country, one language, one flag!" No one can hear it and doubt that the children mean every word and will not be apt to forget that lesson soon.

The industrial school has found a way of dealing with even the truants, of whom it gets more than its share, and the success of it is suggestive. As stated by the teacher in the West Eighteenth Street school who found it out, it is very simple: "I tell them, if they want to play truant to come to me and I will excuse them for the day, and give them a note so that if the truant officer sees them it will be all right." She adds that "only one boy ever availed himself of that privilege." The other boys with few exceptions became interested, as one would expect, and came to school regularly. It was the old story of the boys in the Juvenile Asylum who could be trusted to do guard duty in the grounds when put upon their honor, but the moment they were locked up for the night risked their necks to escape by climbing out of the third-story windows.

But when it has cheated the street and made of the truant a steady scholar, the work of the industrial school is not all done. Next, it hands him over to the public school, clothed and in his right mind, if his time to go to work has not yet come. Last year the thirty-three industrial schools of the Children's Aid Society and the American Female Guardian Society thus dismissed nearly eleven hundred children who, but for their intervention, might never have reached that goal. That their charity had not been allowed to corrupt the children may be inferred from the statement that, with an average daily attendance of 4348 in the Children's Aid Society's schools, 1729 children were depositors in the school savings banks to the aggregate amount of about $800—a very large sum for them—and this in the face of the fact, recorded on the school register, that 938 of the lot came from homes where drunkenness and poverty went hand in hand. It is not in the plan of the industrial school to make paupers, but to develop to the utmost the kernel of self-help that is the one useful legacy of the street. The child's individuality is preserved at any cost. Even the clothes that are given to the poorest in exchange for their rags are of different cut and color, made so with this one end in view. The distressing "institution look" is wholly absent from these schools, and one of the great stumbling blocks of charity administered at wholesale is thus avoided.

The night schools are for the boys and girls already enlisted in the treadmill, and who must pick up what learning they can in their off hours. Together with the day schools they footed up a total enrollment of nearly ten thousand children whom this Society reached in 1891. Upon the basis of the average daily attendance, the cost of their education to the community, which supported the charity, was $24.53 for each child. The cost of sheltering, feeding, and teaching 11,770 boys and girls in the Society's six lodginghouses was $32.76 for each; the expense of sending 2825 children to farm homes $9.96 for each. The average cost per year for each prisoner in the Tombs is $107.75, and for every child maintained in an Asylum, or in the poorhouse, nearly $140.*

* Report for 1891 of Children's Aid Society.

"One of our great difficulties," says the Secretary of the Children's Aid Society, in a recent statement of the Society's aims and purposes, echoing an old grievance, "is with the large boys of the city. There seems to be no place for them in the world as it is. They have grown up in it without any training but that in street trades. The trade unions have kept them from being apprenticed. They are soon too large for street occupations, and are unable to compete with the small boys. They are too old for our lodginghouses. We know not what to do with them. Some succeed well on western farms, but they are usually disliked by their employers because they change places soon; and their occasional offenses and disposition to move about have given us more trouble in the West than any other one thing. Very few people are willing to bear with them, even though a little patience will sometimes bring out excellent qualities in them." They are the boys for whom the street and the saloon have use that shall speedily fashion of their "excellent qualities" a lash to sting the community's purse, if not its conscience, with the memory of its neglect. As 107.75 is to 24.53, or 140 to 9.96, so will be the smart of it compared with the burden of patience that would have turned the scales the other way, to put the matter in a light where the hardheaded man of business can see it without an effort.

There is at least one man of that kind in New York who has seen and understood it to some purpose. His name is Richard T. Auchmuty, and he is by profession an architect. In that capacity he has had opportunity enough of observing how the virtual exclusion of the New York boy from the trades worked to his harm, and he started for his relief an industrial school that deserves to be ranked among the great benefactions of our day, even more for its power to set people to thinking than for the direct benefit it confers upon the boy, great as that is. Once it comes to be thoroughly understood that a chance to learn his father's honest trade is denied the New York boy by a foreign conspiracy, because he is an American lad and cannot be trusted to do its bidding, it is inconceivable that an end should not be put in quick order to this astounding abuse. This thing is exactly what is being done in New York now by the consent of its citizens, who without a protest read in the newspapers that a trade union, one of the largest and strongest in the building trades, has decreed that for two years from a fixed date no apprentice shall be admitted to that trade in New York—decreed, with the consent and connivance of subservient employers, that so many lads who might have become useful mechanics shall grow up tramps and loafers; decreed that a system of robbery of the American mechanic shall go on by which it has come to pass that out of twenty-three millions of dollars paid in a year to the building trades in this city barely six millions are grudgingly accorded the native worker. There is no decree to exclude the mechanic from abroad. He may come and go—and go he does, in shoals, to his home across the sea at the end of each season, with its profits—under the scheme of international comradeship that excludes only the American workman and his boy. I have talked with some of the most intelligent of the labor leaders, men well-known all over the land, to find out if there were any defense to be made for this that I was not aware of, but have got nothing but evasion and sophistries about the "protection of labor" for my answer. A protection, indeed, that has nearly resulted already in the practical extinction of the American mechanic, the best and cleverest in the world, in America's chief city, at the bidding of the Walking Delegate.

Even to Colonel Auchmuty's industrial school this persecution has been extended in a persistent attempt for years to taboo its graduates. In spite of it, the New York trade schools open their twelfth season this winter with six hundred scholars and more, in place of the thirty who sat in the first class eleven years ago. The community's better sense is coming to the rescue, and the opposition to the school is wearing off. In the spring as many hundred young plasterers, printers, tailors, plumbers, stonecutters, bricklayers, carpenters, and blacksmiths will go forth capable mechanics, and with their self-respect unimpaired by the associations of the shop and the saloon under the old apprentice system. In this one respect the trade union may have done them a service it did not intend. Colonel Auchmuty's school has demonstrated what it amounts to by furnishing from among its young men the bricklayers for more than as many handsome buildings in New York as there were pupils in its first class. When a committee of master builders came on from Philadelphia to see what their work was like, the report it brought back was that it looked as if the builders had put their hearts in it, and a trade school was forthwith established in that city. Of that, too, Colonel Auchmuty paid the way from the start.

His wealth has kept the New York school above water since it was started; but this winter a benevolent millionaire, Mr. J. Pierpont Morgan, for whom wealth has other and greater responsibilities than that of ministering to his own comfort, has endowed it with half a million dollars, and Mrs. Auchmuty has added a hundred thousand with the land on First Avenue between Sixty-seventh and Sixty-eighth Streets upon which the school stands, so that it starts out with an endowment sufficient to insure its future. The charges for tuition in the day and evening classes have never been much more than nominal, but these may now, perhaps, be reduced even further to allow the "excellent qualities" of the big boys, of whom the reformer despairs, to be put to their proper use without robbing them of the best of all, their self-respect. Then the gage will have been thrown to the street in good earnest, and the Walking Delegate's day will be nearly spent.

THE OUTCAST
AND THE HOMELESS

Under the heading "Just one of God's Children," one of the morning newspapers told the story last winter of a newsboy at the Brooklyn Bridge, who fell in a fit with his bundle of papers under his arm, and was carried into the waiting room by the bridge police. They sent for an ambulance, but before it came the boy was out selling papers again. The reporters asked the little dark-eyed newswoman at the bridge entrance which boy it was.

"Little Maher it was," she answered.

"Who takes care of him?"

"Oh! no one but God," said she, "and he is too busy with other folks to give him much attention."

Little Maher was the representative of a class that is happily growing smaller year by year in our city. It is altogether likely that a little inquiry into his case could have placed the responsibility for his forlorn condition considerably nearer home, upon someone who preferred giving Providence the job to taking the trouble himself. There are homeless children in New York. It is certain that we shall always have our full share. Yet it is equally certain that society is coming out ahead in its struggle with this problem. In ten years, during which New York added to her population one-fourth, the homelessness of our streets, taking the returns of the Children's Aid Society's lodging-houses as the gauge, instead of increasing proportionally, has decreased nearly one-fifth; and of the Topsy element, it may be set down as a fact, there is an end.

If we were able to argue from this a corresponding improvement in the general lot of the poor, we should be on the high road to the millennium. But it is not so. The showing is due mainly to the perfection of organized charitable effort, that proceeds nowadays upon the sensible principle of putting out a fire, viz., that it must be headed off, not run down, and therefore concerns itself chiefly about the children. We are yet a long, a very long way from a safe port. The menace of the Submerged Tenth has not been blotted from the register of the potter's field, and though the "twenty thousand poor children who would not have known it was Christmas," but for public notice to that effect, be a benevolent fiction, there are plenty whose brief lives have had little enough of the embodiment of Christmas cheer and good will in them to make the name seem like a bitter mockery. Yet, when all is said, this much remains, that we are steering the right course. Against the drift and the headwinds of an unparalleled immigration that has literally drained the pauperism of Europe into our city for two generations, against the false currents and the undertow of the tenement in our social life, we are making headway at last.

Every homeless child rescued from the street is a knot made, a man or a woman saved, not for this day only, but for all time. What if there be a thousand left? There is one less. What that one more on the wrong side of the account might have meant will never be known till the final reckoning. The records of jails and brothels and poorhouses, for a hundred years to come, might but have begun the tale.

When, in 1849, the Chief of Police reported that in eleven wards there were 2955 vagrants and dissolute children under fifteen years of age, the boys all thieves and the girls embryo prostitutes, and that ten per cent of the entire child population of school age in the city were vagrants, there was no Children's Aid Society to plead their cause. There *was* a reformatory, and that winter the American Female Guardian Society was

incorporated, "to prevent vice and moral degradation"; but Mr. Brace had not yet found his lifework,
and little Mary Ellen had not been born. The story of
the legacy her sufferings left to the world of children I
have briefly told, and in the chapter on industrial
schools some of the momentous results of Mr. Brace's
devotion have been set forth. The story is not ended;
it never will be while poverty and want exist in this
great city. His greatest work was among the homeless
and the outcast. In the thirty-nine years during which
he was the life and soul of the Children's Aid Society,
it found safe country homes for 84,318* poor city children. And the work goes on. Very nearly already, the
army thus started on the road to usefulness and independence equals in numbers the whole body of
children that, four years before it took up its march,
yielded its Lost Tenth, as the Chief of Police bore
witness, to the prisons and perdition.

This great mass of children—did they all come from
the street? Not all of them. Not even the larger number. But they would have got there, all of them, had
not the Society blocked the way. That is how the race
of Topsies has been exterminated in New York. That
in this, of all fields, prevention is the true cure and
that a farmer's home is better for the city child that
has none than a prison or the best-managed public institution are the simple lessons it has taught and enforced by example that has carried conviction at last.
The conviction came slowly and by degrees. The degrees were not always creditable to sordid human nature that had put forth no hand to keep the child from
the gutter, and in the effort to rescue it now saw only
its selfish opportunity. There are people yet at this day,
whose offers to accept "a strong and handsome girl of
sixteen or so with sweet temper," as a cheap substitute

---

* In this reckoning is included employment found for many
big boys and girls, who were taken as help, and were thus
given the chance which the city denied them.

for a paid servant—"an angel with mighty strong arms," as one of the officers of the Society indignantly put it once—show that the selfish stage has not been quite passed. Such offers are rejected with the emphatic answer: "We bring the children out because they need you, not because you need them." The Society farms out no girls of sixteen with strong arms. For them it finds ways of earning an honest living at such wages as their labor commands, homes in the West, if they wish it, where good husbands, not hard masters, are waiting for them. But, ordinarily, its effort is to bend the twig at a much tenderer age. And in this effort it is assisted by the growth of a strong humane sentiment in the West, that takes less account of the return the child can make in work for his keep, and more of the child itself. Time was when few children but those who were able to help about the farm could be sure of a welcome. Nowadays babies are in demand. Of all the children sent West in the last two years, 14 per cent were under five years, 43.6 per cent over five and under ten years, 36.8 per cent over ten and under fifteen, and only 5.3 per cent over fifteen years of age. The average age of children sent to Western homes in 1891 by the Children's Aid Society was nine years and forty days, and in 1892 nine years and eight months, or an average of nine years, four months, and twenty days for the two years.

It finds them in a hundred ways—in poverty-stricken homes, on the Island, in its industrial schools, in the street. Often they are brought to its office by parents who are unable to take care of them. Provided they are young enough, no questions are asked. It is not at the child's past, but at its future, that these men look. That it comes from among bad people is the best reason in the world why it should be put among those that are good. That is the one care of the Society. Its faith that the child, so placed, will respond and rise to their level, is unshaken after these many years. Its experience has knocked the bugbear of heredity all to flinders.

So that this one condition may be fulfilled, a constant missionary work of an exceedingly practical and businesslike character goes on in the Western farming communities, where there is more to eat than there are mouths to fill, and where a man's children are yet his wealth. When interest has been stirred in a community to the point of arousing demands for the homeless children, the best men in the place—the judge, the pastor, the local editor, and their peers—are prevailed upon to form a local committee that passes upon all applications, and judges of the responsibility and worthiness of the applicants. In this way a sense of responsibility is cultivated that is the best protection for the child in future years, should he need any, which he very rarely does. On a day set by the committee the agent arrives from New York with his little troop. Each child has been comfortably and neatly dressed in a new suit, and carries in his little bundle a Bible as a parting gift from the Society. The committee is on hand to receive them. So usually are half the mothers of the town, who divide the children among themselves and take them home to be cared for until the next day. If there are any babies in the lot, it is always hard work to make them give them up the next morning, and sometimes the company that gathers in the morning at the town hall, for inspection and apportionment among the farmers, has been unexpectedly depleted overnight. From twenty and thirty miles around, the bighearted farmers come in their wagons to attend the show and to negotiate with the committee. The negotiations are rarely prolonged. Each picks out his child, sometimes two, often more than one the same child. The committee umpires between them. They all know each other, and the agent's knowledge of each child, gained on the way out and perhaps through previous acquaintance, helps to make the best choice. There is no ceremony of adoption. That is left to days to come, when the child and the new home have learned to know each other, and to the watchful care of the local committee. To any questions concerning faith or previous condition that may be asked, the Society's answer is always the same. In substance it is this:

"We do not know. Here is the child. Take him and make a good Baptist, or Methodist, or Christian of any sect of him! That is your privilege and his gain. The fewer questions you ask the better. Let his past be behind him and the future his to work out. Love him for himself."*

And in the spirit in which the advice is given it is usually accepted. Night falls upon a joyous band returning home over the quiet country roads, the little stranger snugly stowed among his new friends, one of them already, with home and life before him.

And does the event justify the high hopes of that home journey? Almost always in the end, if the child was young enough when it was sent out. Sometimes a change has to be made. Oftener the change is of name, in the adoption that follows. Some of the boys get restless as they grow up, and "run about a good deal," to the anguish of the committee. A few are reported as having "gone to the bad." But even these commonly come out all right at last. One of them, of whom mention is made in the Society's thirty-fifth annual report, turned up after long years as Mayor of his town and a

---

* It is inevitable, of course, that such a program should steer clear of the sectarian snags that lie plentifully scattered about. I have a Roman Catholic paper before me in which the Society's "villainous work, which consists chiefly in robbing the Catholic child of his faith," is hotly denounced in an address to the Archbishop of New York. Mr. Brace's policy was to meet such attacks with silence, and persevere in his work. The Society still follows his plan. Catholic or Protestant—the question is never raised. "No Catholic child," said one of its managers once to me, "is ever brought to us. A *poor* child is brought and we care for it."

member of the legislature. "We can think," wrote Mr. Brace before his death, "of little Five Points thieves who are now ministers of the gospel or honest farmers; vagrants and street children who are men in professional life; and women who, as teachers or wives of good citizens, are everywhere respected; the children of outcasts or unfortunates whose inherited tendencies have been met by the new environment, and who are industrious and decent members of society." Only by their losing themselves does the Society lose sight of them. Two or three times a year the agent goes to see them all. In the big ledgers in St. Mark's Place each child who has been placed out has a page to himself on which all his doings are recorded, as he is heard of year by year. There are twenty-nine of these canvas-bound ledgers now, and the stories they have to tell would help anyone who thinks he has lost faith in poor human nature to pick it up with the vow never to let go of it again. I open one of them at random, and copy the page—page 289 of ledger No. 23. It tells the story of an English boy, one of four who were picked up down at Castle Garden twelve years ago. His mother was dead, and he had not seen his father for five years before he came here, a stowaway. He did not care, he said, where they sent him, so long as it was not back to England:

June 15, 1880. James S——, aged fourteen years, English; orphan; goes West with J. P. Brace.

Placed with J. R——, Neosha Rapids, Kan., January 26, 1880, James writes that he gets along pleasantly; wrote to him; twenty-sixth annual report sent August 4th. July 14, 1880, Mr. and Mrs. R—— write that James is impudent and tries them greatly. Wrote to him August 17, 1880; wrote again October 15th. October 21, 1880, Mr. R—— writes that they could not possibly get along with James and placed him with Mr. G. H——, about five miles from his house. Mr. H—— is a good man and has a handsome property. Wrote to James March 8, 1881. May 1, 1883, has left his place and has engaged to work for Mr. H——, of Hartford. James seems to be a pretty wild boy, and the probability is he will turn out badly; is very profane and has a violent temper. April 17, 1887, Mrs. Lyman Fry writes James was crushed to death in Kansas City, where he was employed as brakeman on a freight train.

October 16, 1889. The above is a mistake. James calls today at the office and says that after I saw him he turned over a new leaf, and has made a pretty good character for himself. Has worked steadily and has many friends in Emporia. Has been here three days and wants to look up his friends. Is grateful for having been sent West.

So James came out right after all, and all his sins are forgiven. He was a fair sample of those who have troubled the Society's managers most, occasionally brought undeserved reproach upon them, but in the end given them the sweet joy of knowing that their faith and trust were not put to shame. Many pages in the ledgers shine with testimony to that. I shall mention but a single case, the one to which I alluded in the introduction to the story of the industrial schools. Andrew H. Burke was taken by the Society's agents from the nursery at Randall's Island thirty-three years ago with a number of other boys, and sent out to Nobleville, Ind. They heard from him in St. Mark's Place as joining the Sons of Temperance, then as going to the war, a drummer boy; next of his going to college with a determination "to be somebody in the world." He carried his point. That boy is now the Governor of North Dakota. Last winter he wrote to his kind friends, full of loyalty and gratitude, this message for the poor children of New York:

"To the boys now under your charge please convey my best wishes, and that I hope that their pathways in life will be those of morality, of honor, of health, and industry. With these four attributes as a guidance and incentive, I can bespeak for them an honorable and happy and successful life. The goal is for them as well as for the rich man's son. They must learn to labor and to wait, for 'all things come to him who waits.' Many times will the road be rugged, winding, and long, and the sky overcast with ominous clouds. Still, it will not do to fall by the wayside and give up. If one does, the battle of life will be lost.

"Tell the boys I am proud to have had as humble a beginning in life as they, and that I believe it has been my salvation. I hope my success in life, if it can be so termed, will be an incentive to them to struggle for a respectable recognition among their fellow men. In this country family name cuts but little figure. It is the character of the man that wins recognition, hence I would urge them to build carefully and consistently for the future."

The bigger boys do not always give so good an account of themselves. I have already spoken of the difficulty besetting the Society's efforts to deal with that end of the problem. The street in their case has had the first inning, and the battle is hard, often doubtful. Sometimes it is lost. These are rarely sent West, early consignments of them having stirred up a good deal of trouble there. They go South, where they seem to have more patience with them. "The people there," said an old agent of the Society to me, with an enthusiasm that was fairly contagious, "are the most generous, kindhearted people in the world. And they are more easygoing. If a boy turns out badly, steals and runs away perhaps, a letter comes, asking not for retaliation or upbraiding us for letting him come, but hoping that he will do better, expressing sorrow and concern, and ending usually with the bighearted request that we send them another in his place." And another comes, and, ten to one, does better. What lad is there whose wayward spirit such kindness would not conquer in the end?*

These bigger boys come usually out of the Society's lodginghouses for homeless children. Of these I spoke so fully in the account of the Street Arab in *How the Other Half Lives*, that I shall not here enter into any detailed description of them. There are six, one for girls in East Twelfth Street, lately moved from St. Mark's Place, and five for boys. The oldest and best known of these is the Newsboys' Lodginghouse in Duane Street, now called the Brace Memorial Lodginghouse for Boys. The others are the East Side house in East Broadway, the Tompkins Square house, the West Side house at Seventh Avenue and Thirty-second Street, and the lodginghouse at Forty-fourth Street and Second Avenue. A list of the builders' names emphasizes what I said a while ago about the unostentatious charity of rich New Yorkers. I have never seen them published anywhere except in the Society's reports, but they make good and instructive reading, and here they are in the order in which I gave the houses they built, beginning with the one on East Broadway: Miss Catharine L. Wolfe, Mrs. Robert L. Stuart, John Jacob Astor, Morris K. Jesup. The girls' home in East Twelfth Street, just completed, was built as a memorial to Miss Elizabeth Davenport Wheeler by her family, and is to be known as the Elizabeth Home. The list might be greatly extended by including the twenty-one industrial schools, which are in fact links in the same great chain; but that is not

---

* The Society pleads for a farm of its own, close to the city, where it can organize a "farm school" for the older boys. There they could be taken on probation and their fitness for the West be ascertained. They would be more useful to the farmers and some trouble would be avoided. Two farms, or three, to get as near to the family plan as possible, would be better. The Children's Aid Society of Boston has three farm schools, and its work is very successful.

to the present purpose, and probably I should not be thanked for doing it. I have already transgressed enough. The wealth that seeks its responsibilities among the outcast children in this city, is of the kind that prefers that it should remain unidentified and unheralded to the world in connection with its benefactions.

It is in these lodginghouses that one may study the homelessness that mocks the miles of brick walls which enclose New York's tenements, but not its homes. Only with special opportunities is it nowadays possible to study it anywhere else in New York. One may still hunt up by night waifs who make their beds in alleys and cellars and abandoned sheds. This last winter two stable fires that broke out in the middle of the night routed out little colonies of boys, who slept in the hay and probably set it on fire. But one no longer stumbles over homeless waifs in the street gutters. One has to hunt for them and to know where. The "cruelty man" knows and hunts them so assiduously that the game is getting scarcer every day. The doors of the lodginghouses stand open day and night, offering shelter upon terms no cold or hungry lad would reject: six cents for breakfast and supper, six for a clean bed. They are not pauper barracks, and he is expected to pay; but he can have trust if his pockets are empty, as they probably are, and even a bootblack's kit or an armful of papers to start him in business, if need be. The only conditions are that he shall wash and not swear, and attend evening school when his work is done. It is not possible today that an outcast child should long remain supperless and without shelter in New York, unless he prefers to take his chances with the rats of the gutter. Such children there are, but they are no longer often met. The winter's cold drives even them to cover and to accept the terms they rejected in more hospitable seasons. Even the "dock rat" is human.

It seems a marvel that he is, sometimes, when one hears the story of what drove him to the street. Drunkenness and brutality at home helped the tenement do it, half the time. It drove his sister out to a life of shame, too, as likely as not. I have talked with a good many of the boys, trying to find out, and heard some yarns and some stories that were true. In seven cases out of ten, of those who had homes to go to, it was that, when we got down to hard pan. A drunken father or mother made the street preferable to the house, and to the street they went.* In other cases death, perhaps, had broken up the family and thrown the boys upon the world. That was the story of one of the boys I tried to photograph at a quiet game of "craps" in the hallway of the Duane Street Lodginghouse—James Brady. Father and mother had both died two months after they came here from Ireland, and he went forth from the tenement alone and without a friend, but not without courage. He just walked on until he stumbled on the lodginghouse, and fell into a job of selling papers. James, at the age of sixteen, was being initiated into the mysteries of the alphabet in the evening school. He was not sure that he liked it. The German boy who took a hand in the game, and who made his grub and bed money, when he was lucky, by picking up junk, had just such a career. The third, the bootblack, gave his reasons briefly for running away from his Philadelphia home: "Me muther wuz all the time hittin' me when I cum in the house, so I cum away." So did a German boy I met there, if for a slightly different

---

* I once questioned a class of 71 boys between eight and twelve years old in a reform school, with this result: 22 said they blacked boots; 36 sold papers; 26 did both; 40 "slept out"; but only 3 of them all were fatherless, 11 motherless, showing that they slept out by choice. The father probably had something to do with it most of the time. Three-fourths of the lads stood up when I asked them if they had been to Central Park. The teacher asked one of those who did not rise, a little shaver, if he had never been in the Park. "No, mem!" he replied, "me father he went that time."

reason. He was fresh from over the sea, and had not yet learned a word of English. In his own tongue he told why he came. His father sent him to a gymnasium, but the Latin was "zu schwer" for him, and "der Herr Papa sagt heraus!" He was evidently a boy of good family, but slow. His father could have taken no better course, certainly, to cure him of that defect, if he did not mind the danger of it.

There are always some whom nobody owns. Boys who come from a distance perhaps, and are cast up in our streets with all the other drift that sets toward the city's maelstrom. But the great mass were born of the maelstrom and ground by it into what they are. Of fourteen lads rounded up by the officers of the Society for the Prevention of Cruelty to Children one night this past summer, in the alleys and byways down about the printing offices, where they have their run, two were from Brooklyn, one a runaway from a good home in White Plains, and the rest from the tenements of New York. Only one was really without home or friends. That was perhaps an unusually—I was going to say good—showing; but I do not know that it can be called a good showing that ten boys who had homes to go to should prefer to sleep out in the street. The boy who has none would have no other choice until someone picked him up and took him in. The record of the 84,318 children that have been sent to Western homes in thirty-nine years show that 17,383 of them had both parents living, and therefore presumably homes, such as they were; 5892 only the father, and 11,954 the mother, living; 39,406 had neither father nor mother. The rest either did not know, or did not tell. That again includes an earlier period when the streets were full of vagrants without home ties, so that the statement, as applied to today, errs on the other side. The truth lies between the two extremes. Four-fifths, perhaps, are outcasts, the rest homeless waifs.

The great mass, for instance, of the newsboys who cry their "extrees" in the streets by day, and whom one meets in the Duane Street Lodginghouse or in Theatre Alley and about the post office by night, are children with homes who thus contribute to the family earnings, and sleep out, if they do, because they have either not sold their papers or gambled away the money at "craps," and are afraid to go home. It was for such a reason little Giuseppe Margalto and his chum made their bed in the ventilating chute at the post office on the night General Sherman died, and were caught by the fire that broke out in the mail room toward midnight. Giuseppe was burned to death; the other escaped to bring the news to the dark Crosby Street alley in which he had lived. Giuseppe did not die his cruel death in vain. A much stricter watch has been kept since upon the boys, and they are no longer allowed to sleep in many places to which they formerly had access.

A bed in the street, in an odd box or corner, is good enough for the ragamuffin who thinks the latitude of his tenement unhealthy, when the weather is warm. It is cooler there, too, and it costs nothing, if one can keep out of the reach of the policeman. It is no new experience to the boy. Half the tenement population, men, women, and children, sleep out of doors, in streets and yards, on the roof, or on the fire escape, from May to October. In winter the boys can curl themselves up on the steam pipes in the newspaper offices that open their doors after midnight on secret purpose to let them in. When these fail, there is still the lodginghouse as a last resort. To the lad whom ill treatment or misfortune drove to the street it is always a friend. To the chronic vagrant it has several drawbacks: the school, the wash, the enforced tax for the supper and the bed, that cuts down the allowance for "craps," his all-absorbing passion, and finally the occasional inconvenient habit of mothers and fathers to come looking there for their missing boys. The police send them there, and sometimes they take the trouble to call when the boys have gone to bed, taking them at what they consider a mean disadvantage. However, most of them do not trouble themselves to that extent. They let the strap hang idle till the boy comes back, if he ever does.

Last February Harry Quill, aged fifteen, disappeared from the tenement No. 45 Washington Street, and though he was not heard of again for many weeks, his people never bothered the police. Not until his dead body was fished up from the air shaft at the bottom of which it had lain two whole months was his disappearance explained. But the full explanation came only the other day, in September, when one of his playmates was arrested for throwing him down and confessed to doing it. Harry was drunk, he said, and attacked him on the roof with a knife. In the struggle he threw him into the air shaft. Fifteen years old, and fighting drunk! The mere statement sheds a stronger light on the sources of child vagabondage in our city than I could do, were I to fill the rest of my book with an enumeration of them.

However, it is a good deal oftener the father who gets drunk than the boy. Not all, nor even a majority, of the boys one meets at the lodginghouses are of that stamp. If they were, they would not be there long. They have their faults, and the code of morals proclaimed by the little newsboys, for instance, is not always in absolute harmony with that generally adopted by civilized society. But even they have virtues quite as conspicuous. They are honest after their fashion, and tremendously impartial in a fight. They are bound to see fair play, if they all have to take a hand. It generally ends that way. A good many of them—the great majority in all the other lodginghouses but that in Duane Street—work steadily in shops and factories, making their home there because it is the best they have, and because there they are among friends they know. Two little brothers, John and Willie, attracted my attention in the Newsboys' Lodginghouse by the sturdy way in which they held together, back to back, against the world, as it were. Willie was thirteen and John eleven years old. Their story was simple and soon told. Their mother died, and their father, who worked in a gashouse, broke up the household, unable to maintain it. The boys went out to shift for themselves, while he made his home in a Bowery lodginghouse. The oldest of the brothers was then earning three dollars a week in a factory; the younger was selling newspapers, and making out. The day I first saw him he came in from his route early—it was raining hard—to get dry trousers out for his brother against the time he should be home from the factory. There was no doubt the two would hew their way through the world together. The right stuff was in them, as in the two other lads, also brothers, I found in the Tompkins Square Lodginghouse. Their parents had both died, leaving them to care for a palsied sister and a little brother. They sent the little one to school, and went to work for the sister. Their combined earnings at the shop were just enough to support her and one of the brothers who stayed with her. The other went to the lodginghouse, where he could live for eighteen cents a day, turning the rest of his earnings into the family fund. With this view of these homeless lads, the one who goes much among them is not surprised to hear of their clubbing together, as they did in the Seventh Avenue lodginghouse, to fit out a little ragamuffin, who was brought in shivering from the street, with a suit of clothes. There was not one in the crowd that chipped in who had a whole coat to his back.

It was in this lodginghouse I first saw Buffalo. He was presented to me the night I took the picture of my little vegetable-peddling friend, Edward, asleep on the front bench in evening school. Edward was nine years old and an orphan, but hard at work every day earning his own living by shouting from a peddler's cart. He could not be made to sit for his picture, and I took him at a disadvantage—in a double sense, for he had not made his toilet; it was in the days of the threatened water famine, and the boys had been warned not to waste water in washing, an injunction they cheerfully obeyed. I was anxious not to have the boy disturbed, so the spelling class went right on while I set up the camera. It was an original class, original in its answers as in its looks. This was what I heard while I focused on poor Eddie:

The teacher: "Cheat! spell cheat."

Boy spells correctly.

Teacher: "Right! What is it to cheat?"

Boy: "To skin one, like Tommy—"

The teacher cut the explanation short, and ordering up another boy, bade him spell "nerve." He did it.

"What is nerve?" demanded the teacher; "what does it mean?"

"Cheek! don't you know," said the boy, and at that moment I caught Buffalo blacking my sleeping peddler's face with ink, just in time to prevent his waking him up. Then it was that I heard the disturber's story. He *was* a character, and no mistake. He had run away from Buffalo, whence his name, "beating" his way down on the trains, until he reached New York. He "shined" around until he got so desperately hard up that he had to sell his kit. Just about then he was discovered by an artist, who paid him to sit for him in his awful rags with his tousled hair that had not known the restraint of a cap for months. "Oh! it was a daisy job," sighed Buffalo, at the recollection. He had only to sit still and crack jokes. Alas! Buffalo's first effort at righteousness upset him. He had been taught in the lodginghouse that to be clean was the first requisite of a gentleman, and on his first payday he went bravely, eschewing "craps," and bought himself a new coat and had his hair cut. When, beaming with pride, he presented himself at the studio in his new character, the artist turned him out as no longer of any use to him. I am afraid that Buffalo's ambition to be "like folks," received a shock by this mysterious misfortune that spoiled his career. A few days after that he was caught

by a policeman in the street, at his old game of "craps."
The officer took him to the police court and arraigned
him as a hardened offender. To the judge's question if
he had any home, he said frankly Yes! in Buffalo, but
he had run away from it.

"Now, if I let you go, will you go right back?" asked
the magistrate, looking over the desk at the youthful
prisoner. Buffalo took off his tattered cap and stood up
on the foot rail so that he could reach across the desk
with his hand.

"Put it there, jedge!" he said. "I'll go. Square and
honest, I will."

And he went. I never heard of him again.

The evening classes are a sort of latchkey to knowledge for belated travelers on the road. They make
good use of it, if they are late, as instanced in the class
in history in the Duane Street Lodginghouse, which
the younger boys irreverently speak of as "The Souphouse Gang." I found it surprisingly proficient, if it was
in its shirtsleeves, and there were at least a couple of
pupils in it who promised to make their mark. All of
its members are working lads, and not a few of them
are capitalists in a small but very promising way.
There is a savings bank attached to each lodginghouse,
with the superintendent as president and cashier at
once. No less than $5197 was deposited by the 11,435
boys who found shelter in them in 1891. They were not
all depositors, of course. In the Duane Street Lodginghouse, out of 7614 newsboys who were registered, 1108
developed the instinct of saving, or were able to lay
by something. Their little pile at the end of the year
held the respectable sum of $3162.39.* It is safe to say
that the interest of the Souphouse Gang in it was proportionate to its other achievements. In the West Side

* The lodginghouses are following a noteworthy precedent.
From the Society for the Prevention of Pauperism, organized
in the beginning of this century, sprang the first savings bank
in the country.

lodginghouse, where nearly a thousand boys were taken in during the year, 54 patronized the bank and saved up $360.11. I found a little newsboy there who sells papers in the Grand Central Depot, and whose bankbook showed deposits of $200. Some day that boy, for all he has a "tough" father and mother who made him prefer the lodginghouse as a home at the age of nine years, will be running the news business on the road as the capable "boss" of any number of lads of his present age. He neglects no opportunity to learn what the house has to offer, if he can get to the school in time. On the whole, the teachers report the boys as slow at their books, and no wonder. A glimpse of little Eddie, in from the cart after his day's work and dropping asleep on the bench from sheer weariness, more than excuses him, I think. Eddie may have a chance now to learn something better than peddling apples. They have lately added to the nightly instruction there, I am told, the feature of manual training in the shape of a printing office, to which the boys have taken amazingly and which promises great things.

There was one pupil in that evening class, at whose door the charge of being "slow" could not be laid, indifferent though his scholarship was in anything but the tricks of the street. He was the most hopeless young scamp I ever knew, and withal so aggravatingly funny that it was impossible not to laugh, no matter how much one felt like scolding. He lived by "shinin'" and kept his kit in a saloon to save his dragging it home every night. When I last saw him he was in disgrace for not showing up at the school four successive nights. He explained that the policeman who "collared" him "fur fightin'" was to blame. It was the third time he had been locked up for that offense. When he found out that I wanted to know his history, he set about helping me with a readiness to oblige that was very promising. Did he have any home? Oh, yes, he had.

"Well, where do you live?" I asked.

"Here!" said Tommy, promptly, with just a suspicion of a wink at the other boys who were gathered about watching the examination. He had no father; didn't know where his mother was.

"Is she any relation to you!" put in one of the boys, gravely. Tommy disdained the question. It turned out that his mother had been after him repeatedly and that he was an incorrigible runaway. She had at last given him up for good. While his picture was being "took," one of the lads reported that she was at the door again, and Tommy broke and ran. He returned just when they closed the doors of the house for the night, with the report that "the old woman was a fake."

The crippled boys' brush shop is a feature of the lodginghouse in East Forty-fourth Street. It is the bête noire of the Society, partly on account of the difficulty of making it go without too great an outlay, partly on account of the boys themselves. They are of all the city's outcasts the most unfortunate and the hardest to manage. Their misfortune has soured their temper, and as a rule they are troublesome and head-strong. No wonder. There seems to be no room for a poor crippled lad in New York. There are plenty of institutions that are after the well and able-bodied, but for the cripples the only chance is to shrivel and die in the Randall's Island Asylum. No one wants them. The brush shop pays them wages that enables them to make their way, and the boys turn out enough brushes, if a market could only be found for them. It is a curious and saddening fact that the competition that robs it of its market comes from the prisons, to block the doors of which the Society expends all its energies—the prisons of other States than our own at that. The managers have a good word to say for the trade unions, which have been very kind to them, they say, in this matter of brushes, trying to help the boys, but without much success. The shop is able to employ only a small fraction of the number it might benefit, were it able to dispose of its wares readily. Despite their misfortunes the cripples manage to pick up and enjoy the good things they find in their path as they hobble through life. Last year they challenged the other crippled boys in the hospital on Randall's Island to a champion game of baseball, and beat them on their crutches with a score of 42 to 31. The game was played on the hospital lawn, before an enthusiastic crowd of wrecks, young and old, and must have been a sight to see.

A worse snag than the competition of the prisons is struck by the Society in the cheap Bowery lodging-houses—"hotels" they are called—that attract the homeless boys with their greater promise of freedom. There are no troublesome rules to obey there, no hours to keep, and very little to pay. An ordinance of the Health Department, which exercises jurisdiction over those houses, prohibits the admission of boys under sixteen years old, but the prohibition is easily evaded, and many slip in to encounter there the worst of all company for such as they. The lowest of these houses, which are also the cheapest and therefore the ones the boys patronize, are the nightly rendezvous of thieves and, as the police have more than once pointed out, murderers as well. There should be a much stricter supervision over them—supervision by the police as well as by the health officers—and the age limit should be put at eighteen years instead of sixteen. There is this much to be said for the lodginghouses, however, that it is a ticklish subject to approach until the city as a municipality has swept before its own door. They at least offer a bed, such as it is, and shelter after their fashion. The hospitality the city offers to its homeless poor in the police station lodging rooms is one of the scandals of a civilized age. The moral degradation of an enforced stay in these dens is immeasurable. To say that they are the resort of tramps and "bums" who know and deserve nothing better is begging the question. It is true of the majority, but that very fact consigns the helpless minority, too poor to pay and too proud to beg, to a fate worse than death. I myself picked from the mass of festering human filth in a police station lodging room, one night last winter, six young lads, not one of whom was over eighteen, and who for one reason or another had been stranded there that night. They were not ruffians either, but boys who to all appearances had come from good homes, the memory of which might not efface the lessons learned that night in a lifetime. The scandal has been denounced over and over again by grand juries, by the police commissioners, and by philanthropists who know of the facts, and efforts without end have been made to get the city authorities to substitute some decent system of municipal hospitality for this unutterable disgrace, as other cities have done, but they have all been wrecked by political jobbery or official apathy.

A thing to be profoundly thankful for is the practical elimination of the girl vagrant from our social life. Ten years ago, Broadway from Fourteenth Street up was crowded with little girls who, under the pretense of peddling flowers and newspapers, pandered to the worst immorality. They went in regular gangs, captained and employed by a few conscienceless old harpies, who took the wages of their infamy and paid them with blows and curses if they fell short of their greed. The police and the officers of the Society for the Prevention of Cruelty to Children put an end to this traffic after a long fight, sending the old wretches to jail and some of their victims to the reformatories. One of the gangs that were broken up had a rendezvous in a stable in Thirtieth Street, near Broadway. The girls had latchkeys and went out and in at all hours of the night. Today the flower girl of tender years is scarcely ever met with in New York. Even the newsgirl has disappeared almost entirely and left the field to the boys. Those who are not at work at home or in the shop have been gathered in by the agencies for their rescue, which have multiplied with the growth of the conviction that girl vagrancy is so much more corrosive than boy vagabondism, as it adds sexual immorality to the other dangers of the street. In 1881 the Society's lodginghouse in St. Mark's Place sheltered 1287 girls. Their number has gone down since, as the census has gone up, until last year it had fallen to 335, and even these were no longer vagrants, but wayward daughters brought by their parents to be trained to obedience and industry. In the same period, during which the city's population increased more than one-fourth, the increase being very largely made up of just the material to feed its homelessness, the register of the boys' lodginghouses showed a reduction from 13,155 to 11,435.

In the introductory chapter I pointed out, as a result of the efforts made in behalf of the children in the past generation, not only by the Children's Aid Society, but by many kindred organizations, that the commitments of girls and women for vagrancy fell off between the years 1860 and 1890 from 5880 to

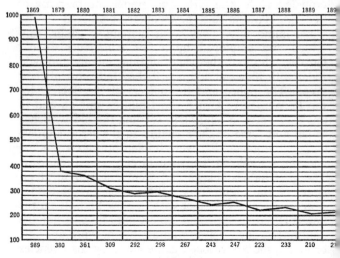

CHART A

1980, or from 1 in every 138½ persons to 1 in every 780 of a population that had more than doubled in the interval, while the commitments of petty girl thieves fell between 1865 and 1890 from 1 in 743 to 1 in 7500. Illustrated by diagram this last statement looks this way, the year 1869 being substituted as the starting point; it had almost exactly the same number of commitments as 1865 (see Chart A).

The year is at the top, and its record of commitments of petty girl thieves at the bottom. The tendency is steadily downward, it will be seen, and downward here is the safe course. The police court arraignments for what is known as juvenile delinquency, which is, in short, all the mischief that is not crime under the code, make the following showing, starting with the year 1875, the upper line representing the boys and the lower the girls:

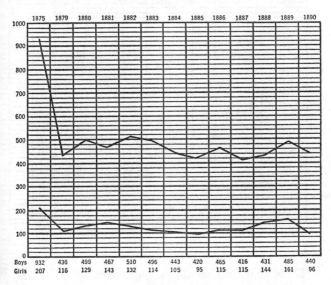

	1875	1879	1880	1881	1882	1883	1884	1885	1886	1887	1888	1889	1890
Boys	932	436	499	467	510	496	443	420	465	416	431	485	440
Girls	207	116	129	143	132	114	105	95	115	115	144	161	96

CHART B

Taking, finally, the commitments of girls under twenty for all causes, in thirteen years, we have this showing:

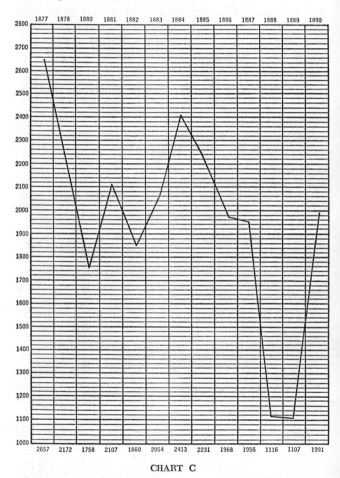

CHART C

These diagrams would be more satisfactory if they always meant exactly what they seem to show. The trouble is that they share in the general inapplicability to the purposes of scientific research of all public reports in this city (save those of the Health Department, which is fortunate in possessing a responsible expert statistician in Dr. Roger S. Tracy) by reason of lack of uniformity or otherwise. When one gets down to the bottom of a slump like that between the years 1888 and 1889, in the last diagram, one is as likely to find a negligent police clerk or some accidental change of classification there as an economic fact. Something like this last is, I believe, hidden in this particular one. The figures for 1891 maintain the point reached in 1887 and in 1890. However, the important thing is that the decrease has gone on more or less steadily through good years and bad since the children's societies took the field, while the population has increased as never before. Had these forms of disorder even held their own, the slope should have been steadily upward, not downward. In this there is encouragement, surely. There is enough left to battle with. The six lodginghouses sheltered in the last twelve years 149,994 children, 8820 of them girls. We are not near the end yet. The problem is a great one, but the efforts on foot to solve it are great and growing. It has been a forty years' fight with poverty and ignorance and crime, and it is only just begun. But the first blow is half the battle, it is said, and it has been struck in New York, and struck to win.

PUTTING A PREMIUM
ON PAUPERISM

In spite of all this labor and effort, in the face of the fact that half of the miseries of society are at last acknowledged to be due to the sundering of the home tie in childhood, and that therefore the remedy lies in restoring it, where that can be done, as early as possible, we have in New York a city of mighty institutions, marshaling a standing army of nearly or quite sixteen thousand children, year in and year out.* Homes they are sometimes called; but too many of them are not homes in the saving sense. Those are, that are merely halfway houses to the ultimate family home that shall restore to the child what it has lost. Failing in that, they become public tenements, with most of the bad features of the tenement left out, but the worst retained: the smothering of the tenant's individuality. He is saved from becoming a tough to become an automaton.

It is money scattered without judgment—not poverty—that makes the pauper. It is money scattered without judgment—not poverty—that marshals the greater part of this army. Money backed up by pharisaical sectarianism. Where two such powerful factors combine, politics is never far in the rear, though modestly invisible to the naked eye. To this irresponsible combination—conspiracy it might be called with-

* That is the average number constantly in asylums. With those that come and go, it foots up quite 25,000 children a year that are a public charge.

out stretching the point far—the care of the defenseless child that comes upon the public for support has been handed over without check or control of any sort. Worse, a premium has been put upon his coming, upon child desertion in our community. What are the causes of this?

They have been stated often and urgently enough by those whose great experience gave weight to their arguments. Clothed in legal phrase, they may be found summed up in the law of 1875, which ordains that a dependent child shall be committed to an institution controlled by persons of the same religious faith as its parents, when that can be done, and that the county shall pay the child's board. It was a tremendous bid for child pauperism, and poverty, ignorance, and greed were not slow to respond. Under this so-called "religious clause," the number of children thrown upon the county, in New York City alone, was swelled, between 1875 and 1890, from 9.363 to 16.358, this statement including only the twenty-nine institutions that can demand or do receive public money toward their support. Some of them, which have come into existence since it was passed, were directly created by the law. It was natural that this should be so, "because it provided exactly the care which parents desired for their children, that of persons of their own religious faith, and supplied ample means for the children's support; while, although the funds were to be derived from public sources, yet since the institutions were to be managed by private persons, the stigma which fortunately attaches to *public* relief was removed. Thus every incentive to parents to place their children upon the public for support was created by the provisions of the law, and every deterrent was removed; for the law demanded nothing from the parent in return for the support of the child, and did not deprive him of any of his rights over the child, although relieving him of every duty toward it."* But New York City went a step further, by having special laws passed securing a stated income from the money raised by local taxation to nine of its largest institutions. This is where the trail of the politician might perhaps be traced with an effort. The amount drawn by the nine in 1890 was nearly a million dollars, while the total so expended footed up in that year over sixteen hundred thousand dollars. New York City today supports one dependent child to each one hundred of its population, and the tax levied, directly and indirectly, for the purpose is about a dollar a head for every man, woman, and child in the city. The state in 1888 supported one child to every 251 of its population. The State of California, which had also gone into the wholesale charity business, supported one dependent child to every 290 of its population, while Michigan, which had gone out of it, taking her children out of the poorhouses and sending them to a state public school, with the proviso that thenceforth parents surrendering their children to be public charges should lose all rights over or to their custody, services, or earnings, had only 1 to every 10,000 of its people.†

That proviso cut the matter to the quick. The law declared the school to be a "temporary home for dependent children, where they shall be detained only until they can be placed in family homes." That is a very different thing from the institution that, with its handsome buildings, its lawns, and its graveled walks, looks to the poor parent like a grand boarding school where his child can be kept, free of charge to him, and taught on terms that seem alluringly like the privileges enjoyed by the rich, until it shall be old enough

* Report upon the Care of Dependent Children in New York City and elsewhere, to the State Board of Charities, by Commissioner Josephine Shaw Lowell. December 1889.

† Mrs. Josephine Shaw Lowell on Dependent Children. Report of 1889.

to earn wages and help toward the family support; very different from the plan of sending the boy to the asylum to be managed the moment parental authority fails at home. To what extent these things are done in New York may be inferred from the statement of the Superintendent of the Juvenile Asylum, which contains an average of a thousand children, that three-fourths of the inmates could not be sent to free homes in the West because their relatives would not consent to their going.* It was only last summer that my attention was attracted, while on a visit to this Juvenile Asylum, to a fine-looking little fellow who seemed much above the average of the class in which I found him. On inquiring as to the causes that had brought him to that place, I was shocked to find that he was the son of a public official, well-known to me, whose income from the city's treasury was sufficient not only to provide for the support of his family, but to enable him to gratify somewhat expensive private tastes as well. The boy had been there two years, during which time the Asylum had drawn for his account from the public funds about $240, at the per capita rate of $110 for each inmate and his share of the school money. His father, when I asked him why the boy was there, told me that it was because he would insist upon paying unauthorized visits to his grandmother in the country. There was no evidence that he was otherwise unmanageable. Seeing my surprise, he put the

---

* Anna T. Wilson: Some Arguments for the Boarding-out of Dependent Children in the State of New York. This opposition the Superintendent explains in his report for 1891, to be due in part to the lying stories about abuse in the West, told by bad boys who return to the city. He adds, however, that "oftentimes the most strenuous opposition . . . is made by stepmothers, uncles, aunts, and cousins," and is "due in the majority of cases not to any special interest in the child's welfare, but to self-interest, the relative wishing to obtain a situation for the boy in order to get his weekly wages."

question, as if that covered the ground: "Well, now! where would you put him in a better place?" It was a handsome compliment to the Asylum, which as a reform school it perhaps deserved; but it struck me, all the same, that he could hardly have put him in a worse place, on all accounts.

I do not know how many such cases there were in the Asylum then. I hope not many. But it is certain that our public institutions are full of children who have parents amply able, but unwilling, to support them. From time to time enough such cases crop out to show how common the practice is. Reference to cases 59,703; 59,851; and 60,497 in the report of the Society for the Prevention of Cruelty to Children (1892), will discover some striking instances that were ferreted out by the Society's officers. All of the offenders were in thriving business. One of them kept a store in Newark—in another state—and was not even a resident of the city. He merely "honored it with the privilege of paying his children's boarding-school expenses in the institution." They were all Italians. These people seem to consider that it is their right to thus feed at the public crib. Perhaps it is the first quickening of the seed of municipal politics that sprouts so energetically among them in the slums, under the teaching of their Irish patrons.

When Mrs. Lowell inspected the New York City institutions in 1889, she found "that of 20,384 individual children sheltered in them, 4139 had been that year returned to parents or friends, that is, to the persons who had given them up to be paupers; that there were only 1776 orphans among them, and 4987 half orphans, of whom 2247 had living fathers, who presumably ought to have been made to support their children themselves." Three years later, the imperfect returns to a circular inquiry sent out by the State Board of Charities, showed that of 18,556 children in institutions in this state, 3671, or less than twenty per cent, were orphans. The rest then had, or should have, homes. Doubtless, many were homes of which they were well rid; but all experience shows that there must have been far too many of the kind that were well rid of *them*, and to that extent the taxpayers were robbed and the parents and the children pauperized. And that even that other kind were much better off in the long run, their being in the institution did not guarantee. Children, once for all, cannot be successfully reared in regiments within the narrow rules and the confinement of an asylum, if success is to be measured by the development of individual character. Power to regulate or shorten their stay is not vested to any practical extent or purpose in any outside agency. Within, with every benevolent desire to do the right, every interest of the institution as a whole tends to confuse the perception of it. The more children, the more money; the fewer children, the less money. A thousand children can be more economically managed for $110,000 than five hundred for half the money. The fortieth annual report of the Juvenile Asylum (1891) puts it very plainly, in this statement on page 23: "Until the capacity of the Asylum was materially increased, an annual deficit ranging between $5000 and $10,000 had to be covered by appeals to private contributors." Now, it runs not only the New York house but its western agency as well on its income.

The city pays the bills, but exercises no other control over the institutions. It does not even trouble itself with counting the children.* The committing

---

* It will do so hereafter. This autumn the discovery was made that the city was asked to pay for more children than there ought to be in the institutions according to the record of commitments. The comptroller sent two of his clerks to count all the children. The result was to show slipshod bookkeeping, if nothing worse, in certain cases. Hereafter the ceremony of counting the children will be gone through every six months.

magistrate consults and is guided more or less by the officers of the Society for the Prevention of Cruelty to Children in his choice of the institution into which the child is put. But both are bound by the law that imposes the "faith test." The faith test, as enforced by civil law anywhere, is absurd. The parents of the eighty per cent of children in institutions who were not orphans, split no theological hairs in ridding themselves of their support. Backed by the money sacks of a great and wealthy city, it is injurious humbug. This is not the perfection of organized charitable effort for the rescue of the children of which I spoke, but rather the perversion of it.

It is reasonable to ask that if the public is to pay the piper, the public should have the hiring of him too. A special city officer is needed to have this matter in charge. Nearly six years ago Commissioner Lowell submitted a draft for a bill creating a department for the care of dependent children in New York City, with a commissioner at the head whose powers would have been an effective check upon the evil tendencies of the present law. But we travel slowly along the path of municipal reform, and the commissioner is yet a dream. Someday we may wake up and find him there, and then we shall be ready, by and by, to carry out the ideal plan of placing those children, for whom free homes cannot be found, out at board in families where they shall come by their rights, denied them by institution life. Then, too, we shall find, I think, that there is a good deal less of the problem than we thought. The managers of the Union Temporary Home in Philadelphia decided, after thirty-one years of work, to close the house and put the children out to board, because experience had convinced them

---

Nothing could more clearly show the irresponsible character of the whole business and the need of a change, lest we drift into corporate pauperism in addition to encouraging the vice in the individual.

that "life in the average institution is not so good for children as life in the average home." The intelligence of the conclusion, and the earnestness with which they presented it, guaranteed that their "home" had been above the average.

"The testimony of two gentlemen on our board of council," they reported, "both experienced as heads of great industrial enterprises, is that institution boys are generally the least desirable apprentices. They have been dulled in faculty, by not having been daily exercised in the use of themselves in small ways; have marched in platoons; have done everything in squads; have had all the particulars of life arranged for them; and, as a consequence, they wait for someone else to arrange every piece of work, and are never ready for emergencies, nor able to 'take hold.'" But when they came to actually board the children out, all but the parents of nine were suddenly able to take good care of them themselves, and of the rest three found a way before final arrangements were made. There were seventy children in the home. Pauperism runs in the same ruts in New York as in Pennsylvania, and the motive power is the same—ill-spent money.

THE VERDICT OF THE
POTTER'S FIELD

Looking back now over the field we have traversed, what is the verdict? Are we going backward or forward? To be standing still would be to lose ground. Nothing stands still in this community of ours, with its ever-swelling population, least of all the problem of the children of the poor. It got the start of our old indifference once, and we have had a long and wearisome race of it, running it down.

But we have run it down. We are moving forward, and indifference will not again trap us into defeat. Evidence is multiplying on every hand to show that interest in the children is increasing. The personal service that counts for so infinitely much more than money is more freely given day by day, and no longer as a fashionable fad, but as a duty too long neglected. From the colleges young men and women are going forth to study the problem in a practical way that is full of promise. Charity is forgetting its petty jealousies and learning the lesson of organization and co-operation. "Looking back," writes the secretary of the Charity Organization Society, "over the progress of the last ten years, the success seems large, while looking at our hopes and aims it often seems meagre." The Church is coming up, no longer down, to its work among the poor. In the multiplication of brotherhoods and sisterhoods, of societies of Christian Endeavor, of King's Daughters, of efforts on every hand to reach the masses, the law of love, the only law that has real power to protect the poor, is receiving fresh illustration day by day.

The Fresh Air Work, the Boys' Clubs, the Society for the Prevention of Cruelty to Children, bear witness to it, and to the energy and resources that shall yet win the fight for us. They were born of New York's plight. The whole world shares in the good they have wrought.

Kindergartens, industrial schools, baby nurseries are springing up everywhere. We have children's playgrounds, and we shall be getting more, if the promised small parks are yet in the future. Municipal progress has not kept step with private benevolence, but there *is* progress. New schools have been built this year and others are planned. We are beginning to understand that there are other and better ways of making citizens and voters than to grind them out through the political naturalization mill at every election. If the rum power has not lost its grip, it has not tightened it, at all events, in forty years. Then there was one saloon to every 90.8 inhabitants; today there is one to every 236.42.* The streets in the tenement districts, since I penned the first lines of this book, have been paved and cleaned as never before, and new standards of decency set up for the poor who live there and for their children. Jersey Street, Poverty Gap, have disappeared, and an end has been put, for a time at least, to the foul business of refuse gathering at the dumps. Nothing stands still in New York. Conditions change so suddenly, under the pressure of new exigencies, that it is sometimes difficult to keep up with

---

* In 1854, with a population of 605,000, there were 6657 licensed and unlicensed saloons in the city, or 1 to every 90.8 of its inhabitants. At the beginning of 1892, with a population of 1,706,500, there were 7218 saloons, or 1 to every 236.42. Counting all places where liquor was sold by license, including hotels, groceries, steamboats, etc., the number was 9050, or 1 to every 188.56 inhabitants.

them. The fact that it is generally business which prompts the changes for the better has this drawback, that the community, knowing that relief is coming sooner or later, gets into the habit of waiting for it to come that way as the natural one. It is not always the natural way, and though relief comes with bustle and stir at last, it is sometimes too long delayed.

Another mischievous habit, characteristic of the American people, preoccupied with so many urgent private concerns, is to rise up and pass a law that is loudly in demand, and let it go with that, as if all social evils could be cured by mere legal enactment. As a result, some of the best and most necessary laws are dead letters on our statute books. The law is there, but no one thinks of enforcing it. The beginning was made at the wrong end; but we shall reach around to the other in season.

The chief end has been gained in the recognition of the child problem as the all-important one, of the development of individual character as the strongest barrier against the evil forces of the street and the tenement. Last year I had occasion to address a convention at the National Capital, on certain phases of city poverty and suffering, and made use of the magic lantern to enforce some of the lessons presented. The last picture put on the screen showed the open trench in the potter's field. When it had passed, the secretary of the convention, a clergyman whose life has been given to rescue work among homeless boys, told how there had just come to join him in his work the man who had until very lately been in charge of this potter's field. His experience there had taught him that the waste before which he stood helpless at that end of the line, looking on without power to check or relieve, must be stopped at its source. So he had turned from the dead to the living, pledging the years that remained to him to that effort.

It struck me then, and it has seemed to me since, that this man's position to the problem was most comprehensive. The evidence of his long-range view was convincing. Society had indeed arrived at the same diagnosis some time before. Reasoning by exclusion, as doctors do in doubtful diseases, the symptoms of which are clearer than their cause, it had conjectured that if the "tough" whom it must maintain in idleness behind prison bars, to keep him from preying upon it, was a creature of environment, not justly to blame, the community must be, for allowing him to grow up a "tough." So, in self-defense, it had turned its hand to the forming of character in proportion as it had come to own its failure to reform it. To that failure the trench in the potter's field bore unceasing witness. Its claim to be heard in evidence was incontestable.

Now that it has been heard, its testimony confirms the judgment that had already experience to back it. There is no longer room for doubt that with the children lies the solution of the problem of poverty, as far as it can be reached under existing forms of society and with our machinery for securing justice by government. The wisdom of generations that were dust two thousand years ago made this choice. We have been long in making it, but not too long if our travail has made it clear at last that for all time to come it must be the only safe choice. And this, whether from the standpoint of the Christian or the unbeliever, from that of humanity or mere business. If the matter is reduced to a simple sum in arithmetic, so much for so much—child rescue, as the one way of balancing waste with gain, loss with profit, becomes the imperative duty of society, its chief bulwark against bankruptcy and wreck.

Thus, through the gloom of the potter's field that has levied such heavy tribute on our city in the past—even the tenth of its life—brighter skies, a new hope, are discerned beyond. They brighten even the slum tenement, and shine into the home which just now we despaired of reaching by any other road than that of pulling it down. Tireless, indeed, the hands need be that have taken up this task. Flag their efforts ever so little, hard-won ground is lost, mischief done. But we are gaining, no longer losing, ground. Seen from the tenement, through the framework of injustice and greed that cursed us with it, the outlook seemed little less than despairing. Groping vainly, with unseeing eyes, we said: There is no way out. The children, upon whom the curse of the tenement lay heaviest, have found it for us. Truly it was said: "A little child shall lead them."

REGISTER OF CHILDREN'S CHARITIES

AS PUBLISHED BY THE
CHARITY ORGANIZATION SOCIETY

In addition to the charities given here, seventy-eight churches of all denominations conduct weekly industrial and sewing classes, generally on Saturdays, for which see the Directory of the Charity Organization Society, under Churches, where may also be found the register of thirty-two fresh-air funds not recorded below, and of some kindergartens and clubs established by various churches for the children of their congregations.

NURSERIES

	Ages Received
Ahawath Chesed Sisterhood, 71 East 3d St.	3 to 6 yrs.
Bethany Day Nursery, 453 East 57th St.	2 weeks to 6 yrs.
Beth-El Society, 355 East 62d St.	2½ to 6 yrs.
Bethlehem Day Nursery, 249 East 30th St.	1 week to 7 yrs.
Children's Charitable Union, 70 Ave. D	3 to 7 yrs.
Day Nursery and Babies' Shelter, 118 West 21st St.	1 to 5 yrs.
Ecole Française Gratuite and Salle d'Asile, 69 Washington Square	2 to 11 yrs.
Emanu-El Sisterhood, 159 East 74th St.	3 to 6 yrs.
Grace House Day Nursery, 94 Fourth Ave.	1 to 8 yrs.
Hope Nursery, 226 Thompson St.	
Jewell Day Nursery, 20 MacDougal St.	2 to 5 yrs.
Manhattan Working Girls' Association, 440 East 57th St.	2 weeks to 10 yrs.

Ages Received

Memorial Day Nursery, 275 East B'way	1 to 6 yrs.
Riverside Day Nursery, 121 West 63d St.	1 mo. to 8 yrs.
St. Agnes' Day Nursery, 7 Charles St.	8 days to 6 yrs.
St. Barnabas' House, 304 Mulberry St.	4 weeks to 8 yrs.
St. Chrysostom Chapel Nursery, 224 West 38th St.	
St. John's Day Nursery, 223 East 67th St.	1 to 6 yrs.
St. Joseph's Day Nursery, 473 West 57th St.	2 weeks to 7 yrs.
St. Stephen's Equity Club, Kindergarten and Nursery, 59 West 46th St.	
St. Thomas' Day Nursery, 231 East 59th St.	— to 6 yrs.
Salle d'Asile et Ecole Primaire, 2 South 5th Ave.	3 to 8 yrs.
Silver Cross Day Nursery, 2249 Second Ave.	2 weeks to 10 yrs.
Sunnyside Day Nursery, 51 Prospect Pl.	2 weeks to 7 yrs.
Virginia Day Nursery, 632 5th St.	6 mos. to 6 yrs.
Wayside Day Nursery, 216 East 20th St.	2 mos. to 7 yrs.
West Side Day Nursery, 266 West 40th St.	18 mos. to 7 yrs.
Wilson Industrial School Day Nursery, 125 St. Mark's Pl.	1 mo. to 6 yrs.

KINDERGARTENS

Ahawath Chesed Sisterhood Free Kindergarten	71 East 3d St.
All Souls' Church Free Kindergarten	70th St. East of Lexington Ave.
Beth-El Society Free Kindergarten	355 East 62d St.
Central Presbyterian Church Free Kindergarten	454 West 42d St.
Cherry Street Kindergarten	340 Cherry St.
Children's Charitable Union Kindergarten	70 Ave. D.
East Side Chapel and Bible Women's Association Kindergarten	404 East 15th St.
East Side House Kindergarten	Foot of East 76th St.
Emanu-El Sisterhood Kindergarten	159 E. 74th St.
Free Kindergarten Ass'n of Harlem, No. 1 School	2048 First Ave.
Free Kindergarten of St. John's Chapel	Varick near Beach.
French Free School	69 South Washington Sq.
Hebrew Free School Association	East B'way and Jefferson St.
Kindergarten of Madison Square Presbyterian Church House	Third Ave. and 30th St.

Kindergarten of St. George's Ave. A Mission	253 Ave. A.
Kindergarten of St. George's Chapel	130 Stanton St.
Kindergarten of Shearith Israel Congregation	5 West 19th St.
Ladies' Bikur Cholim Society Kindergarten	177 East B'way.
Neighborhood Guild Kindergarten	146 Forsyth St.
N. Y. Foundling Hospital Kindergarten	175 East 68th St.

N. Y. Kindergarten Association Schools:

No. 1	221 East 51st St.
No. 2, Alumnæ Kindergarten	cor. 63d St. and First Ave.
No. 3	228 West 35th St.
No. 4	348 West 26th St.
No. 5, Shaw Memorial	61 Henry St.
No. 6, McAlpine	62 Second St.
No. 7	Ave. A and 15th St.
St. Andrews' Free Kindergarten	2067 Second Ave.
St. Bartholomew's Kindergarten	209 East 42d St.
St. James' Free Kindergarten	Ave. A and 78th St.
St. Mary's Kindergarten	438 Grand St.
Shaaray Tefilla Sisterhood Kindergarten	127 West 44th St.
Silver Cross Sisterhood Kindergarten	2249 Second Ave.
Society for Ethical Culture Kindergarten	109 West 54th St.
Temple Israel Sisterhood Kindergarten	125th St. and 5th Ave.
Trinity Church Ass'n Kindergarten	209 Fulton St.
Wilson Industrial School Kindergarten	125 St. Mark's Pl.

INDUSTRIAL SCHOOLS

Abigail School and Kindergarten	242 Spring St.
American Female Guardian Society	Office, 32 East 30th St.
Home School	29 East 29th St.

Industrial Schools:

No. 1	552 First Ave., cor. 32d St.
No. 2 (*Rose Memorial*)	418 West 41st St.
No. 3	124 West 26th St.
No. 4	34 Willett St.
No. 5	220 West 36th St.
No. 6	125 Allen St.
No. 7	234 East 80th St.
No. 8	463 West 32d St.
No. 9	East 60th St. and Boulevard.
No. 10	125 Lewis St.
No. 11	52d St. and Second Ave.
No. 12	2247 Second Ave.

Children's Aid Society   Office, 24 St. Mark's Pl.
   Industrial Schools—

Astor Memorial	256 Mott St.
Ave. B	607 East 14th St.
Cottage Place	208 Bleecker St.
Brace Memorial	9 Duane St.
East River	247 East 44th St.
East Side	287 East Broadway.
Eleventh Ward	295 Eighth St.
Fourth Ward	73 Monroe St.
Fifth Ward	36 Beach St.
Fifty-second Street	573 West 52d St.
German	272 Second St.
Henrietta	215 East 21st St.
Italian	156 Leonard St.
Jones Memorial	407 East 73d St.
Lord	135 Greenwich St.
Park	68th St. near Broadway.
Phelps	314 East 35th St.
Rhinelander	350 East 88th St.
Sixteenth Ward	211 West 18th St.
Sixth Street	632 Sixth St.
West Side	201 West 32d St.
West Side Italian	24 Sullivan St.

   Night Schools—

German	272 Second St.
Italian	156 Leonard St.
Brace Memorial (*Newsboys*)	9 Duane St.
Eleventh Ward	295 8th St.
East Side	287 East Broadway.
Lord	135 Greenwich St.
Jones Memorial	407 East 73d St.
Fifty-second Street	573 West 52d St.
West Side	400 Seventh Ave.

Church Society for Promoting Christianity among Jews	
(*Industrial School for Girls*)	68 East 7th St.
Eighth Ward Mission School	1 Charlton St.
Five Points House of Industry	155 Worth St.
Five Points Mission	63 Park St.
Free German School	140 East 4th St.
Hebrew Free School Assn	East B'way and Jefferson St.
Italian Mission (*P. E. School for Girls*)	309 Mulberry St.
Industrial Christian Alliance	113 MacDougal St.

Louis Downtown Sabbath and Daily School (*Hebrew*)
                                    267 Henry St.
Mission of the Immaculate Virgin
                        Lafayette Pl. and Great Jones St.
Mission School of All Souls' Church   213 East 21st St.
New York Bible and Tract Mission (*School for Girls*)
                                    422 East 26th St.
New York House and School of Industry   120 West 16th St.
Sisterhood of the Good Shepherd (P. E.) 419 West 19th St.
St. Barnabas' House   304 Mulberry St.
St. Vincent de Paul Industrial School   346 West 43d St.
St. Elizabeth Industrial School   235 East 14th St.
Spanish Industrial School   1345 Lexington Ave.
Trinity Industrial School   90 Trinity Pl.
St. George's Industrial School   Teutonia Hall.
Trinity Chapel Industrial School   15 West 25th St.
St. Augustine's Chapel Industrial School   105 East Houston St.
St. Mary's   Lawrence St., Manhattanville.
West Side Industrial School   266 West 40th St.
Wilson Industrial School   125 St. Mark's Pl.
United Hebrew Charities (*Industrial School for Girls*)
                                    128 Second Ave.
Zion and St. Timothy Industrial School   332 West 57th St.

FRESH AIR WORK

The Tribune Fresh-Air Fund   Tribune Building.
Bartholdi Creche   21 University Pl.
Children's Aid Society—Health Home   West Coney Island.
Children's Aid Society—Summer Home   Bath Beach.
The King's Daughters Tenement-House Committee
                                    77 Madison St.
New York Infirmary for Women and Children   5 Livingston Pl.
New York City Mission and Tract Society 106 Bible House.
St. John's Guild   501 Fifth Ave.
St. John's Guild—Floating Hospital
                        (every weekday but Saturday).
St. John's Guild—Seaside Hospital   Cedar Grove, Staten Island.
Sanitarium for Hebrew Children   124 East 14th St.
Society for Ethical Culture   109 West 54th St.
New York Association for Improving the Condition
   of the Poor (*Ocean Parties*)   79 Fourth Ave.

St. Barnabas Fresh-Air Fund	38 Bleecker St.
The Little Mothers' Aid Society	305 East 17th St.
New York Bible and Tract Mission	416 East 26th St.
New York Society for Parks and Playgrounds for Children	36 Union Square.
American Female Guardian Society	Summer Home at Oceanport, N. J.
Summer Shelter	Morristown, N. J.

(*Apply to Charity Organization Society, 21 University Pl.*)

BOYS' CLUBS AND READING ROOMS

Ascension Memorial Chapel (P. E.)	330 West 43d St.
Avenue C Club	65 East 14th St.
Bethany Church	Tenth Ave., bet. 35th and 36th Sts.
Calvary Parish	344 East 23d St.
Chapel of the Comforter	814 Greenwich St.
Christ Chapel	West 65th St. near Amsterdam Ave.
Church of the Archangel (P. E.)	117th St. and St. Nicholas Ave.
Church of the Redeemer	Park Ave. and 81st St.
College Settlement	95 Rivington St.
Covenant Chapel	310 East 42d St.
DeWitt Chapel	160 West 29th St.
East Side House	Foot of 76th St. and East River.
Free Reading Rooms	8 West 14th St., 330 Fourth Ave., and 590 Seventh Ave.
Grace Mission	640 East 13th St.
Holy Communion (P. E.) Church	49 West 20th St.
Holy Cross Lyceum	43d St., bet. Eighth and Ninth Aves.
Holy Cross Mission	300 East Fourth St.
Lafayette Club (*Middle Collegiate Church*)	14 Lafayette Pl.
Mission Chapel of Madison Ave. Church	440 East 57th St.
Madison Square Church House	Third Ave., cor. 30th St.
Manor Chapel	348 West 26th St.
Memorial Baptist Church	Washington Square, South.
Monday Night Club (*Church of Holy Communion*)	49 West 20th St.
Neighborhood Guild	147 Forsyth St.
New Jerusalem Church	114 East 35th St.
North Side Boys' Club	79 MacDougal St.
St. Bartholomew's Parish House	207 East 42d St.

St. George's (P. E.) Church (*Memorial House*)

207 East 16th St.

St. Luke's M. E. Church (*Knights of St. Luke*)

108 West 41st St.

St. Mary's   Lawrence St., Manhattanville.
West Side   Vermilye Chapel, 794 Tenth Ave.
Wilson Mission Building (*Ave. A Club*)   125 St. Mark's Pl.

CHILDREN'S LODGINGHOUSES

Brace Memorial   9 Duane St.
Girls' Temporary Home   307–309 East 12th St.
Tompkins Square   295 8th St.
East Side   287 East Broadway.
Forty-fourth Street   247 East 44th St.
West Side   400 Seventh Ave.
Mission of the Immaculate Virgin

Lafayette Pl. and Great Jones St.

CHILDREN'S HOMES—TEMPORARY AND PERMANENT

Asylum of St. Vincent de Paul   215 West 39th St.
Asylum of Sisters of St. Dominic (*House of Reception*)

137 Second St.

Berachah Orphanage (*Gospel Tabernacle*)   692 Eighth Ave.
Bethlehem Orphan and Half-Orphan Asylum, College Point, L. I.
  (*Controlled by thirteen Lutheran churches of New York and
  vicinity.*)
Children's Fold   92d St. and Eighth Ave.
Colored Orphan Asylum   West 143d St. and Boulevard.
Free Home for Destitute Young Girls   23 East 11th St.
Dominican Convent of Our Lady of the Rosary   329 East 63d St.
Five Points House of Industry   155 Worth St.
German Odd Fellows' Orphanage

Apply at Home, 82 Second Ave.

Hebrew Benevolent and Orphan Asylum

Amsterdam Ave. and 136th St.

Hebrew Sheltering Guardian Orphan Asylum

Eleventh Ave. and 151st St.

Holy Angels' Orphan Asylum (*for Italian Children from New
  York*)   West Park-on-the-Hudson.

House of Mercy   81st St. and Madison Ave.
Ladies' Deborah Nursery and Child's Protectory, Male Department, 95 East B'way and 83 Henry St.; Female Department, East 162d St., near Eagle Ave.
Leake and Watts Orphan House   Ludlow Station, Hudson R. R.
Messiah Home for Little Children   4 Rutherford Pl.
Mission of the Immaculate Virgin for Homeless and Destitute Children   Lafayette Pl. and Great Jones St.
St. Joseph's Home for Destitute Children
                    House of Reception, 143 West 31st St.
New York Foundling Hospital (*Asylum of Sisters of Charity*)
                              175 East 68th St.
New York Infant Asylum   Amsterdam Ave. and 61st St.
Orphanage of the Church of the Holy Trinity   400 East 50th St.
Orphan Asylum Society   Riverside Drive and West 73d St.
Orphans' Home and Asylum of Protestant Episcopal Church
                          49th St. near Lexington Ave.
Roman Catholic Orphan Asylum   Madison Ave. and 51st St.
St. Agatha's Home for Children   209 West 15th St.
St. Ann's Home for Destitute Children   Ave. A, cor. 90th St.
St. Benedict's Home for Colored Children
                    House of Reception, 120 MacDougal St.
St. Christopher's Home   Riverside Drive and 112th St.
St. James' Home   21 Oliver and 26 James St.
St. Joseph's Orphan Asylum   89th St. and Ave. A.
Shepherd's Fold (P. E. Church)   92d St. and Eighth Ave.
Protestant Half-Orphan Asylum   Manhattan Ave. near 104th St.
Home for Seamen's Children (*New York and vicinity*)
                              West New Brighton, S. I.
Society for the Prevention of Cruelty to Children
                              100 East 23d St.

REFORMATORY INSTITUTIONS

Burnham Industrial Farm   Office, 135 East 15th St.
Hebrew Sheltering Guardian Society
                          Eleventh Ave. and 151st St.
New York Catholic Protectory   Office, 415 Broome St.
New York Juvenile Asylum   176th St. and Amsterdam Ave.
St. James' Home   21 Oliver St.
House of Refuge   Randall's Island.
House of the Holy Family   132 Second Ave.

CHILDREN'S HOSPITALS AND DISPENSARIES

All Saints' Convalescent Home for Men and Boys (*Holy Cross Mission*)   Avenue C and 4th St.
Babies' Hospital of the City of New York   657 Lexington Ave.
Babies' Ward, Post-Graduate Hospital   226 East 20th St.
Children's Hospital   Randall's Island.
New York Infirmary for Women and Children   5 Livingston Pl.
Five Points House of Industry Infirmary   147 Worth St.
Good Samaritan Diakonissen (*Hahnemann Hospital*)   Park Ave. and 67th St.
Infants' Hospital   Randall's Island.
Laura Franklin Free Hospital for Children   19 East 111th St.
New York Foundling Hospital   175 East 68th St.
Nursery and Child's Hospital   Lexington Ave. and 51st St.
St. Mary's Free Hospital for Children   405 West 34th St.
Harlem Dispensary for Women and Children   2331 Second Ave.
Sick Children's Mission of Children's Aid Society   287 East B'way.
Yorkville Dispensary and Hospital for Women and Children   1307 Lexington Ave.
New York Orthopedic Hospital   126 East 59th St.
New York Ophthalmic Hospital   201 East 23d St.

ASYLUMS FOR DEFECTIVE CHILDREN

Crippled Boys' Home (*Forty-fourth Street Lodginghouse*)   247 East 44th St.
Institution for the Improved Instruction of Deaf-Mutes   Lexington Ave. and 67th St.
Idiot Asylum   Randall's Island.
New York Institution for the Blind   Ninth Ave. and 34th St.
New York Institution for the Instruction of the Deaf and Dumb   Eleventh Ave. and 163d St.
New York Society for the Relief of the Ruptured and Crippled   Lexington Ave. and 42d St.
St. Joseph's Institution for the Improved Instruction of Deaf-Mutes   772 East 188th St.
Sheltering Arms   Amsterdam Ave. and 129th St.
Society of St. Johnland   Apply at Calvary Chapel, 220 East 23d St.

Syracuse State School for Feeble-Minded
                    (*Apply to Superintendent of Outdoor Poor.*)
Children's Aid Society   Haxtun Cottage, Bath Beach, L. I.
House of St. Giles the Cripple   422 Degraw St., Brooklyn.

A TEN YEARS' WAR

An Account of the Battle
with the Slum in New York

THE BATTLE
WITH THE SLUM

The slum is as old as civilization. Civilization implies a race to get ahead. In a race there are usually some who for one cause or another cannot keep up, or are thrust out from among their fellows. They fall behind, and when they have been left far in the rear they lose hope and ambition, and give up. Thenceforward, if left to their own resources, they are the victims, not the masters, of their environment; and it is a bad master. They drag one another always farther down. The bad environment becomes the heredity of the next generation. Then, given the crowd, you have the slum ready-made.

The battle with the slum began the day civilization recognized in it her enemy. It was a losing fight until conscience joined forces with fear and self-interest against it. When common sense and the golden rule obtain among men as a rule of practice, it will be over. The two have not always been classed together, but here they are plainly seen to belong together. Justice to the individual is accepted in theory as the only safe groundwork of the commonwealth. When it is practiced in dealing with the slum, there will shortly be no slum. We need not wait for the millennium to get rid of it. We can do it now. All that is required is that it shall not be left to itself. That is justice to it and to us, since its grievous ailment is that it cannot help itself. When a man is drowning, the thing to do is to pull him out of the water; afterward there will be time for talking it over. We got at it the other way in deal-

ing with our social problems. The doctrinaires had
their day, and they decided to let bad enough alone;
that it was unsafe to interfere with "causes that operate sociologically," as one survivor of these unfittest
put it to me. It was a piece of scientific humbug that
cost the age which listened to it dear. "Causes that
operate sociologically" are the opportunity of the
political and every other kind of scamp who trades
upon the depravity and helplessness of the slum, and
the refuge of the pessimist who is useless in the fight
against them. We have not done yet paying the bills
he ran up for us. Some time since we turned to, to
pull the drowning man out, and it was time. A little
while longer, and we should have been in danger of
being dragged down with him.

The slum complaint had been chronic in all ages,
but the great changes which the nineteenth century
saw, the new industry, political freedom, brought on
an acute attack which threatened to become fatal. Too
many of us had supposed that, built as our commonwealth was on universal suffrage, it would be proof
against the complaints that harassed older states; but
in fact it turned out that there was extra hazard in
that. Having solemnly resolved that all men are
created equal and have certain inalienable rights,
among them life, liberty, and the pursuit of happiness,
we shut our eyes and waited for the formula to work.
It was as if a man with a cold should take the doctor's
prescription to bed with him, expecting it to cure him.
The formula was all right, but merely repeating it
worked no cure. When, after a hundred years, we
opened our eyes, it was upon sixty cents a day as the
living wage of the working woman in our cities; upon
"knee pants" at forty cents a dozen for the making;
upon the potter's field taking tithe of our city life, ten
per cent each year for the trench, truly the Lost Tenth
of the slum. Our country had grown great and rich;
through our ports was poured food for the millions of
Europe. But in the back streets multitudes huddled

in ignorance and want. The foreign oppressor had been vanquished, the fetters stricken from the black man at home; but his white brother, in his bitter plight, sent up a cry of distress that had in it a distinct note of menace. Political freedom we had won; but the problem of helpless poverty, grown vast with the added offscourings of the Old World, mocked us, unsolved. Liberty at sixty cents a day set presently its stamp upon the government of our cities, and it became the scandal and the peril of our political system.

So the battle began. Three times since the war that absorbed the nation's energies and attention had the slum confronted us in New York with its challenge. In the darkest days of the great struggle it was the treacherous mob; later on, the threat of the cholera, which found swine foraging in the streets as the only scavengers, and a swarming host, but little above the hog in its appetites and in the quality of the shelter afforded it, peopling the back alleys. Still later, the mob, caught looting the city's treasury with its idol, the thief Tweed, at its head, drunk with power and plunder, had insolently defied the outraged community to do its worst. There were meetings and protests. The rascals were turned out for a season; the archthief died in jail. I see him now, going through the gloomy portals of the Tombs, whither, as a newspaper reporter, I had gone with him, his stubborn head held high as ever. I asked myself more than once, at the time when the vile prison was torn down, whether the comic clamor to have the ugly old gates preserved and set up in Central Park had anything to do with the memory of the "martyred" thief, or whether it was in joyful celebration of the fact that others had escaped. His name is even now one to conjure with in the Sixth Ward. He never "squealed," and he was "so good to the poor"—evidence that the slum is not laid by the heels by merely destroying Five Points and the Mulberry Bend. There are other fights to be fought in that war, other victories to be won, and it is slow work. It was nearly ten years after the great robbery before decency got the upper grip in good earnest. That was when the civic conscience awoke in 1879.

In that year the slum was arraigned in the churches. The sad and shameful story was told of how it grew and was fostered by avarice, that saw in the homeless crowds from over the sea only a chance for business, and exploited them to the uttermost, making sometimes a hundred per cent on the capital invested—always most out of the worst houses, from the tenants of which "nothing was expected" save that they pay the usurious rents; how Christianity, citizenship, human fellowship, shook their skirts clear of the rabble that was only good enough to fill the greedy purse, and how the rabble, left to itself, improved such opportunities as it found after such fashion as it knew; how it ran elections merely to count its thugs in, and fattened at the public crib; and how the whole evil thing had its root in the tenements, where the home had ceased to be sacred—those dark and deadly dens in which the family ideal was tortured to death, and character was smothered; in which children were "damned rather than born" into the world, thus realizing a slum kind of foreordination to torment, happily brief in many cases. The Tenement House Committee long afterward called the worst of the barracks "infant slaughter houses," and showed, by reference to the mortality lists, that they killed one in every five babies born in them.

The story shocked the town into action. Plans for a better kind of tenement were called for, and a premium was put on every ray of light and breath of air that could be let into it. Money was raised to build model houses, and a bill to give the health authorities summary powers in dealing with tenements was sent to the legislature. The landlords held it up until the last day of the session, when it was forced through by an angered public opinion. The power of the cabal was broken. The landlords had found their Waterloo.

Many of them got rid of their property, which in a large number of cases they had never seen, and tried to forget the source of their ill-gotten wealth. Light and air did find their way into the tenements in a half-hearted fashion, and we began to count the tenants as "souls." That is one of our milestones in the history of New York. They were never reckoned so before; no one ever thought of them as "souls." So, restored to human fellowship, in the twilight of the air shaft that had penetrated to their dens, the first Tenement House Committee was able to make them out "better than the houses" they lived in, and a long step forward was taken. The Mulberry Bend, the wicked core of the "bloody Sixth Ward," was marked for destruction, and all slumdom held its breath to see it go. With that gone, it seemed as if the old days must be gone too, never to return. There would not be another Mulberry Bend. As long as it stood, there was yet a chance. The slum had backing, as it were.

The civic conscience was not very robust yet, and required many and protracted naps. It slumbered fitfully eight long years, waking up now and then with a start, while the politicians did their best to lull it back to its slumbers. I wondered often, in those years of delay, if it was just plain stupidity that kept the politicians from spending the money which the law had put within their grasp; for with every year that passed a million dollars that could have been used for small park purposes was lost. But they were wiser than I. I understood when I saw the changes which letting in the sunshine worked. We had all believed it, but they knew it all along. At the same time, they lost none of the chances that offered. They helped the landlords, who considered themselves greatly aggrieved because their property was thereafter to front on a park instead of a pigsty, to transfer the whole assessment of half a million dollars for park benefit to the city. They undid in less than six weeks what it had taken considerably more than six years to do; but the park was cheap at the price. We could afford to pay all it cost to wake us up. When finally, upon the wave of wrath excited by the Parkhurst and Lexow disclosures, reform came with a shock that dislodged Tammany, it found us wide awake, and, it must be admitted, not a little astonished at our sudden access of righteousness.

The battle went against the slum in the three years that followed, until it found backing in the "odium of reform" that became the issue in the municipal organization of the greater city. Tammany made notes. Of what was done, how it was done, and why, during those years, I shall have occasion to speak further in these pages. Here I wish to measure the stretch we have come since I wrote *How the Other Half Lives*, ten years ago. Some of it we came plodding, and some at full speed; some of it in the face of every obstacle that could be thrown in our way, wresting victory from defeat at every step; some of it with the enemy on the run. Take it altogether, it is a long way. Most of it will not have to be traveled over again. The engine of municipal progress, once started as it has been in New York, may slip many a cog with Tammany as the engineer; it may even be stopped for a season; but it can never be made to work backward. Even Tammany knows that, and is building the schools she so long neglected, and so is hastening the day when she shall be but an unsavory memory.

How we strove for those schools, to no purpose! Our arguments, our anger, the anxious pleading of philanthropists who saw the young on the East Side going to ruin, the warning year after year of the superintendent of schools that the compulsory education law was but an empty mockery where it was most needed, the knocking of uncounted thousands of children for whom there was no room—uncounted in sober fact; there was not even a way of finding out how many were adrift—brought only the response that the tax rate must be kept down. Kept down it was. "Waste" was successfully averted at the spigot; at the bunghole it went on unchecked. In a swarming population like that you must have either schools or jails, and the jails waxed fat with the overflow. The East Side, which had been orderly, became a hotbed of child crime. And when, in answer to the charge made by a legislative committee that the father forced his child into the shop on a perjured age certificate to labor when he ought to have been at play, that father, bent and heavy-eyed with unceasing toil, flung back the charge with the bitter reproach that we gave him no other choice, that it was either the street or the shop for his boy, and that perjury for him was cheaper than the ruin of the child, we were mute. What, indeed, was there to say? The crime was ours, not his. That was but yesterday. Today we can count the months to the time when every child who knocks shall find a seat in our schools. We have a school census to tell us of the need. In that most crowded neighborhood in all the world, where the superintendent lately pleaded in vain for three new schools, five have been built, the finest in this or any other land—great light and airy structures, with playgrounds on the roof; and all over the city the like are going up. The briefest of our laws, every word of which is like the blow of a hammer driving the nails home in the coffin of the bad old days, says that never one shall be built without its playground. So the boy is coming to his rights.

The streets are cleaned—not necessarily clean just now; Colonel Waring is dead, with his doctrine of putting a man instead of a voter behind every broom, killed by politics, he and his doctrine both—but cleaned. The slum has even been washed. We tried that on Hester Street years ago, in the age of cobblestone pavements, and the result fairly frightened us. I remember the indignant reply of a well-known citizen, a man of large business responsibility and experience in the handling of men, to whom the office of street-cleaning commissioner had been offered, when I asked him if he would accept. "I have lived," he said, "a blameless life for forty years, and have a character in the community. I cannot afford—no man with a reputation can afford—to hold that office; it will surely wreck it." That was then. It made Colonel Waring's reputation. He took the trucks from the streets. Tammany, in a brief interregnum of vigor under Mayor Grant, had laid the ax to the unsightly telegraph poles and begun to pave the streets with asphalt, but it left the trucks and the ash barrels to Colonel Waring as hopeless. Trucks have votes; at least their drivers have. Now that they are gone, the drivers would be the last to bring them back; for they have children, too, and the rescued streets gave them their first playground. Perilous, begrudged by policeman and storekeeper, though it was, it was still a playground.

But one is coming in which the boy shall rule unchallenged. The Mulberry Bend Park kept its promise. Before the sod was laid in it, two more were under way in the thickest of the tenement house crowding, and each, under the law which brought them into existence, is to be laid out in part as a playground. They are not yet finished, but they will be; for the people have taken to the idea, and the politician has made a note of the fact. He saw a great light when the play piers were opened. In half a dozen localities where the slum was striking its roots deep into the soil, such piers are now being built, and land is being acquired for small parks. We shall yet settle the "causes that operated sociologically" on the boy with a lawn mower and a sand heap. You have got your boy, and the heredity of the next one, when you can order his setting.

Even while I am writing, a bill is urged in the legislature to build in every senatorial district in the city a gymnasium and a public bath. It matters little whether it passes at this session or not. The important thing is that it is there. The rest will follow. A people's

club is being organized, to crowd out the saloon that
has had a monopoly of the brightness and the cheer
in the tenement streets too long. The labor unions are
bestirring themselves to deal with the sweating curse,
and the gospel of less law and more enforcement sits
enthroned at Albany. Theodore Roosevelt will teach
us again Jefferson's forgotten lesson, that "the whole
art of government consists in being honest." With a
back door to every ordinance that touched the lives
of the people, if indeed the whole thing was not the
subject of open ridicule or the vehicle of official blackmail, it seemed as if we had provided a perfect municipal machinery for bringing the law into contempt
with the young, and so for wrecking citizenship by the
shortest cut.

Of free soup there is an end. It was never food for
free men. The last spoonful was ladled out by yellow
journalism with the certificate of the men who fought
Roosevelt and reform in the police board that it was
good. It is not likely that it will ever plague us again.
Our experience has taught us a new reading of the old
word that charity covers a multitude of sins. It does.
Uncovering some of them has kept us busy since our
conscience awoke, and there are more left. The worst
of them all, that awful parody on municipal charity,
the police station lodging room, is gone, after twenty
years of persistent attack upon the foul dens—years
during which they were arraigned, condemned, indicted by every authority having jurisdiction, all to no
purpose. The stale beer dives went with them and
with the Bend, and the grip of the tramp on our
throat has been loosened. We shall not easily throw it
off altogether, for the tramp has a vote, too, for which
Tammany, with admirable ingenuity, has found a new
use, since the ante-election inspection of lodginghouses
has made them less available for colonization purposes than they were. Perhaps I should say a new
way of very old use. It is simplicity itself. Instead of
keeping tramps in hired lodgings for weeks at a daily

outlay, the new way is to send them all to the island
on short commitments during the canvass, and vote
them from there *en bloc* at the city's expense. Time
and education must solve that, like so many other
problems which the slum has thrust upon us. They
are the forces upon which, when we have gone as far
as our present supply of steam will carry us, we must
always fall back; and this we may do with confidence
so long as we keep stirring, if it is only marking time,
as now. It is in the retrospect that one sees how far
we have come, after all, and from that gathers courage for the rest of the way. Twenty-nine years have
passed since I slept in a police station lodginghouse,
a lonely lad, and was robbed, beaten, and thrown out
for protesting; and when the vagrant cur that had
joined its homelessness to mine, and had sat all night
at the door waiting for me to come out—it had been
clubbed away the night before—snarled and showed
its teeth at the doorman, raging and impotent I saw
it beaten to death on the step. I little dreamed then
that the friendless beast, dead, should prove the undoing of the monstrous wrong done by the maintenance of these evil holes to every helpless man and
woman who was without shelter in New York; but it
did. It was after an inspection of the lodging rooms,
when I stood with Theodore Roosevelt, then president
of the police board, in the one where I had slept that
night, and told him of it, that he swore they should
go. And go they did, as did so many another abuse in
those two years of honest purpose and effort. I hated
them. It may not have been a very high motive to furnish power for municipal reform; but we had tried
every other way, and none of them worked. Arbitration is good, but there are times when it becomes necessary to knock a man down and arbitrate sitting on
him, and this was such a time. It was what we started
out to do with the rear tenements, the worst of the
slum barracks, and it would have been better had we
kept on that track. I have always maintained that we

made a false move when we stopped to discuss damages with the landlord, or to hear his side of it at all. His share in it was our grievance; it blocked the mortality records with its burden of human woe. The damage was all ours, the profit all his. If there are damages to collect, he should foot the bill, not we. Vested rights are to be protected, but no man has a right to be protected in killing his neighbor.

However, they are down, the worst of them. The community has asserted its right to destroy tenements that destroy life, and for that cause. We bought the slum off in the Mulberry Bend at its own figure. On the rear tenements we set the price, and set it low. It was a long step. Bottle Alley is gone, and Bandits' Roost. Bone Alley, Thieves' Alley, and Kerosene Row —they are all gone. Hell's Kitchen and Poverty Gap have acquired standards of decency; Poverty Gap has risen even to the height of neckties. The time is fresh in my recollection when a different kind of necktie was its pride; when the boy murderer—he was barely nineteen—who wore it on the gallows took leave of the captain of detectives with the cheerful invitation to "come over to the wake. They will have a high old time." And the event fully redeemed the promise. The whole Gap turned out to do the dead bully honor. I have not heard from the Gap, and hardly from Hell's Kitchen, in five years. The last news from the Kitchen was when the thin wedge of a column of negroes, in their uptown migration, tried to squeeze in, and provoked a race war; but that in fairness should not be laid up against it. In certain local aspects it might be accounted a sacred duty; as much so as to get drunk and provoke a fight on the anniversary of the battle of the Boyne. But on the whole the Kitchen has grown orderly. The gang rarely beats a policeman nowadays, and it has not killed one in a long while.

So, one after another, the outworks of the slum have been taken. It has been beaten in many battles; but its reserves are unimpaired. More tenements are be-

ing built every day on twenty-five-foot lots, and however watchfully such a house is planned, if it is to return to the builder the profit he seeks, it will have that
within it which, the moment the grasp of official sanitary supervision is loosened, must summon up the
ghost of the slum. The common type of tenement today is the double-decker, and the double-decker is
hopeless. In it the crowding goes on at a constantly
increasing rate. This is the sore spot, and as against
it, all the rest seems often enough unavailing. Yet it
cannot be. It is true that the home, about which all
that is to work for permanent progress must cluster,
is struggling against desperate odds in the tenement,
and that the struggle has been reflected in the morals
of the people, in the corruption of the young, to an
alarming extent; but it must be that the higher standards now set up on every hand, in the cleaner streets,
in the better schools, in the parks and the clubs, in the
settlements, and in the thousand and one agencies for
good that touch and help the lives of the poor at as
many points, will tell at no distant day, and react upon
the homes and upon their builders. To anyone who
knew the East Side, for instance, ten years ago, the
difference between that day and this in the appearance of the children whom he sees there must be
striking. Rags and dirt are now the exception rather
than the rule. Perhaps the statement is a trifle too
strong as to the dirt; but dirt is not harmful except
when coupled with rags; it can be washed off, and
nowadays is washed off where such a thing would
have been considered affectation in the days that
were. Soap and water have worked a visible cure already, that must go more than skin-deep. They are
moral agents of the first value in the slum. And the
day must come when rapid transit will cease to be a
football between contending forces in a city of three
million people, and the reason for the outrageous
crowding will cease to exist with the scattering of the
centers of production to the suburb. That day may

be a long way off, measured by the impatience of the philanthropist, but it is bound to come. Meanwhile, philanthropy is not sitting idle and waiting. It is building tenements on the humane plan that wipes out the lines of the twenty-five-foot lot, and lets in sunshine and air and hope. It is putting up hotels deserving of the name for the army that but just now had no other home than the cheap lodginghouses which Inspector Byrnes fitly called "nurseries of crime." These also are standards from which there is no backing down, even if coming up to them is slow work; and they are here to stay, for they pay. That is the test. Not charity, but justice—that is the gospel which they preach.

Flushed with the success of many victories, we challenged the slum to a fight to the finish a year ago, and bade it come on. It came on. On our side fought the bravest and best. The man who marshaled the citizen forces for their candidate had been foremost in building homes, in erecting baths for the people, in directing the self-sacrificing labors of the oldest and worthiest of the agencies for improving the condition of the poor. With him battled men who had given lives of patient study and effort to the cause of helping their fellow men. Shoulder to shoulder with them stood the thoughtful workingman from the East Side tenement. The slum, too, marshaled its forces. Tammany produced her notes. She pointed to the increased tax rate, showed what it had cost to build schools and parks and to clean house, and called it criminal recklessness. The issue was made sharp and clear. The war cry of the slum was characteristic: "To hell with reform!" We all remember the result. Politics interfered, and turned victory into defeat. We were beaten. I shall never forget that election night. I walked home through the Bowery in the midnight hour, and saw it gorging itself, like a starved wolf, upon the promise of the morrow. Drunken men and women sat in every doorway, howling ribald songs and curses. Hard faces I had not seen for years showed themselves about the dives. The mob made merry after its fashion. The old days were coming back. Reform was dead, and decency with it.

A year later, I passed that same way on the night of election. The scene was strangely changed. The street was unusually quiet for such a time. Men stood in groups about the saloons, and talked in whispers, with serious faces. The name of Roosevelt was heard on every hand. The dives were running, but there was no shouting, and violence was discouraged. When, on the following day, I met the proprietor of one of the oldest concerns in the Bowery—which, while doing a legitimate business, caters necessarily to its crowds, and therefore sides with them—he told me with bitter reproach how he had been stricken in pocket. A gambler had just been in to see him, who had come on from the far West in anticipation of a wide-open town, and had got all ready to open a house in the Tenderloin. "He brought $40,000 to put in the business, and he came to take it away to Baltimore. Just now the cashier of —— Bank told me that two other gentlemen—gamblers? yes, that's what you call them—had drawn $130,000 which they would have invested here, and had gone after him. Think of all that money gone to Baltimore! That's what you've done!"

I went over to police headquarters, thinking of the sad state of that man, and in the hallway I ran across two children, little tots, who were inquiring their way to "the commissioner." The older was a hunchback girl, who led her younger brother (he could not have been over five or six years old) by the hand. They explained their case to me. They came from Allen Street. Some undesirable women tenants had moved into the tenement, and when complaint was made that sent the police there, the children's father, who was a poor Jewish tailor, was blamed. The tenants took it out of the boy by punching his nose till it bled. Whereupon the children went straight to Mulberry Street to see the commissioner and get justice. It was the first time in twenty years that I had known Allen Street to come to police headquarters for justice; and in the discovery that the new idea had reached down to the little children, I read the doom of the slum, despite its loud vauntings.

No, it was not true that reform was dead, with decency. It was not the slum that had won; it was we who had lost. We were not up to the mark—not yet. But New York is a many times cleaner and better city today than it was ten years ago. Then I was able to grasp easily the whole plan for wresting it from the neglect and indifference that had put us where we were. It was chiefly, almost wholly, remedial in its scope. Now it is preventive, constructive, and no ten men could gather all the threads and hold them. We have made, are making headway, and no Tammany has the power to stop us. She knows it, too, and is in such frantic haste to fill her pockets while she has time that she has abandoned her old ally, the tax rate, and the pretense of making bad government cheap government. She is at this moment engaged in raising taxes and assessments at one and the same time to an unheard-of figure, while salaries are being increased lavishly on every hand. We can afford to pay all she charges us for the lesson we are learning. If to that we add common sense, we shall discover the bearings of it all without trouble. Yesterday I picked up a book— a learned disquisition on government—and read on the title page, "Affectionately dedicated to all who despise politics." That was not common sense. To win the battle with the slum, we must not begin by despising politics. We have been doing that too long. The politics of the slum is apt to be like the slum itself, dirty. Then it must be cleaned. It is what the fight is about. Politics is the weapon. We must learn to use it so as to cut straight and sure. That is common sense, and the golden rule as applied to Tammany.

Some years ago, the United States Government conducted an inquiry into the slums of great cities. To its staff of experts was attached a chemist, who gathered and isolated a lot of bacilli with fearsome Latin names in the tenements where he went. Among those he labeled were the *Staphylococcus pyogenes albus,* the *Micrococcus fervidosus,* the *Saccharomyces rosaceus,* and the *Bacillus buccalis fortuitus.* I made a note of the names at the time, because of the dread with which they inspired me. But I searched the collection in vain for the real bacillus of the slum. It escaped science, to be identified by human sympathy and a conscience-stricken community with that of ordinary human selfishness. The antitoxin has been found, and is applied successfully. Since justice has replaced charity on the prescription, the patient is improving. And the improvement is not confined to him; it is general. Conscience is not a local issue in our day. A few years ago, a United States Senator sought re-election on the platform that the decalogue and the golden rule were glittering generalities that had no place in politics, and lost. We have not quite reached the millennium yet, but today a man is governor in the Empire State who was elected on the pledge that he would rule by the ten commandments. These are facts that mean much or little, according to the way one looks at them. The significant thing is that they are facts, and that, in spite of slipping and sliding, the world moves forward, not backward. The poor we shall have always with us, but the slum we need not have. These two do not rightfully belong together. Their present partnership is at once poverty's worst hardship and our worst fault.

THE TENEMENT-HOUSE BLIGHT

In a Stanton Street tenement, the other day, I stumbled upon a Polish capmaker's home. There were other capmakers in the house, Russian and Polish, but they simply "lived" there. This one had a home. The fact proclaimed itself the moment the door was opened, in spite of the darkness. The rooms were in the rear, gloomy with the twilight of the tenement, although the day was sunny without, but neat, even cosy. It was early, but the day's chores were evidently done. The teakettle sang on the stove, at which a bright-looking girl of twelve, with a pale but cheery face, and sleeves brushed back to the elbows, was busy poking up the fire. A little boy stood by the window, flattening his nose against the pane and gazing wistfully up among the chimney pots where a piece of blue sky about as big as the kitchen could be made out. I remarked to the mother that they were nice rooms.

"Ah yes," she said, with a weary little smile that struggled bravely with hope long deferred, "but it is hard to make a home here. We would so like to live in the front, but we can't pay the rent."

I knew the front with its unlovely view of the tenement street too well, and I said a good word for the air shaft—yard or court it could not be called, it was too small for that—which rather surprised myself. I had found few virtues enough in it before. The girl at the stove had left off poking the fire. She broke in the moment I finished, with eager enthusiasm: "Why, they have the sun in there. When the door is opened the light comes right in your face."

"Does it never come here?" I asked, and wished I had not done so, as soon as the words were spoken. The child at the window was listening, with his whole hungry little soul in his eyes.

Yes, it did, she said. Once every summer, for a little while, it came over the houses. She knew the month and the exact hour of the day when its rays shone into their home, and just the reach of its slant on the wall. They had lived there six years. In June the sun was due. A haunting fear that the baby would ask how long it was till June—it was February then—took possession of me, and I hastened to change the subject. Warsaw was their old home. They kept a little store there, and were young and happy. Oh, it was a fine city, with parks and squares, and bridges over the beautiful river—and grass and flowers and birds and soldiers, put in the girl breathlessly. She remembered. But the children kept coming, and they went across the sea to give them a better chance. Father made fifteen dollars a week, much money; but there were long seasons when there was no work. She, the mother, was never very well here—she hadn't any strength; and the baby! She glanced at his grave white face, and took him in her arms. The picture of the two, and of the pale-faced girl longing back to the fields and the sunlight, in their prison of gloom and gray walls, haunts me yet. I have not had the courage to go back since. I recalled the report of an English army surgeon, which I read years ago, on the many more soldiers that died—were killed would be more correct—in barracks into which the sun never shone than in those that were open to the light.

The capmaker's case is the case of the nineteenth century, of civilization, against the metropolis of America. The home, the family, are the rallying points of civilization. But long since the tenements of New York earned for it the ominous name of "the homeless city."

In its 40,000 tenements its workers, more than half of
the city's population, are housed. They have no other
chance. There are, indeed, wives and mothers who,
by sheer force of character, rise above their environment and make homes where they go. Happily, there
are yet many of them. But the fact remains that hitherto their struggle has been growing ever harder, and
the issue more doubtful.

The tenement itself, with its crowds, its lack of privacy, is the greatest destroyer of individuality, of character. As its numbers increase, so does "the element
that becomes criminal for lack of individuality and
the self-respect that comes with it." Add the shiftless
and the weak who are turned out by the same process,
and you have its legitimate crop. In 1880 the average
number of persons to each dwelling in New York was
16.37; in 1890 it was 18.52. In 1895, according to the
police census, 21.2. The census of 1900 will show the
crowding to have gone on at an equal if not at a
greater rate. That will mean that so many more tenements have been built of the modern type, with four
families to the floor where once there were two. I shall
not weary the reader with many statistics. They are
to be found, by those who want them, in the census
books and in the official records. I shall try to draw
from them their human story. But, as an instance of
the unchecked drift, let me quote here the case of the
Tenth Ward, that East Side district known as the most
crowded in all the world. In 1880, when it had not
yet attained that bad eminence, it contained 47,554
persons, or 432.3 to the acre. In 1890 the census
showed a population of 57,596, which was 522 to the
acre. The police census of 1895 found 70,168 persons
living in 1514 houses, which was 643.08 to the acre.
Lastly, the Health Department's census for the first
half of 1898 gave a total of 82,175 persons living in
1201 tenements, with 313 inhabited buildings yet to
be heard from. This is the process of doubling up—
literally, since the cause and the vehicle of it all is the

double-decker tenement—which in the year 1895 had crowded a single block in that ward at the rate of 1526 persons per acre, and one in the Eleventh Ward at the rate of 1774.* It goes on not in the Tenth Ward or on the East Side only, but throughout the city. When, in 1897, it was proposed to lay out a small park in the Twenty-second Ward, up on the far West Side, it was shown that five blocks in that section, between Forty-ninth and Sixty-second streets and Ninth and Eleventh avenues, had a population of more than 3000 each. The block between Sixty-first and Sixty-second streets, Tenth and Eleventh avenues, harbored 3580, which meant 974.6 persons to the acre.

If we have here to do with forces that are beyond the control of the individual or the community, we shall do well at least to face the facts squarely and know the truth. It is no answer to the charge that New York's way of housing its workers is the worst in the world to say that they are better off than they were where they came from. It is not true, in most cases, as far as the home is concerned: a shanty is better than a flat in a cheap tenement, any day. Even if it were true, it would still be beside the issue. In Poland my capmaker counted for nothing. Nothing was expected of him. Here he ranks, after a few brief years, politically equal with the man who hires his labor. A citizen's duty is expected of him, and home and citizenship are convertible terms. The observation of the Frenchman who had watched the experiment of herding two thousand human beings in eight tenement barracks in Paris, that the result was the "exasperation of the tenant against society," is true the world over. We have done as badly in New York.

---

* Police census of 1895: Block bounded by Canal, Hester, Eldridge, and Forsyth streets: size 375 × 200, population 2628, rate per acre 1526. Block bounded by Stanton, Houston, Attorney, and Ridge streets: size 200 × 300, population 2244, rate per acre 1774.

Social hatefulness is not a good soil for citizenship to grow in, where political equality rules.

Nor will the old lie about the tenants being wholly to blame cover the ground. It has long been overworked in defense of landlord usury. Doubtless there are bad tenants. In the matter of renting houses, as in everything else, men have a trick of coming up to what is expected of them, good or bad; but as a class the tenants have been shown all along to be superior to their surroundings. "Better than the houses they live in," said the first Tenement-House Commission; and the second gave as its verdict that "they respond quickly to improved conditions." That is not an honest answer. The truth is that if we cannot check the indraught to the cities, we can, if we choose, make homes for those who come, and at a profit on the investment. Nothing has been more clearly demonstrated in our day, and it is time that it should be said so that everybody can understand. It is not a case of transforming human nature in the tenant, but of reforming it in the landlord builder. It is a plain question of the per cent he is willing to take.

So that we may get the capmaker's view and that of his fellow tenants—for, after all, that is the one that counts; the state and the community are not nearly so much interested in the profits of the landlord as in the welfare of the workers—suppose we take a stroll through a tenement-house neighborhood and see for ourselves. We were in Stanton Street. Let us start there, then, going east. Towering barracks on either side, five, six stories high. Teeming crowds. Push-cart men "moved on" by the policeman, who seems to exist only for the purpose. Forsyth Street: there is a church on the corner, Polish and Catholic, a combination that strikes one as queer here on the East Side, where Polish has come to be synonymous with Jewish. I have cause to remember that corner. A man killed his wife in this house, and was hanged for it. Just across the street, on the stoop of that brownstone tenement, the tragedy was re-enacted the next year; only the murderer saved the county trouble and expense by taking himself off, also. That other stoop in the same row witnessed a suicide. Why do I tell you these things? Because they are true. The policeman here will bear me out. They belong to the ordinary setting of life in a crowd such as this. It is never so little worth living, and therefore held so cheap along with the fierce, unceasing battle that goes on to save it. You will go no further unless I leave it out? Very well; I shall leave out the murder after we have passed the block yonder. The tragedy of that is of a kind that comes too close to the everyday life of tenement-house people to be omitted. The house caught fire in the night, and five were burned to death—father, mother, and three children. The others got out; why not they? They stayed, it seems, to make sure none was left; they were not willing to leave one behind to save themselves. And then it was too late; the stairs were burning. There was no proper fire escape. That was where the murder came in; but it was not all chargeable to the landlord, nor even the greater part. More than thirty years ago, in 1867, the state made it law that the stairs in every tenement four stories high should be fireproof, and forbade the storing of any inflammable material in such houses. I do not know when the law was repealed, or if it ever was. I only know that in 1892 the Fire Department, out of pity for the tenants and regard for the safety of its own men, forced through an amendment to the building law, requiring the stairs of the common type of five-story tenements to be built of fireproof material, and that today they are of wood, just as they always were. Only last spring I looked up the Superintendent of Buildings and asked him what it meant. I showed him the law, which said that the stairs should be "built of slow-burning construction or fireproof material"; and he put his finger upon the clause that follows, "as the Superintendent of Buildings shall decide." The law gave him discretion, and that is how he used it. "Hard wood burns slowly," said he.

The fire of which I speak was a "cruller fire," if I remember rightly, which is to say that it broke out in the basement bakeshop, where they were boiling crullers (doughnuts) in fat, at four A.M., with a hundred tenants asleep in the house above them. The fat went into the fire, and the rest followed. I suppose that I had to do with a hundred such fires, as a police reporter, before, under the protest of the Tenement-House Committee and the Good Government Clubs, the boiling of fat in tenement bakeshops was forbidden. The chief of the Fire Department, in his testimony before the committee, said that "tenements are erected mainly with a view of returning a large income for the amount of capital invested. It is only after a fire in which great loss of life occurs that any interest whatever is taken in the safety of the occupants." The Superintendent of Buildings, after such a fire in March 1896, said that there were thousands of tenement firetraps in the city. My reporter's notebook bears witness to the correctness of his statement, and it has many blank leaves that are waiting to be put to that use yet. The reckoning for eleven years showed that, of 35,844 fires in New York, 53.18 per cent were in tenement houses, though they were only a little more than 31 per cent of all the buildings, and that 177 occupants were killed, 523 maimed, and 625 rescued by the firemen. Their rescue cost the lives of three of these brave men, and 453 were injured in the effort. And when all that is said, not the half is told. A fire in the night in one of those human beehives, with its terror and woe, is one of the things that live in the recollection ever after as a terrible nightmare. Yet the demonstration of the Tenement-House Committee, that to build tenements fireproof from the ground up would cost little over ten per cent more than is spent upon the firetrap and would more than return the interest on the extra outlay in the saving of insurance and repairs and in the better building every way, has found no echo in legislation or in the practice of builders. That was the fire chief's way to avoid "the great destruction of life"; but he warned the committee that it would "meet with strong opposition from the different interests should legislation be requested." The interest of the man who pays the rent will not be suspected in this, so he must have meant the man who collects it.

Here is a block of tenements inhabited by poor Jews. Most of the Jews who live over here are poor; and the poorer they are, the higher rent do they pay, and the more do they crowd to make it up between them. "The destruction of the poor is their poverty." It is only the old story in a new setting. The slum landlord's profits were always the highest. He spends nothing for repairs, and lays the blame on the tenant. The "district leader" saves him, in these days of Tammany rule come back, unless he is on the wrong side of the political fence, in which case the Sanitary Code comes handy to chase him into camp. A big "order" on his house is a very effective way of making a tenement-house landlord discern political truth on the eve of an important election. Just before the last, when the election of Theodore Roosevelt was threatened, the sanitary force displayed such activity as it has not since, up to the raid on the elevated roads, in the examination of tenements belonging very largely, as it happened, to sympathizers with the gallant Rough Rider's cause; and those who knew did not marvel much at the large vote polled by the Tammany candidate in the old city.

The halls of these tenements are dark. Under the law, there should be a light burning, but it is one of the rarest things to find one. The thing seems well-nigh impossible of accomplishment. Two years ago, when the Good Government Clubs set about backing up the Board of Health in its efforts to work out this reform, which comes close to being one of the most necessary of all—such untold mischief is abroad in the darkness of these thoroughfares—the sanitary police reported 12,000 tenement halls unlighted by night, even, and brought them, by repeated orders, down to less than 1000 in six months. I do not believe the light burns in 1000 of them all today. It is so easy to put it out when the policeman's back is turned, and save the gas.

We had a curious instance at the time of the difficulties that sometimes beset reform. Certain halls that were known to be dark were reported sufficiently lighted by the policeman of the district, and it was discovered that it was his standard that was vitiated. He himself lived in a tenement, and was used to its gloom. So an order was issued defining darkness to the sanitary police: if the sink in the hall could be made out, and the slops overflowing on the floor, and if a baby could be seen on the stairs, the hall was light; if, on the other hand, the baby's shrieks were the first warning that it was being trampled upon, the hall was dark. Some days later, the old question arose about an Eldridge Street tenement. The policeman had reported the hall light enough. The president of the Board of Health, to settle it once for all, went over with me, to see for himself. The hall was very dark. He sent for the policeman.

"Did you see the sink in that hall?" he asked.

The policeman said he did.

"But it is pitch dark. How did you see it?"

"I lit a match," said the policeman.

Four families live on these floors, with Heaven knows how many children. It was here the police commissioners were requested, in sober earnest, some years ago, by a committee of very practical women philanthropists, to have the children tagged, so as to save the policemen wear and tear in taking them back and forth between the Eldridge Street police station and headquarters when they got lost. If tagged, they could be assorted at once and taken to their homes.

Incidentally, the city would save the expense of many meals. It was shrewdly suspected that the little ones were lost on purpose in a good many cases, as a way of getting them fed at the public expense.

That the children preferred the excitement of the police station, and the distinction of a trip in charge of a brass-buttoned guardian to the Ludlow Street flat, is easy enough to understand. A more unlovely existence than that in one of these tenements it would be hard to imagine. Everywhere is the stench of the kerosene stove that is forever burning, serving for cooking, heating, and ironing alike, until the last atom of oxygen is burned out of the close air. Oil is cheaper than coal. The air shaft is too busy carrying up smells from below to bring any air down, even if it is not hung full of washing in every story, as it ordinarily is. Enterprising tenants turn it to use as a refrigerator as well. There is at least a draught of air, such as it is. When fire breaks out, this draught makes of the air shaft a flue through which the fire roars fiercely to the roof, so transforming what was meant for the good of the tenants into their greatest peril. The stuffy rooms seem as if they were made for dwarfs. Most decidedly, there is not room to swing the proverbial cat in any one of them. In one I helped the children, last holiday, to set up a Christmas tree, so that a glimpse of something that was not utterly sordid and mean might for once enter their lives. Three weeks after, I found the tree standing yet in the corner. It was very cold, and there was no fire in the room. "We were going to burn it," said the little woman, whose husband was then in the insane asylum, "and then I couldn't. It looked so kind o' cheery-like there in the corner." My tree had borne the fruit I wished.

It remained for the New York slum landlord to assess the exact value of a ray of sunlight—upon the tenant, of course. Here are two back-to-back rear tenements, with dark bedrooms on the south. The flat on the north gives upon a neighbor's yard, and a hole two feet square has been knocked in the wall, letting in air and sunlight; little enough of the latter, but what there is is carefully computed in the lease. Six dollars for this flat, six and a half for the one with the hole in the wall. Six dollars a year per ray. In half a dozen houses in this block have I found the same rate maintained. The modern tenement on the corner goes higher: for four front rooms, "where the sun comes right in your face," seventeen dollars; for the rear flat of three rooms, larger and better every other way, but always dark, like the capmaker's, eleven dollars. From the landlord's point of view, this last is probably a concession. But he is a landlord with a heart. His house is as good a one as can be built on a twenty-five-foot lot. The man who owns the corner building in Orchard Street, with the two adjoining tenements, has no heart. In the depth of last winter, I found a family of poor Jews living in a coop under his stairs, an abandoned piece of hallway, in which their baby was born, and for which he made them pay eight dollars a month. It was the most outrageous case of landlord robbery I had ever come across, and it gave me sincere pleasure to assist the sanitary policeman in curtailing his profits by even this much. The hall is not now occupied.

The Jews under the stairs had two children. The shoemaker in the cellar next door has three. They were fighting and snarling like so many dogs over the coarse food on the table before them, when we looked in. The baby, it seems, was the cause of the row. He wanted it all. He was a very dirty and a very fierce baby, and the other two children were no match for him. The shoemaker grunted fretfully at his last, "Ach, he is all de time hungry!" At the sight of the policeman, the young imp set up such a howl that we beat a hasty retreat. The cellar "flat" was undoubtedly in violation of law, but it was allowed to pass. In the main hall, on the ground floor, we counted seventeen children. The facts of life here suspend ordinary land-

lord prejudices to a certain extent. Occasionally it
is the tenant who suspends them. The policeman
laughed as he told me of the case of a mother who
coveted a flat into which she well knew her family
would not be admitted; the landlord was particular.
She knocked, with a troubled face, alone. Yes, the flat
was to let; had she any children? The woman heaved
a sigh. "Six, but they are all in Greenwood." The landlord's heart was touched by such woe. He let her have
the flat. By night he was amazed to find a flock of half
a dozen robust youngsters domiciled under his roof.
They had indeed been in Greenwood; but they had
come back from the cemetery to stay. And stay they
did, the rent being paid.

High rents, slack work, and low wages go hand in
hand in the tenements as promoters of overcrowding.
The rent is always one fourth of the family income,
often more. The fierce competition for a bare living
cuts down wages; and when loss of work is added, the
only thing left is to take in lodgers to meet the landlord's claim. The Jew usually takes them singly, the
Italian by families. The midnight visit of the sanitary
policeman discloses a state of affairs against which he
feels himself helpless. He has his standard: 400 cubic
feet of air space for each adult sleeper, 200 for a child.
That in itself is a concession to the practical necessities of the case. The original demand was for 600
feet. But of 28,000 and odd tenants canvassed in New
York, in the slumming investigation prosecuted by the
general government in 1894, 17,047 were found to
have less than 400 feet, and of these 5526 slept in
unventilated rooms with no windows. No more such
rooms have been added since; but there has come
that which is worse.

It was the boast of New York, till a few years ago,
that at least that worst of tenement depravities, the
one-room house, too familiar in the English slums, was
practically unknown here. It is not so any longer. The
evil began in the old houses in Orchard and Allen

streets, a bad neighborhood, infested by fallen women and the thievish rascals who prey upon their misery— a region where the whole plan of humanity, if plan there be in this disgusting mess, jars out of tune continually. The furnished-room house has become an institution here, speeded on by a conscienceless Jew who bought up the old buildings as fast as they came into the market, and filled them with a class of tenants before whom charity recoils, helpless and hopeless. When the houses were filled, the crowds overflowed into the yard. In one case, I found, in midwinter, tenants living in sheds built of odd boards and roof tin, and paying a dollar a week for herding with the rats. One of them, a red-faced German, was a philosopher after his kind. He did not trouble himself to get up, when I looked in, but stretched himself in his bed—it was high noon—responding to my sniff of disgust that it was "sehr schoen! ein bischen kalt, aber was!" His neighbor, a white-haired old woman, begged, trembling, not to be put out. She would not know where to go. It was out of one of these houses that Fritz Meyer, the murderer, went to rob the poorbox in the Redemptorist Church, the night when he killed policeman Smith. The policeman surprised him at his work. In the room he had occupied I came upon a brazen-looking woman with a black eye, who answered the question of the officer, "Where did you get that shiner?" with a laugh. "I ran up against the fist of me man," she said. Her "man," a big, sullen lout, sat by, dumb. The woman answered for him that he was a mechanic.

"What does he work at?" snorted the policeman, restraining himself with an effort from kicking the fellow.

She laughed scornfully. "At the junk business." It meant that he was a thief.

Young men, with blotched faces and cadaverous looks, were loafing in every room. They hung their heads in silence. The women turned their faces away at the sight of the uniform. They cling to these wretches, who exploit their starved affections for their own ease, with a grip of desperation. It is their last hold. Women have to love something. It is their deepest degradation that they must love these. Even the wretches themselves feel the shame of it, and repay them by beating and robbing them as their daily occupation. A poor little baby in one of the rooms gave a shuddering human touch to it all.

The old houses began it, as they began all the tenement mischief that has come upon New York. But the opportunity that was made by the tenant's need was not one to be neglected. In some of the newer tenements, with their smaller rooms, the lodger is by this time provided for in the plan, with a special entrance from the hall. "Lodger" comes, by an easy transition, to stand for "family." Only the other night I went with the sanitary police on their midnight inspection through a row of Elizabeth Street tenements which I had known since they were built, fifteen or sixteen years ago. That is the neighborhood in which the recent Italian immigrants crowd. In the house which we selected for examination, in all respects the type of the rest, we found forty-three families where there should have been sixteen. Upon each floor were four flats, and in each flat three rooms that measured respectively 14 × 11, 7 × 11, and 7 × 8½ feet. In only one flat did we find a single family. In three there were two to each. In the other twelve each room had its own family living and sleeping there. They cooked, I suppose, at the one stove in the kitchen, which was the largest room. In one big bed we counted six persons, the parents and four children. Two of them lay crosswise at the foot of the bed, or there would not have been room. A curtain was hung before the bed in each of the two smaller rooms, leaving a passageway from the hall to the main room. The rent for the front flats was twelve dollars; for that in the rear ten dollars. The social distinctions going with the advantage of location were rigidly observed, I suppose. The three steps across a tenement hall, from the front to "the back," are often a longer road than from Ludlow Street to Fifth Avenue.

They were sweaters' tenements. But I shall keep that end of the story until I come to speak of the tenants. The houses I have in mind now. They were Astor leasehold property, and I had seen them built upon the improved plan of 1879, with air shafts and all that. There had not been water in the tenements for a month then, we were told by the one tenant who spoke English that could be understood. The cold snap had locked the pipes. Fitly enough, the lessee was an undertaker, an Italian himself, who combined with his business of housing his people above and below the ground that of the padrone, to let no profit slip. He had not taken the trouble to make many or recent repairs. The buildings had made a fair start; they promised well. But the promise had not been kept. In their premature decay they were distinctly as bad as the worst. I had the curiosity to seek out the agent, the middleman, and ask him why they were so. He shrugged his shoulders. With such tenants nothing could be done, he said. I have always held that Italians are most manageable, and that, with all the surface indications to the contrary, they are really inclined to cleanliness, if cause can be shown, and I told him so. He changed the subject diplomatically. No doubt it was with him simply a question of the rent. They might crowd and carry on as they pleased, once that was paid; and they did. It used to be the joke of Elizabeth Street that when the midnight police came, the tenants would keep them waiting outside, pretending to search for the key, until the surplus population of men had time to climb down the fire escape. When the police were gone, they came back. We surprised them all in bed.

Like most of the other tenements we have come across on our trip, these were double-deckers. That is the type of tenement that is responsible for the crowding that goes on unchecked. It is everywhere replacing the older barracks, as they rot or are torn down.

This double-decker was thus described by the Tenement-House Committee of 1894: "It is the one hopeless form of tenement construction. It cannot be well ventilated, it cannot be well lighted; it is not safe in case of fire. It is built on a lot 25 feet wide by 100 or less in depth, with apartments for four families in each story. This necessitates the occupation of from 86 to 90 per cent of the lot's depth. The stairway, made in the center of the house, and the necessary walls and partitions reduce the width of the middle rooms (which serve as bedrooms for at least two people each) to nine feet each at the most, and a narrow light and air shaft, now legally required in the center of each side wall, still further lessens the floor space of these middle rooms. Direct light is only possible for the rooms at the front and rear. The middle rooms must borrow what light they can from dark hallways, the shallow shafts, and the rear rooms. Their air must pass through other rooms or the tiny shafts, and cannot but be contaminated before it reaches them. A five-story house of this character contains apartments for eighteen or twenty families, a population frequently amounting to 100 people, and sometimes increased by boarders or lodgers to 150 or more."

The committee, after looking in vain through the slums of the Old World cities for something to compare the double-deckers with, declared that, in their setting, the separateness and sacredness of home life were interfered with, and evils bred, physical and moral, that "conduce to the corruption of the young." The statement needs no argument to convince.

Yet it is for these that the "interests" of which the fire chief spoke rush into battle at almost every session of the legislature, whenever a step, no matter how short and conservative, is to be taken toward their improvement. No winter has passed, since the awakening conscience of the people of New York City manifested itself in a desire to better the lot of the other half, that has not seen an assault made, in one shape or another, on the structure of tenement-house law built up with such anxious solicitude. Once a bill to exempt from police supervision, by withdrawing them from the tenement-house class, the very worst of the houses, whose death rate threatened the community, was sneaked through the legislature all unknown, and had reached the executive before the alarm was sounded. The governor, put upon his guard, returned the bill, with the endorsement that he was unable to understand what could have prompted a measure that seemed to have reason and every argument against it, and none for it. But the motive is not so obscure, after all. It is the same old one of profit without conscience. It took from the Health Department the supervision of the light, ventilation, and plumbing of the tenements, which by right belonged there, and put it in charge of a compliant Building Department, "for the convenience of architects and their clients, and the saving of time and expense to them." For the convenience of the architect's client, the builder, the lot was encroached upon, until of one big block which the Tenement-House Committee measured only 7 per cent was left uncovered for the air to struggle through; 93 per cent of it was covered with brick and mortar. Rear tenements, to the number of nearly 100, have been condemned as "slaughterhouses," with good reason, but this block was built practically solid. The average of space covered in 34 tenement blocks was shown to be 78.13 per cent. The law allowed only 65. The "discretion" that pens tenants in a burning tenement with stairs of wood for the builder's "convenience" cut down the chance of life of their babies unmoved. Sunlight and air mean just that, where three thousand human beings are packed into a single block. That was why the matter was given into the charge

of the health officials, when politics was yet kept out
of their work.

Of such kind are the interests that oppose betterment of the worker's hard lot in New York; that
dictated the appointment by Tammany of a commission composed of builders to revise its code of building laws, and that sneer at the "laughable results of
the late Tenement-House Committee." Those results
made for the health and happiness and safety of a
million and a half of souls, and were accounted, on
every humane ground, the longest step forward that
had yet been taken by this community. For the old
absentee landlord, who did not know what mischief
was afoot, we have got the speculative builder, who
does know, but does not care so long as he gets his
pound of flesh. Half of the just laws that have been
passed for the relief of the people he has paralyzed
with his treacherous discretion clause, carefully nursed
in the school of practical politics to which he gives
faithful adherence. The thing has been the curse of
our city from the day when the earliest struggle toward better things began. Among the first manifesta-
tions of that was the prohibition of soap factories
below Grand Street by the act of 1797, which created
a Board of Health with police powers. The act was
passed in February, to take effect in July; but long
before that time the same legislature had amended it
by giving the authorities discretion in the matter. And
the biggest soap factory of them all is down there to
this day, and is even now stirring up a rumpus among
the latest immigrants, the Syrians, who have settled
about it. No doubt it is all a question of political education; but are not a hundred years enough to settle
this much, that compromise is out of place where the
lives of the people are at stake, and that it is time
our years of "discretion" were numbered?

And, please God, the time is at hand. Here, set in
its frame of swarming tenements, is a wide open
space, sometime, when enough official red tape has

been unwound, to be a park, with flowers and grass and birds to gladden the hearts of those to whom such things have been as tales that are told all these dreary years, and with a playground in which the children of yonder big school may roam at will, undismayed by landlord or policeman. Not all the forces of reaction can put back the barracks that were torn down as one of the "laughable results" of that very Tenement-House Committee's work, or restore to the undertaker his profits from Bone Alley of horrid memory. It was the tenant's turn to laugh, that time. Down half a dozen blocks, among even denser swarms, is another such plot, where football and a skating pond are being planned by the children's friends. We shall hear the story of these yet, and rejoice that the day of reckoning is coming for the builder without a soul. Till then let him deck the fronts of his tenements with bravery of plate glass and brass to hide the darkness within. He has done his worst.

We can go no further. Yonder lies the river. A full mile we have come, through unbroken ranks of tenements with their mighty, pent-up multitudes. Here they seem, with a common impulse, to overflow into the street. From corner to corner it is crowded with girls and children dragging babies nearly as big as themselves, with desperate endeavor to lose nothing of the show. There is a funeral in the block. Unnumbered sewing machines cease for once their tireless rivalry with the flour mill in the next block, which is forever grinding in a vain effort to catch up. Heads are poked from windows. On the stoops hooded and shawled figures have front seats. The crowd is hardly restrained by the policeman and the undertaker in holiday mourning, who clear a path by force to the plumed hearse. The eager haste, the frantic rush to see—what does it not tell of these starved lives, of the quality of their aims and ambitions? The mill clatters loudly: there is one mouth less to fill. In the midst of

it all, with clamor of urgent gong, the patrol wagon
rounds the corner, carrying two policemen precari-
ously perched upon a struggling "drunk," a woman.
The crowd scatters, following the new sensation. The
tragedies of death and life in the slum have met together.

Many a mile I might lead you along these rivers,
east and west, through the island of Manhattan, and
find little else than we have seen. The great crowd is
yet below Fourteenth Street, but the northward
march knows no slackening of pace. As the tide sets
uptown, it reproduces faithfully the scenes of the older
wards, though with less of their human interest than
here where the old houses, in all their ugliness, have
yet some imprint of the individuality of their tenants.
Only on feast days does Little Italy, in Harlem, recall
the Bend when it put on holiday attire. Anything
more desolate and disheartening than the unending
rows of tenements, all alike and all equally repellent,
of the uptown streets, it is hard to imagine. Hell's
Kitchen in its ancient wickedness was picturesque, at
least, with its rocks and its goats and shanties. Since
the negroes took possession it is only dull, except
when, as happened last summer, the remnant of the
Irish settlers make a stand against the intruders. Vain
hope! Perpetual eviction is their destiny. Negro,
Italian, and Jew, biting the dust with many a bruised
head under the Hibernian's stalwart fist, resistlessly
drive him before them, nevertheless, out of house and
home. The landlord pockets the gate money. The old
robbery still goes on. Where the negro pitches his tent,
he pays more rent than his white neighbor next door,
and is a better tenant. And he is good game forever.
He never buys the tenement, as the Jew or the Italian
is likely to do, when he has scraped up money enough
to re-enact, after his own fashion, the trick taught him
by his oppressor. The black column has reached the
hundredth street on the East Side, and the sixties on

the West,* and there for the present it halts. Jammed
between Africa, Italy, and Bohemia, the Irishman has
abandoned the East Side uptown. Only west of Central Park does he yet face his foe, undaunted in defeat
as in victory. The local street nomenclature, in which
the directory has no hand—Nigger Row, Mixed Ale
Flats, etc.—indicates the hostile camps with unerring
accuracy.

Uptown or downtown, as the tenements grow taller,
the thing that is rarest to find is the home of the olden
days, even as it was in the shanty on the rocks. "No
home, no family, no morality, no manhood, no patriotism!" said the old Frenchman. Seventy-seven per
cent of their young prisoners, say the managers of the
state reformatory, have no moral sense, or next to
none. "Weakness, not wickedness, ails them," adds
the prison chaplain; no manhood, that is to say. Years
ago, roaming through the British Museum, I came
upon an exhibit that riveted my attention as nothing
else had. It was a huge stone arm, torn from the shoulder of some rock image, with doubled fist and every
rigid muscle instinct with angry menace. Where it
came from or what was its story I do not know. I did
not ask. It was its message to us I was trying to read.
I had been spending weary days and nights in the
slums of London, where hatred grew, a noxious crop,
upon the wreck of the home. Lying there, mute and
menacing, the great fist seemed to me like a shadow
thrown from the gray dawn of the race into our busy
day with a purpose, a grim, unheeded warning. What
was it? In the slum the question haunts me yet. They
perished, the empires those rock-hewers built, and the
governments reared upon their ruins are long since
dead and forgotten. They were born to die, for they
were not built upon human happiness, but upon

---

* There is an advanced outpost of blacks as far up as One
Hundred and Forty-fifth Street, but the main body lingers yet
among the sixties.

human terror and greed. We built ours upon the bedrock, and its cornerstone is the home. With this bitter mockery of it that makes the slum, can it be that the warning is indeed for us?

THE TENEMENT: CURING ITS BLIGHT

I stood at Seven Dials and heard the policeman's account of what it used to be. Seven Dials is no more like the slum of old than is the Five Points today. The conscience of London wrought upon the one as the conscience of New York upon the other. A mission house, a children's refuge, two big schools, and, hard by, a public bath and a washhouse stand as the record of the battle with the slum, which, with these forces in the field, has but one ending. The policeman's story rambled among the days when things were different. Then it was dangerous for an officer to go alone there at night.

Around the corner there came from one of the side streets a procession with banners, parading in honor and aid of some church charity. We watched it pass. In it marched young men and boys with swords and battle axes, and upon its outskirts skipped a host of young roughs—so one would have called them but for the evidence of their honest employment—who rattled collection boxes, reaping a harvest of pennies from far and near. I looked at the battle axes and the collection boxes, and thought of forty years ago. Where were the Seven Dials of that day, and the men who gave it its bad name? I asked the policeman.

"They were druv into decency, sor," he said, and answered from his own experience the question ever asked by fainthearted philanthropists. "My father, he done duty here afore me in forty-five. The worst dive was where that church stands. It was always full of thieves"—whose sons, I added mentally, have become collectors for the church. The one fact was a whole chapter on the slum.

London's way with the tenant we adopted at last in New York with the slum landlord. He was "druv into decency." We had to. Moral suasion had been stretched to the limit. The point had been reached where one knock-down blow outweighed a bushel of arguments. It was all very well to build model tenements as object lessons to show that the thing could be done; it had become necessary to enforce the lesson by demonstrating that the community had power to destroy houses which were a menace to its life. The rear tenements were chosen for this purpose.

They were the worst as they were the first of New York's tenements. The double-deckers of which I have spoken had, with all their evils, at least this to their credit, that their death rate was not nearly as high as that of the old houses. That was not because of any virtue inherent in the double-deckers, but because the earlier tenements were old, and built in a day that knew nothing of sanitary restrictions, and cared less. Hence the showing that the big tenements had much the lowest mortality. The death rate does not sound the depths of tenement house evils, but it makes a record that is needed when it comes to attacking property rights. The mortality of the rear tenements had long been a scandal. They are built in the backyard, generally back to back with the rear buildings on abutting lots. If there is an open space between them, it is never more than a slit a foot or so wide, and gets to be the receptacle of garbage and filth of every kind; so that any opening made in these walls for purposes of ventilation becomes a source of greater danger than if there were none. The last count that was made, in 1898, showed that among the 40,958 tenements in New York there were still 2379 rear houses left. Where they are, the death rate rises, for reasons that are apparent. The sun cannot reach them. They are damp and dark, and the tenants, who are always the poorest and most crowded, live "as in a cage open only toward the front," said the Tenement-House Committee. A canvass made of the mortality records by Dr. Roger S. Tracy, the registrar of records, showed that while in the First Ward (the oldest), for instance, the death rate in houses standing singly on the lot was 29.03 per 1000 of the living, where there were rear houses it rose to 61.97. The infant death rate is a still better test: that rose from 109.58 in the single tenements of the same ward to 204.54 where there were rear houses. One in every five babies had to die, that is to say; the house killed it. No wonder the committee styled the rear tenements "slaughterhouses," and called upon the legislature to root them out, and with them every old, ramshackle, disease-breeding tenement in the city.

A law which is in substance a copy of the English act for destroying slum property was passed in the spring of 1895. It provides for the seizure of buildings that are dangerous to the public health or unfit for human habitation, and their destruction upon proper proof, with compensation to the owner on a sliding scale down to the point of entire unfitness, when he is entitled only to the value of the material in his house. Up to that time, the only way to get rid of such a house had been to declare it a nuisance under the sanitary code; but as the city could not very well pay for the removal of a nuisance, to order it down seemed too much like robbery; so the owner was allowed to keep it. It takes time and a good many lives to grow a sentiment such as this law expressed. The Anglo-Saxon respect for vested rights is strong in us, also. I remember going through a ragged school in London, once, and finding the eyes of the children in the infant class red and sore. Suspecting some contagion, I made inquiries, and was told that a collar factory next door was the cause of the trouble. The fumes from it poisoned the children's eyes.

"And you allow it to stay, and let this thing go on?"
I asked, in wonder.

The superintendent shrugged his shoulders. "It is
their factory," he said.

I was on the point of saying something that might
not have been polite, seeing that I was a guest, when
I remembered that, in the newspaper which I carried
in my pocket, I had just been reading a plea of some
honorable M.P. for a much-needed reform in the system of counsel fees, then being agitated in the House
of Commons. The reply of the solicitor general had
made me laugh. He was inclined to agree with the
honorable member, but still preferred to follow precedent by referring the matter to the Inns of Court.
Quite incidentally, he mentioned that the matter had
been hanging fire in the House two hundred years. It
seemed very English to me then; but when we afterward came to tackle our rear tenements, and in the
first batch there was a row which I knew to have been
picked out by the sanitary inspector, twenty-five years
before, as fit only to be destroyed, I recognized that
we were kin, after all.

That was Gotham Court. It was first on the list, and
the Mott Street Barracks came next, when, as executive officer of the Good Government Clubs, I helped
the Board of Health put the law to the test the following year. The Health Department kept a list of 66 old
houses, with a population of 5460 tenants, in which
there had been 1313 deaths in a little over five years
(1889–94). From among them we picked our lot, and
the department drove the tenants out. The owners
went to law, one and all; but, to their surprise and
dismay, the courts held with the health officers. The
moral effect was instant and overwhelming. Rather
than keep up the fight, with no rent coming in, the
landlords surrendered at discretion. In consideration
of this, compensation was allowed them at the rate of
about a thousand dollars a house, although they were
really entitled only to the value of the old material.

The buildings all came under the head of "wholly unfit." Gotham Court, with its sixteen buildings, in which, thirty-five years ago, a health inspector counted 146 cases of sickness, including "all kinds of infectious disease," was bought for $19,750, and Mullen's Court, adjoining, for $7251. They had been under civilized management since, but nothing decent could be made out of them. To show the character of all, let two serve; in each case it is the official record, upon which seizure was made, that is quoted:

No. 98 Catherine Street: "The floor in the apartments and the wooden steps leading to the second-floor apartment are broken, loose, saturated with filth. The roof and eaves gutters leak, rendering the apartments wet. The two apartments on the first floor consist of one room each, in which the tenants are compelled to cook, eat, and sleep. The back walls are defective; the house wet and damp, and unfit for human habitation. It robs the surrounding houses of light."

"The sunlight never enters" was the constant refrain.

No. 17 Sullivan Street: "Occupied by the lowest whites and negroes, living together. The houses are decayed from cellar to garret, and filthy beyond description—the filthiest, in fact, we have ever seen. The beams, the floors, the plaster on the walls, where there is any plaster, are rotten and alive with vermin. They are a menace to the public health, and cannot be repaired. Their annual death rate in five years was 41.38."

The sunlight enters where these stood, at all events, and into 58 other yards that once were plague spots. Of 94 rear tenements seized that year, 60 have been torn down, 33 of them voluntarily by the owners; 29 were remodeled and allowed to stand, chiefly as workshops; 5 other houses were standing empty, and yielding no rent, in March 1899. The worst of them all, the Mott Street Barracks, are yet in the courts; but all the judges and juries in the land have no power to put them back. It is a case of "They can't put you in jail for that"—"Yes, but I am in jail." They are gone, torn down under the referee's decision that they ought to go, before the Appellate Division called a halt. In 1888 I counted 360 tenants in these tenements, front and rear, all Italians, and the infant death rate of the Barracks that year was 325 per 1000. There were forty babies, and one in three of them had to die. The general infant death rate for the whole tenement-house population that year was 88.38. In the four years following, during which the population and the death rate of the houses were both reduced with an effort, fifty-one funerals went out of the Barracks. With entire fitness, a cemetery corporation held the mortgage upon the property. The referee allowed it the price of opening one grave, in the settlement, gave one dollar to the lessee and one hundred and ten dollars to the landlord, who refused to collect, and took his case to the Court of Appeals, where it is to be argued this summer. The only interest that attaches to it, since the real question has been decided by the wrecker ahead of time, is the raising of the constitutional point, perchance, and the issue of that is not doubtful. The law has been repeatedly upheld, and in Massachusetts, where similar action has been taken since, the constitutionality of it has in no case been attacked, so far as I know.

I have said before that I do not believe in paying the slum landlord for taking his hand off our throats, when we have got the grip on him in turn. Mr. Roger Foster, who as a member of the Tenement-House Committee drew the law, and as counsel for the Health Department fought the landlords successfully in the courts, holds to the opposite view. I am bound to say that instances turned up in which it did seem a hardship to deprive the owners of even such prop-

erty. I remember especially a tenement in Roosevelt
Street, which was the patrimony and whole estate of
two children. With the rear house taken away, the income from the front would not be enough to cover the
interest on the mortgage. It was one of those things
that occasionally make standing upon abstract principle so very uncomfortable. I confess I never had the
courage to ask what was done in their case. I know
that the tenement went, and I hope—Well, never mind
what I hope. It has nothing to do with the case. The
house is down, and the main issue decided upon its
merits.

In the 94 tenements (counting the front houses in;
they cannot be separated from the rear tenements in
the death registry) there were in five years 956 deaths,
a rate of 62.9 at a time when the general city death
rate was 24.63. It was the last and heaviest blow aimed
at the abnormal mortality of a city that ought, by reason of many advantages, to be one of the healthiest
in the world. With clean streets, pure milk, medical
school inspection, antitoxin treatment of deadly diseases, and better sanitary methods generally; with the
sunlight let into its slums, and its worst plague spots
cleaned out, the death rate of New York came down
from 26.32 per 1000 inhabitants in 1887 to 19.53 in
1897. Inasmuch as a round half million was added to
its population within the ten years, it requires little
figuring to show that the number whose lives were
literally saved by reform would people a city of no
mean proportions. The extraordinary spell of hot
weather, two years ago, brought out the full meaning
of this. While many were killed by sunstroke, the population as a whole was shown to have acquired, in
better hygienic surroundings, a much greater power of
resistance. It yielded slowly to the heat. Where two
days had been sufficient, in former years, to send the
death rate up, it now took five; and the infant mortality remained low throughout the dreadful trial. Perhaps the substitution of beer for whisky as a summer

drink had something to do with it; but Colonel Waring's broom and unpolitical sanitation had more. Since it spared him so many voters, the politician ought to have been grateful for this; but he was not. Death rates are not as good political arguments as tax rates, we found out. In the midst of it all, a policeman whom I knew went to his Tammany captain to ask if Good Government Clubs were political clubs within the meaning of the law, which prohibits policemen from joining such. The answer he received set me to thinking: "Yes, the meanest, worst kind of political clubs, they are." Yet they had done nothing worse than to save the babies, the captain's with the rest.

The landlord read the signs better. He learned his lesson quickly. All over the city, he made haste to set his house to rights, lest it be seized or brought to the bar in other ways. The Good Government Clubs did not rest content with their first victory. They made war upon the dark hall in the double-decker, and upon the cruller bakery. They opened small parks, exposed the abuses of the civil courts, the "poor man's courts," urged on the building of new schools, compelled the cleaning of the Tombs prison and hastened the demolition of the wicked old pile, and took a hand in evolving a sensible and humane system of dealing with the young vagrants who were going to waste on free soup. The proposition to establish a farm colony for their reclamation was met with the challenge at Albany that "we have had enough reform in New York City," and, as the event proved, for the time being we had really gone as far as we could. But even that was a good long way. Some things had been nailed that could never again be undone; and hand in hand with the effort to destroy had gone another to build up that promised to set us far enough ahead to appeal at last successfully to the self-interest of the builder, if not to his humanity; or, failing that, to compel him to decency. If that promise has not been kept, the end is not yet. I believe it will be kept.

The movement for reform, in the matter of housing the people, had proceeded upon a clearly outlined plan that apportioned to each of several forces its own share of the work. At a meeting held under the auspices of the Association for Improving the Condition of the Poor, early in the days of the movement, the field had been gone over thoroughly. To the Good Government Clubs fell the task, as already set forth, of compelling the enforcement of the existing tenement-house laws. D. O. Mills, the philanthropic banker, declared his purpose to build hotels which should prove that a bed and lodging as good as any could be furnished to the great army of homeless men at a price that would compete with the cheap lodginghouses, and yet yield a profit to the owner. On behalf of a number of well-known capitalists, who had been identified with the cause of tenement-house reform for years, Robert Fulton Cutting, the president of the Association for Improving the Condition of the Poor, offered to build homes for the working people that should be worthy of the name, on a large scale. A company was formed, and chose for its president Dr. Elgin R. L. Gould, author of the government report on the Housing of the Working People, the standard work on the subject. A million dollars was raised by public subscription, and operations were begun at once.

Two ideas were kept in mind as fundamental: one, that charity that will not pay will not stay; the other, that nothing can be done with the twenty-five-foot lot. It is the primal curse of our housing system, and any effort toward better things must reckon with it first. Nineteen lots on Sixty-eighth and Sixty-ninth streets, west of Tenth Avenue, were purchased of Mrs. Alfred Corning Clark, who took one tenth of the capital stock of the City and Suburban Homes Company; and upon these was erected the first block of tenements. This is the neighborhood toward which the population has been setting with ever-increasing congestion. Already in 1895 the Twenty-second Ward contained nearly 200,000 souls. Between Forty-ninth and Sixty-second streets, west of Ninth Avenue, there are at least five blocks with more than 3000 tenants in each, and the conditions of the notorious Tenth Ward are certain to be reproduced here, if indeed they are not exceeded. In the Fifteenth Assembly District, some distance below, but on the same line, the first sociological canvass of the Federation of Churches had found the churches, schools, and other educational agencies marshaling a frontage of 756 feet on the street, while the saloon fronts stretched themselves over nearly a mile; so that, said the compiler of these pregnant facts, "saloon social ideals are minting themselves in the minds of the people at the ratio of seven saloon thoughts to one educational thought." It would not have been easy to find a spot better fitted for the experiment of restoring to the home its rights.

The Alfred Corning Clark Buildings, as they were called in recognition of the support of this public-spirited woman, have been occupied a year. When I went through them, the other day, I found all but five of the 373 apartments they contain occupied, and a very large waiting list of applicants for whom there was no room. The doctor alone, of all the tenants, had moved away, disappointed. He had settled on the estate, hoping to build up a practice among so many; but he could not make a living. The plan of the buildings, for which Ernest Flagg, a young and energetic architect, with a very practical interest in the welfare of the Other Half, has the credit, seems to me to realize the ideal of making homes under a common roof. The tenants appeared to take the same view of it. They were a notably contented lot. Their only objection was to the use of the common tubs in the basement laundry—a sign that, to my mind, was rather favorable than otherwise, though it argued ill for the scheme of public washhouses on the Glasgow plan that has seemed so promising. They were selected tenants as to trustworthiness and desirability on that score, but they were all of the tenement-house class. The rents are a little lower than for much poorer quarters in the surrounding tenements. The houses are built around central courts, with light and air in abundance, with fireproof stairs and steam-heated halls. There is not a dark passage anywhere. Within, there is entire privacy for the tenant; the partitions are deadened, so that sound is not transmitted from one apartment to another. Without, the houses have none of the discouraging barrack look. The architecture is distinctly pleasing. The few and simple rules laid down by the management have been readily complied with, as making for the benefit of all. A woman collects the rents, which are paid weekly in advance. The promise that the property will earn the five per cent to which the company limits its dividends seems certain to be kept. There is nothing in sight to prevent it, everything to warrant the prediction.

The capital stock has since been increased to $2,000,000, and the erection has been begun of a new block of buildings in East Sixty-fourth Street, within hail of Battle Row, of anciently warlike memory. James E. Ware & Son, the architects who, in the competition of 1879, won the prize for the improved tenements that marked the first departure from the boxlike barracks of old, drew the plans, embodying all the good features of the Clark Buildings with attractions of their own. A suburban colony is being developed by the company, in addition. It is not the least promising feature of its work that a very large proportion of its shareholders are workingmen, who have invested their savings in the enterprise, thus bearing witness to their faith and interest in it. Of the entire number of shareholders at the time of the first annual report, forty-five per cent held less than ten shares each.

The success of these and previous efforts at the building of model tenements has had the desired effect of encouraging other attempts in the same direction. They represent the best that can be done in fighting the slum within the city. Homewood, the City and Suburban Homes Company's settlement in the country, stands for the way out that must eventually win the fight. That is the track that must be followed, and will be when we have found in rapid transit the key to the solution of our present perplexities. "In the country" hardly describes the site of the colony. It is within the Greater City, on Long Island, hardly an hour's journey by trolley from the City Hall, and only a short walk from the bay. Here the company has built a hundred cottages, and has room for two or three hundred more. Of the hundred houses, seventy-two had been sold when I was there last winter. They are handsome and substantial little houses, the lower story of brick, the upper of timber and stucco, each cottage standing in its own garden. The purchaser pays for the property in monthly payments extending over twenty years. A plan of life insurance, which protects the family and the company alike in the event of the death of the breadwinner, is included in the arrangement. The price of the cottages which so far have found owners has averaged about $3100, and the monthly installment, including the insurance premium, a trifle over $25. It follows that the poorest have not moved to Homewood. Its settlers include men with an income of $1200 or $1500 a year—policemen, pilots, letter carriers, clerks, and teachers. This is as it should be. They represent the graduating class, as it were, from the city crowds. It is the province of the philanthropic tenement to prepare the next lot for moving up and out. Any attempt to hasten the process by taking a short cut could result only in failure and disappointment. The graduating class is large enough, however, to guarantee that it will not be exhausted by one Homewood. Before the houses were contracted for, without advertising or effort of any kind to make the thing known, more than eight hundred wage earners had asked to have their names put on the books as applicants for suburban homes.

Others had built model tenements and made them pay, but it was left to Mr. D. O. Mills to break ground in the field which Lord Rowton had filled with such signal success in London. The two Mills Houses, in Bleecker and Rivington streets, are as wide a departure as could well be imagined from the conventional type of lodginghouses in New York. They are large and beautiful structures, which, for the price of a cot in one of the Bowery barracks, furnish their lodgers with as good a bed in a private room as the boarder in the Waldorf-Astoria enjoys. Indeed, it is said to be the very same in make and quality. There are baths without stint, smoking and writing rooms and games, and a free library; a laundry for those who can pay for having their washing done, and a separate one for such as prefer to do it themselves. There is a restaurant in the basement, in which a regular dinner of good quality is served at fifteen cents. The night's lodging is twenty cents. The dearest Bowery lodginghouses charge twenty-five cents. The bedrooms are necessarily small, but they are clean and comfortable, well lighted and heated. The larger house, No. 1, in Bleecker Street, has room for 1554 guests; No. 2, in Rivington Street, for 600. Though this represents more than twelve per cent of the capacity of all the cheap lodginghouses in the city, both have been filled since they were opened, and crowds have often been turned away. The Bowery "hotels" have felt the competition. Their owners deny it, but the fact is apparent in efforts at improvements with which they were not justly chargeable before. Only the lowest, the ten-cent houses, are exempt from this statement. These attract a class of custom for which the Mills Houses do not compete. The latter are intended for the large number of decent mechanics, laborers, and men of small means, hunting for work, who are always afloat in a large city, and who neither seek nor wish charity.

The plan and purpose of the builder cannot be better put than in his own words at the opening of the first house.

"No patron of the Mills Hotel," he said, "will receive more than he pays for, unless it be my hearty goodwill and good wishes. It is true that I have devoted thought, labor, and capital to a very earnest effort to help him, but only by enabling him to help himself. In doing the work on so large a scale, and in securing the utmost economies in purchases and in administration, I hope to give him a larger equivalent for his money than has hitherto been possible. He can, without scruple, permit me to offer him this advantage; but he will think better of himself and will be a more self-reliant, manly man and a better citizen if he knows that he is honestly paying for what he gets."

Mr. Mills's faith that the business of housing the homeless crowds in decency and comfort could be made to pay just as well as that of housing families in model tenements has been justified. Besides providing a fund sufficient for deterioration and replacement, the two houses have made a clear three per cent profit on the investment of $1,500,000 which they represent. Beyond this, they have borne, and will bear increasingly, their own hand in settling with the saloon, which had no rival in the cheerlessness of the cheap lodginghouse or the boardinghouse back bedroom. Every philanthropic effort to fight it on that ground has drawn renewed courage and hope from Mr. Mills's work and success.

While I am writing, subscriptions are being made to the capital stock of a Woman's Hotel Company, which will endeavor to do for the self-supporting single women of our own city what Mr. Mills has done for the men. It is proposed to erect, at a cost of $800,-000, a hotel capable of sheltering over 500 guests, at a price coming within reach of women earning wages as clerks, stenographers, nurses, etc. The number of women whose needs an establishment of the kind would meet is said to exceed 40,000. The Young Women's Christian Association alone receives every year requests enough for quarters to fill a score of such hotels, and can only refer the applicants to boardinghouses. Experience in other cities shows that a woman's hotel or club can be managed and made profitable, and there seems to be little doubt that New York will be the next to furnish proof of it. It was the dream of A. T. Stewart, the merchant prince, to do this service for his city, just as he planned Garden City for a home colony for his clerks. It came out differently. The Long Island town became a cathedral city, and the home of wealth and fashion; his woman's boardinghouse a great public hotel, far out of the reach of those he sought to benefit. It may be that the success of the banker's philanthropy will yet realize the dream of the merchant before the end of the century that saw his wealth, his great business, his very name, vanish as if they had never been, and even his bones denied, by ghoulish thieves, a rest in the grave. I like to think of it as a kind of justice to his memory, more eloquent than marble and brass in the empty crypt. Mills House No. 1 stands upon the site of Mr. Stewart's old home, where he dreamed his barren dream of benevolence to his kind.

Of all these movements the home is the keynote. That is the cheerful sign that shows light ahead. To the home it comes down in the end—good government, bad government, and all the rest. As the homes of a community are, so is the community. New York has still the worst housing system in the world. Eight fifteenths of its people live in tenements, not counting the better class of flats, though legally they come under the definition. The blight of the twenty-five-foot lot remains, with the double-decker. But we can now destroy what is not fit to stand; we have done it, and our republic yet survives. The slum landlord would have had us believe that it must perish with his rookeries. We knew that to build decently improved a neighborhood, made the tenants better and happier, and reduced the mortality. Model tenement-house building is now proving daily that such houses can be built safer and better every way for less money than the double-decker, by crossing the lot line. The dark hall is not a problem in the tenement built around a central court, for there is no common hall. The plan of the double-decker is shown to be wasteful of space and wall and capital. The model tenement pays, does not deteriorate, and keeps its tenants. After the lapse of ten years, I was the other day in Mr. A. T. White's Riverside Buildings in Brooklyn, which are still the best I know of, and found them, if anything, better houses than the day they were built. The stone steps of the stairways were worn: that was all the evidence of deterioration I saw. These, and Mr. White's other block of buildings on Hicks Street, which was built more than twenty years ago—occupied, all of them, by distinctly poor tenants—have paid their owner over five per cent right along. Practically every such enterprise has the same story to tell. Dr. Gould found that only six per cent of all the great model housing operations had failed to pay. All the rest were successful. That was the showing of Europe. It is the same here. Only the twenty-five-foot lot is in the way in New York.

It will continue to be in the way. A man who has one lot will build on it: it is his right. The state, which taxes his lot, has no right to confiscate it by forbidding him to make it yield him an income, on the plea that he might build something which would be a nuisance. But it can so order the building that it shall not be a nuisance: that is not only its right, but its duty. The best which can be made out of a twenty-five-foot lot is not good, but even that has not been made out of it yet. I have seen plans drawn by two young women architects in this city, the Misses Gannon and Hands, and approved by the Building Department, which let in an amount of light and air not dreamed of in the conventional type of double-decker, while providing detached stairs in a central court. It was not pretended that it was an ideal plan—far from it; but it indicated clearly the track to be followed in dealing with the twenty-five-foot lot, seeing that we cannot get rid of it. The demand for light and air space must be sharpened and rigidly held to, and "discretion" to cut it down on any pretext must be denied, to the end of discouraging at least the building of double-deckers by the speculative landlord who has more than one lot, but prefers to build in the old way, in order that he may more quickly sell his houses, one by one.

With much evidence to the contrary in the big blocks of tenements that are going up on every hand, I think still we are tending in the right direction. I come oftener, nowadays, upon three tenements built on four lots, or two on three lots, than I used to. Indeed, there was a time when such a thing would have been considered wicked waste, or evidence of unsound mind in the builder. Houses are built now, as they were then, for profit. The business element must be there, or the business will fail. Philanthropy and five per cent belong together in this field; but there is no more reason for allowing usurious interest to a man who makes a living by providing houses for the poor than for allowing it to a lender of money on security. In fact, there is less; for the former draws his profits from a source with which the welfare of the commonwealth is indissolubly bound up. The Tenement-House Committee found that the double-deckers yield the landlord an average of ten per cent, attack the home, and are a peril to the community. Model tenements pay a safe five per cent, restore the home, and thereby strengthen the community. It comes down, then, as I said, to a simple question of the per cent the builder will take. It should help his choice to know, as he cannot now help knowing, that the usurious profit is the price of good citizenship and human happiness, which suffer in the proportion in which the home is injured.

The problem of rent would be solved by the same formula, but not so readily. In the case of the builder, the state can add force to persuasion, and so urge him along the path of righteousness. The only way to reach the rent collector would be for the municipality to enter the field as a competing landlord. Doubtless relief could be afforded that way. The Tenement-House Committee found that the slum landlord charged the highest rents, sometimes as high as twenty-five per cent. He made no repairs. Model tenement-house rents are lower, if anything, than those of the double-decker, with more space and better accommodations. Such a competition would have to be on a very large scale, however, to avail, and I am glad that New York has shown no disposition to undertake it yet. I would rather we, as a community, learned first a little more of the art of governing ourselves without scandal. Present relief from the burden that taxes the worker one fourth of his earnings for a roof over his head must be sought in the movement toward the suburbs that will follow the bridging of our rivers, and real rapid transit. On the island, rents will always remain high, on account of the great land values. But I have often thought that if the city may not own new tenements, it might with advantage manage the old to the extent of licensing them to contain so many tenants on the basis of the air space, and no more. The suggestion was made when the tenement-house question first came up for discussion, thirty years ago, but it was rejected then. The same thing is now proposed for rooms and workshops, as the means of getting the best of the sweating nuisance. Why not license the whole tenement, and with the money collected in the way of fees pay for the supervision of them by night and day? The squad of sanitary policemen now comprises for the Greater City some ninety men. Forty-one thousand tenements in the Borough of Manhattan alone, at three dollars each for the license, would pay the salaries of the entire body, and leave a margin. Seeing that their services are going exclusively to the tenements, it would not seem to be an unfair charge upon the landlords.

The home is the key to good citizenship. Unhappily for the great cities, there exists in them all a class that has lost the key or thrown it away. For this class, New York, until three years ago, had never made any provision. The police station lodging rooms, of which I have spoken, were not to be dignified by the term. These vile dens, in which the homeless of our great city were herded, without pretense of bed, of bath, of food, on rude planks, were the most pernicious parody on municipal charity, I verily believe, that any civilized community had ever devised. To escape physical and moral contagion in these crowds seemed humanly impossible. Of the innocently homeless lad they made a tramp by the shortest cut. To the old tramp they were indeed ideal provision, for they enabled him to spend for drink every cent he could beg or steal. With the stale beer dive, the free lunch counter, and the police lodging room at hand, his cup of happiness was full. There came an evil day, when the stale beer dive shut its doors and the free lunch disappeared for a season. The beer pump, which drained the kegs dry and robbed the stale beer collector of his ware, drove the dives out of business; the Raines law forbade the free lunch. Just at this time Theodore Roosevelt shut the police lodging rooms, and the tramp was literally left out in the cold, cursing reform and its fruits. It was the climax of a campaign a generation old, during which no one had ever been found to say a word in defense of these lodging rooms; yet nothing had availed to close them.

The city took lodgers on an old barge in the East River that winter, and kept a register of them. We learned something from that. Of nearly 10,000 lodgers, one-half were under thirty years old and in good health—fat, in fact. The doctors reported them "well nourished." Among 100 whom I watched taking their compulsory bath one night, only two were skinny; the others were stout, well-fed men, abundantly able to do a man's work. They all insisted that they were willing, too; but the moment inquiries began with a view of setting such to work as really wanted it, and sending the rest to the island as vagrants, their number fell off most remarkably. From between 400 and 500 who had crowded the barge and the pier sheds, the attendance fell on March 16, the day the investigation began, to 330, on the second day to 294, and on the third day to 171; by March 21 it had been cut down to 121. The problem of the honestly homeless, who were without means to pay for a bed even in a ten-cent lodginghouse and who had a claim upon the city by virtue of residence in it, had dwindled to surprisingly small proportions. Of 9386 lodgers, 3622 were shown to have been here less than sixty days, and 968 less than a year. The old mistake that there is always a given amount of absolutely homeless destitution in a city and that it is to be measured by the number of those who apply for free lodging had been reduced to a demonstration. The truth is that the opportunity furnished by the triple alliance of stale beer, free lunch, and free lodging at the police station was the open door to permanent and hopeless vagrancy.

A city lodginghouse was established, with decent beds, baths, and breakfast, and a system of investigation of the lodger's claim that is yet to be developed to useful proportions. The link that is missing is a farm school for the training of young vagrants to habits of industry and steady work as the alternative of the workhouse. Efforts to forge this link have failed so far, but in the good time that is coming, when we shall have learned the lesson that the unkindest thing that can be done to a young tramp is to let him go on tramping, and when magistrates shall blush to discharge him on the plea that "it is no crime to be poor in this country," they will succeed, and the tramp also we shall then have "druv into decency." When I look back now to the time, ten or fifteen years ago, when, night after night, with every police station filled, I found the old tenements in the "Bend" jammed with a reeking mass of human wrecks that huddled in hall and yard, and slept, crouching in shivering files, all the way up the stairs to the attic, it does seem as if we had come a good way, and as if all the turmoil and the bruises and the fighting had been worthwhile.

THE TENANT

We have considered the problem of the tenement. Now about the tenant. How much of a problem is he? And how are we to go about solving his problem?

The government "slum inquiry," of which I have spoken before, gave us some facts about him. In New York it found 62.58 per cent of the population of the slum to be foreign-born, whereas for the whole city the percentage of foreigners was only 43.23. While the proportion of illiteracy in all was only as 7.69 to 100, in the slum it was 46.65 per cent. That, with nearly twice as many saloons to a given number, there should be three times as many arrests in the slum as in the city at large need not be attributed to nationality, except indirectly in its possible responsibility for the saloons. I say "possible" advisedly. Anybody, I should think, whose misfortune it is to live in the slum might be expected to find in the saloon a refuge. I shall not quarrel with the other view of it. I am merely stating a personal impression. The fact that concerns us here is the great proportion of the foreign-born. Though the inquiry covered only a small section of a tenement district, the result may be accepted as typical.

We shall not, then, have to do with an American element in discussing this tenant, for even of the "natives" in the census, by far the largest share is made up of the children of the immigrant. Indeed, in New York only 4.77 per cent of the slum population canvassed were shown to be of native parentage. The parents of 95.23 per cent had come over the sea, to better themselves, it may be assumed. Let us see what they brought us, and what we have given them in return.

The Italians were in the majority where this census taker went. They were from the south of Italy, avowedly the worst of the Italian immigration which in the eight years from 1891 to 1898 gave us more than half a million of King Humbert's subjects. The exact number, as registered by the Emigration Bureau, was 502,592. In 1898, 58,613 came over, 36,086 of them with New York as their destination. The official year ends with June. In the six months from July 1 to December 31, the immigrants were sorted out upon a more intelligent plan than previously. The process as applied to the 30,470 Italians who were landed during that term yielded this result: from northern Italy, 4762; from southern Italy, 25,708. Of these latter a number came from Sicily, the island of the absentee landlord, where peasants die of hunger. I make no apology for quoting here the statement of an Italian officer, on duty in the island, to a staff correspondent of the *Tribuna* of Rome, a paper not to be suspected of disloyalty to United Italy. I take it from the *Evening Post*:

"In the month of July I stopped on a march by a threshing floor where they were measuring grain. When the shares had been divided, the one who had cultivated the land received a single *tumolo* (less than a half bushel). The peasant, leaning on his spade, looked at his share as if stunned. His wife and their five children were standing by. From the painful toil of a year this was what was left to him with which to feed his family. The tears rolled silently down his cheeks."

These things occasionally help one to understand. Over against this picture there arises in my memory one from the Barge Office, where I had gone to see an Italian steamer come in. A family sat apart, ordered to wait by the inspecting officer; in the group an old man, worn and wrinkled, who viewed the turmoil with the calmness of one having no share in it. The younger members formed a sort of bulwark around him.

"Your father is too old," said the official.

Two young women and a boy of sixteen rose to their feet at once. "Are not we young enough to work for him?" they said. The boy showed his strong arms.

It is charged against this Italian immigrant that he is dirty, and the charge is true. He lives in the darkest of slums, and pays rent that ought to hire a decent flat. To wash, water is needed; and we have a law which orders tenement landlords to put it on every floor, so that their tenants may have the chance. And it is not yet half a dozen years since one of the biggest tenement-house landlords in the city, the wealthiest church corporation in the land, attacked the constitutionality of this statute rather than pay a couple of hundred dollars for putting water into two old buildings, as the Board of Health had ordered, and came near upsetting the whole structure of tenement-house law upon which our safety depends. He is ignorant, it is said, and that charge is also true. I doubt if one of the family in the Barge Office could read or write his own name. Yet would you fear especial danger to our institutions, to our citizenship, from these four? He lives cheaply, crowds, and underbids even the Jew in the sweatshop. I can myself testify to the truth of these statements. Only this spring I was the umpire in a quarrel between the Jewish tailors and the factory inspector whom they arraigned before the Governor on charges of inefficiency. The burden of their grievance was that the Italians were underbidding them in their own market, which of course the factory inspector could not prevent. Yet, even so, the evidence is not that the Italian always gets the best of it. I came across a family once working on "knee pants." "Twelve pants, ten cents," said the tailor, when there was work.

"Ve work for dem sheenies," he explained. "Ven dey has work, ve gets some; ven dey hasn't, ve don't." He was an unusually gifted tailor as to English, but apparently not as to business capacity. In the Astor tenements, in Elizabeth Street, where we found forty-three families living in rooms intended for sixteen, I saw women finishing "pants" at thirty cents a day. Some of the garments were of good grade, and some of poor; some of them were soldiers' trousers, made for the government; but whether they received five, seven, eight, or ten cents a pair, it came to thirty cents a day, except in a single instance, in which two women, sewing from five in the morning till eleven at night, were able, being practiced hands, to finish forty-five "pants" at three and a half cents a pair, and so made together over a dollar and a half. They were content, even happy. I suppose it seemed wealth to them, coming from a land where a Parisian investigator of repute found three lire (not quite sixty cents) *per month* a girl's wages.

I remember one of those flats, poor and dingy, yet with signs of the instinctive groping toward orderly arrangement which I have observed so many times and take to be evidence that in better surroundings much might be made of these people. Clothes were hung to dry on a line strung the whole length of the room. Upon couches by the wall some men were snoring. They were the boarders. The "man" was out shoveling snow with the midnight shift. By a lamp with brown paper shade over at the window sat two women sewing. One had a baby on her lap. Two sweet little cherubs, nearly naked, slept on a pile of unfinished "pants," and smiled in their sleep. A girl of six or seven dozed in a child's rocker between the two workers, with her head hanging down on one side; the mother propped it up with her elbow as she sewed. They were all there, and happy in being together even in such a place. On a corner shelf burned a night lamp before a print of the Mother of God, flanked by two green bottles, which, seen at a certain angle, made quite a festive show.

Complaint is made that the Italian promotes child labor. His children work at home on "pants" and flowers at an hour when they ought to have been long in bed. Their sore eyes betray the little flowermakers when they come tardily to school. Doubtless there are such cases, and quite too many of them; yet, in the very block which I have spoken of, the investigation conducted for the Tenement House Committee by the University Department of Sociology of Columbia College, under Professor Franklin H. Giddings, discovered of 196 children of school age only 23 at work or at home, and in the next block only 27 out of 215. That was the showing of the foreign population all the way through. Of 225 Russian Jewish children only 15 were missing from school, and of 354 little Bohemians only 21. The overcrowding of the schools and their long waiting lists occasionally furnished the explanation why they were not there. Professor Giddings reported, after considering all the evidence: "The foreign-born population of the city is not, to any great extent, forcing children of legal school age into money-earning occupations. On the contrary, this population shows a strong desire to have its children acquire the common rudiments of education. If the city does not provide liberally and wisely for the satisfaction of this desire, the blame for the civic and moral dangers that will threaten our community, because of ignorance, vice, and poverty, must rest on the whole public, not on our foreign-born residents." It is satisfactory to know that the warning has been heeded, and that soon there will be schools enough to hold all the children who come. Now, since September 1, 1899, the new factory law reaches also the Italian flowermaker in his home, and that source of waste will be stopped.

He is clannish, this Italian; he gambles and uses a knife, though rarely on anybody not of his own people; he "takes what he can get," wherever anything is free,

as who would not, coming to the feast like a starved
wolf? There was nothing free where he came from.
Even the salt was taxed past a poor man's getting any
of it. Lastly, he buys fraudulent naturalization papers,
and uses them. I shall plead guilty for him to every
one of these counts. They are all proven. Gambling is
his besetting sin. He is sober, industrious, frugal, en-
during beyond belief, but he will gamble on Sunday
and quarrel over his cards, and when he sticks his
partner in the heat of the quarrel, the partner is not
apt to tell. He prefers to bide his time. Yet there has
lately been evidence once or twice in the surrender of
an assassin by his countrymen that the old vendetta is
being shelved, and a new idea of law and justice is
breaking through. As to the last charge: our Italian is
not dull. With his intense admiration for the land
where a dollar a day waits upon the man with a
shovel, he can see no reason why he should not accept
the whole "American plan" with ready enthusiasm. It
is a good plan. To him it sums itself up in the statement: a dollar a day for the shovel; two dollars for
the shovel with a citizen behind it. And he takes the
papers and the two dollars.

He came here for a chance to live. Of politics, social
ethics, he knows nothing. Government in his old home
existed only for his oppression. Why should he not
attach himself with his whole loyal soul to the plan of
government in his new home that offers to boost him
into the place of his wildest ambition, a "job on the
streets"—that is, in the Street-Cleaning Department
—and asks no other return than that he shall vote as
directed? Vote! Not only he, but his cousins and
brothers and uncles will vote as they are told, to get
Pietro the job he covets. If it pleases the other man,
what is it to him for whom he votes? He is after the
job. Here, ready-made to the hand of the politician,
is such material as he never saw before. For Pietro's
loyalty is great. As a police detective, one of his own
people, once put it to me: "He got a kind of an idea,

or an old rule: an eye for an eye; do to another as you'd be done by; if he don't squeal on you, you stick by him, no matter what the consequences." This "kind of an idea" is all he has to draw upon for an answer to the question if the thing is right. But the question does not arise. Why should it? Was he not told by the agitators whom the police jailed at home that in a republic all men are made happy by means of the vote? And is there not proof of it? It has made him happy, has it not? And the man who bought his vote seems to like it. Well, then?

Very early Pietro discovered that it was every man for himself, in the chase of the happiness which this powerful vote had in keeping. He was robbed by the padrone—that is, the boss—when he came over, fleeced on his steamship fare, made to pay for getting a job, and charged three prices for board and lodging and extras while working in the railroad gang. The boss had a monopoly, and Pietro was told that it was maintained by his "divvying" with some railroad official. Rumor said a very high-up official and that the railroad was in politics in the city; that is to say, dealt in votes. When the job gave out, the boss packed him into the tenement he had bought with his profits on the contract; and if Pietro had a family, told him to take in lodgers and crowd his flat, as the Elizabeth Street tenements were crowded, so as to make out the rent, and to never mind the law. The padrone was a politician and had a pull. He was bigger than the law, and it was the votes he traded in that did it all. Now it was Pietro's turn. With his vote he could buy what to him seemed wealth. In the muddle of ideas, that was the one which stood out. When citizen papers were offered him for $12.50, he bought them quickly, and got his job on the street.

It was the custom of the country. If there was any doubt about it, the proof was furnished when Pietro was arrested through the envy and plotting of the opposition boss last fall. Distinguished counsel, em-

ployed by the machine, pleaded his case in court.
Pietro felt himself to be quite a personage, and he was
told that he was safe from harm, though a good deal
of dust might be kicked up; because, when it came
down to that, both the bosses were doing the same
kind of business. I quote from the report of the State
Superintendent of Elections of January 1899: "In
nearly every case of illegal registration, the defendant
was represented by eminent counsel who were identified with the Democratic organization, among them
being three assistants to the Corporation counsel. My
deputies arrested Rosario Calecione and Giuseppe
Marrone, both of whom appeared to vote at the fifth
election district of the Sixth Assembly District; Marrone being the Democratic captain of the district, and,
it was charged, himself engaged in the business of
securing fraudulent naturalization papers. In both of
these cases Farriello had procured the naturalization
papers for the men for a consideration. They were
subsequently indicted. Marrone and Calecione were
bailed by the Democratic leader of the Sixth Assembly
District."

The business, says the State Superintendent, is carried on "to an enormous extent." It appears, then, that
Pietro has already "got on to" the American plan as
the slum presented it to him, and has in good earnest
become a problem. I guessed as much from the statement of a Tammany politician to me, a year ago, that
every Italian voter in his district got his "old two" on
election day. He ought to know, for he held the purse.
Suppose, now, we speak our minds as frankly, for
once, and put the blame where it belongs. Will it be
on Pietro? And upon this showing, who ought to be
excluded, when it comes to that?

The slum census taker did not cross the Bowery.
Had he done so, he would have come upon the refugee Jew, the other economic marplot of whom complaint is made with reason. If his Nemesis has overtaken him in the Italian, certainly he challenged that

fate. He did cut wages by his coming. He was starving, and he came in shoals. In fourteen years more than 400,000 Jewish immigrants have landed in New York.* They had to have work and food, and they got both as they could. In the strife they developed qualities that were anything but pleasing. They herded like cattle. They had been so herded by Christian rulers, a despised and persecuted race, through the centuries. Their very coming was to escape from their last inhuman captivity in a Christian state. They lied, they were greedy, they were charged with bad faith. They brought nothing—neither money nor artisan skill —nothing but their consuming energy, to our land, and their one gift was their greatest offense. One might have pointed out that they had been trained to lie, for their safety; had been forbidden to work at trades, to own land; had been taught for a thousand years, with the scourge and the stake, that only gold could buy them freedom from torture. But what was the use? The charges were true. The Jew was—he still is—a problem of our slum.

And yet, if ever there was material for citizenship, this Jew is such material. Alone of all our immigrants he comes to us without a past. He has no country to renounce, no ties to forget. Within him there burns a passionate longing for a home to call his, a country which will own him, that waits only for the spark of such another love to spring into flame which nothing can quench. Waiting for it, all his energies are turned into his business. He is not always choice in method; he often offends. But he succeeds. He is the yeast of any slum, if given time. If it will not let him go, it must rise with him. The charity managers in London said it, when we looked through their slums some years ago: "The Jews have renovated Whitechapel." I, for

---

* According to the register of the United Hebrew Charities, between October 1, 1884, and March 1, 1899, the number was 402,181.

one, am a firm believer in this Jew, and in his boy. Ignorant they are, but with a thirst for knowledge that surmounts any barrier. The boy takes all the prizes in the school. His comrades sneer that he will not fight. Neither will he when there is nothing to be gained by it. But I believe that, should the time come when the country needs fighting men, the son of the despised immigrant Jew will resurrect on American soil, the first that bade him welcome, the old Maccabee type, and set an example for all the rest of us to follow.

For fifteen years he has been in the public eye as the vehicle and promoter of sweating, and much severe condemnation has been visited upon him with good cause. He had to do something, and he took to the clothesmaker's trade as that which was most quickly learned. The increasing crowds, the tenement, and his grinding poverty made the soil wherein the evil thing grew rank. Yet the real sweater is the manufacturer, not the workman. It is just a question of expense to the manufacturer. By letting out his work on contract, he can save the expense of running his factory and delay longer making his choice of styles. The Jew is the victim of the mischief quite as much as he has helped it on. Back of the manufacturer there is still another sweater—the public. Only by its sufferance of the bargain counter and of sweatshop-made goods has the nuisance existed as long as it has. I am glad to believe that its time is passing away. The law has driven the sweatshops out of the tenements, and so deprived them of one of their chief props: there was no rent at all to pay there. Child labor, which only four years ago the Reinhard Committee characterized as "one of the most extensive evils now existing in the city of New York, a constant and grave menace to the welfare of its people," has been practically banished from the tailoring trade. What organization among the workers had failed to effect is apparently going to be accomplished by direct pressure of an outraged public opinion. Already manufacturers are returning to their own factories, and making capital of the fact among their customers. The new law, which greatly extends the factory inspector's power over sweatshops, is an expression of this enlightened sentiment. It will put New York a long stride ahead, and quite up to Massachusetts. The inspector's tag has proved, where the law was violated, an effective weapon. It suspends all operation of the shop and removal of the goods until the orders of the inspector have been obeyed. But the tag which shall finally put an end to sweating, and restore decent conditions, is not the factory inspector's, I am persuaded, but a trade-union label, which shall deserve public confidence and receive it. We have much to learn yet, all of us. I think I can see the end of this trouble, however, when the Italian's triumph in the sweatshop shall have proved but a barren victory, to his own gain.

In all I have said so far, in these papers, I have not gone beyond the limits of the old city—of Manhattan Island, in fact. I want now to glance for a moment at the several attempts made at colonizing refugee Jews in this part of the country. Brownsville was one of the earliest. Its projector was a manufacturer, and its motive profit. The result was the familiar one—as nasty a little slum as ever the East Side had to show. We have it on our hands now in the Greater City—it came in with Brooklyn—and it is not a gain. Down in southern New Jersey several colonies were started, likewise by speculators, in the persecution of the early eighties, and these also failed. The soil was sandy and poor, and, thrown upon their own resources in a strange and unfriendly neighborhood, with unfamiliar and unremunerative toil, the colonists grew discouraged and gave up in despair. The colonies were approaching final collapse, when the managers of the Baron de Hirsch Fund in New York, who had started and maintained a successful colony at Woodbine, in the same neighborhood, took them under the arms and inaugurated a new plan. They persuaded several large clothing contractors in this city to move their plants down to the villages, where they would be assured of steady hands, not so easily affected by strikes. For strikes in sweatshops are often enough the alternative of starvation. Upon the land there would be no starvation. The managers of the Fund built factories, bought the old mortgages on the farms, and put up houses for the families which the contractors brought down with them. This effort at transplanting the crowd from the Ghetto to the soil has now been going on for a year. At latest account, eight contractors and two hundred and fifty families had been moved out. The colonies had taken on a new lease of life and apparent prosperity. While it is yet too early to pass sober judgment, there seems to be good ground for hoping that a real way out has been found that shall restore the Jew, at least in a measure, to the soil from which he was barred so long. The experiment is of exceeding interest. The hopes of its projectors that a purely farming community might be established have not been realized. Perhaps it was too much to expect. By bringing to the farmers their missing market, and work to the surplus population, the mixed settlement plan bids fair to prove a step in the desired direction.

Some 18,500 acres are now held by Jewish colonists in New Jersey. In the New England States, in the last eight years, 600 abandoned farms have been occupied and are cultivated by refugees from Russia. As a dairy farmer and a poultry raiser, the Jew has more of an immediate commercial grip on the situation and works with more courage. At Woodbine, sixty-five boys and girls are being trained in an agricultural school that has won the whole settlement the friendly regard of the neighborhood. Of its pupils, eleven came out of tailor shops, and ten had been office boys, messengers, or newsboys. To these, and to the trade schools now successfully operated by the De Hirsch Fund, we are to look in the next generation for the answer to the old taunt that the Jew is a trader, and not fit to be either farmer or craftsman, and for the solution of the problem which he now presents in the slum.

I have spoken at length of the Jew and the Italian because they are our present problem. Yesterday it was the Irishman and the Bohemian. Tomorrow it may be the Greek, who already undersells the Italian from his pushcart in the Fourth Ward, and the Syrian, who can give Greek, Italian, and Jew points at a trade. From Dalmatia a new immigration has begun to come, and there are signs of its working further east in the Balkan states, where there is no telling what is in store for us. How to absorb them all safely is the question. Doubtless the Irishman, having absorbed us politically, would be glad to free us from all concern on that score by doing a like favor for them. But we should not get the best of the slum that way; it would get the best of us, instead. Would I shut out the newcomers? Sometimes, looking at it from the point of view of the Barge Office and the sweatshop, I think I would. Then there comes up the recollection of a picture of the city of Prague that hangs in a Bohemian friend's parlor, here in New York. I stood looking at it one day, and noticed in the foreground cannon that pointed in over the city. I spoke of it, unthinking, and said to my host that they should be trained, if against an enemy, the other way. The man's eye flashed fire. "Ha!" he cried, "here, yes!" When I think of that, I do not want to shut the door.

Again, there occurs to me an experience the police had last summer in Mulberry Street. They were looking for a murderer, and came upon a nest of Italian thugs who lived by blackmailing their countrymen. They were curious about them, and sent their names to Naples with a request for information. There came back such a record as none of the detectives had ever seen or heard of before. All of them were notorious criminals, who had been charged with every conceivable crime, from burglary to kidnapping and "maiming," and some not to be conceived of by the American mind. Five of them together had been sixty-three times in jail, and one no less than twenty-one times. Yet, though they were all "under special surveillance," they had come here without let or hindrance within a year. When I recall that, I want to shut the door quick. I sent the exhibit to Washington at the time. But then, again, when I think of Mrs. Michelangelo in her poor mourning for one child run over and killed, wiping her tears away and going bravely to work to keep the home together for the other five until the oldest shall be old enough to take her father's place; and when, as now, there strays into my hand the letter from my good friend, the "woman doctor" in the slum, when her father had died, in which she wrote: "The little scamps of the street have been positively pathetic; they have made such shy, boyish attempts at friendliness. One little chap offered to let me hold his top while it was spinning, in token of affection"—when I read that, I have not the heart to shut anybody out.

Except, of course, the unfit, the criminal and the pauper, cast off by their own, and the man brought over here merely to put money into the pockets of the steamship agent, the padrone, and the mine owner. We have laws to bar these out. Suppose we begin by being honest with ourselves and the immigrant, and enforcing our own laws. In spite of a healthy effort at the port of New York—I can only speak for that—under the present administration, that has not yet been done. When the door has been shut and locked against the man who left his country for his country's good, whether by its "assistance" or not, and when trafficking in the immigrant for private profit has been stopped, then, perhaps, we shall be better able to decide what degree of ignorance in him constitutes unfitness for citizenship and cause for shutting him out. Perchance then, also, we shall hear less of the cant about his being a peril to the republic. Doubtless ignorance is a peril, but the selfishness that trades upon ignorance is a much greater. He came to us without a country, ready to adopt such a standard of patriotism as he found, at its face value, and we gave him the rear tenement and slum politics. If he accepted the standard, whose fault was it? His being in such a hurry to vote that he could not wait till the law made him a citizen was no worse, to my mind, than the treachery of the "upper class" native, who refuses to go to the polls for fear he may rub up against him there. This last let us settle with first, and see what remains of our problem. We can approach it honestly, then, at all events.

When the country was in the throes of the silver campaign, the newspapers told the story of an old laborer who went to the subtreasury and demanded to see the "boss." He undid the strings of an old leathern purse with fumbling fingers, and counted out more than two hundred dollars in gold eagles, the hoard of a lifetime of toil and self-denial. They were for the government, he said. He had not the head to understand all the talk that was going, but he gathered from what he heard that the government was in trouble, and that somehow it was about not having gold enough. So he had brought what he had. He owed it all to the country, and now that she needed it he had come to give it back. The man was an Irishman. Very likely he was enrolled in Tammany and voted her ticket.

I remember a tenement at the bottom of a back alley over on the East Side, where I once went visiting with the pastor of a mission chapel. Up in the attic there was a family of father and daughter in two rooms that had been made out of one by dividing off the deep dormer window. It was midwinter, and they had no fire. He was a peddler, but the snow had stalled his pushcart and robbed them of their only other source of income, a lodger who hired cot room in the attic for a few cents a night. The daughter was not able to work. But she said, cheerfully, that they were "getting along." When it came out that she had not tasted solid food for many days, was starving, in fact—indeed, she died within a year, of the slow starvation of the tenements that parades in the mortality returns under a variety of scientific names which all mean the same thing—she met her pastor's gentle chiding with the excuse, "Oh, your church has many poorer than I. I don't want to take your money." These were Germans, ordinarily held to be close-fisted; but I found that in their dire distress they had taken in a poor old man who was past working, and had kept him all winter, sharing with him what they had. He was none of theirs; they hardly even knew him, as it appeared. It was enough that he was "poorer than they," and lonely and hungry and cold.

It was over here that the children of Dr. Elsing's Sunday school gave out of the depth of their poverty fifty-four dollars in pennies to be hung on the Christmas tree as their offering to the persecuted Armenians. One of their teachers told me of a Bohemian family that let the holiday dinner she brought them stand and wait, while they sent out to bid to the feast four little ragamuffins of the neighborhood who else would have gone hungry. I remember well a teacher in one of the Children's Aid Society's schools, herself a tenement child, who, with breaking heart, but brave face, played and sang the children's Christmas carols with them rather than spoil their pleasure, while her only sister lay dying at home.

I might keep on and fill many pages with instances of that kind, which simply go to prove that our poor human nature is at least as robust on Avenue A as up on Fifth Avenue, if it has half a chance, and often enough to restore one's faith in it, with no chance at all; and I might set over against it the product of sordid and mean environment which one has never far to seek. Good and evil go together in the tenements as in the fine houses, and the evil sticks out sometimes merely because it lies nearer the surface. The point is that the good does outweigh the bad, and that the virtues that turn the balance are after all those that make for good citizenship anywhere, while the faults are oftenest the accidents of ignorance and lack of training, which it is the business of society to correct. I recall my discouragement when I looked over the examination papers of a batch of candidates for police appointment—young men largely the product of our public schools in this city and elsewhere—and read in them that five of the original New England States were "England, Ireland, Scotland, Belfast, and Cork"; that the Fire Department ruled New York in the absence of the Mayor—I have sometimes wished it did, and that he would stay away awhile; and that Lincoln was murdered by Ballington Booth. But we shall agree, no doubt, that the indictment of these papers was not of the men who wrote them, but of the school that stuffed its pupils with useless trash, and did not teach them to think. Neither have I forgotten that it was one of these very men who, having failed, and afterward got a job as a bridge policeman, on his first payday went straight from his post, half frozen as he was, to the settlement worker who had befriended him and his sick father, and gave him five dollars for "some one who was poorer than they." Poorer than they! What worker among the poor has not heard it? It is the charity of the tenement that covers a multitude of sins. There were thirteen in this policeman's family, and his wages were the biggest item of income in the house.

Jealousy, envy, and meanness wear no fine clothes and masquerade under no smooth speeches in the slums. Often enough it is the very nakedness of the virtues that makes us stumble in our judgment. I have in mind the "difficult case" that confronted some philanthropic friends of mine in a rear tenement on Twelfth Street, in the person of an aged widow, quite seventy I should think, who worked uncomplainingly for a sweater all day and far into the night, pinching and saving and stinting herself, with black bread and chicory coffee as her only fare, in order that she might carry her pitiful earnings to her big, lazy lout of a son in Brooklyn. He never worked. My friends' difficulty was a very real one, for absolutely every attempt to relieve the widow was wrecked upon her mother heart. It all went over the river. Yet one would not have had her different.

Sometimes it is only the unfamiliar setting that shocks. When an East Side midnight burglar, discovered and pursued, killed a tenant who blocked his way of escape, a few weeks ago, his "girl" gave him up to the police. But it was not because he had taken human life. "He was good to me," she explained to the captain whom she told where to find him, "but since he robbed the church I had no use for him." He had stolen, it seems, the communion service in a Staten Island church. The thoughtless laughed. But in her ignorant way she was only trying to apply the standards of morality as they had been taught her. Stunted, bemuddled, as they were, I think I should prefer to take my chances with her rather than with the woman of wealth and luxury who, some years ago, gave a Christmas party to her lap dog, as on the whole the sounder of the two, and by far the more hopeful.

All of which is merely saying that the country is all right, and the people are to be trusted with the old faith in spite of the slum. And it is true, if we remember to put it that way—in spite of the slum. There is nothing in the slum to warrant that faith save human nature as yet uncorrupted. How long it is to remain so is altogether a question of the sacrifices we are willing to make in our fight with the slum. As yet, we are told by the officials having to do with the enforcement of the health ordinances, which come closer to the life of the individual than any other kind, that the poor in the tenements are "more amenable to the law than the better class." It is of the first importance, then, that we should have laws deserving of their respect, and that these laws should be enforced, lest they conclude that the whole thing is a sham. Respect for law is a very powerful bar against the slum. But what, for instance, must the poor Jew understand, who is permitted to buy a live hen at the market, yet neither to kill nor keep it in his tenement, and who on his feast day finds a whole squad of policemen detailed to follow him around and see that he does not do any of the things with his fowl for which he must have bought it? Or the day laborer, who drinks his beer in a "Raines law hotel," where brick sandwiches, consisting of two pieces of bread with a brick between, are set out on the counter, in derision of the state law which forbids the serving of drinks without "meals"? (The Stanton Street saloonkeeper who did that was solemnly acquitted by a jury.) Or the boy who may buy fireworks on the Fourth of July but not set them off? These are only ridiculous instances of an abuse that pervades our community life to an extent that constitutes one of the gravest perils. Insincerity of that kind is not lost on our fellow citizen by adoption, who is only anxious to fall in with the ways of the country; and especially is it not lost on his boy.

We shall see how it affects him. He is the one for whom we are waging the battle with the slum. He is the tomorrow that sits today drinking in the lesson of the prosperity of the big boss who declared with pride upon the witness stand that he rules New York, that judges pay him tribute, and that only when *he* says so a thing "goes"; and that it is all for what he can get out of it, "just the same as everybody else." He sees corporations today pay blackmail and rob the people in return, quite according to the schedule of Hester Street. Only there it is the police who charge the peddler twenty cents, while here it is the politicians taking toll of the franchises, twenty per cent. Wall Street is not ordinarily reckoned in the slum, because of certain physical advantages; but, upon the evidence of the day, I think we shall have to conclude that the advantage ends there. The boy who is learning such lessons—how is it with him?

The president of the Society for the Prevention of Cruelty to Children says that children's crime is increasing, and he ought to know. The managers of the Children's Aid Society, after forty-six years of wrestling with the slum for the boy, in which they have lately seemed to get the upper hand, say in this year's report that on the East Side children are growing up in certain districts "entirely neglected," and that the number of such children "increases beyond the power of philanthropic and religious bodies to cope properly with their needs." In the Tompkins Square Lodginghouse the evening classes are thinning out, and the keeper wails: "Those with whom we have dealt of late have not been inclined to accept this privilege; how to make night school attractive to shiftless, indifferent street boys is a difficult problem to solve."

Perhaps it is only that he has lost the key. Across the square, the Boys' Club of St. Mark's Place, that began with a handful, counts five thousand members today, and is seeking a place to build a house of its own. The school census man announces that no boy in that old stronghold of the "bread or blood" brigade need henceforth loiter in the street because there is not room in the public school, and the brigade has disbanded for want of recruits. The shop is being shut against the boy, and the bars let down at the playground. But from Tompkins Square, nevertheless, came Jacob Beresheim, whose story I shall tell you presently.

JUSTICE
FOR THE BOY

—

Sometimes, when I see my little boy hugging himself with delight at the near prospect of the kindergarten, I go back in memory forty years and more to the day when I was dragged, a howling captive, to school, as a punishment for being bad at home. I remember, as though it were yesterday, my progress up the street in the vengeful grasp of an exasperated servant, and my reception by the aged monster—most fitly named Madame Bruin—who kept the school. She asked no questions, but led me straightway to the cellar, where she plunged me into an empty barrel and put the lid on over me. Applying her horn goggles to the bunghole, to my abject terror, she informed me, in a sepulchral voice, that that was the way bad boys were dealt with in school. When I ceased howling from sheer fright, she took me out and conducted me to the yard, where a big hog had a corner to itself. She bade me observe that one of its ears had been slit half its length. It was because the hog was lazy, and little boys who were that way minded were in danger of similar treatment; in token whereof she clipped a pair of tailor's shears suggestively close to my ear. It was my first lesson in school. I hated it from that hour.

The barrel and the hog were never part of the curriculum in any American boy's school, I suppose; they seem too freakish to be credited to any but the demoniac ingenuity of my home ogre. But they stood for a comprehension of the office of school and teacher which was not patented by any day or land. It is not so long since the notion yet prevailed that the schools were principally to lock children up in for the convenience of their parents, that we should have entirely forgotten it. Only the other day a clergyman from up the state came into my office to tell of a fine reform school they had in his town. They were very proud of it.

"And how about the schools for the good boys in your town?" I asked, when I had heard him out. "Are they anything to be proud of?"

He stared. He guessed they were all right, he said, after some hesitation. But it was clear that he did not know.

It is not necessary to go back forty years to find us in the metropolis upon the clergyman's platform, if not upon Madame Bruin's. Ten will do. They will bring us to the day when roof playgrounds were contemptuously left out of the estimates for an East Side school, as "frills" that had nothing to do with education; when the Board of Health found but a single public school in more than sixscore that was so ventilated as to keep the children from being poisoned by foul air; when the authority of the Talmud had to be invoked by the Superintendent of School Buildings to convince the president of the Board of Education, who happened to be a Jew, that seventy-five or eighty pupils were far too many for one classroom; when a man who had been dead a year was appointed a school trustee of the Third Ward, under the moldy old law surviving from the day when New York was a big village, and filled the office as well as if he had been alive, because there were no schools in his ward; when manual training and the kindergarten were yet the fads of yesterday, looked at askance; when fifty thousand children roamed the streets for whom there was no room in the schools, and the only defense of the School Commissioners was that they "didn't know" there were so many; and when we mixed truants and thieves in a jail with entire unconcern. Indeed, the jail filled the title role in the educational cast of that day. Its inmates were well lodged and cared for, while the sanitary authorities twice condemned the Essex Market school across the way as wholly unfit for children to be in, but failed to catch the ear of the politician who ran things unhindered. When (in 1894) I denounced the "system" of enforcing—or not enforcing—the compulsory education law as a device to make thieves out of our children by turning over their training to the street, he protested angrily; but the experts of the Tenement-House Committee found the charge fully borne out by the facts. They were certainly plain enough in the sight of us all, had we chosen to see.

When at last we saw, we gave the politician a vacation for a season. To say that he was to blame for all the mischief would not be fair. We were to blame for leaving him in possession. He was only a link in the chain which our indifference had forged; but he was always and everywhere an obstruction to betterment—sometimes, illogically, in spite of himself. Successive Tammany mayors had taken a stand for the public schools, when it was clear that reform could not be delayed much longer; but they were helpless against a system of selfishness and stupidity of which they were the creatures, though they posed as its masters. They had to go with it as unfit, and upon the wave that swept out the last of the rubbish came reform. The Committee of Seventy took hold, the Good Government Clubs, the Tenement-House Committee, and the women of New York. Five years we strove with the powers of darkness, and look now at the change. The New York school system is not yet the ideal one—it may never be; but the jail, at least, has been cast out of the firm. We have a compulsory education law under which it will be possible, when a seat has been provided for every child, to punish the parent for the boy's truancy, unless he surrenders him as unmanageable; and we can count the months now till every child shall find the latchstring out on the school door. We have had to put our hands deep into our pockets to get to that point, but we are nearly there now. Since 1895 the expenditure of twenty-two and a half millions of dollars for new schools in the old city has been authorized by law, and two-thirds of the money has been spent. Fifty-odd new buildings have been put up, or are going up while I am writing, every one of them with its playground, which will by and by be free to all the neighborhood. The idea is at last working through that the schools belong to the people, and are primarily for the children and their parents; not mere vehicles of ward patronage, or for keeping an army of teachers in office and pay.

The silly old regime is dead. The ward trustee is gone with his friend the alderman, loudly proclaiming the collapse of our liberties in the day that saw the schools taken from "the people's" control. They were "the people." Experts manage our children's education, which was supposed in the old plan to be the only thing that did not require any training. To superintend a brickyard demanded some knowledge, but anybody could run the public schools. It cost us an election to take that step. One of the Tammany district leaders, who knew what he was talking about, said to me after it was all over: "I knew we would win. Your bringing those foreigners here did the business. Our people believe in home rule. We kept account of the teachers you brought from out of town, and who spent the money they made here out of town, and who it got to be the talk among the tenement people in my ward that their daughters would have no more show to get to be teachers. That did the business. We figured the school vote in the city at forty-two thousand, and I knew we could not lose." The "foreigners" were teachers from Massachusetts and other states, who had achieved a national reputation at their work.

There lies upon my table a copy of the minutes of the Board of Education of January 9, 1895, in which is underscored a report on a primary school in the

Bronx. "It is a wooden shanty," is the inspector's account, "heated by stoves, and is a regular tinder box; cellar wet, and under one classroom only. This building was erected in order, I believe, to determine whether or not there was a school population in the neighborhood to warrant the purchase of property to erect a school on."

That was the way then of taking a school census, and the result was the utter failure of the compulsory education law to compel anything. Today we have a biennial census, ordained by law, which, when at last it gets into the hands of some one who can count, will tell us how many Jacob Beresheims are drifting upon the shoals of the street. And we have a truant school to keep them safe in. To it, says the law, no thief shall be committed. It is not yet five years since the burglar and the truant—who, having been refused admission to the school because there was not room for him, inconsequently was locked up for contracting idle ways—were herded in the Juvenile Asylum, and classified there in squads of those who were four feet, four feet seven, and over four feet seven! I am afraid I scandalized some good people, during the fight for decency in this matter, by insisting that it ought to be considered a good mark for Jacob that he despised such schools as were provided for him. But it was true. Except for the risk of the burglar, the jail was preferable by far. A woman has now had charge of the truant school for fourteen months, and she tells me that of quite twenty-five hundred boys scarce sixty were rightly called incorrigible, and even these a little longer and tighter grip would probably win over. For such, a farm school is yet to be provided. The rest responded promptly to an appeal to their pride. She "made it a personal matter" with each of them, and the truant vanished; the boy was restored. The burglar, too, made it a personal matter in the old contact, and the result was two burglars for one. In common with nearly all those who have paid attention to this matter, Mrs. Alger believes that the truant school strikes at the root of the problem of juvenile crime. After thirty years of close acquaintance with the child population of London, Mr. Andrew Drew, chairman of the Industrial Committee of the School Board, declared his conviction that "truancy is to be credited with nearly the whole of our juvenile criminality." But for years there seemed to be no way of convincing the New York School Board that the two had anything to do with each other. As executive officer of the Good Government Clubs, I fought that fight to a finish. We got the school, and in Mrs. Alger, at the time a truant officer, a person singularly well qualified to take charge of it. She has recently been removed, that her place might be given to a man. It is the old scheme come back—a voter behind the broom—and the old slough waiting to overwhelm us again.

But it will not get the chance. I have my own idea of how this truancy question is going to be solved. Yesterday I went with Superintendent Snyder through some of the new schools he is building, upon what he calls the letter H plan, in the crowded districts. It is the plan of the Hôtel de Cluny in Paris, and to my mind as nearly perfect as it is possible to make a schoolhouse. There is not a dark corner in the whole structure, from the splendid gymnasium under the red-tiled roof to the indoor playground on the ground floor, which, when thrown in one with the two open-air playgrounds that lie embraced in the arms of the H, will give the children nearly an acre of asphalted floor space from street to street to romp on. Seven such schools are going up today, each a beautiful palace, and within the year sixteen thousand children will be housed in them. When I think of the old Allen Street school, where the gas had to be kept burning even on the brightest days, recitations suspended every half hour, and the children made to practice calisthenics so that they should not catch cold while the windows were opened to let in fresh air; of the dark playground downstairs, with the rats keeping up such a racket that one could hardly hear himself speak at times, or of the other East Side playground where the boys "weren't allowed to speak above a whisper," so as not to disturb those studying overhead, I fancy that I can make out both the cause and the cure of the boy's desperation. "We try to make our schools pleasant enough to hold the children," wrote the Superintendent of Schools in Indianapolis to me once, and added that they had no truant problem worth bothering about. With the kindergarten and manual training firmly engrafted upon the school course, as they are at last, and with it reaching out to enlist also the boy's play through playground and vacation schools, I shall be willing to turn the boy who will not come in over to the reformatory. They will not need to build a new wing to the jail for his safekeeping.

All ways lead to Rome. The reform in school building dates back, as does every other reform in New York, to the Mulberry Bend. It began there. The first school that departed from the soulless old tradition, to set beautiful pictures before the child's mind as well as dry figures on the slate, was built there. At the time I wanted it to stand in the park, hoping so to hasten the laying out of that; but although the Small Parks law expressly permitted the erection on park property of buildings for "the instruction of the people," the officials upon whom I pressed my scheme could not be made to understand that as including schools. Perhaps they were right. I catechized thirty-one Fourth Ward girls in a sewing school about that time, twenty-six of whom had attended the public schools of the district more than a year. One wore a badge earned for excellence in her studies. In those days every street corner was placarded with big posters of Napoleon on a white horse riding through fire and smoke. There was one right across the street. Yet only one of the thirty-one knew who Napoleon was. She "thought she had heard of the gentleman before." It

came out that the one impression she retained of what
she had heard was that "the gentleman" had two
wives. They knew of Washington that he was the first
President of the United States and cut down a cherry
tree. They were sitting and sewing at the time almost
on the identical spot where he lived and held office.
To the question who ruled before Washington the
answer came promptly: no one; he was the first. They
agreed reluctantly, upon further consideration, that
there was probably "a King of America" before his
day, and the Irish damsels turned up their noses at the
idea. The people of Canada, they thought, were
copper-colored. The same winter I was indignantly
bidden to depart from a school in the Fourth Ward
by a trustee who had heard that I had written a book
about the slum and spoken of "his people" in it.

Those early steps in the reform path stumbled sadly
at times over obstacles that showed how dense was
the ignorance and how rank were the prejudices we
had to fight. When I wrote that the Allen Street school
was overrun by rats, which was a fact anyone might
observe for himself by spending five minutes in the
building, I was called sharply to account by the Mayor
in the Board of Estimate and Apportionment. There
were no rats, he said. The Allen Street school was the
worst of them all, and I determined that the time had
come to make a demonstration. I procured a rat trap,
and was waiting for an idle hour to go over and catch
one of the rats, so that I might have it stuffed and
sent to the board over which the Mayor presided, as
a convincing exhibit; but before I got so far reform
swept the whole conspiracy of ignorance and jobbery
out of the City Hall.

That was well enough as far as it went; but that
the broom was needed elsewhere we learned later,
when the Good Government Clubs fought for the inspection of the schools and of the children by trained
oculists. The evidence was that the pupils were made
both near-sighted and stupid by the want of proper

arrangement of their seats and of themselves in the
classroom. The fact was not denied, and the scheme
was strongly endorsed by the Board of Health and
by some of the ablest and best known oculists in the
city; but it was wrecked upon an opposition in which
we heard the ignorant and selfish cry that it would "interfere with private practice," and so curtail the profits
of the practitioner. The proposal to inspect the classes
daily for evidence of contagious disease—which, carried
out, has proved a most effective means of preventing the spread of epidemics, and one of the greatest
blessings—had been opposed, happily unsuccessfully,
with the same arguments.* It is very well to prate
about the rapacity of politicians, but these things came
often enough to show what they meant by the claim
that they were "closer to the people" than we who
were trying to help them; and they were all the more
exasperating because they came rarely from below—
the tenement people, when they were not deliberately
misled, were ready and eager to fall in with any plan
for bettering things, notably where it concerned the
schools—but usually from those who knew better, and
from whom we had a right to expect support and
backing.

Speaking of that reminds me of a mishap I had in
the Hester Street school—the one with the "frills" which
the Board of Education cut off. I happened to pass
it after school hours, and went in to see what sort
of a playground the roof would have made. I met no
one on the way, and, finding the scuttle open, climbed

---

* I set down reluctantly this censure of an honored profession, to individual members of which I have been wont, in a
long succession of troubled years, to go for advice and help in
public matters, and never in vain. The statement of the chief
sanitary officer of the Health Department, reaffirmed at the
time I am writing, is, however, positive to the effect that to this
opposition, and this only, was due the failure of that much-
needed reform which had for years been with me a pet measure.

out and up the slant of the roof to the peak, where I sat musing over our lost chance, when the janitor came to close up. He must have thought I was a crazy man, and my explanation did not make it any better. He haled me down, and but for the fortunate chance that the policeman on the beat knew me, I should have been taken to the lockup as a dangerous lunatic —all for dreaming of a playground on the roof of a schoolhouse.

Janitor and Board of Commissioners to the contrary notwithstanding, the dream became real. There stands another school in Hester Street today within easy call that has a playground measuring more than twelve thousand square feet on the roof, one of half that size down on the ground, and an asphalted indoor playground as big as the one on the roof. Together they measure a trifle less than thirty thousand feet. To the indignant amazement of my captor, the janitor, his school was thrown open to the children in the last summer vacation, and in the winter they put a boys' club in to worry him. What further indignities there are in store for him in this day of "frills" there is no telling. A resolution is on record which states, under date of May 18, 1897, that "it is the sense of the Board of Superintendents that the schoolhouses may well be used in the cause of education as neighborhood centers, providing reading rooms, branch offices of public libraries, etc." And to cut off all chance of relapse into the old doubt whether "such things are educational," which laid so many of our hopes on the dusty shelf of the circumlocution office, the state legislature has expressly declared that the commonwealth will take the chance, which Boards of Education shunned, of a little amusement creeping in. The schools may be used for "purposes of recreation." To the janitor it must seem that the end of all things is at hand.

In the crowded districts, the school playgrounds were thrown open to the children during the long vacation last year, with kindergarten teachers to amuse them, and half a score of vacation schools tempted more than four thousand children from the street into the cool shade of the classrooms. They wrought in wood and iron, they sang and they played and studied nature—out of a barrel, to be sure, that came twice a week from Long Island filled with "specimens"; but toward the end we took a hint from Chicago and let the children gather their own specimens on excursions around the bay and suburbs of the city. That was a tremendous success. The mere hint that money might be lacking to pay for the excursions this summer set the St. Andrew's Brotherhood men on Long Island to devising schemes for inviting the schoolchildren out on trolley and shore trips. With the Christian Endeavor, the Epworth League, and kindred societies looking about for something to try their young strength and enthusiasm on, we may be here standing upon the threshold of something which shall bring us nearer to a universal brotherhood than all the consecrations and badges that have yet been invented.

The mere contact with nature, even out of a barrel, brought something to those starved child lives that struck a new note. Sometimes it rang with a sharp and jarring sound. The boys in the Hester Street school could not be made to take an interest in the lesson on wheat until the teacher came to the effect of drought and a bad year on the farmer's pocket. Then they understood. They knew the process. Strikes cut into the earnings of Hester Street, small enough at the best of times, at frequent intervals, and the boys need not be told what a bad year means. No other kind ever occurs there. They learned the lesson on wheat in no time after that. Oftener it was a gentler note that piped timidly in the strange place. A barrel of wild roses came one day, instead of the expected "specimens," and these were given to the children. They took them greedily. "I wondered," said the teacher, "if it was more love of the flower, or of getting something for nothing, no matter what." But even if it were largely the latter, there was still the rose. Nothing like it had come that way before, and without a doubt it taught its own lesson. The Italian child might have jumped for it more eagerly, but its beauty was not wasted in Jew-town, either. The baby kissed it, and it lay upon more than one wan cheek, and whispered who knows what thought of hope and courage that were nearly gone. Even in Hester Street the wild rose from the hedge was not wasted.

The result of it all was wholesome and good, because it was common sense. The way to fight the slum in the children's lives is with sunlight and flowers and play, which their child hearts crave, if their eyes have never seen them. The teachers reported that the boys were easier to manage, more quiet, and played more fairly than before. The police reports showed that fewer were arrested or run over in the streets than in other years. A worse enemy was attacked than the trolley car or the truck. In the kindergarten at the Hull House in Chicago there hangs a picture of a harvest scene, with the man wiping his brow, and a woman resting at his feet. The teacher told me that a little girl with an old face picked it out among all the rest, and considered it long and gravely. "Well," she said, when her inspection was finished, "he knocked her down, didn't he?" A two hours' argument for kindergartens or vacation schools could not have put it stronger or better.

The awakening of the civic conscience is nowhere more plainly traced than in our public schools. The last five years have set us fifty years ahead, and there is now no doubling on the track we have struck. We have fifty kindergartens today where five years ago we had one, and their method has invaded the whole system of teaching. Cooking, the only kind of temperance preaching that counts for anything in a school course, is taught in the girls' classes. Five years ago a minister of justice declared in the Belgian Chamber that the nation was reverting to a new form of barbarism, which he described by the term "alcoholic barbarism," and pointed out as its first cause the "insufficiency of the food procurable by the working classes." He referred to the quality, not the quantity. The United States experts, who lately made a study of the living habits of the poor in New York, spoke of it as a common observation that "a not inconsiderable amount of the prevalent intemperance can be traced to poor food and unattractive home tables." The toasting fork in Jacob's sister's hand beats preaching in the campaign against the saloon, just as the boys' club beats the police club in fighting the gang.

The cram and the jam are being crowded out as common-sense teaching steps in and takes their place, and the "three H's," the head, the heart, and the hand —a whole boy—are taking the place too long monopolized by the "three R's." There was need of it. It had seemed sometimes as if, in our anxiety lest he should not get enough, we were in danger of stuffing the boy to the point of making a hopeless dunce of him. It is a higher function of the school to teach principles than to impart facts merely. Teaching the boy municipal politics and a thousand things to make a good citizen of him, instead of so filling him with love of his country and pride in its traditions that he is bound to take the right stand when the time comes, is as though one were to attempt to put all the law of the state into its constitution to make it more binding. The result would be hopeless congestion and general uselessness.

It comes down to the teacher in the end, and there are 5600 of them in the old city alone, 10,000 for the greater city;* the great mass faithful and zealous, but yoked to the traditions of a day that is past. Half the machine teaching, the wooden output of our public schools in the past, I believe was due to the practical

* The exact number for April 1899, was 9989; number of pupils registered, 401,761; average daily attendance, 370,722.

isolation of the teachers between the tyranny of politics and the distrust of those who had good cause to fear the politician and his work. There was never a more saddening sight than that of the teachers standing together in an almost solid body to resist reform of the school system as an attack upon them. There was no pretense on their part that the schools did not need reform. They knew better. They fought for their places. Throughout the fight no word came from them of the children's rights. They imagined that theirs were in danger, and they had no thought for anything else. We gathered then the ripe fruit of politics, and it will be a long while, I suppose, before we get the taste out of our mouths. But the grip of politics on our schools has been loosened, if not shaken off altogether, and the teacher's slavery is at an end, if she herself so wills it. Once hardly thought worthy of a day laborer's hire, she will receive a policeman's pay for faithful service* in the school year now begun, with his privilege of a half-pay pension on retirement. Within three weeks after the passage of the salary bill forty-two teachers in the boroughs of Manhattan and Bronx had applied for retirement. The training schools are hard at work filling up the gaps. The windows of the schoolhouse have been thrown open, and life let in there, too, with the sunlight. The day may be not far distant when ours shall be schools "for discovering aptitude," in Professor Felix Adler's wise plan. The problem is a vast one, even in its bulk; every year seats must be found on the school benches for twenty thousand additional children. However deep we have gone down into our pockets to pay for new schools, there are to-day in the greater city nearly thirty thousand children in half-day or part-time classes, waiting their chance. But that it can and will be solved the experience of the last five years fully warrants.

---

* The teacher's pay, under the new act, is from $600 to $1400. The policeman's pay is $1400.

In the solution the women of New York will have had no mean share. In the struggle for school reform they struck the telling blows, and the credit for the victory was justly theirs. The Public Education Association, originally a woman's auxiliary to Good Government Club E, has since worked as energetically with the school authorities as it before worked against them. It has opened many windows for little souls by hanging schoolrooms with beautiful casts and pictures, and forged at the same time new and strong links in the chain that bound the boy all too feebly to the school. At a time when the demand of the boys of the East Side for club room, which was in itself one of the healthiest signs of the day, had reached an exceedingly dangerous pass, the Public Education Association broke ground that will prove the most fertile field of all. The Raines law saloon, quick to discern in the new demand the gap that would divorce it by and by from the man, attempted to bridge it by inviting the boy in under its roof. Occasionally the girl went along. A typical instance of how the scheme worked was brought to my attention at the time by the manager of the College Settlement. The back room of the saloon was given to the club free of charge, with the understanding that the boy members should "treat." As a means of raising the needed funds, the club hit upon the plan of fining members ten cents when they "got funny." To defeat this device of the devil some way must be found; but club room was scarce among the tenements. The Good Government Clubs proposed to the Board of Education that it open the empty classrooms at night for the children's use. It was my privilege to plead their cause before the School Board, and to obtain from it the necessary permission, after some hesitation and doubt as to whether "it was educational." The Public Education Association promptly assumed the responsibility for "the property," and the Hester Street school was opened. There are now two schools that are given over to evening clubs. The property has not been molested, but the boys who have met under Miss Winifred Buck's management have learned many a lesson of self-control and practical wisdom that has proved "educational" in the highest degree. Her plan is simplicity itself. Through their play—the meeting usually begins with a romp—in quarters where there is not too much elbow room, the boys learn the first lesson of respecting one another's rights. The subsequent business meeting puts them upon the fundamentals of civilized society, as it were. Out of the debate of the question, Do we want boys who swear, steal, gamble, and smoke cigarettes? grow convictions as to why these vices are wrong that put "the gang" in its proper light. Punishment comes to appear, when administered by the boys themselves, a natural consequence of law breaking, in defense of society; and the boy is won. He can thenceforward be trusted to work out his own salvation. If he does it occasionally with excessive unction, remember how recent is his conversion. "*Resolved*, that wisdom is better than wealth," was rejected as a topic for discussion by one of the clubs, because "everybody knows it is." This was in the Tenth Ward. If temptation had come that way in the shape of a pushcart with pineapples—we are all human! Anyway, they had learned the right.

With the women to lead, the school has even turned the tables on the jail and invaded it bodily. For now nearly two years the Public Education Association has kept school in the Tombs for the boys locked up there awaiting trial. Of thirty-one pupils on this school register the other day, twelve were charged with burglary, four with highway robbery, and three with murder. That was the gang run to earth at last. Better late than never. The windows of their prison overlooked the spot where the gallows used to stand that cut short many a career such as they pursued. They were soberly attentive to their studies, which were of a severely practical turn. Their teacher, Mr. David Willard, who was a resident of the University Settlement in its old Delancey Street home—the fact that the forces for good one finds at work in the slum usually lead back to the settlements shows best that they have so far escaped the peril of stiffening into mere institutions—has his own sound view of how to head off the hangman. Daily and nightly he gathers about him in the house on Chrystie Street, where he makes his home, three hundred boys and girls, whom he meets as their friend, on equal terms. The club is the means of getting them there, and so it is in its right place.

Once a week another teacher comes to the Tombs school and tells the boys of our city's history, its famous buildings and great men, trying so to arouse their interest as a first step toward a citizen's pride. This one also is sent by a club of women, the City History Club, which in three years has done strange things among the children. It sprang from the proposition of Mr. Robert Abbe that the man and the citizen has his birth in the boy, and that to love a thing one must know it first. The half-dozen classes that were started for the study of our city's history have swelled into nearly a hundred, with quite eighteen hundred pupils. The pregnant fact was noted early by the teachers, that the immigrant boy easily outstrips in interest for his adopted home the native, who perchance turns up his nose at him, and later very likely complains of the "unscrupulousness" of the Jew who forged ahead of him in business as well.

"Everything takes ten years." Looking back from the closing year of the century, one is almost tempted to turn Mr. Hewitt's phrase about, and say that everything has been packed into ten years. The tenth winter of the free lectures, which the city provides to fill up in a measure those gaps which the earlier years left, has just passed. When the first course showed an attendance of 22,149 upon 186 lectures, we were all encouraged; but the last season saw 1923 lectures delivered upon every topic of human interest, from the care of our bodies and natural science to literature, astronomy, and music, and a multitude of 519,411 persons, chiefly workingmen and their wives, the parents of the schoolboy, heard them. Forty-eight schools and halls were employed for the purpose. The People's Institute adds to this program a forum for the discussion of social topics, nineteenth-century history, and "present problems" on a wholly nonpartisan, unsectarian basis. The Institute was launched upon its educational mission within six weeks after the disastrous Greater New York election in 1897. It has since drawn to the platform of the Cooper Institute audiences, chiefly of workingmen more or less connected with the labor movement, that have filled its great hall. The spirit that animates its work is shown in its review of the field upon the threshold of its third year. Speaking of the social issues that are hastening toward a settlement, it says: "Society is about to be organized, gradually, wisely, on the lines of the recognition of the brotherhood of man. The People's Institute holds to-day, as no other institution in this city, the confidence of all classes of the working people; also of the best minds among the well-to-do classes. It can throw all its influence upon the side of removing misunderstandings, promoting mutual confidence. . . . This is its great work." A great undertaking, truly, but one in which no one may rashly say it shall not succeed. As an installment, it organized last spring, for study, discussion, and social intercourse, the first of a chain of People's Clubs, full of a strong and stirring life, which within three months had a membership of three hundred and fifty, and a list of two hundred and fifty applicants.

While the Institute's plan has met with this cordial reception downtown, uptown, among the leisure classes, its acceptance has been nothing like so ready. Selfish wealth has turned a cold shoulder to the brotherhood of man, as so often in the past. Still the proffered hand is not withdrawn. In a hundred ways it is held out with tender of help and sympathy and friendship these days, where distrust and indifference were once the rule. The People's University Extension Society, leaving the platform to its allies, invades the home, the nursery, the kindergarten, the club, wherever it can, with help and counsel. Down on the lower East Side, the Educational Alliance conducts from the Hebrew Institute an energetic campaign among the Jewish immigrants that reaches fully six thousand souls, two-thirds of them children, every day in the week. Sixty-two clubs alone hold meetings in the building on Saturday and Sunday. Under the same roof the Baron Hirsch Fund has taught sixteen thousand children of refugee Jews in nine years. It passes them on to the public schools within six months of their landing, the best material they receive from anywhere.

So the boy is being got ready for dealing, in the years that are to come, with the other but not more difficult problems of setting his house to rights, and ridding it of the political gang which now misrepresents him and us. And justice to Jacob is being evolved. Not yet without obstruction and dragging of feet. The excellent home library plan that proved so wholesome in the poor quarters of Boston has failed in New York, except in a few notable instances, through the difficulty of securing the visitors upon whom the plan depends for its success. The same want has kept the boys' club from reaching the development that would apply the real test to it as a barrier against the slum. There are fifteen clubs for every Winifred Buck that is in sight. From the City History Club, the Charity Organization Society, from everywhere, comes the same complaint. The hardest thing in the world to give is still one's self. But it is all the time getting to be easier. There are daily more women and men who, thinking of the boy, can say, and do, with my friend of the College Settlement, when an opportunity to enter a larger field was offered her, "No, I am content to stay here, to be ready for Johnnie when he wants me."

Justice for the boy, and for his father. An itinerant Jewish glazier, crying his wares, was beckoned into a stable by the foreman, and bidden to replace a lot of broken panes, enough nearly to exhaust his stock. When, after working half the day, he asked for his pay, he was driven from the place with jeers and vile words. Raging and impotent, he went back to his poor tenement cursing a world in which there was no justice for a poor man. If he had next been found ranting with anarchists against the social order, would you have blamed him? He found instead, in the Legal Aid Society, a champion that pleaded his cause and compelled the stableman to pay him his wages. For a hundred thousand such—more shame to us—this society has meant all that freedom promised: justice to the poor man. It too has earned a place among the forces that are working out through the new education the brighter day, for it has taught the lesson which all the citizens of a free state need most to learn—respect for law.

REFORM BY
HUMANE TOUCH

I have sketched in outline the gains achieved in the metropolis since its conscience awoke. Now, in closing this account, I am reminded of the story of an old Irishman who died here a couple of years ago. Patrick Mullen was an honest blacksmith. He made guns for a living. He made them so well that one with his name on it was worth a good deal more than the market price of guns. Other makers went to him with offers of money for the use of his stamp; but they never went twice. When sometimes a gun of very superior make was brought to him to finish, he would stamp it P. Mullen, never Patrick Mullen. Only to that which he himself had wrought did he give his honest name without reserve. When he died, judges and bishops and other great men crowded to his modest home by the East River, and wrote letters to the newspapers telling how proud they had been to call him friend. Yet he was, and remained to the end, plain Patrick Mullen, blacksmith and gunmaker.

In his life he supplied the answer to the sigh of dreamers in all days: when will the millennium come? It will come when every man is a Patrick Mullen at his own trade; not merely a P. Mullen, but a Patrick Mullen. The millennium of municipal politics, when there shall be no slum to fight, will come when every citizen does his whole duty as a citizen; not before. As long as he "despises politics," and deputizes another to do it for him, whether that other wears the stamp of a Croker or of a Platt—it matters little which—we shall

have the slum, and be put periodically to the trouble
and the shame of draining it in the public sight. A citizen's duty is one thing that cannot be farmed out
safely; and the slum is not limited by the rookeries of
Mulberry or Ludlow streets. It has long roots that
feed on the selfishness and dullness of Fifth Avenue
quite as greedily as on the squalor of the Sixth Ward.
The two are not nearly so far apart as they look.

I am not saying this because it is anything new, but
because we have just had an illustration of its truth
in municipal politics. Waring and Roosevelt were the
Patrick Mullens of the reform administration which
Tammany has now replaced with her insolent platform, "To hell with reform." It was not an ideal
administration, but it can be said of it, at least, that
it was up to the times it served. It made compromises
with spoils politics, and they were wretched failures.
It took Waring and Roosevelt on the other plan, on
which they insisted, of divorcing politics from the
public business, and they let in more light than even
my small parks over on the East Side. For they
showed us where we stood and what was the matter
with us. We believed in Waring when he demonstrated the success of his plan for cleaning the streets:
not before. When Roosevelt announced his program
of enforcing the excise law because it *was* law, a howl
arose that would have frightened a less resolute man
from his purpose. But he went right on doing the duty
he was sworn to do. And when, at the end of three
months of clamor and abuse, we saw the spectacle of
the saloonkeepers formally resolving to help the police
instead of hindering them; of the prison ward in
Bellevue Hospital standing empty for three days at a
time, an astonishing and unprecedented thing, which
the warden could only attribute to the "prompt closing
of the saloons at one A.M."; and of the police force
recovering its lost self-respect, we had found out more
and greater things than whether the excise law was a

good or a bad law. We understood what Roosevelt meant when he insisted upon the "primary virtues" of honesty and courage in the conduct of public business. For the want of them in us, half the laws that touched our daily lives had become dead letters or vehicles of blackmail and oppression. It was worth something to have that lesson taught us in that way; to find out that simple, straightforward, honest dealing as between man and man is after all effective in politics as in gunmaking. Perhaps we have not mastered the lesson yet. But we have not discharged the teacher, either.

Courage, indeed! There were times during that stormy spell when it seemed as if we had grown wholly and hopelessly flabby as a people. All the outcry against the program of order did not come from the lawless and the disorderly, by any means. Ordinarily decent, conservative citizens joined in counseling moderation and virtual compromise with the lawbreakers—it was nothing else—to "avoid trouble." The old love of fair play had been whittled down by the jackknife of all-pervading expediency to an anemic desire to "hold the scales even"; that is a favorite modern device of the devil for paralyzing action in men. You cannot hold the scales even in a moral issue. It inevitably results in the triumph of evil, which asks nothing better than the even chance to which it is not entitled. When the trouble in the Police Board had reached a point where it seemed impossible not to understand that Roosevelt and his side were fighting a cold and treacherous conspiracy against the cause of good government, we had the spectacle of a Christian Endeavor Society inviting the man who had hatched the plot, the bitter and relentless enemy whom the Mayor had summoned to resign, and afterward did his best to remove as a fatal obstacle to reform—inviting this man to come before it and speak of Christian citizenship! It was a sight to make the bosses hug themselves with glee. For Christian citizenship is their nightmare, and nothing is so cheering to them as evidence that those who profess it have no sense.

Apart from the moral bearings of it, what this question of enforcement of law means in the life of the poor was illustrated by testimony given before the Police Board very recently. A captain was on trial for allowing the policy swindle to go unchecked in his precinct. Policy is a kind of penny lottery, with alleged daily drawings which never take place. The whole thing is a pestilent fraud, which is allowed to exist only because it pays heavy blackmail to the police and the politicians. Expert witnesses testified that eight policy shops in the Twenty-first Ward, which they had visited, did a business averaging about thirty-two dollars a day each. The Twenty-first is a poor Irish tenement ward. The policy sharks were getting two hundred and fifty dollars or more a day of the hard-earned wages of those poor people, in sums of from one and two cents to a quarter, without making any return for it. The thing would seem incredible, were it not too sadly familiar. The saloonkeeper got his share of what was left, and rewarded his customer by posing as the "friend of the poor man" whenever his business was under scrutiny; I have yet in my office the record of a single week during the hottest of the fight between Roosevelt and the saloons as showing of what kind that friendship is. It embraces the destruction of eight homes by the demon of drunkenness: the suicide of four wives, the murder of two others by drunken husbands, the killing of a policeman in the street, and the torture of an aged woman by her rascal son, who "used to be a good boy till he took to liquor, when he became a perfect devil." In that role he finally beat her to death for giving shelter to some evicted fellow tenants who else would have had to sleep in the street. Nice friendly turn, wasn't it?

And yet there was something to be said for the saloonkeeper. He gave the man the refuge from his tenement which he needed. I say needed, purposely. There has been a good deal of talk lately about the saloon as a social necessity. About all there is to that is that the saloon is there, and the necessity too. Man is a social animal, whether he lives in a tenement or in a palace. But the palace has resources; the tenement has not. It is a good place to get away from at all times. The saloon is cheery and bright, and never far away. The man craving human companionship finds it there. He finds, too, in the saloonkeeper one who understands his wants much better than the reformer who talks civil service in the meetings. "Civil service" to him and his kind means yet a contrivance for keeping them out of a job. The saloonkeeper knows the boss, if he is not himself the boss or his lieutenant, and can steer him to the man who will spend all day at the City Hall, if need be, to get a job for a friend, and all night pulling wires to keep him in it, if trouble is brewing. Mr. Beecher used to say, when pleading for bright hymn tunes, that he didn't want the devil to have the monopoly of all the good music in the world. The saloon has had the monopoly up to date of all the cheer in the tenements. If its owner has made it pan out to his own advantage and the boss's, we at least have no just cause of complaint. We let him have the field all to himself.

As to this boss, of whom we hear so much, what manner of man is he? That depends on how you look at him. I have one in mind, a district boss, whom you would accept instantly as a type, if I were to mention his name, which I shall not do for a reason which I fear will shock you: he and I are friends. In his private capacity I have real regard for him. As a politician and a boss I have none at all. I am aware that this is taking low ground in a discussion of this kind, but perhaps the reader will better understand the relations of his "district" to him, if I let him into mine. There is no political bond between us, of either district or party; just the reverse. It is purely personal.

He was once a police justice—at that time he kept a saloon—and I never knew one with more common sense, which happens to be the one quality especially needed in that office. Up to the point where politics came in I could depend upon him entirely. At that point he let me know bluntly that he was in the habit of running his district to suit himself. The way he did it brought him under the just accusation of being guilty of every kind of rascality known to politics. When next our paths would cross each other, it would very likely be on some errand of mercy, to which his feet were always swift. I recall the distress of a dear and gentle lady at whose dinner table I once took his part. She could not believe that there was any good in him; what he did must be done for effect. Some time after that she wrote asking me to look after an East Side family that was in great trouble. It was during the severe cold spell of last winter, and there was need of haste. I went over at once; but although I had lost no time, I found my friend the boss ahead of me. It was a real pleasure to me to be able to report to my correspondent that he had seen to their comfort, and to add that it was unpolitical charity altogether. The family was that of a Jewish widow with a lot of little children. He is a Roman Catholic. There were no men, consequently no voters, in the house, which was far outside of his district, too; and as for effect, he was rather shamefaced at my catching him at it. I do not believe that a soul has ever heard of the case from him to this day.

My friend is a Tammany boss. During that same cold spell a politician of the other camp came into my office and gave me a hundred dollars to spend as I saw fit among the poor. His district was miles uptown, and he was most unwilling to disclose his identity, stipulating in the end that no one but I should know where the money came from. He was not seeking notoriety. The plight of the suffering had appealed to him, and he wanted to help where he could, that was all.

Now, I have not the least desire to glorify the boss in this. He is not glorious to me. He is simply human. Often enough he is a coarse and brutal fellow, in his morals as in his politics. Again, he may have some very engaging personal traits that bind his friends to him with the closest of ties. The poor man sees the friend, the charity, the power that is able and ready to help him in need; is it any wonder that he overlooks the source of this power, this plenty—that he forgets the robbery in the robber who is "good to the poor"? Anyhow, if anybody got robbed, it was "the rich." With the present ethical standards of the slum, it is easy to construct even a scheme of social justice out of it that is very comforting all round, even to the boss himself, though he is in need of no sympathy or excuse. "Politics," he will tell me in his philosophic moods, "is a game for profit. The city foots the bills." Patriotism means to him working for the ticket that shall bring more profit. "I regard," he says, lighting his cigar, "a repeater as a shade off a murderer, but you are obliged to admit that in my trade he is a necessary evil." I am not obliged to do anything of the kind, but I can understand his way of looking at it. He simply has no political conscience. He has gratitude, loyalty to a friend—that is part of his stock in trade— fighting blood, plenty of it, all the good qualities of the savage; nothing more. And a savage he is, politically, with no soul above the dross. He would not rob a neighbor for the world; but he will steal from the city—though he does not call it by that name— without a tremor, and count it a good mark. When I tell him that, he waves his hand toward Wall Street as representative of the business community, and toward the office of his neighbor, the padrone, as representative of the railroads, and says with a laugh, "Don't they all do it?"

The boss believes in himself. It is one of his strong

points. And he has experience to back him. In the fall of 1894 we shook off boss rule in New York, and set up housekeeping for ourselves. We kept it up three years, and then went back to the old style. I should judge that we did it because we were tired of too much virtue. Perhaps we were not built to hold such a lot at once. Besides, it is much easier to be ruled than to rule. That fall, after the election, when I was concerned about what would become of my small parks, of the Health Department in which we took such just pride, and of a dozen other things, I received one unvarying reply to my anxious question, or rather two. If it was the Health Department, I was told: "Go to Platt. He is the only man who can do it. He is a sensible man, and will see that it is protected." If small parks, it was: "Go to Croker. He will not allow the work to be stopped." A playgrounds bill was to be presented in the legislature, and everybody advised: "Go to Platt. He won't have any objection: it is popular." And so on. My advisers were not politicians. They were businessmen, but recently honestly interested in reform. I was talking one day with a gentleman of very wide reputation as a philanthropist about the unhappy lot of the old fire-engine horses—which, after lives of toil that deserve a better fate, are sold for a song to drag out a weary existence hauling some huckster's cart around—and wishing that they might be pensioned off to live out their years on a farm, with enough to eat and a chance to roll in the grass. He was much interested, and promptly gave me this advice: "I tell you what you do. You go and see Croker. He likes horses." No wonder the boss believes in himself. He would be less than human if he did not. And he is very human.

I had voted on the day of the Greater New York election—the Tammany election, as we learned to call it afterward—in my home out in the Borough of Queens, and went over to the depot to catch the train for the city. On the platform were half a dozen of my neigh-

bors, all businessmen, all "friends of reform." Some
of them were just down from breakfast. One I remembered as introducing a resolution, in a meeting
we had held, about the discourtesy of local politicians.
He looked surprised when reminded that it was election day. "Why, is it today?" he said. "They didn't
send any carriage," said another regretfully. "I don't
see what's the use," said the third; "the roads are just
as bad as when we began talking about it." (We had
been trying to mend them.) The fourth yawned and
said: "I don't care. I have my business to attend to."
And they took the train, which meant that they lost
their votes. The Tammany captain was busy hauling
his voters by the cartload to the polling place. Over
there stood a reform candidate who had been defeated
in the primary, and puffed out his chest. "The politicians are afraid of me," he said. They slapped him on
the back, as they went by, and told him that he was a
devil of a fellow.

So Tammany came back. The Health Department
is wrecked. The police force is worse than before
Roosevelt took hold of it, and we are back in the mud
out of which we pulled ourselves with such an effort.
And we are swearing at it. But I am afraid we are
swearing at the wrong fellow. The real Tammany is
not the conscienceless rascal that plunders our treasury
and fattens on our substance. That one is a mere
counterfeit. It is the voter who waits for a carriage to
take him to the polls, the man who "doesn't see what's
the use"; the businessman who says "business is
business," and has no time to waste on voting; the
citizen who "will wait to see how the cat jumps, because he doesn't want to throw his vote away"; the
cowardly American who "doesn't want to antagonize"
anybody; the fool who "washes his hands of politics."
These are the real Tammany, the men after the
boss's own heart. For every one whose vote he buys,
there are two of these who give him theirs for nothing.
We shall get rid of him when these withdraw their

support, when they become citizens of the Patrick Mullen stamp, as faithful at the polling place as he was at the forge; not before.

The true work of reform is at the top, not at the bottom. The man in the slum votes according to his light, and the boss holds the candle. But the boss is in no real sense a leader. He follows instead, always as far behind the moral sentiment of the community as he thinks is safe. He has heard it said that a community will not be any better than its citizens, and that it will be just as good as they are, and he applies the saying to himself. He is no worse a boss than the town deserves. I can conceive of his taking credit to himself as some kind of a moral instrument by which the virtue of the community may be graded, though that is most unlikely. He does not bother himself with the morals of anything. But right here is his Achilles heel. The man has no conscience. He cannot tell the signs of it in others. It always comes upon him unawares. Reform to him simply means the "outs" fighting to get in. The real thing he will always underestimate. Such a man is not the power he seems. He is formidable only in proportion to the amount of shaking it takes to rouse the community's conscience.

The boss is like the measles, a distemper of a self-governing people's infancy. When we shall have come of age politically, he will have no terrors for us. Meanwhile, being charged with the business of governing, which we left to him because we were too busy making money, he follows the track laid out for him, and makes the business pan out all that is in it. He fights when we want to discharge him. Of course he does. No man likes to give up a good job. He will fight or bargain, as he sees his way clear. He will give us small parks, play piers, new schools, anything we ask, to keep his place, while trying to find out "the price" of this conscience which he does not understand. Even to the half of his kingdom he will give, to be "in" on the new deal. He has done it before, and there is no reason that he can see why it should not be done again. And he will appeal to the people whom he is plundering to trust him because they know him.

Odd as it sounds, this is where he has his real hold. I have shown why this is so. To the poor people of his district the boss is a real friend in need. He is one of them. He does not want to reform them; far from it. No doubt it is very ungrateful of them, but the poor people have no desire to be reformed. They do not think they need to be. They consider their moral standards quite as high as those of the rich, and resent being told that they are mistaken. The reformer comes to them from another world to tell them these things, and goes his way. The boss lives among them. He helped John to a job on the pipes in their hard winter, and got Mike on the force. They know him as a good neighbor, and trust him to their harm. He drags their standard ever farther down. The question for those who are trying to help them is how to make them transfer their allegiance, and trust their real friends instead.

It ought not to be a difficult question to answer. Any teacher could do it. He knows, if he knows anything, that the way to get and keep the children's confidence is to trust them, and let them know that they are trusted. They will almost always come up to the demand thus made upon them. Preaching to them does little good; preaching at them still less. Men, whether rich or poor, are much like children. The good in them is just as good as it is said to be, and the bad, considering their enlarged opportunities for mischief, not so much worse than it is called. A vigorous optimism, a stout belief in one's fellow man, is better equipment in a campaign for civic virtue than stacks of tracts and arguments, economic and moral, are. There is good bottom, even in the slum, for that kind of an anchor to get a grip on. A year ago I went to see a boxing match there had been much talk about. The hall was jammed with a rough and noisy crowd, hotly intent upon its favorite. His opponent, who hailed, I think, from somewhere in Delaware, was greeted with hostile demonstrations as a "foreigner." But as the battle wore on, and he was seen to be fair and manly, while the New Yorker struck one foul blow after another, the attitude of the crowd changed rapidly from enthusiastic approval of the favorite to scorn and contempt; and in the last round, when he knocked the Delawarean over with a foul blow, the audience rose in a body and yelled to have the fight given to the "foreigner," until my blood tingled with pride. For the decision would leave it practically without a cent. It had staked all it had on the New Yorker. "He is a good man," I heard on all sides, while the once favorite sneaked away without a friend. "Good" meant fair and manly to that crowd. I thought, as I went to the office the next morning, that it ought to be easy to appeal to such a people with measures that were fair and just, if we could only get on common ground. But the only hint I got from my reform paper was an editorial denunciation of the brutality of boxing, on the same page that had an enthusiastic review of the college football season. I do not suppose it did any harm, for the paper was probably not read by one of the men it had set out to reform. But suppose it had been, how much would it have appealed to them? Exactly the qualities of robust manliness which football is supposed to encourage in college students had been evoked by the trial of strength and skill which they had witnessed. As to the brutality, they knew that fifty young men are maimed or killed at football to one who fairs ill in a boxing match. Would it seem to them common sense, or cant and humbug?

It comes down in the end to a question of common sense and common honesty. For how many failures of reform effort is insincerity not to blame! Last spring I attended a meeting at Albany that had been called by the governor to discuss the better enforcement of the labor laws. We talked the situation over, and Mr. Roosevelt received from those present their ready promise to aid him in every way in making effective the laws that represented so much toil and sacrifice, yet had until then been in too many instances barren of results. Some time after, a workingman told me with scorn how, on our coming home, one of our party had stopped in at the factory inspector's office to urge him to "let up" on a friend, a cigar manufacturer, who was violating a law for which the labor organizations had fought long years as absolutely necessary to secure human conditions in the trade. How much stock might he and his fellows be supposed to take in a movement that had such champions? "You scratch my back and I'll scratch yours," is a kind of politics in which the reformer is no match for the boss. The boss will win on that line every time. A saving sense of humor might have avoided that and many other pitfalls. I am seriously of the opinion that a professional humorist ought to be attached to every reform movement to keep it from making itself ridiculous by either too great solemnity or too much conceit. As it is, the enemy sometimes employs him with effect. Failing the adoption of that plan, I would recommend a decree of banishment against photographers, press-clippings men, and the rest of the congratulatory staff. Why should the fact that a citizen has done a citizen's duty deserve to be celebrated in print and picture as if something extraordinary had happened? The smoke of battle had not cleared away after the victory of reform, in the fall of 1894, before the citizens' committee and all the little subcommittees rushed pell-mell to the photographer's to get themselves on record as the men who did it. The spectacle might have inspired in the humorist the advice to get two sets made, while they were about it—one to serve by and by as an exhibit of the men who didn't; and, as the event proved, he would have been right.

But it is easy to find fault, and on that tack we get no farther. Those men did a great work, and they did it well. The mileposts they set up on the road to better things will guide another generation to the goal, however the present may go astray. Good schools, better homes, and a chance for the boy are arguments that are not lost upon the people. They wear well. It may be that, like Moses and his followers, we of the present day shall see the promised land only from afar and with the eye of faith, because of our sins; that to a younger and sturdier tomorrow it shall be given to blaze the path of civic righteousness that was our dream. I like to think that it is so, and that that is the meaning of the coming of men like Roosevelt and Waring at this time with their simple appeal to the reason of honest men. Unless I greatly err in reading the signs of the times, it is indeed so, and the day of the boss and of the slum is drawing to an end. Our faith has felt the new impulse; rather, I should say, it has given it. The social movements, and that which we call politics, are but a reflection of what the people honestly believe, a chart of their aims and aspirations. Charity in our day no longer means alms, but justice. The social settlements are substituting vital touch for the machine charity that reaped a crop of hate and beggary. They are passenger bridges, it has been truly said, not mere "shoots" for the delivery of coal and groceries; bridges upon which men go over, not down, from the mansion to the tenement. We have learned that we cannot pass off checks for human sympathy in settlement of our brotherhood arrears. The church, which once stood by indifferent, or worse, is hastening to enter the life of the people. In the memory of men yet living, one church, moving uptown away from the crowd, left its old Mulberry Street home to be converted into tenements that justly earned the name of "dens of death" in the Health Department's records, while another became the foulest lodginghouse in an unclean city. It was a church corporation which in those bad days owned the worst underground dive downtown, and turned a deaf ear to all remonstrances. The church was "angling for souls." But souls in this world live in bodies endowed with reason. The results of that kind of fishing were empty pews and cold hearts, and the conscience-stricken cry that went up, "What shall we do to lay hold of this great multitude that has slipped from us?"

Ten years have passed, and today we see the churches of every denomination uniting in a systematic canvass of the city to get at the facts of the people's life of which they had ceased to be a part, pleading for parks, playgrounds, kindergartens, libraries, clubs, and better homes. There is a new and hearty sound to the word "brother" that is full of hope. The cry has been answered. The gap in the social body, between rich and poor, is no longer widening. We are certainly coming closer together. Ten years ago, when the King's Daughters lighted a Christmas tree in Gotham Court, the children ran screaming from Santa Claus as from a "bogey man." Last Christmas the boys in the Hebrew Institute's schools nearly broke the bank laying in supplies to do him honor. I do not mean that the Jews are deserting to join the Christian church. They are doing that which is better—they are embracing its spirit; and they and we are the better for it. God knows we waited long enough; and how close we were to each other all the while without knowing it! Last Christmas a clergyman, who lives out of town and has a houseful of children, asked me if I could not find for them a poor family in the city with children of about the same ages, whom they might visit and befriend. He worked every day in the office of a foreign mission in Fifth Avenue, and knew little of the life that moved about him in the city. I picked out a Hungarian widow in an East Side tenement, whose brave struggle to keep her little flock together had enlisted my sympathy and strong admiration. She was a cleaner in an office building; not until all the arrangements had been made did it occur to me to ask where. Then it turned out that she was scrubbing floors in the missionary society's house, right at my friend's door. They had passed each other every day, each in need of the other, and each as far from the other as if oceans separated them instead of a doorstep four inches wide.

Looking back over the years that lie behind with their work, and forward to those that are coming, I see only cause for hope. As I write these last lines, in a far distant land in the city of my birth the children are playing under my window, and calling to one another with glad cries in my sweet mother tongue, even as we did in the long ago. Life and the world are before them, bright with the promise of morning. So to me seem the skies at home. Not lightly do I say it, for I have known the toil of rough-hewing it on the pioneer line that turns men's hair gray; but I have seen also the reward of the toil. New York is the youngest of the world's great cities, barely yet out of its knicker-bockers. It may be that the dawning century will see it as the greatest of them all. The task that is set it, the problem it has to solve and which it may not shirk, is the problem of civilization, of human progress, of a people's fitness for self-government that is on trial among us. We shall solve it by the world-old formula of human sympathy, of humane touch. Somewhere in these pages I have told of the woman in Chicago who accounted herself the happiest woman alive because she had at last obtained a playground for her poor neighbors' children. "I have lived here for years," she said to me, "and struggled with principalities and powers, and have made up my mind that the most and the best I can do is to live right here with my people and smile with them—keep smiling; weep when I must, but smile as long as I possibly can." And the tears shone in her gentle old eyes as she said it. When we have learned to smile and weep with the poor, we shall have mastered our problem. Then the slum will have lost its grip and the boss his job.

Until then, while they are in possession, our business is to hold taut and take in slack right along; never letting go for a moment.

BIBLIOGRAPHICAL NOTE

Considerable manuscript material of Jacob Riis including letters, his notes on slum conditions, library clippings, copies of resolutions he helped to frame are in Russell Sage Library (*Jacob A. Riis Papers*); additional manuscript material is in the possession of the Riis family, and with the recent death of Mrs. Jacob A. Riis (August 1967) will go to the Russell Sage Library. The Jacob A. Riis Collection, Museum of the City of New York, is a rich collection of *memorabilia* of his era. A complete bibliography of Jacob A. Riis is in Louise Ware, *Jacob A. Riis* (New York: D. Appleton-Century, 1939), and includes his contributions to periodicals (pp. 303-8). For historical background on the urban slum, see Marshall B. Clinard, *Slums and Community Development* (New York: Free Press, 1966), and Anselm L. Strauss, ed., *The American City* (Chicago: Aldine, 1967). For companion tableaux to the portraits of Riis, see Hutchins Hapgood, *The Spirit of the Ghetto*, ed. by Moses Rischin (Cambridge: Harvard University Press, 1967); and Allon Schoener, *Portal to America: The Lower East Side, 1870–1925* (New York: Holt Rinehart and Winston, 1967). For the immigrant school child, see Leonard Covello, *The Social Background of the Italo-American School Child: A Study of the Southern Italian Mores and Their Effect on the School Situation in Italy and America*, edited and with an introduction by F.

Cordasco (Leiden, The Netherlands: E. J. Brill, 1967); and Morris I. Berger, *The Settlement, the Immigrant, and the Public School* (unpublished Ph.D. dissertation, Columbia University, 1956).